THE NAVAL WAR IN THE BALTIC

1939–1945

The German cruiser *Köln* rigging camouflage nets in Copenhagen Freeport, June 1941. (Søren Bang)

THE NAVAL WAR IN
THE BALTIC
1939–1945

POUL GROOSS

Seaforth
PUBLISHING

Copyright © Poul Grooss 2014
English translation © Seaforth Publishing 2017

First published in the English language in Great Britain in 2017 by
Seaforth Publishing,
A division of Pen & Sword Books Ltd,
47 Church Street,
Barnsley S70 2AS

www.seaforthpublishing.com

First published Denmark in 2014 under the title *Krigen I Østersøen 1939–1945*,
supported by the Krista & Viggo Petersen Foundation.

British Library Cataloguing in Publication Data
A catalogue record for this book is available from the British Library

ISBN 978 1 5262 0000 1 (HARDBACK)
ISBN 978 1 5267 0003 2 (EPUB)
ISBN 978 1 5267 0001 8 (KINDLE)

Unless otherwise indicated, the illustrations are from the Digital Archives of the Library of
the Danish Defence Forces – www.foto.fak.dk.
It has not been possible to find or get in touch with the legal holder of the copyright for
some of the illustrations. If any copyright has been violated in this way, it has happened
involuntarily and unintentionally. Lawful demands in this regard will be honoured in the
same way as if permission had been given in advance.

Translation from the Danish by David Young

Typeset and designed by JCS Publishing Services Ltd, www.jcs-publishing.co.uk
Printed and bound in Great Britain by CPI Group (UK) Ltd, Croydon, CR0 4YY

To my four grandchildren,
in the ardent hope that they never
have to experience anything like this.

Contents

FINLAND

Lake Ladoga

• Vyborg

Kotka

Turku Åbo

Helsinki

Hogland

Karelian Isthmus

Kronstadt

• Leningrad (St Petersburg)

•Porkkala

Gulf of Finland

Kronstadt Naval Base is situated at the southeastern tip of the Kotlin Island

Hanko

Narva

Ivangorod

Tallinn

Hiiumaa/Dagø

Muhu Sound

ESTONIA

Lake Peipus

Novgorod •

Lake Ilmen

Saaremaa/ Øsel

Pernau

Irben Strait

U S S R

dau tspils)•

Courland

Gulf of Riga

Tukums •

Riga

LATVIA

•Libau (Liepāja)

•Memel (Klaipėda)

LITHUANIA

• Vitebsk

• Tilsit

Kaunas

• Wilno

sberg

emmersdorf (ayakovskoye)

enburg (Kętrzyn)

• Minsk

AST SSIA

N   D

0   50   100 miles

Foreword

Although events in the Baltic Sea played a significant part in the Second World War, and this was a theatre which saw intense action and great tragedy, not many books have been written on the subject and thus knowledge about the events of the war in the area is limited. This book is an attempt to correct this state of affairs and it demonstrates that what happened in the Baltic Sea may have had a greater impact on the war than previously thought. My own interest in the area stems from sailing patrols in Danish ships during the Cold War and subsequent service in the Danish Defence Intelligence Service, where the area's military activities were under constant surveillance. In the course of naval visits to Leningrad and official journeys to the Soviet Union, I have had the opportunity of studying the Soviet side of the course of the war and after my retirement, as a travel guide on military historical tours, I have visited some of the most important areas of the Eastern Front. It has helped me very much in my understanding of the events of the war.

I do not at all pretend to be a professional historian, but I have studied the events of the war from many different sources, partly during my time at the Centre for Military History at the Royal Danish Defence College. As a lecturer, I have often had to explain the war to a civilian audience and one of my goals with this book is to explain to a non-military audience why the war went as it did. It is my intention both to describe the background to the action and the inter-relationships between the different decisions made during the course of the war. The book is therefore built up chronologically around the sequence of events between 1939 and 1945. This chronology gives rise to some necessary leaps from place to place, and throughout the book I have tried to insert appropriate comments to build up the picture for the reader and explain events in a wider context. Initially, the book covers broader periods of time, while the final four months (approximately) of the war have been summarised month by month.

The book has had a long journey, in that I have been taking notes for over forty years, but it is only since my appointment as a military historian at the Royal Danish Defence College in 2002 that a little structure has been applied to the many details.

Thanks are due to the following: Søren Nørby MA from the Naval Library/ Defence Library and the Royal Danish Defence College for access to a rich photographic archive, as well as for proofreading and good advice; Martin Cleemann Rasmussen MA for proofreading and good advice along the way; my now former boss, Niels Bo Poulsen from the Centre for Military History, for his patience with the project, exceptionally good advice along the way and for taking responsibility for production of the book; the Royal Danish Defence College for a study trip to St Petersburg and London, and especially for being the host for the entire project in the ten years I was employed there; Anastasia Lomagina for complete replies to my many strange questions in St Petersburg, and not least my wife Lone for advice, guidance, proofreading and patience.

Thanks to Samuel Svärd and Peter Wilkinson for the maps. Also thanks to Svenkst Militärhistoriskt Biblioteks Förlag, the author Anders Frankson and Captain Gustaf von Hofsten for illustrations, comments and assistance that could be used in the Swedish and the English editions of the book.

For the English edition, I would like to thank the translator David Young and his wife Lotte for a challenging and inspiring collaboration. Finally, a warm thank you to my indefatigable great-cousin Christian Williams for his tenacity and all his hard work behind the curtain.

Introduction

The original intention of this book was to describe the events in the naval war in the Baltic from 1939 to 1945. Even though the naval war is the book's main subject, it quickly became apparent that this could not be looked at in isolation, but had to be seen in the context of the fighting on land and in the air. This meant moving into an area which in modern English is called 'joint warfare', ie operations involving two or more services. In this context, the following aspects of the war years can be added: foreign policy, security, economy, ideology, espionage and the deciphering of codes.

In recent years, a number of books on the Second World War have been published. Specifically, I have been able to draw on the overwhelming volume of titles released in Sweden, but previously unknown material has also been released from the Soviet side. There is a lot of conflicting information within the sources, and this book therefore references several sources and comments on the information. Some of the statistical information has been produced from widely different backgrounds, and is thus not always comparable. Inaccuracies in the source material have also astounded me: there are discrepancies about dates, events, the number of fatalities and injured, and much more. The main sources are shown in the list of references in the Bibliography. Attempts have been made to verify the specified information as far as possible.

The use of sources has not been without its problems. If, for example, one were to read the existing books on the German navy, the Kriegsmarine, in the Baltic Sea during the war, one would probably get a picture of what the Kriegsmarine would itself regard as a worthy legacy, but not necessarily an accurate account of what happened. Similarly, Soviet publications shortly after the war only drew the picture of events which the Communist Party of the Soviet Union (CPSU) regarded as politically expedient. Later books, especially after 1991, have corrected this aspect somewhat.

The demarcation of 'the Baltic Sea' should not be taken literally. A series of events outside the Baltic Sea have been included, among other things, in the North Sea, the Skagerrak and Norway. War events outside the Baltic region are mentioned when they have affected the situation in the Baltic Sea area. In this respect, the activities of the German pocket battleship *Admiral Graf*

Spee in the South Atlantic in the autumn of 1939 were an actual contributing factor to the German occupation of Norway and Denmark. The surviving crew members from the British merchant ships sunk in the South Atlantic were transferred from the pocket battleship to the tanker *Altmark*, which was boarded by a British destroyer crew on 16 February 1940 in Norwegian territorial waters; the prisoners were brought home to Britain. Hitler had previously discussed plans with the Kriegsmarine's commander-in-chief about an occupation of Norway; now he became so angry that he demanded a drawing up of plans.

The Battle of the Atlantic was a pivotal event during the Second World War which has been described in detail by historians. A conservative estimate indicates that 102,200 seamen[1] from the warring parties were killed. If one tries to determine a similar estimate of how many people perished at sea in the Baltic Sea during the war, one arrives at a conservative estimate of 61,000, but the real figure is probably significantly higher. No one knows and we will never know. On the other hand, most of these casualties were not sailors, but civilians fleeing or under evacuation. In addition, there were a large number of concentration camp prisoners: 33,000 German refugees perished on refugee transports westward between January and May 1945; 18,000 concentration camp prisoners died in the Baltic Sea during evacuations from concentration camps in the last days of the war, and at least 10,000 people were killed during the Soviet evacuation of Tallinn in 1941 – a total of at least 61,000 people. These figures do not include those on board well over a thousand ships sunk, and hundreds of downed aircraft, as well as the Soviet evacuation from their base at Hanko. This last operation probably cost 6,000 lives. The latest figure for the evacuation of Tallinn is 14,000 dead and this figure excludes the crews from more than fifty missing submarines. The total toll on the Baltic Sea could thus well be around the toll in the Atlantic, but there is great uncertainty about this.

The war on the Eastern Front was a 'total war', where civilians were hit just as hard as the military forces. It has surprised me that more has not been written about all these events but, partly as a result of Günter Grass's novel *Crabwalk*, published in 2002, about the sinking of the *Wilhelm Gustloff*, and a number of German TV broadcasts about the final days of the war, there has been more discussion in recent years. German reticence about the events of 1945 is, of course, related to the large number of German war crimes – mainly carried out in Poland and the Soviet Union. In the years immediately after the war, there was not much compassion and sympathy for the German

---

1   36,200 men from the Royal Navy, 36,000 men from the British merchant navy and 30,000 men from the Kriegsmarine, mainly submarine crews, a total of 102,200 men.

population, which was moved west in the final months of the war with great loss and suffering.

When the Third Reich went under in total destruction in the spring of 1945, unimaginable tragedies were played out in the Baltic Sea. The background and the events are described in this book. The most violent events in the Baltic Sea took place just after the German attack on the Soviet Union in June 1941 and in the last four months of the war in 1945. Thick books have been written about the fighting on the Eastern Front, but knowledge of the conditions as seen from the Soviet side is probably modest in the West. There is, to my knowledge, no overall Danish presentation of the events regarding the naval warfare in and around the Baltic Sea from 1939 to 1945, and it has not been easy to acquire an overview. In order to put it into a larger context, I also had to include fighting in the coastal areas and to set all the events in the larger context of the war. The book is therefore an account of the whole war in the Baltic region. The level of detail and the descriptions are more comprehensive for the eastern areas, since the conditions here are probably less well known than they are, for example, for Denmark and Sweden.

The book was not originally intended as an attack directed at Sweden, but the extent of Swedish efforts in favour of Germany, and the extent of Swedish benevolence, surprised me during the writing process, and this is why Sweden takes up so much space in the book. Sweden's political manoeuvring under threat has not been without its problems.

The book is my take on the progress of the war in the areas that were close to my own country, Denmark. The country was spared serious fighting because of events over which Denmark had no influence. The degree of collaboration with the occupation forces in the occupied countries in Europe varied greatly and, during the war, circumstances were constantly changing. At government level in Denmark, it was not possible to enter into a kind of sham collaboration with the Germans and then surreptitiously support the Allies. From Denmark's point of view, export of agricultural and industrial goods meant that the country could receive fuel (coal and oil) and other raw materials, but in the bigger picture, Denmark was, of course, quite clearly supporting the German war effort. Collaboration with the occupying forces could not be avoided, but the participants were involved in some grey areas concerning legislation as well as morality and ethics, spanning topics as diverse as passive and active resistance, self-sacrifice, national sentiment and patriotism, and continuing into personal gain, profit, active participation in the war, and treason. The government wanted to preserve the welfare state and keep the means of production intact. Unemployment and social problems were helped by work in Germany and work on German installations in Denmark. Shipowners wanted to make money, but not to lose their ships, and the list of problems and dilemmas is potentially neverending. This is well described in the anthology *Over stregen – under besættelsen* (*Overstepping the Mark – Under Occupation*). It is no glorious tale and it was not without danger for the participants. Among others, the home fleet – the merchant ships that were in home waters on 9 April 1940 – took part in this. The 'external fleet', namely the merchant ships which initially went to an Allied or a neutral port, was able to support the Allied cause during the war. It was Denmark's most important contribution to the Allied victory and the contribution that exacted most victims. Those efforts have been described elsewhere. It is my hope that all the efforts of the 'maritime area' – the contribution of those we today call 'the blue Denmark' (shipowners, seafarers, fishermen, navy personnel, pilots, harbourmasters and others) – will be appreciated by future generations. Their work has been put into a much larger context in this book.

My aim has been to describe the war with the Baltic Sea at the centre and look at the events in the surrounding area from there. To understand the progress of the war, an overview is necessary and I hope that the book will provide the reader with this. At the same time, I have tried to describe the essential and decisive events in detail. A shift in the level of detail will therefore sometimes occur, especially with some more bizarre incidents, which I have a predilection for including. Finally, I have allowed myself to call the people of the Soviet Union 'Russians', which is wrong in principle, but common in Danish speech; for example, when talking about 'the Russians on Bornholm in 1945'.

All place names with several names in different languages have been cross-referenced alphabetically in Appendix 3.

Insofar as the significance of the names of the naval vessels mentioned is known, they are referred to in the text or footnotes. Sometimes the names of merchant ships are also explained. The naming of naval and merchant ships will often hint at the values most cherished by the country or regime in question.

Military ranks in English, German, Danish and Swedish are generally mentioned in the original language, while other ranks have been translated into English equivalents. Wherever possible, people are mentioned with the titles and the ranks they had at the point in time when they are mentioned. An overview of rank designations and what they correspond to in the British defence forces is shown in Appendix 2.

If any errors should occur in the book, they can be attributed to me alone.

Hellerup, February 2017

1

The Baltic

Geography and History

Sea areas

The Skagerrak and the Kattegat have at times been regarded as transitional areas for the Baltic Sea – the Baltic Sea proper begins with the three Danish straits. In the Middle Ages, it was known as the Baltic Sea or the Baltic Salt; the latter name is still used in the Faroese language. In Latin, the sea was called Codan, or Mare Balticum. The North Sea in the Danish King Frederik II's time (1559–1588) was referred to in Danish as the Western Sea, while the Baltic waters west of the Baltic states and Finland were also known in the local languages as the Western Sea.

In the eastern Baltic, there are three waterways that are partially closed or which are easy to close off against a military opponent. The first is the Gulf of Bothnia, which includes the Sea of Åland, the Bothnian Sea and the Bay of Bothnia. Next is the Gulf of Finland, which is a long, narrow area of sea between Estonia and Finland. At the eastern end of the gulf lies St Petersburg, which for many years has been Russia's and the Soviet Union's capital and second largest city respectively. The third area is the Gulf of Riga. The main seaward approach is via the Irben/Irbe Strait south of the southern tip of the island of Saaremaa, but you can also sail in and out through a narrow channel inside an Estonian archipelago through Muhu (Moon) Sound, which connects the Gulf of Finland to the Gulf of Riga. This brings you out to the east of Saaremaa, Hiiumaa and some smaller islands. All three areas are affected by the formation of ice, which may make it impossible to sail through from December to May. Since the Gulf of Finland and the Gulf of Riga are usually closed by ice for long periods, Russia and the Soviet Union have had a need for ice-free ports for their fleets along the Baltic coast.

After passing through the Danish straits and past the German island of Fehmarn, there are seven major islands in the Baltic Sea: Rügen, Bornholm, Öland, Gotland, Åland, Saaremaa and Hiiumaa. Near some of these islands are small islands or archipelagos. In the Sea of Åland, there are numerous islands and skerries.

Straits and canals

From ancient times, there have been three routes for sailing in and out of the Baltic Sea: the Sound (Øresund) between Denmark and Sweden; the Great Belt between the two largest Danish islands of Zealand and Funen; and the Little Belt between Funen and Jutland. In the Viking Age, ships could sail up the Schlei to Hedeby near Schleswig, where the army road went in a north–south direction. From here a cargo could be transported the short distance over land and shipped onward into the North Sea on another ship. From the Middle Ages until the Napoleonic Wars, shipping went almost exclusively through the Sound. Accurate hydrographic surveys were not taken in the Great Belt until around 1806 by the Royal Navy, as Great Britain at that time had extensive commercial and military interests in the Baltic Sea. Because of its narrow and winding course, the Little Belt has never had any special significance as an international sea route.

In the Sound, there are three passage options. On the Swedish side, there is Flinterenden (in Swedish, Flintrännan), east of Saltholm. Flinterenden was not sounded during the Great Northern War of 1700–1720, but on one occasion the Swedish navy made use of it, even though it resulted in some ships running aground. On the Danish side, west of Saltholm, there

The German battleship SMS *Zähringen* of the *Wittelsbach* class in the Kaiser Wilhelm Canal.

is a channel at Drogden. From the south, it splits into two northbound channels. One of them runs east of Middelgrunden (Middle Ground) and is called Hollænderdybet (Dutchman's Deep), while the other goes west of Middelgrunden and is called Kongedybet (King's Deep). In the eighteenth century, one of the Danish navy's quandaries was whether they should focus on ships of the line with two battery decks which could pass through Drogden, or on those with three battery decks which could not pass through Drogden, but had to go north of Zealand and into the Baltic Sea via the more precarious route through the Great Belt.

   In 1895, Germany opened the Kaiser Wilhelm Canal, today referred to as the Kiel Canal. It was built for military purposes, so that the Imperial German Navy could be sent into either the North Sea or the Baltic Sea according to military needs without being exposed during a passage, particularly in relation to the Royal Navy. The canal is 61 miles/98km long and has locks at both ends. Immediately after the canal opened, the number of shipwrecks on the west coast of Jutland fell considerably. Besides the element of risk when operating in the North Sea, the canal reduces the sailing time between the Baltic Sea and the North Sea. From Kiel to Brunsbüttel, where the two locks are, there are 55 nautical miles through the canal, compared with 575 nautical miles (1 nautical mile = 1.15 land miles = 1,852m) around the Scaw (Skagen). The channel has continuously been deepened and allows the passage of ships with a draught of 33ft/10m. It was widened in the summer of 1914 so that the largest German warships could use it.

Territorial waters

Discussions about territorial waters and the high seas in the eighteenth century concluded in a general acceptance of the rights of coastal states to a distance of approximately one cannon shot from shore and this developed further into an understanding of about three nautical miles. Some countries claimed three nautical miles, others four.

   Maritime territory consists of the inner and the outer territorial waters. A state can demand that outer territorial waters be respected which extend out to at most twelve nautical miles from the baseline, which is the line between the outermost points of the coastline. In a large bay, the baseline will thus follow the coast at a distance of the width of the territorial limit, while in a small bay it will follow the line between the outermost points of the bay.

In its maritime territory – underwater and in the air space above it – a coastal state has, in principle, full jurisdiction *inter alia* to enforce its legislation, just as it does on land, including the laying of sea mines. The coastal state must, though, observe the right of foreign ships to innocent passage in external territorial waters. Innocent passage in internal territorial waters, where the coastal state has sovereignty, may not be demanded. Special regulations apply for international straits, ie straits that connect one part of the high seas with another part of the high seas.

Danish and Norwegian territorial waters were important for the war at the beginning, while they played a decisive role in Sweden during the entire period. Sweden has claimed four nautical miles since the eighteenth century. During the First World War, the Germans violated the Swedish limit, and in 1916, a German court in Berlin ruled that Germany would respect a fishing limit of four nautical miles, but a neutrality limit of only three nautical miles. After the verdict, the Germans laid mines right up to three nautical miles of the coast near Falsterbo, but Sweden still insisted on its four nautical miles of territorial waters.

In 1933, the Soviet Union opened the White Sea Canal or Stalin Canal, a 141-mile/227km excavated canal with nineteen locks, which allows navigation between Leningrad and the White Sea via the large lakes of Ladoga and Onega. The canal is ice-bound from October to May. It was the Soviet Union's first project to be completed by slave labour from the later infamous Gulag system. The prisoners were known as ZEK[1] in prison slang. The canal is also restricted by a maximum draught, originally 16ft/5m (now 11ft/3.5m), and a lock width of 58ft/17.6m. The Russians had earlier solved this problem by, for example, mounting a larger vessel or a large submarine on a large, broad, flat-bottomed floating dock with less than 16ft/5m draught. Then the floating dock is towed through the canal system. From Lake Onega, further passage is possible along the Volga–Baltic Waterway which goes down to the Sea of Azov via the River Don and from there into the Black Sea.

Finally, it is possible to sail from Gothenburg along the Göta Canal through Sweden to the south of Stockholm, via Lakes Vänern and Vättern. However, the canal with its fifty-eight locks is only passable for small vessels with a draught of less than 9ft/2.8m and a length of up to 105ft/32m. The canal is ice-bound for four months of the year. Because of acts of war close

---

1   Originally Z/K, which orally became ZEK = Заключённый каналоармеец = 'a canal soldier behind lock and key'.

to Swedish territory at the beginning of the Second World War, the Swedish government implemented the construction of the Falsterbo Canal so that Swedish shipping could sail along the coast within Swedish territorial waters. The Kogrund Canal served a similar purpose. If one sails east of the Kogrund Canal along Scania's southwest coast, one can remain within Swedish territorial waters. If an enemy respected the territorial waters, one could thus sail without the risk of mines along this route.

Power struggles around the Baltic Sea – a historical perspective

The Viking Age and the Middle Ages
Excavations in the major Nordic Viking towns of Hedeby, also known as Haithabu (in Schleswig), and Birka (near Stockholm), and at other sites have revealed an extensive trade in the Viking Age from the Baltic region and further down towards the Black Sea along the many river systems. Novgorod in Russia occupied a central place in the Vikings' trading network. From 1157, Finland was under the Swedish crown.

Cape Arkona was conquered in 1168 from the local Wendic tribes and the whole island of Rügen became a Danish fiefdom which was included in the diocese of Roskilde until 1325. During the reign of Valdemar the Conqueror in the thirteenth century, parts of current Estonia were subjected to the Danish crown. The capital was called Tallinn, which is derived from the Estonian words *Taani Linn*, meaning 'Danish town'. The conquest was encouraged by the Catholic Church, which at the time was seeking to increase its power and influence eastwards. From the opposite side, the Slavic population was spreading the Greek/Russian Orthodox faith and for centuries the River Narva was the border between these two faiths. The River Narva runs from Lake Peipus northwards and flows into the Gulf of Finland. It was on the west bank of Lake Peipus in 1242 that the canonised Russian national hero Alexander Nevsky defeated the German knights.

From 1241, the Hanseatic League, and above all Lübeck, started to be an economic power in the region. It lasted for the next three hundred years. Visby on Gotland played a special role as a natural centre for the Baltic trade – Gotland was Danish from 1361 to 1645. Danzig (now the Polish town of Gdańsk) later evolved into the centre for all trade in cereals in northern Europe, and the German knightly orders and the Hanseatic League were firmly in the driving seat in this part of the economy. The power of the orders of knights began to wane in the 1550s as a result of the Reformation.

The Danish King Frederik II restored the Danish presence in Estonia in 1559 when he bought the diocese, which included Saaremaa and Hiiumaa.

Near the mouth of the River Narva lie two towns: Estonian Narva on the west side and Russian Ivangorod on the east. There is a fort belonging to each settlement. Danes, Swedes, Poles and Russians have fought in this area throughout the centuries for land, trade and ports. Narva was founded in 1222 by Valdemar the Conqueror and remained in Danish hands until Valdemar IV Atterdag's sale of Estonia to the Teutonic Order in 1346. Among the Estonian regions, the island of Saaremaa remained in Danish hands the longest – right up to the Peace of Brömsebro in 1645.

Sound dues and power relationships in the Baltic Sea
From 1429, the Danish king extracted 'Sound dues' from ships that passed Kronborg at Elsinore (Helsingør). Almost all transportation of large amounts of goods over longer distances took place by ship. As maritime and trading nations, the Netherlands and England were very interested in the significant trade in the area. This gave rise to the classic problems of power and rights. Those coastal states which were strong enough wanted to enforce a principle of *mare clausum*, ie a closed sea, where only the coastal states were involved in the trading. The weaker powers and the intruders wanted a *mare liberum*, a free sea where trading was open to all. This battle for dominance of the Baltic Sea affected Danish and Swedish foreign policy and the Latin name was often used: *Dominum Maris Baltici*. It led to wars for hundreds of years and the Netherlands and England, in particular, used their naval power to support a policy in favour of the weak powers in the Baltic Sea. The aim was to ensure that no single nation got total dominion over the coastal reaches in the straits. The wars between Sweden and Denmark were mainly about trading rights in the Baltic Sea and all rights were based on the power that each state could put behind its demands.

Poland and Lithuania
From 1386 right up to Poland's dissolution in 1795, Poland and Lithuania were united and at times the two countries formed a strong polity. Formally, it was the Kingdom of Poland and the Grand Duchy of Lithuania, a union in which Poland was the dominant partner. The Teutonic knightly orders were kept in check by the Polish king, who defeated them at Tannenberg in 1410; Moscow was captured and was under the domination of the union from 1610 to 1612 – the nation stretched all the way to the shores of the Black Sea at certain periods.

The Swedish wars
From about 1560 until 1660, Sweden carried out a dramatic expansion of its territories and consolidated its power in what are now Finland, Estonia, Latvia, Lithuania, Poland, Germany, Denmark and Norway. A large part of the Baltic

coast thus fell into Swedish hands. The Swedish army was partly financed by export earnings from iron and arms. Generally speaking, the Swedish armies were very strong, but the Swedish navy was sometimes poorly led and in a worse shape than the Danish. In 1644, the Danish navy was almost wiped out by a Swedish-Dutch fleet and the subsequent Peace of Brömsebro was the beginning of the collapse of Denmark's foreign policy. When the next war broke out, the King of Sweden came from Torun, in what is now Poland. He gathered together some scattered Swedish forces and immediately marched west. A strong Danish-Norwegian fleet could usually maintain the security of the Danish islands, but not Jutland and Scania, and when in 1658 Danish territorial waters became ice-bound, the Swedish army crossed the ice and thereby won the war. In this way, Denmark lost the provinces of Scania, Halland and Blekinge in southern Sweden, all of which had constituted an integral part of Denmark since the Viking age. The Swedish wars were very much about the right to maritime trade. Shipping paid Sound dues to the Danish king. During the Scanian War of 1675–1679, the Danish-Norwegian navy transported a large army over to Scania, but it was defeated.

Russia becomes a Baltic power

In 1558, Russia fought her way out to Narva and started trading from there. The Swedes captured Narva in 1581 and forced the Russians back from the Baltic Sea again. One of the reasons for the Great Northern War from 1700 to 1720 was a Russian desire to regain access to the Baltic Sea and thereby to the extensive trade in the area. During this war, Sweden was crushed as a great power. Because of the intervention of the great powers, Denmark did not get its lost lands back, despite a renewed attempt at reconquering Scania. Russia captured the River Neva estuary in 1703. The Baltic states were incorporated into the Tsarist Empire in 1721 and from this year, Russia became a significant power in the Baltic Sea.

The Napoleonic wars

The Napoleonic wars also reached the Baltic region. In 1801, Britain had prepared a punitive action against the second League of Armed Neutrality. This consisted of the three naval powers of Russia, Sweden and Denmark, which, thanks to a joint convoy system, were earning enormous sums trading with everyone, including the warring parties. The action against Sweden and Russia was called off after the Battle of Copenhagen in 1801, when it became known that the Russian Tsar Paul I had just been murdered.

The siege of Copenhagen and the subsequent bombardment in 1807 was due to British demands for the surrender of the Danish-Norwegian fleet, together with the merchant fleet, both of which Britain did not want to fall into Napoleon's hands, as this would pose a significant threat to Britain, particularly of French invasion across the English Channel. The subsequent gunboat war in Danish and Norwegian waters was a series of pinprick operations directed against Royal Navy and commercial ships. Britain had to obtain imports of hemp, mast poles, timber and much more from the Baltic ports to maintain the Royal Navy, as well as her merchant ships, and it was too expensive and too dangerous to sail around the North Cape and obtain the goods in Arkhangelsk. But the Danish-Norwegian resistance did not have any significant impact on Britain, whose fleet sailed in and out of the Baltic Sea with large convoys. The Royal Navy was simply too strong.

In 1809, Sweden had to cede Finland, which then became a Grand Duchy with the Russian tsar as Grand Duke. At the conclusion of peace in 1814, Sweden got Norway as compensation for the loss of Finland.

The Schleswig Wars and the Crimean War

Prussia and Denmark fought two wars over the duchy of Schleswig-Holstein (Slesvig-Holsten). The end of the First Schleswig War from 1848 to 1850 was

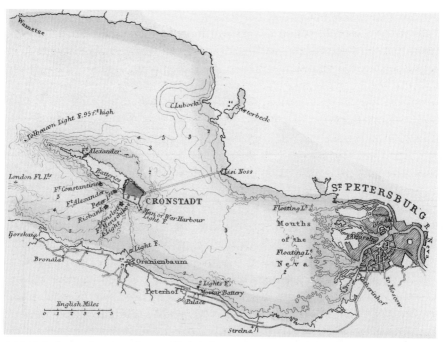

A historical map showing the naval base of Kronstadt, Systerbäck (Russian Sestroretsk – the border river), the Peterhof Palace, which became German headquarters, and Oranienbaum, which was never conquered by the Germans between 1941 and 1945. (Distances in English miles)

not brought about by the action of the Danish army and navy – Russian diplomatic pressure, supported by a strong Russian Baltic Fleet, persuaded Prussia to end the war.

The Crimean War (1853–1856) took a small detour to the Baltic Sea, when British and French naval forces bombarded the Russian forts at Bomarsund on Åland and in Helsinki. This event revealed Denmark's impotence: two major naval powers just sailed through the Danish straits and did what they pleased. It was the direct reason for the United States demanding the abolition of the Sound dues. They were lifted in 1857 after an international conference.

During the Second Schleswig War in 1864, Prussia only had a modest fleet, and therefore the Austrian fleet in the Adriatic was called in to provide assistance. At the Battle of Heligoland on 9 May 1864, the force was turned back by a Danish squadron under Orlogskaptajn Edouard Suensson before it came into the Baltic Sea, but this war was lost on the ground to an army against which the Danish forces were powerless. From the Danish point of view, the naval victory was the only bright spot of the war, but irrelevant when peace terms were dictated.

Germany rearms at sea

In the late nineteenth century, Germany began a naval rearmament which was primarily directed against Britain and France. It was also intended to support Germany's ambitions for empire and its growing number of colonies in China, the Pacific Islands and Africa.

Russia and its fleets

In relation to Russia, the Baltic Sea should not be seen in isolation, but also considered in conjunction with the country's ambitions in other maritime areas. The Russian tsars sought for years to get access to the oceans. Russia started as a small city-state around the city of Moscow and was expanded gradually and very slowly during centuries of struggle against diverse invading forces, such as the Mongols, the Teutonic orders of knighthood, Swedes, Turks, Lithuanians and Poles. From 1555, it was possible to establish maritime trade with English merchants from Arkhangelsk via the tsar's newly established Muscovy Company,[2] but the area was not inviting for either industry or traffic on a large scale. Peter the Great's victories over Sweden gave Russia access to the sea in the Baltic. In 1703, Peter founded the new city

2   In 1555, the English were granted trading privileges by Tsar Ivan IV (Ivan the Terrible). He gave them the right to trade in the area of the northern River Dvina estuary. (There are two Dvina rivers. The western Dvina flows into the Gulf of Riga.)

of St Petersburg on the estuary of the River Neva, which became the country's capital as early as 1712. From here, Russia had access to conduct maritime trade in the ice-free periods from May to December. English merchants could now buy their Russian goods via St Petersburg and avoid the expensive and dangerous voyage up to the Barents Sea.

The two oldest Russian fleets are the Baltic Fleet and the Black Sea Fleet, which originated during Peter the Great's reign. The Pacific Fleet was established in 1860, but after the defeat by the Japanese in 1905, it was not re-established until 1932. In the northern area, a naval force was established in 1916 that could co-operate with the Allied transports. In 1933, it received the status of a flotilla and in 1937 of an independent fleet, the Northern Fleet. At the outbreak of war in 1941, a modest number of submarines and destroyers were based here.

The outcome of the Russo-Japanese War 1904/1905 was a disaster for Russia and its population and it contributed to both the February and the October revolutions in St Petersburg in 1917.[3] The human sacrifices and the economic consequences were both enormous. When the Pacific Fleet was defeated by the Japanese fleet, the entire Baltic Fleet was sent to Vladivostok and Port Arthur. It was a relocation which took more than seven months, as most units had to sail south of Africa. In the end, the naval force was destroyed by an inferior, but ably-led, Japanese naval force in the Battle of Tsushima Strait in May 1905. After 1905, Russia thus had no Baltic Fleet, and there were therefore no forces available to protect St Petersburg.

Russian analyses in 1909 concluded that an attack on the capital would naturally come by sea. Following a major commission, work was begun in 1914 on the Peter the Great naval fortress in what is now Finland and Estonia. The plans also included sketches for a small fleet. In this way, according to the plan, it would be possible – with limited use of warships – to hold an invading enemy at a distance from St Petersburg simply by fortifying the entire entrance to the Gulf of Finland. Twenty-five forts were built on the Finnish side and seventeen on the Estonian side, where the artillery had a calibre of between 2in/57mm and 14in/355mm. In 1912, the Russian State Duma adopted a long-term building programme which should have lasted over eighteen years. Twenty-four battleships, twelve battlecruisers, twenty-four light cruisers, 108 destroyers and thirty-six large submarines were to be built.

---

3   According to the old Russian calendar (the Julian), they took place in February and October 1917, but going by the current calendar (the Gregorian), they took place in March and November. The correction in the twentieth century was thirteen days.

The Baltic Sea during and after the First World War

When the First World War broke out, the German navy got its best ships ready for the battle against the Royal Navy, while they could make do with the older and outdated vessels against the Russians. To relieve the Russians, but also to put maximum pressure on the German economy, industry and fleet, the Royal Navy from 1915 onwards sent a number of submarines in through the Sound to the Baltic Sea. These submarines were supported at Russian bases.

Russian military participation slowly ground to a standstill because of domestic social upheavals near the end of the war. The Germans made a very large and successful landing in October 1917, when a landing force of 23,000 men captured Saaremaa and the nearby island of Muhu. The Germans actually won the war on the Eastern Front, partly because of Lenin's seizure of power in Russia one month later, but the outcome of the war was decided on the Western Front where the Germans lost during 1918. With the end of the war and the Russian Revolution, a special situation arose in the Baltic region. Two of the losers from the First World War were no longer strong naval powers. As losers, they came together in co-operation during the following decade.

In Sweden, German naval rearmament leading up to the First World War had been followed with some concern, because this development had reduced Sweden to a secondary power. Russia had been Sweden's natural enemy for centuries and, with the revolution and Russia in chaos, this threat was suddenly eliminated. Sweden could therefore save on military spending after the First World War and went towards apparently problem-free times in the 1920s and 1930s.

2

Political Manoeuvring Between the Wars

The Baltic states and Finland

A number of new countries emerged as a result of the October Revolution in 1917 and the defeat of Germany in the First World War in 1918. In the Baltic region, a new Poland reappeared after the conclusion of peace. In 1795, the country had been wiped off the map by Russia, Prussia and Austria, which were all losers in the First World War (with Germany as the heir of Prussia). In the Baltic area, three countries rose again which had been under Russian rule since 1721: Lithuania, Latvia and Estonia. Before that they had been Swedish.

North of here lay the Grand Duchy of Finland. Finland declared independence on 6 December 1917, but had to go through a bloody civil war from 27 January to 15 May 1918. On the Red side, about thirty thousand men (Russians and Finns) were killed. On the White side, about five thousand Finns and five hundred Germans died. Many of these died in captivity, not in direct combat. With the Treaty of Tartu in 1920, Finland received a coastal area of the Barents Sea with the harbour at Petsamo, and Norway and Russia no longer had a common border.

Poland

Poland became independent in 1905 with Marshal Józef Piłsudski as head of state. He founded Poland's new army and also became its commander-in-chief. He had previously served five years of internment in Siberia. During the war against Russia in 1920/21, where the Polish army beat the Red Army under the leadership of the People's Commissar Trotsky and General Tukhachevsky, the Poles captured large tracts of land. Galicia was captured from the Ukraine, and Minsk and Bobruysk from Belarus. Piłsudski's plan was to offer the newly won Polish territories to the Allies, so these could intervene against the new Bolshevik threat from there. France supported Poland's fight against Ukraine with a large number of aircraft. The new Polish nation was not popular with either the Russians or the Germans who – not completely without reason – perceived the Polish regime as very provocative. When the Germans marched into the Sudetenland in

Poland became independent in 1918 with Marshal Józef Piłsudski as head of state. He founded Poland's new army and also became its commander-in-chief.

Czechoslovakia in 1938, Poland used the occasion to annex the town of Těšín (now Polish Cieszyn) from Czechoslovakia.

The Baltic states and Russia

From November 1918 until 1920, Britain supported the Baltic states' struggle against revolutionary Russia and the Whites' fight against the Reds. Lenin's opponents were supported with deliveries of equipment and small army forces were also sent. The most important action came from the Royal Navy which sent a large naval force. Copenhagen was used as a forward base for British warships.

British naval operations included aircraft carriers, which ferried a lot of aircraft to bases in Estonia, numerous cruisers, destroyers, submarines and, not least, minesweepers, since there were still a lot of mines in the area from the war and even more were now being laid. Their opponents were Russian revolutionaries with battleships, cruisers, destroyers and submarines. During the attacks, the British sent small torpedo boats right into the naval port at Kronstadt, which was the Red Fleet's main base. The battleships *Petropavlovsk* (later renamed *Marat*) and *Andrei Pervozvanny*[1] were sunk and subsequently

---

1   The somewhat unusual name arises because Russian naval ships during the time of the tsars were often named after apostles and saints. The ship's name meant 'Andrew, the first

The battleship *Marat* (ex-*Petropavlovsk*) from the Soviet Baltic Fleet. (Old Ship Picture Galleries)

The Russian battleship *Andrei Pervozvanny* anchored or moored to a buoy in Copenhagen harbour in September 1912.

lay on the bottom of the harbour. The large number of private armies and foreign intervention forces did not work together and that was the only reason that Lenin's revolution was not defeated.

Finnish-Estonian defence preparations

When Estonia and Finland became independent after the First World War, the plan utilising the Peter the Great naval fortress was reversed: it was now possible jointly – with the same coastal forts which the Russians had built – to prevent the Russians from coming out from their bases at the eastern end of the Gulf of Finland. Apart from the forts, Finland and Estonia planned to make use of their mines and submarines, and they practised blocking the passages between Porkkala and Naissaar. The last joint submarine exercise was held between 17 and 21 July 1939. Initially, the two new Baltic Sea countries considered Russia as the enemy in the long term, and Germany as a possible ally. Another result of the Russian Revolution was that Åland was no longer Russian, but Finnish. The population of the islands consisted predominantly of Swedish-speaking Finns.

Memel's special status

Memel (now Klaipėda in Lithuania) was an old Hanseatic city situated on the estuary of the River Niemen. It was German until 1918 and had a predominantly German population. It was then administered by French authorities under a mandate from the League of Nations. After 1924, the city became self-governing, but was assigned to Lithuania. During the next fifteen years, numerous problems arose between the German population in Memel and the Lithuanian authorities. A state of emergency was declared on two occasions. When the Nazis came to power during the 1930s, the picture changed. In the elections of December 1938, the Nazis won twenty-six of the twenty-nine seats on the city council and this set off the Jewish exodus from the city in earnest. From March 1939, the German fleet was ready to carry out an invasion of Memel, but it was not necessary because the Lithuanian government bowed to Hitler's threats and demands. On 21 March 1939, Memel was 'incorporated into the Reich', amid great rejoicing, as Hitler's last bloodless conquest.

---

called', after Jesus's first disciple.

Alliances

The three Baltic states and Poland sought security through alliances. The four countries now all had strained relationships with both Hitler's Germany and Stalin's Soviet Union. Polish intelligence, for example, was split: one half worked on the threat from Germany, the other with the threat from the Soviet Union. Poland had had an alliance with France since 1920. It included military co-operation in the case of aggression from either Russia or Germany and was gradually expanded, but in trying to keep up with rearmament in Germany after 1933, France was finding it harder to back up its support with a corresponding military capability. After Germany had begun rearming its fleet, it was no longer possible for France to maintain its obligations to Poland without itself making any significant investments in its fleet. Similarly, Britain could not live up to its promises and intentions, and demonstrate power and presence in the Baltic region. The view was also confirmed to the Danish Prime Minister Thorvald Stauning by the British prime minister on a visit to London in April 1937. On 31 March 1939,

The German Foreign Minister, Joachim von Ribbentrop; the General Secretary of the CPSU, Joseph Vissarionovich Stalin; and the Soviet Foreign Minister, Vyacheslav Mikhailovich Molotov, in Moscow on 23 August 1939 during the signing of the Molotov–Ribbentrop Pact. (SMB arkiv)

Britain, France and Poland signed a treaty of mutual military support in the event of German aggression. It was also prompted by Hitler's annexation of Czechoslovakia. This treaty was extended on 25 August 1939 in response to the Molotov–Ribbentrop agreement in Moscow two days earlier.

The Molotov–Ribbentrop Pact of 23 August 1939

The background to the Molotov–Ribbentrop Pact was partly that Stalin felt betrayed by the Munich Agreement of 1938. By making a pact with Germany, the Soviet Union was buying time to prepare for a future showdown with Germany. This infamous pact was signed in Moscow on 23 August 1939 and was, in fact, Hitler's prerequisite for attacking Poland and thereby initiating the Second World War. The pact contained a secret additional protocol, which described the signatory powers' spheres of interest, which in practice meant an internal statement of the areas that Germany and the Soviet Union respectively could occupy. Western Poland and Lithuania were included in the German area, but soon after Hitler accepted Stalin's wish that Lithuania be 'ceded' to him. The Soviet Union could hereafter freely decide over Finland, Estonia, Latvia and Lithuania, as well as the remainder of Poland. The Soviet Union denied the existence of the secret additional protocol right up to 1989.

3

Naval Developments Between the Wars

The development of the Soviet Baltic fleet after the October Revolution of 1917

After the civil war, the Baltic Fleet had, broadly speaking, been wiped out. The few remaining ships could not be manned adequately by the available crews: there were simply too few sailors and they were too poorly trained to operate and maintain the vessels. Furthermore, supplies of fuel were so sparse that they could not afford to fire up the boilers. They were therefore compelled to allow some of the former Tsarist Empire's naval officers to continue in the new fleet. The Baltic Fleet had a very distinguished record,[1] but initially not very much equipment.

The starting signal for Lenin's revolution was given from the Baltic Fleet's old cruiser *Aurora*, which was one of the few ships that had not been sunk by the Japanese in 1905 after sailing from the Baltic to Tsushima Strait, when the ship sought haven in a neutral port. The sailors of the fleet took an active part in the revolution in 1917, but on 1 March 1921, a rebellion broke out among the sailors at the base at Kronstadt on Kotlin Island. They made numerous demands on the regime – for freedom of expression, reforms, secret ballots, a multi-party system, etc – and the ruling elite could not allow that. The People's Commissar of Defence (Defence Minister) Leon Trotsky gave his most talented general, the later Marshal Mikhail Nikolayevich Tukhachevsky, the task of putting down the rebellion, which he did most harshly. The revolt was crushed after two failed attacks from the Red Army, and after the battles, the Cheka – the secret police – made sure that those who had not already died were killed. The number of victims from the rebellion in Kronstadt has never been fully clarified. Over twenty thousand sailors have been named as killed, but recent research suggests that approximately two thousand sailors were executed, and six to eight thousand fled across the ice to Finland. In

---

1 Since 1965, the Soviet Baltic Fleet has been designated in Russian as Дважды Краснознаменный Балтиский Флот, which means 'The Baltic Fleet, twice awarded the Order of the Red Banner.' The three other Soviet fleets have only received one corresponding order. The Baltic Fleet was awarded the first for its participation in the October Revolution of 1917 and the second for its contribution during the Great Patriotic War from 1941 to 1945.

The cruiser *Aurora*, which today is a museum ship in St Petersburg. (Old Ship Picture Galleries)

addition, many thousands – perhaps ten thousand soldiers from the Red Army – fell during the attacks over the ice.

In the 1920s, the naval policies of Russia and the Soviet Union were marked by bad experiences from the Russo-Japanese War, the First World War and the Civil War, and the fleet was in a miserable condition. At the conferences in Riga in 1923 and in Rome in 1924, Russia and the newly-formed Soviet Union respectively tried unsuccessfully to make the Baltic Sea a *mare clausum* (a closed sea), reserved for the coastal states. The following year, a concerned editor of *Izvestia*[2] wrote that Denmark's dredging of the channel at Drogden was aimed at facilitating Britain's access to the Baltic Sea.

The few who understood naval strategy suggested as early as 1925 that the Soviet Union should acquire a fleet of aircraft carriers. They would be crucial if a conflict arose with the Western powers, especially Britain, which from the mid-1920s to the early 1930s was regarded as the most obvious adversary – after their experiences in the Civil War. The fleet just scraped by with its existing ships until 1928, when Stalin launched the first of many five-year plans.

---

2   The two largest newspapers in the Soviet Union were *Pravda* and *Izvestia*. *Pravda* was the mouthpiece of the Communist Party, while *Izvestia* was the voice of the Soviet government.

The five-year plans and the fleet programmes

The first five-year plan ran from 1928 to 1932. The Commissar (Minister) for the Navy, Romuald Adamovich Muklevich, stated in a top-secret document in connection with the fleet discussions in 1928/29, especially about the Baltic Fleet, that the budgets for new construction and maintenance did not measure up to the plans for the defence of the Soviet Union (perhaps not a completely new phenomenon for military planners). The problem for the promoters of the first five-year plan was that it had to both redress the country's dire economy and be a political success. World revolution was still in the party programme, but it quickly became clear that it would not be possible to build cruisers, battleships and aircraft carriers, and train the crews, in the space of just a few years. The few large vessels that had been taken over from the tsarist era had to be rebuilt and modernised, and that was difficult enough.

In the end, the first five-year plan only included a fleet programme with light vessels and naval aircraft. From a technological point of view, these units were relatively straightforward to build, and many of them were built, but the quality of the equipment could not measure up to that of Western Europe, and the training in the navy was initially very poor.

With the second five-year plan (which only lasted from 1 January 1933 to 1 April 1937),[3] a large submarine-building programme was initiated which, by the end of 1937, had given the Soviet Union a submarine fleet of about 145 boats, the largest in the world. When the Spanish Civil War broke out, the Soviet Union had no large ships to send as escorts or patrol vessels and it had to take into account that its opponents sank at least one of the Soviet transport vessels in Spanish waters without it being able to intervene. Large ocean-going vessels which could be decisive in battle would be built during the next five-year plan from 1938 to 1942. In the run-up to the Second World War, the Soviet Union had a number of ambitious naval programmes, including giant battleships of 70,000 tonnes, but in reality only very few, modest-sized new constructions saw the light of day. On paper, the Soviet navy had a lot of submarines and smaller vessels at the start of the war, but they were spread over four geographically separate fleets.[4]

Since about 1925, there had been discussions about the character of the future Soviet fleet. Should it be ocean-going or consist of smaller vessels

---

3   The objectives of this five-year plan, according to Stalin, had already been achieved after four years and three months (one of the great triumphs of socialism).

4   The Northern Fleet in the Barents Sea, the Baltic Fleet, the Black Sea Fleet and the Pacific Fleet.

built for coastal operations? The young school – *Jeune École*,[5] or in Russian, *Molodaya Shkola* – was in favour of a fleet with a lot of light units such as submarines, naval aircraft and torpedo boats, supported by destroyers. There were no cruisers or battleships in this rationale. Criticism by the Mahan supporters,[6] predominantly surviving naval officers from the tsarist era, increased in 1927 and 1928, but it was the *Jeune École* supporters who won, which is reflected in the fleet's new fighting instructions[7] from 1930. Now there was not so much talk about demonstrating naval power on the oceans, but about operating in coastal areas, carrying out coastal defence and joint operations with the Red Army. In 1937, the fighting instructions were revised again and now more emphasis was put on co-operation with other armed forces and on types of weapons, as well as on operations directed against an enemy's maritime supply lines. The navy's offensive potential was especially emphasised. If Stalin's purges had not taken place, the navy would probably have changed character during the third five-year plan from a *Jeune École* fleet with light units to a more Mahan-influenced fleet of large ocean-going vessels with heavy artillery.

The later Marshal Tukhachevsky, as head of the Leningrad military district, took part in a series of exercises which also had a maritime component. He had previously been opposed to large ships, but in 1932 he admitted that aircraft carriers would be a great advantage if the Baltic Fleet was going to operate at a great distance from Leningrad. The Soviet navy's commander-in-chief during the same period, Admiral Lev Mikhailovich Galler, had doubts about whether the operational plans actually measured up to the ambitions. According to him, the naval infantry could not solve offensive tasks, and the minesweepers were technically unable to sweep modern mines. The decision-makers were thus far from being in agreement about plans and operations during this period, but the biggest problem for the Baltic Fleet was clear: since the revolution and the loss of Estonia and Finland, the fleet could easily become locked in at the eastern end of the Gulf of Finland. When the Soviet navy was established in 1928 on the remains of the Russian navy, the majority of the vessels were in the Baltic Sea. Three of the navy's four old battleships were here, along with two of the four cruisers, twelve of the seventeen destroyers and nine of the seventeen submarines.

---

5   The term *Jeune École* comes from the French defence debate in the late nineteenth century, in which they were trying to prevent a naval race with the British. A *Jeune École* fleet has a large number of small, effective units.

6   The American naval theorist, Rear Admiral Alfred Thayer Mahan, emphasised that sea power is based on the large ships which decide battles, such as battleships and cruisers. His works were written between 1890 and 1914.

7   Fighting instructions (in Russian *bojevoj ustav*) are the navy's general directives for action, use of weapons, etc.

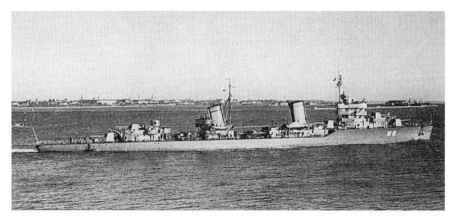

Two powerful destroyers – 'destroyer leaders' (a mixture of a cruiser and a destroyer) – joined the Baltic Fleet in 1936 and 1939 respectively. They were a Soviet attempt to copy the destroyers of the French *Vauquelin* class. The two ships, *Leningrad* and *Minsk*, were heavily armed with five 5in/130mm guns, but they were not very stable. The ship shown here is *Minsk*. (Old Ship Picture Galleries)

When Germany began building the aircraft carriers *Graf Zeppelin* and *Peter Strasser* in 1936,[8] Stalin a little later somewhat reluctantly launched a ten-year construction programme, where consideration was given to beginning the building of four aircraft carriers. The Russians were aware of their inferiority to the Kriegsmarine[9] in the Baltic Sea, so in 1939 the Soviets invited both the French navy and the Royal Navy to participate in joint manoeuvres in the Baltic Sea, but nothing ever came of it.

During the third five-year plan from 1 April 1937 up until the beginning of the Great Patriotic War, it was decided to begin construction of a high-seas fleet (an ocean-going fleet). Keels were laid[10] for two battleships in Leningrad and one in Nikolayevsk (on the Black Sea). They were to be of 35,000 tonnes each and have 16in guns (406mm) – France was asked about supply of the guns. These very ambitious plans were updated every fiscal year until 1940. The target was a high-seas fleet which could measure up to the three largest fleets in the world (from Britain, the USA and Japan). Because of the looming prospect of war against Germany, the programme was stopped by decree on 19 October 1940, and the funds were channelled to construction programmes for smaller units which could be produced faster.

---

8   Graf (Count) Ferdinand von Zeppelin was a German general and airship designer, and Fregattenkapitän Peter Strasser headed the Imperial German Navy's fleet of airships. Strasser was shot down and killed over the British east coast on 5 August 1918.

9   The term Kriegsmarine is used when mentioning the German navy during the war.

10 The construction of a large steel ship begins with keel-laying in a dock and the ribs are built up from that. After this the ship begins to take shape.

The minelayer *Marti*, formerly the Imperial Russian yacht *Shtandart*. Immediately after the revolution, the ship's name was changed to *18 Marta* (18 March) and later to *Marti*. (Old Ship Picture Galleries)

The Soviet cruiser *Kirov* was commissioned on 26 September 1938. The main armament was four gun turrets, each with three 7in/180mm guns. (Old Ship Picture Galleries)

The aircraft carriers previously mentioned were also included in the plan, but construction of them was to be started at the end of the five-year plan, around 1942. They were complicated to design and the associated aircraft also needed to be developed. Four aircraft carriers should have been built, one for each fleet, before 1948. US assistance was desired for the construction of both the aircraft carriers and the battleships, but the US Congress was not happy supporting a totalitarian (ie Communist) regime. The Soviet navy's leadership would also have liked to have accelerated aircraft carrier production.

In 1935, the construction of a series of cruisers had begun, two of which were intended for the Baltic Fleet. They were *Kirov*[11] and *Maxim Gorky*.[12] They were built at the Ordzhonikidze shipyard in Leningrad with technical assistance from Italy. The collaboration resulted in vessels with very beautiful

11 Named after Sergei Mironovich Kirov, who was assassinated (possibly at Stalin's behest) in 1934. He was one of Stalin's competitors.
12 Named after the Soviet writer Aleksei Maksimovich Peshkov (1868–1936), who wrote under the pseudonym of Maxim Gorky.

lines. They were the first large units to join the fleet after the revolution and to have been built in the Soviet Union. The cruisers were developed from the Italian cruiser *Raimondo Montecuccolli*; *Kirov* was commissioned on 26 September 1938, and *Maxim Gorky* on 12 December 1940.

At the outbreak of war in 1941, the Baltic Fleet had a very large minelayer, which was the former Imperial Russian yacht *Shtandart* (Standard), of 5,600 tonnes.[13] *Shtandart* was renamed *Marti* during the war, when the ship got an armament of four 5in/130mm guns, and the maximum mine load was between 320 and 780 mines, depending on the type of mine.

Political control and purges in the Baltic Fleet

While the revolution was at its peak in January 1918, Rear-Admiral Alexei Mikhailovich Shchastnyi, chief of staff of the Russian Baltic Fleet, offered to conduct evacuations from Tallinn and Helsinki, so the fleet's equipment did not fall into the hands of the White forces. His conditions for co-operation with Lenin's people were simple: there was to be no interference by political commissars. In a skilful manoeuvre, he got the fleet's equipment back to Petrograd through heavy ice and large minefields. As a reward, Trotsky appointed him commander-in-chief of the Baltic Fleet, but soon after he fell into disgrace and Trotsky had him liquidated as a counter-revolutionary in June 1918.[14]

The political officers kept a wary eye on the navy, where they had had to use a large number of naval officers from the tsar's time because it was not possible to train commanding officers of ships and fleets right away without them acquiring a certain amount of experience in advance of promotion. Naval officers were regarded as aristocrats. It was easier to push young people through the training system in the Red Army and thereby obtain politically reliable army officers with a minimal professional military background. With the introduction of political commissars, the military command situation became chaotic. These commissars (deputy chiefs in political affairs, in Russian shortened to *zampolit* or *politruk*) had no prerequisites whatsoever for participating in operational discussions or decisions. They 'helped' the commanding officers and force commanders to make the right decisions on the party's behalf and their presence was supposed to ensure uniformity and loyalty in the leading cadres. In addition to the great purges that took the

---

13 *Shtandart* was originally commissioned from the B&W shipyard in Copenhagen in 1893, while Maria Feodorovna was Tsarina of Russia (the Danish-born Empress Dagmar). The vessel was delivered in 1896, but by then Maria Feodorovna had become a widow and her son had inherited the throne. The ship was not broken up until 1963.

14 Admiral Shchastnyi was rehabilitated in 1995.

lives of many of the navy's people in 1937 and 1938, there were special purges in the fleet after the Kronstadt revolt in 1921, in 1926 and again in 1930.

Stalin's purges in the armed forces culminated in 1937/38 and thereafter there were, broadly speaking, no naval officers from the tsar's time remaining in the fleet. The purges affected all levels of society, but especially people in leadership positions. Some were shot, others put in labour camps in the Gulag system. The navy's losses during the purges were proportionately larger than those of the army. During the purges, a special court was set up, the Baltic Fleet Revolutionary Tribunal, but the archives for exactly the years 1935–1938 have disappeared and it is therefore very difficult to put a figure on the importance of the purges for the Baltic Fleet. The commander-in-chief of the Baltic Fleet, Admiral Alexander Kuzmich Sivkov, was convicted and executed on 22 February 1938. His chief of staff, Vice-Admiral Ivan Stepanovich Isakov, had complained in 1937 about the purges when his chief planning officer had been arrested, and all project work concerning the third five-year plan had therefore come to a complete standstill.

Soviet submarine programmes

Submarine construction comprised some very different types. In 1919, the Royal Navy lost the minelaying submarine *L-55* on the island of Seiskaari (Russian: Seskar) west of Kronstadt during the fighting against the Red forces. In 1928, the Russians salvaged this submarine and it became operational again in 1931. Moreover, they copied the design and build their own 'L'-class submarines. By 1926, Soviet submarine designers had had contacts with German submarine experts who acted through foreign countries. German submarine engineers came to Leningrad in 1934. The first submarine was built in 1936 and was called the 'S' class, where 'S' stood for *srednaja* (medium-sized), but later the 'S' came to designate the *Stalinets* class.[15] A slightly smaller type of submarine was called the 'Shch' class. The first unit was named *Shchuka* (pike) and the Russian term for the first letter of the name (Щ = shch) became the name of the class. In the 1930s, they also developed a small type of submarine, called the 'M' class – 'M' stood for *malaya/malyutka* (small/baby). Finally, they developed a very large submarine, which was classified as 'K'-class, where 'K' stood for *kreiserskaya* (cruiser/submarine cruiser). At the beginning of the Second World War on 1 September 1939, the number of Soviet submarines had reached 181 and, at the time of the German attack on the Soviet Union on 22 June 1941, that figure had grown to 212.

---

15 Soviet submarine classifications changed from specifying the size to specifying the class designation.

In 1919, the Royal Navy lost the minelaying submarine *L-55* on the island of Seiskaari (Russian: Seskar) west of Kronstadt during the fighting against the Red forces. In 1928, the Soviet Navy salvaged this submarine and it became operational again in 1931, now under the name *Bezbozhnik* (Atheist). It was used as a basis of design for the Soviet 'L'-class submarine. Here it is shown in British waters. (WIO)

Baltic Fleet plans and ships up to the start of the war

In September 1939, there were 239 Soviet warships under construction, including three battleships, two battlecruisers, ten cruisers, forty-five destroyers and ninety-one submarines. Soviet defences in the Baltic Sea were based – with minor modifications – on the thinking of the First World War. The somewhat optimistic plans for the future fleet had in 1930 counted on the Baltic Fleet having one battleship, four cruisers, an aircraft carrier, twelve large destroyers and about fifty submarines by around 1943, as well as a large number of smaller vessels. The Gulf of Finland was to be blocked off at the island of Osmussaar (Odensholm), between Hanko and Tallinn. West of this line, the Soviet Union could take up offensive positions with submarines and naval fighter planes. When control had been gained over the situation, offensive sorties could be undertaken with cruisers and destroyers which could lay a large number of mines. East of the line, the heavy artillery units and shore batteries would take up the fight against an invader. Large numbers of sea mines were included in the defensive plans. With the de facto Soviet occupation of the three Baltic countries in 1939/40, the Soviet Union had an opportunity to create more depth in their defensive positions and thereby ensure the defence of Leningrad, in particular. A number of modern coastal batteries were established, with guns with a calibre from 5in/130mm to 11in/280mm. Naval bases were constructed in the major ports, along with about twenty airfields constructed for the Baltic Fleet air force, but the preparations were nowhere near completion when the war suddenly broke out. In particular, it came as a surprise to the Russians that the German attack in 1941 also emanated from Finland, which meant that Leningrad was threatened from the first days of the war.

The reconstruction of German military forces after the First World War

A good deal of the German re-equipment programmes which influenced the Second World War began long before Hitler came to power. They were based on German dissatisfaction with the Versailles Treaty of 1919, leading to a circumvention of its provisions. Germany and the Soviet Union had found a form of co-operation where German trials were carried out in Soviet exercise areas. These included the development of aircraft and tanks. Similarly, the navy circumvented the provisions by developing submarines and building warships larger than those permitted. Under the Treaty of Versailles of 1919, Germany was not permitted to build warships with a displacement of more than 10,000 tonnes. Cruisers were not allowed to exceed 6,000 tonnes and the Germans were not allowed to have submarines. The provisions of the

The German battleship *Bayern* sinking in Scapa Flow on 21 June 1919 after being scuttled by her own crew.

Treaty of Versailles also stipulated that Germany was not allowed to possess long-range artillery. This was a provision that France had had inserted because of the bombardment of Paris in the final year of the First World War. Since there was nothing in the treaty about rockets, in 1929 the army began to research long-range rockets for bombardment.

After the First World War, most of the German warships interned in Scapa Flow were scuttled by their own crews. The remaining fleet consisted of just eight pre-dreadnought battleships,[16] eight light cruisers, thirty-two destroyers and torpedo boats, as well as some minesweepers and auxiliaries.

The German navy's overall plans

German naval thinking up to the Second World War was in many ways a repeat of ideas from the First World War, enhanced by wartime experience. Initially, it was constrained by the limitations of the Treaty of Versailles for submarines and larger vessels, but they slowly got over these constraints in various ways. The plan was still that the Baltic Sea should be kept free of the British and the French, who would possibly ally with the Poles. This could be done by preventing enemies sailing through the Danish straits, which could best be blocked with mines. It was especially important that British submarines did not penetrate the straits again. On the world's oceans, German cruisers or auxiliary cruisers/commerce raiders (very heavily armed ships that looked like merchant ships) could conduct trade wars against the colonial powers, France and Britain. Submarines could support these operations, as well as blockade the island kingdom of Great Britain. If war against the Soviet Union arose, they could either defeat the technologically backward Soviet vessels at sea or bottle them up inside their bases with mines. The German North Sea ports could easily be blockaded by the British, so several alternative bases were required. Experience from the First World War emphasised southern Norway as a base area, and in this context, a partial or total occupation of Denmark could be seen as a possibility.

Grossadmiral Erich Raeder and the reconstruction of the German navy

In 1924, 48-year-old Vizeadmiral Erich Raeder became commander-in-chief of the German navy's Baltic Fleet. He came from the naval staff in Berlin where he had been in charge of naval training. At the end of the First World

---

16 That is, built before the ground-breaking British battleship HMS *Dreadnought* (1906).

War, he had been a staff officer for Admiral Franz von Hipper. After the war, in 1920, he was accused of having participated in the so-called Kapp Putsch, or coup, directed against the Weimar government and he was therefore ordered to lie low in the navy library, where he wrote the history of the Imperial German Navy during the war. It was here that he began to see how enormously important the German commerce raiders had been. His books on naval warfare led to the University of Kiel awarding him an honorary doctorate.

In 1928 he was appointed admiral and commander-in-chief of the Reichsmarine. This took place at the same time as the construction of a number of Panzerkreuzer (armour-plated cruisers) was being planned to replace the navy's oldest and largest vessels. These were ships that could operate on the oceans as commerce raiders (armed merchant cruisers, or ships targeting the enemy's merchant fleet), based on experience from the First World War. The German Social Democratic Party (SPD) wanted 'food instead of Panzerkreuzer' but the building programme was slowly forced through. To save weight, they were welded instead of riveted. Their diesel engines could give them a speed of 26 knots and, with two triple 11in/280mm gun turrets, they could defeat targets which they would not be able to outrun ('they could outgun every cruiser and outrun every battleship'). The limit was 10,000 tonnes, but they ended up actually at 14,890 tonnes displacement. The treaty was also violated in the submarine area. The Reichsmarine had already set

Naval review in Kiel before the war; from the right: *Admiral Graf Spee*, *Deutschland* and two light cruisers.

up a company in the Netherlands in 1922, via German businesses, called Ingenieurskantoor voor Scheepsbouw (Engineering Office for Shipbuilding). It designed submarines with a view to developing prototypes for future German submarines – expertise was provided and submarines were built for Turkey, Spain, Finland and the Soviet Union. Incidentally, Raeder's appointment in 1928 came in the backwash of a financial scandal which had cost his predecessor the position. Kapitän zur See Walther Lohmann was the head of all the Reichsmarine's secret equipment programmes and the scandal came close to revealing the systematic circumvention of the Treaty of Versailles, but the press were only aware of Lohmann's poor financial transactions – not of their actual purpose.

In May 1935, the Reichsmarine changed its name to the Kriegsmarine. At that time, there was keen competition for funding within the armed forces. When the Luftwaffe was established in 1935, Hermann Göring was its commander-in-chief and he was at the same time number two in the Nazi Party. The German army was clearly the first priority and after that came Göring's Luftwaffe. Grossadmiral Raeder was last in the queue when funds for the military forces were being distributed. The Kriegsmarine tried a few times to get its own naval air force established, but Reichsmarschall Hermann Göring had stated that '*Alles, was fliegt, gehört mir*' ('everything that flies belongs to me'), and that was how it stayed. In practice, the Kriegsmarine only had the few aircraft aboard its larger ships at its disposal. The rest were land-based and therefore subject to Göring.

German military precautions against political developments

Poland and France were included in German war preparations from an early point, but from November 1937, Britain was also included in their plans. If there was a man who was surprised at the coming war, it was the German navy's commander-in-chief, Grossadmiral[17] Erich Raeder. On 29 January 1939, Raeder presented the so-called Z-Plan to Hitler. It was the Kriegsmarine's own plan for the reconstruction of the fleet. Several times, both on 29 January 1939 and also as late as August 1939, Raeder received assurances from Hitler that a war with France or Britain would not be considered before 1944 at the earliest. He therefore had ample time to build a powerful fleet in accordance with the Z-plan.

The German army, however, was immediately ready to go to war. The army had evolved from a Reichswehr of 100,000 men in 1933 to an offensive

---

17 Promoted from Generaladmiral to Grossadmiral on 1 April 1939.

formation that eight and a half years later, on the Eastern Front alone, could field three million men on the front and one million men in the hinterland. Purely from a training point of view, it was in itself a huge achievement.

Hitler broke the ban on a German air force contained in the Treaty of Versailles and founded the Luftwaffe on 26 February 1935. Since Hitler's usurpation of power, Göring had been commander-in-chief of the Reichsluftfahrtministerium (Reich aviation ministry), which had been a stalking-horse for a new German air force. It was here that trials and planning of production of future aircraft could be held. The new German air force therefore had no aircraft which were more than four years old when the war started, while some of their opponents' aircraft were ten or twenty years old.

The introduction of Panzerkreuzer, battleships and cruisers

The first Panzerkreuzer was *Schiff A*, or *Ersatz*[18] *Preussen*, and it was named *Deutschland* (launched on 19 May 1931). The next was *Schiff B*, *Ersatz Lothringen*, which was named *Admiral Scheer* (keel laid down on 25 June 1931). The third and last was *Schiff C, Ersatz Braunschweig*, which was named *Admiral Graf Spee* (launched on 30 June 1934).

With Hitler's takeover of power, the circumstances were changed. Now the German navy began on a *Schiffbauersatzplan* (shipbuilding replacement programme), which was not only, as the name might suggest, a plan for the construction of replacement ships. The plan was kept secret and involved yet another violation of the Treaty of Versailles by beginning with a new type of *Schlachtkreuzer* (battlecruiser). There should have been five, but only two were begun: *Schiff D, Scharnhorst*, the keel of which was laid in 1934 (launched in October 1936), and *Schiff E, Gneisenau* in 1935 (launched in December 1936). France represented the probable enemy.

Between 1925 and 1929, the Reichsmarine gained five light cruisers with 6in/150mm artillery: *Emden, Karlsruhe, Köln, Königsberg* and *Leipzig*. In 1934, they received one additional light cruiser, *Nürnberg*.

In the middle of the 1930s, the keels were laid for five identical heavy cruisers which had a very varied fate.

Lützow[19] became part of the German-Soviet trade-offs between 1939 and 1941, and the ship came in an unfinished state to the Soviet Union with German guns and ammunition, but without fire-control systems, and its propulsion machinery had not been tested. The ship was first named *Petropavlovsk*, but in 1944 it was changed to *Tallinn*.

---

18 Replacement.
19 Not to be confused with the pocket battleship of the same name.

Four German VIPs at a parade in Berlin in 1938. The three generals to the left are General der Luftwaffe Erhard Milch, General der Artillerie Wilhelm Keitel and Generaloberst Walther von Brauchitsch. Next to them is Generaladmiral Erich Raeder. (Krigsarkivet, Sweden)

The German Panzerschiff *Deutschland*. The photo was taken before the war. The ship is seen here flying an admiral's flag. On 15 November 1939, the ship's name was changed to *Lützow*; from a propaganda point of view, it would have been unfortunate if a ship with its country's name went down. Due to its heavy armour, the type was also called a pocket battleship. On 16 April 1945, *Lützow* was subjected to an air raid by the RAF with Tallboy bombs. She was badly damaged and put aground in the Kaiser Canal at Swinemünde, from where she fired on Soviet troops right up to 4 May 1945 when her ammunition ran out.

The light cruiser *Königsberg* at Langelinie, Copenhagen, in 1932: the first German naval visit to Copenhagen after the First World War.

Seydlitz should have followed *Lützow* to the Soviet Union, but the outbreak of war in 1941 came in the way. As submarines were given top priority in the early war years, the completion of the cruiser was put on ice, and in 1942 it was decided to rebuild her as an aircraft carrier. Lack of materials put an end to that in January 1943 and the ship was towed to Königsberg (now the Russian city of Kaliningrad), where it was sunk on 10 April 1945 during the Soviet conquest of the city. The three other heavy cruisers, *Prinz Eugen*, *Blücher* and *Admiral Hipper* all participated in the war and will be discussed later.

In 1936, the keels were laid for *Schiff F*, *Ersatz Hannover*, which became *Bismarck*, and *Schiff G*, *Ersatz Schleswig-Holstein*, eventually named *Tirpitz*. The crews were approximately 2,400 men, and *Bismarck* was designed for a displacement of 41,700 tonnes, while *Tirpitz* was 42,900 tonnes. These two ships were designed to fight French battleships of the *Richelieu* class. In addition, plans were made for six battleships known as *H*, *J*, *K*, *L*, *M* and *N*. The first two had their keels laid in 1938, but the unfinished hulls were scrapped in 1940 because Germany had apparently already won the war.

The building of German aircraft carriers

In December 1936, the construction began at Deutsche Werk in Kiel of the 23,200-tonne aircraft carrier *Graf Zeppelin*, with a flight deck of 787ft/240m. The crew was to consist of 1,760 men and it was to deploy around forty-three aircraft: twenty Fieseler Fi 167s (with torpedoes or bombs or equipped as reconnaissance aircraft), thirteen Junkers Ju 87Cs (dive-bombers) and ten Messerschmitt Bf-109s for air defence. The carrier was launched in December 1938. Work was stopped on 29 April 1940 because of shortages of materials, when the construction was 85 per cent complete, and in July 1940, the ship was towed to Gotenhafen (now the Polish port of Gdynia) and used as a timber warehouse. On 5 December 1942, the stop on construction was rescinded and the ship was towed back to Kiel, but seven weeks later, construction was once again halted. In April 1943, the ship was towed to Stettin (in Polish, Szczecin), where she remained until 24 April 1945, when she was run aground and blown up. In 1946 she was refloated by the Russians and towed to Leningrad on 7 April 1947 to be used as a target for Soviet aircraft and ships and sunk later that year. The wreckage was rediscovered on the bottom of the Baltic Sea in 2006 in 285ft/87m of water. The second aircraft carrier, *Peter Strasser*, had already been broken up on the slipway in 1940.

Submarine construction and submarine training

On 18 June 1935, after a bilateral naval conference between Britain and Germany, the Treaty of London abolished some of the restrictions for the reconstruction of the German navy. It was now permissible for Germany to build submarines and surface vessels amounting to 35 per cent, measured by displacement,[20] of British submarine and surface fleet tonnage. The French government was angry that Britain had given Germany permission to partially lift restrictions imposed by the Treaty of Versailles without even consulting France. The submarine *U-1* was launched only eleven days after the treaty, which suggests thorough advance preparations on the German side. The first twelve submarines had already been laid down in February 1935. Submarine training was led by Kapitän zur See Karl Dönitz, and the training programme was highly formalised. Each submarine crew had to be

---

20 The size of warships is often stated as displacement in tonnes, that is, the weight of the water the ship displaces, or in other words, the weight of the ship itself. Submarines therefore have two indications of displacement: the weight of the ship on the surface and the weight of the ship submerged (with full tanks) respectively.

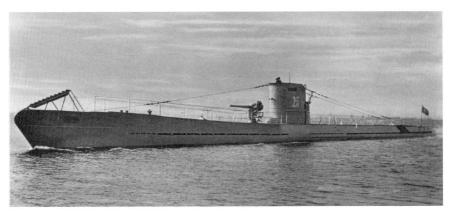

The German submarine *U-25* of the Type IA class.

The large German minesweeper *M36*. (SMB arkiv)

trained for nine months and sixty-six attacks had to be carried out. When war broke out, the submarine strength consisted of only fifty-seven boats.

Destroyers, torpedo boats, Schnellboote, Räumboote and minelayers

At the start of the war, the German navy possessed over twenty-two modern destroyers (*Zerstörer*) with a displacement of 2,171 tonnes (1934 class). These were *Z1* to *Z22*, which in addition to the 'Z' designation also bore the names of sailors from the Imperial German Navy killed and wounded during the First World War. They each had five 5in/127mm guns and eight torpedo tubes. The subsequent destroyers with 'Z'-names only had a number and no name. *Z23* to *Z30* were laid down between 1938 and 1940, and *Z31* to *Z39* from 1940

A German *Räumboot*. They could be used both as minesweepers and minelayers, and also as patrol boats which carried depth charges. During minelaying operations, they were covered by more offensive units.

to 1941. The latter were very heavily armed with a total of five 6in/150mm guns, but the weight of the armament made them unstable and they had poor seaworthiness.

A torpedo-boat force was established, comprising a number of large torpedo boats of 600–800 tonnes. The torpedo boats became even larger though during the war. From 1941, a new type was introduced with *T22* as the first. They were in reality small destroyers of 1,754 tonnes displacement. Furthermore, construction of a fast motor torpedo-boat force (*Schnellboote* or *S-Boote*)[21] was begun, with boats of approximately 100 tonnes.

Large minesweepers of 700 tonnes were built and they were designated with an 'M'. Smaller minesweepers were called *Räumboote* and could also be used for a variety of other purposes – they were designated with an 'R'.

Many of the German minelayers had been requisitioned from the merchant navy, often ferries or government ships which flew the *Reichsflagge* (the national flag).

Seaworthiness

German shipbuilders and naval officers were not always satisfied with the ships. A *Marinebaurat* (shipbuilder), talking about the ships in the Kriegsmarine, said: '*Wir bauen Süsswasserschiffe, bildschön anzusehen, aber für den Atlantik nicht geeignet.*' (We build freshwater ships that look great, but are unsuitable for the Atlantic). Some of the cruisers, and especially the

---

21 The British called them E-boats ('E' for 'enemy').

destroyers, sailed badly. For example, the heavy cruiser *Prinz Eugen* had a very poor bunker capacity (fuel oil stock) and a large fuel oil consumption – and therefore a poor operational radius – and several of the destroyers had poor stability. On the other hand, the artillery armaments, hulls, shock protection,[22] damage control, and the machinery generally, was better in the German ships than in the British. In the last year of the war, seaworthiness did not, however, play a decisive role, as the large vessels were used exclusively within the Baltic Sea, where the height of the waves is modest.

The Z-plan

The Z-plan encapsulated the wish of the Kriegsmarine to achieve a fleet of ten battleships, four aircraft carriers, three battlecruisers, five heavy cruisers, sixty light cruisers, sixty-eight destroyers, ninety torpedo boats and 249 submarines. Kapitän zur See Karl Dönitz calculated that Germany required 250–300 submarines. With that number in a war against Britain, they would always be able to keep about a hundred submarines on patrol, and that would be enough to close Britain's supply routes. The remainder of the submarines would be on the way to and from patrol areas, at a shipyard or on exercise. The Z-plan was never given the importance intended. From the viewpoint of the German naval planners, the war against Britain and France came much earlier than anticipated. Shortly after the start of the war, submarines were given top priority and big ships got second priority.

Polish warships and forts

In 1939, the Polish navy was of a relatively modest size and consisted basically of four destroyers, five submarines, one minelayer and twelve torpedo boats. Navy personnel included around three hundred officers and 3,200 sailors and NCOs. In addition there were the fort garrisons. The two oldest destroyers were *Wicher* (Gale) and *Burza* (Storm), which had been built in France and delivered in 1930 and 1932. They were each 1,900 tonnes and had four 5in/130mm guns. In 1937, Poland purchased two new destroyers from a British shipyard, *Grom* (Thunder) and *Blyskawica* (Lightning). They were very fast in relation to contemporary destroyers, with a top speed of about 39 knots, a large operational radius and good artillery weapons. They displaced

---

22 Shock protection protects the ship against damage from nearby explosions such as mines and close artillery and bomb hits. Good shock protection reduces damage to the engine foundations, electric switchboards, shaft brackets, bearings, etc.

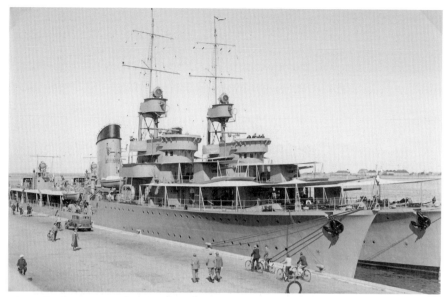

The two British-built Polish destroyers *Grom* and *Blyskawica* at Langelinie in Copenhagen on 23 August 1938. The ships escaped to Britain on the first day of the war.

2,400 tonnes, were armed with seven Bofors 5in/120mm guns and could each carry forty-four mines.

The five Polish submarines were primarily acquired as large minelaying submarines. The first three were ordered in 1926 at a French shipyard and the first was commissioned in 1932. Their surface displacement was 980 tonnes, 1,250 tonnes submerged. They were called *Wilk* (Wolf), *Ryś* (Lynx) and *Żbik* (Wildcat), were armed with six 53cm torpedo tubes and a 4in/100mm gun, and they could each carry thirty-eight mines. Their maximum speed was 14 knots on the surface and 9 knots submerged. The crews, each of fifty-four men, had been trained in Toulon. After some years of experience with the French-built submarines, it was decided to order two ocean-going submarines at Dutch yards, but as can be seen from the following, they only came to take part in the impending war by a hair's breadth. The first one was partly paid for by funds from a public collection. This was *Orzeł* (Eagle), which was built at the Schelde shipyard in Vlissingen and was commissioned on 2 February 1939. The second submarine was named *Sęp* (Vulture). It was built at a shipyard in Rotterdam, where the workers mostly had German sympathies: they delayed the completion of the submarine and that created fear and uncertainty among the Poles. On 2 April 1939, the submarine was supposed to go out on sea trials for the shipyard and instead of returning, the boat sailed home to a Polish port. It ran out of fuel, however, and had to be towed the last 100 nautical miles to Gdynia, still with stunned and angry Dutch shipyard workers on board. It arrived at Gdynia on 18 April 1939. The two new boats had eight 21in/53cm torpedo tubes, a 4in/100mm gun and a 1.5in/40mm gun and could carry forty mines. Displacement was 1,092 tonnes on the surface and 1,450 tonnes submerged.

From the Bofors factory: a 6in/152mm gun produced for Poland, the Netherlands and Sweden. This type was used for the Laskowski Battery at the eastern tip of the Hel Peninsula. (SMB arkiv)

The Polish submarine *Orzeł*. (Old Ship Picture Galleries)

In 1937, at the tip of a long spit of land known as Hel, the Poles constructed an important fort with four Swedish 6in/152mm Bofors guns, which could cover large parts of Gdańsk (Danzig) Bay. It was called the Batteri Laskowski after the naval officer who had been in charge of the construction, but had died the year before.

Finland

After Finland's independence from Russia, there followed a bloody civil war. In 1920, peace was made with Russia and thereafter Finland presided over only a very modest fleet. There were approximately thirty old Russian warships as spoils of war in the Finnish ports, but they were in poor condition. During a storm in 1925, the navy lost an old torpedo boat, which went down with all fifty-three men on board. That started a debate which in 1927 led to a new law about the navy. In the years up until 1939, a fleet was constructed in which the main units were two coastal monitors (armour-plated ships), four torpedo boats and five submarines. The two coastal monitors were commissioned in

The Finnish monitor *Väinämöinen* photographed at Langelinie in Copenhagen on 25 May 1937. The ship's powerful main armament is evident from the photo. It has a double turret both fore and aft with 10in/254mm Bofors guns. The main armament was so powerful that it could fight the largest Soviet warships in the Baltic Sea. *Väinämöinen* was handed over to the Russians on 5 June 1947 as part of the peace agreement. The ship subsequently joined the Baltic Fleet under the name of *Vyborg*. It was probably decommissioned around 1960 and was broken up in 1966.

The small Finnish submarine *Vesikko* was in service in the Finnish navy until 1946 and is today a museum submarine at the Suomenlinna Fortress (Sveaborg Fortress) in Helsinki. (Old Ship Picture Galleries)

1932 and 1934. They were given the names *Väinämöinen* and *Ilmarinen* (after mythological figures in the Finnish national epic poem 'Kalevala'). They were constructed at the Crichton-Vulcan shipyard in Turku from Dutch drawings. They were not good as ocean-going ships, but that was not their purpose. In times of war, they were chiefly intended to sail in the archipelago and combat invasion attempts, and possibly relieve the Åland Islands. They had a modest draught of 15ft/4.5m, strong armour-plating and a displacement of almost 4,000 tonnes. After the Winter War against the Soviet Union, the ships' air defence armament was improved. In 1941, their weaponry consisted of two twin 10in/254mm Swedish Bofors guns, four twin 4in/105mm Bofors guns, four Bofors 1.5in/40mm anti-aircraft guns and eight Danish Madsen 0.75in/20mm anti-aircraft guns.

In the period from 1926 to 1931, Finland built three submarines at the Crichton-Vulcan shipyard: *Vetehinen* (Water Sprite), *Vesihiisi* (Water Devil) and *Iku-Turso* (Eternal Sea Monster). They were designed on the basis of German experience with the UB III class from the First World War and became the prototype of the German Type VII, which was the most important German submarine type in the Atlantic during the Second World War.

The next Finnish submarine was *Vesikko* (Mink). It was built as a secret German prototype in 1932 – that is, before Hitler took power – but not officially purchased by the Finns until 1936. It went under the name *Submarine 707*. Rumour said that it was going to be taken over by Estonia. The Germans contributed Korvettenkapitän Barttenburg and a technician to the Finnish naval staff. The German supply ship *Grille* brought a complete

German submarine crew, except for four hands from the engine room who were Finnish. This gave a new German submarine crew half a year's experience in the Finnish navy every six months from 1932 to 1936. *Vesikko* was built as a coastal submarine based on the German drawings developed from the UB II class from the First World War and it became the prototype of the German coastal submarine Type II during the Second World War. The small submarine *Saukko* (Otter) was actually built for Lake Ladoga, where the limit, according to the Treaty of Tartu of 1920, was 100 tonnes, but it ended up being 114 tonnes displacement on the surface. It proved to be unfit for sailing on the surface in heavy seas and in icy conditions.

The navies of the three Baltic states

Apart from the two Estonian and the two Latvian submarines, the three Baltic states' fleets were irrelevant. The Estonian navy took delivery of two British-built submarines, named *Kalev* and *Lembit*, from Vickers-Armstrong in 1936.[23] Built as minelaying submarines, they could each carry twenty-four mines; their displacement was 600 tonnes on the surface and 820 tonnes submerged, and each had a crew of thirty men. *Lembit* is now a museum submarine in Estonia. In addition, there was a torpedo boat, *Sulev*, dating from 1916. The fleet had a number of motor torpedo boats on order from the Thornycroft shipyard in Britain in 1939, but they were never delivered. The rest of the fleet consisted of icebreakers and small vessels. When the war started, Latvia's fleet had 450 men in the navy's permanent personnel and 200 conscripts. There were two submarines, *Ronis* (Seal) and *Spidola* (a mythical character), built in France in 1926. They were relatively small, with 390 tonnes displacement on the surface and 514 tonnes submerged. The crew of each submarine was twenty-eight men. The gunboat *Virsaitis* was from 1917. In addition, there were two small minesweepers, *Viesturs* and *Imanta*, and six naval aircraft. Lithuania had just one former German minesweeper or guard ship, *Antanas Smetona* (named after the country's president from 1926 to 1940). All these vessels fell to the Soviet Union in 1940.

The Swedish navy

Sweden made it through the First World War without getting involved. When rearmament in Germany and the Soviet Union began to take off

---

23 In the Estonian national epic poem, Kalev was the country's first king, and Lembit was a heroic freedom fighter who fell in battle in 1217.

The Swedish coastal fleet on exercise in the Sound in 1937. In front is the minelaying cruiser *Gotland*.

in the 1930s, Sweden did not follow suit and at the outbreak of war found itself with a weakened fleet. They had finished building three armour-plated ships of the *Sverige* class just after the First World War: *Gustav V*, *Sverige* (Sweden) and *Drottning Victoria* (Queen Victoria). In addition, there were five older armour-plated ships named *Oscar II*, *Äran* (Honour), *Manligheten* (Manliness), *Tapperheten* (Bravery) and *Wasa*, as well as the old cruiser *Fylgia*. In the mid-1930s, the aircraft-carrying cruiser and minelayer *Gotland* was built. The rest of the fleet consisted of sixteen submarines, eight modern destroyers and seven minesweepers.

The Danish navy

Like Sweden, Denmark had weathered the storm of the First World War and, based on a relative position of strength, had been able to avoid interference from the major powers. Danish waters had been mined, partly at German behest, and there was a certain understanding in Britain that Denmark had acted in the shadow of its powerful neighbour to the south when Britain itself could not give Denmark any safeguards. With the defence reorganisation of 1922, which drastically cut down on military capabilities and personnel, and the next reorganisation in 1932, the politicians in reality precluded any possibility of maintaining neutrality based on a minimum of

The Danish torpedo boat *Glenten* (Kite), which early on the morning of 9 April 1940 reported that the German ships in the Great Belt had battle-dressed troops on board. In February 1941, *Glenten* and the other five units of the *Dragen* (Dragon)/*Glenten* class were handed over to the Germans, who used them for torpedo recovery. Their top speed was too slow and their torpedoes too small (17.7in/45cm) for the Kriegsmarine to use them as offensive vessels. None of the vessels could be brought back into a usable condition after the war.

The artillery ship *Niels Iuel* leaving the Holmen naval base in Copenhagen for the last time – 16 August 1943. After an air strike in Isefjorden on 29 August 1943, the ship was run aground near Nykøbing on Zealand. The Kriegsmarine took it over as the training ship *Nordland*. It was scuttled in Eckernförde Fjord near Schleswig on 3 May 1945 by its German crew.

military capability. A panic stopgap solution in 1937 with some additional funding for minesweepers, submarines and torpedo boats did not have time to have any effect. At the outbreak of war in 1939, the Royal Danish Navy had nine modern submarines, but only with small 17.7in/45cm torpedoes. The artillery ship *Niels Iuel* (named after a Danish admiral from the seventeenth century) had ten 6in/150mm guns, but the ship was a political compromise, and should originally have had significantly larger guns and a higher speed. The armour-plated ship *Peder Skram* (named after a Danish naval hero from the sixteenth century), which was launched in 1908, was out of date by 1939. The six torpedo boats also had torpedoes which were too small. The naval air force had a total of thirty-four aircraft, but only two could drop torpedoes. Compared with the First World War, the navy's striking force had been reduced to nothing.

Norway

The Norwegian navy was of a very modest size. There were four old coastal armour-plated ships from the turn of the century named *Eidsvold*, *Norge* (Norway), *Harald Haarfagre* and *Tordenskjold*. In addition, there were two large minelayers, three large torpedo boats, nine old submarines and approximately twenty small torpedo boats. The minelayer *Olav Tryggvasson* was taken over by the Kriegsmarine after the German occupation, under the name *Brummer*. The large torpedo boat, *Gyller*, was taken over as *Löwe*.

4

The Attack on Poland

Background to the war with Poland

In May 1939, Denmark, Estonia and Latvia entered into non-aggression pacts with Germany. This took place after political pressure from US President Franklin D Roosevelt following the dissolution of Czechoslovakia. The idea was that Germany should not be allowed to engulf more small states. Poland was now seriously concerned about Gdańsk, which had a somewhat special status. Like Memel, the city was an old Hanseatic town with a predominantly German population, but after the Treaty of Versailles of 1919, it became a free city under the protection of the League of Nations.

At its establishment as an independent nation, Poland had been given the so-called 'Polish corridor' of approximately 19 miles/30km of coastline (plus the peninsula of Hel), and the Poles tried to develop the port here at Gdynia. The corridor separated East Prussia from the rest of Germany and, with its increased power, the Germans now began to pressurise Poland: a German railway and a motorway were going to be built across the corridor. On 24 October 1938, the Polish Ambassador in Berlin, Jozef Lipski, was invited to a meeting with the German Foreign Minister Joachim von Ribbentrop, at which the proposal about the rail and road links, as well as Danzig's status, was raised. In return, Germany would renew its non-aggression pact with Poland. The proposal was flatly rejected by Ambassador Lipski and five days later, on 29 October 1938, Hitler ordered the German army to prepare a surprise operation aimed at Danzig.

On 21 March 1939, the same day as Germany took possession of Memel, Hitler again demanded of Poland that the free city of Danzig should be reunited with Germany and that a connection be established between East Prussia and the rest of Germany over Polish territory. On 26 March, the negotiations foundered and two days later Hitler gave notice of the termination of the German-Polish non-aggression pact from 1934. Three days after this, France and Britain promised to support Poland if the country should become a victim of German aggression. This support would spark off the Second World War five months later. Already, on 3 April 1939, Hitler had ordered the OKW to prepare a set of plans for attacking the whole of Poland.

On 23 August 1939, the German requirements for the attack on Poland fell into place. The Molotov–Ribbentrop Pact was signed in Moscow and, in a secret additional protocol, the two countries had agreed on a division of Poland. The German invasion of Poland was scheduled for 26 August 1939 at 0430, but on the afternoon of 25 August, Hitler received two pieces of bad news. The first was that the alliance mapped out between Poland and Great Britain had been formalised in London with signatures that same day. The second was that Benito Mussolini had informed Hitler that, because of the Italian military engagement in Albania and Libya, Italy would not be able to participate in a war on the German side.

If there was to be a major conflict, it was important to get merchant ships home. Early on the morning of 25 August 1939, German merchant ship captains received a telegram from Berlin with the text 'QWA7', which meant: 'Abandon journey and make for home port.' Two days later, ships on long voyages were notified to leave international routes within the next four days and make their way to Italian, Spanish, Japanese or Soviet ports – in an emergency, a US port could also be used.

Hitler withdrew his attack order, but not everyone got the message. In what became know as the Jablunkov (Polish: Jabłonków) Incident, one military group did as ordered and detonated their bombs at an important railway tunnel during the night of 25/26 August, when Polish forces, moreover, offered resistance. The Germans had to explain it away by saying 'that it was probably some fanatical people who had over-reacted.' On 31 August, a German radio station at Gleiwitz (now the Polish town of Gliwice) near the border with Poland was apparently attacked by Polish soldiers. They made a brief anti-German speech on the radio, but then they were all killed. This was to be the provocation that justified Hitler's invasion of Poland. The incident at Gleiwitz proved much later to be a purely German affair. A Polish national named Franciszek Honiok had been arrested by the Gestapo in the border area the day before. He and a number of German concentration camp prisoners had then been fitted out with Polish uniforms and were shot near the radio station. A new attack order was issued by Hitler on 31 August at 0400. The attack would now start on 1 September at 0445.

The overall German plan

The German attack on Poland on 1 September 1939 had been planned by the chief of the general staff for the army, Generaloberst Franz Halder and implemented under the leadership of the Oberbefehlshaber des Heeres (army commander-in-chief), Generalfeldmarschall Walther von Brauchitsch. The operation was called *Fall Weiss* (Operation White) and was originally a plan from 1928 which had been adjusted on an ongoing basis: 1,850,000 men were to take part in the current operation, marshalled in fifty-seven divisions. The premise of the plan was for the attack to be carried out without prior declaration of war and before a Polish mobilisation could be achieved. The Germans had a thorough knowledge of Polish infrastructure, which they had themselves created in the former German territories. Necessary intelligence could be obtained via German-speaking groups all over Poland.

The attack on Poland was a violent and sudden invasion across the borders from the north, west and south with large German army forces, supported by a powerful air force. Looking at contemporary maps, it is clear that Poland was more or less surrounded by Germany. The key to German success was co-ordination between fast tank units and tactical air forces. The German forces were to advance against Warsaw from different directions and defeat the Polish forces west of the River Vistula.

The army forces consisted of two army groups: Army Group North (General-oberst Fedor von Bock), comprising the 3rd Army (General der Artillerie Georg von Küchler) and the 4th Army (General der Artillerie Günther von Kluge), attacked from East Prussia and Pomerania. Army Group South (Generaloberst Gerd von Rundstedt), comprising the 8th Army (General der Infanterie Johannes Albrecht Blaskowitz), the 10th Army (General der Artillerie Walter von Reichenau) and the 14th Army (Generaloberst Wilhelm List), attacked from southeastern Germany and from Slovakia.

In addition, the Luftwaffe deployed 2,085 aircraft which very quickly cut off the main railway lines and neutralised the Polish air force. Of the 435 Polish aircraft, 327 were destroyed in combat or on the ground. Ninety-eight Polish aircrew succeeded in escaping to internment in Romania before the German occupation.

The Kriegsmarine only played a marginal role in this operation. A blockade of Polish ports had to be established in Danzig Bay, and maritime traffic between East Prussia and the rest of Germany had to be maintained. In addition, the Kriegsmarine had to support army operations. The relatively modest Polish fleet had to be neutralised in the initial phase.

The German build-up at the borders had to be done secretly and quickly. In order to conceal their ultimate aim, the Germans planned two memorial ceremonies. One was a big parade at Tannenberg in East Prussia on the twenty-fifth anniversary of the brilliant German victory over two Russian armies in late August 1914. The parade included units from IV Panzer Brigade, which were transported openly on the decks of German merchant ships to East Prussia. The second was a naval visit to Danzig by a cruiser. The cruiser was to participate in the city's observance of the twenty-fifth

THE ATTACK ON POLAND 49

anniversary of the loss of the cruiser *Magdeburg*[1] in 1914. Those members of *Magdeburg*'s crew who had died were buried in Danzig. The German general staff considered, however, that the cruiser's artillery was too weak to defeat the Polish fort of Westerplatte at the entrance to Danzig harbour, and therefore sent *Schleswig-Holstein*, the old armour-plated warship from 1906 which had two twin 11in/280mm guns, instead.

The Kriegsmarine's strike force

The commander-in-chief of the German naval forces during the attack on Poland was Vizeadmiral Hermann Densch, his flag flying on the light cruiser *Nürnberg*. The force consisted of the three light cruisers, *Nürnberg*, *Leipzig* and *Köln*, ten destroyers, six motor torpedo boats, twenty-one minesweepers, five smaller escort vessels and ten submarines, in addition to *Schleswig-Holstein* in Danzig harbour. When the war started, the German navy had at its disposal two battleships, three pocket battleships, one heavy cruiser, six light cruisers, thirty-four destroyers and large torpedo boats and fifty-seven submarines. There were also two old armour-plated warships, a number of minesweepers and miscellaneous auxiliary vessels. Of the fifty-seven submarines the Kriegsmarine had at its disposal at the outbreak of war, only thirty-one were ocean-going: that is, suitable for operations outside the Baltic Sea.

The Polish navy's precautionary measures

The Polish government had already issued a warning on the radio on 30 August 1939 that Polish waters were mined up to three nautical miles from the coast. The minelaying had admittedly not started yet, but about a thousand mines were ready. Ships that were going to dock at Polish ports had to request a pilot on board. Since there was a prospect of war, the Polish navy's commander-in-chief, Rear-Admiral Jerzy Swirski, decided that the destroyers *Blyskawica*, *Burza* and *Grom* should leave for British ports before war broke out as they would not be able to be of any significant use if they

---

1 The German cruiser *Magdeburg* ran aground off the island of Osmussaar in the Gulf of Finland on 26 August 1914, where two Russian cruisers, *Bogatyr* (Knight) and *Pallada* (Pallas Athene) found it and shot it to pieces. Fifteen men from the crew were killed and the rest picked up by the German destroyer *V26*. The code books were thrown overboard but discovered by Russian divers. The British were given the code books and could thereafter read some of the German naval messages transmitted by radio.

ORP *Blyskawica* arriving in port, here refitted with British 4in/102mm guns. (Old Ship Picture Galleries)

were sunk during a German attack. The naval chief of staff, Rear-Admiral Jozef Unrug, launched Plan Peking, which was the order to seek haven in British ports. He wrote some very detailed instructions to the commanding officers of the three destroyers. The fourth destroyer, *Wicher*, was in Gdynia with engine trouble. On 30 August, the Polish destroyers were escorted past Bornholm by four German destroyers, *Z8 Bruno Heinemann*, *Z14 Friedrich Ihn*, *Z15 Erich Steinbrinck* and *Z16 Friederich Eckoldt*, the commanding officers

The Polish naval chief of staff, Rear-Admiral Jozef Unrug, launched Plan Peking, which was the order to the destroyers to seek haven in British ports. He wrote some very detailed instructions to the commanding officers of the three destroyers. In the First World War he was a submarine commanding officer in the Imperial German Navy and the German authorities tried in vain to recruit him for war service. (Kungl Örlogsmannasälskapet)

of which did not know, for good reasons, that war was going to break out one and a half days later. The German naval command at this time probably had no inkling, either, that Britain would immediately afterwards be involved in the coming war against Poland. Had this been known, they would hardly have allowed the Polish destroyers to escape to Britain without a fight, but would have shadowed them until 1 September at 0447 when the war became a fact and they could engage them. His Majesty's Ships *Wanderer* and *Wallace* met *Grom*, *Burza* and *Blyskawica* in the North Sea on 1 September 1939 and escorted them to Leith. They were sent on to Rosyth that same evening

The Polish forts at Westerplatte and Hel

In a decision made on 9 December 1925, the League of Nations had allowed Poland to maintain a fort at Westerplatte with a maximum garrison of eighty-eight men, but in March 1939 this permission had been extended to 138 men. Just before the outbreak of war, the Poles had smuggled extra troops in, while the civilian barracks workers had been put in uniform and ordered into service. Westerplatte thus had a garrison of 205 men when war broke out. German intelligence assessments were that there were probably a little over two hundred men in the fort. The fort's modest armament consisted of an older mobile French 3in/75mm gun, two 1.5in/37mm Bofors anti-tank guns, four mortars and some machine guns. The fort's main building was constructed of reinforced concrete.

Rear-Admiral Unrug was in command of the defence of Hel Peninsula, which consisted of four incomplete forts where only the Laskowski Battery was ready with four 6in/152mm Bofors guns. Unrug had formerly been an officer in the Imperial German Navy during the First World War. Towards the end of the war, he had been in charge of an exercise unit for submarines, where one of his talented pupils had been Karl Dönitz, later commander-in-chief of the German submarine forces and, eventually, Hitler's successor.

The attacks on Westerplatte, Hel and the few Polish surface ships

The commanding officer of *Schleswig-Holstein*, Kapitän zur See Gustav Kleikamp, gave the order to begin the shelling of the fort at Westerplatte on 1 September 1939 at 0447 and, with that, the first shots in the Second World War were fired. He had been ordered to remain in low water on the morning of 1 September, so that even if the ship had been struck, it would not have sunk but just have sat on the harbour bottom. On board the ship

The festive arrival of *Schleswig-Holstein* at Danzig 25 August 1939. A week later it fired the opening rounds of the Second World War. (SMB arkiv)

The first shots of the war: the armour-plated warship *Schleswig-Holstein* opens fire on the Polish fort at Westerplatte on 1 September 1939 at 0447. The ship was anchored in the harbour channel close to the fort. (Old Ship Picture Galleries)

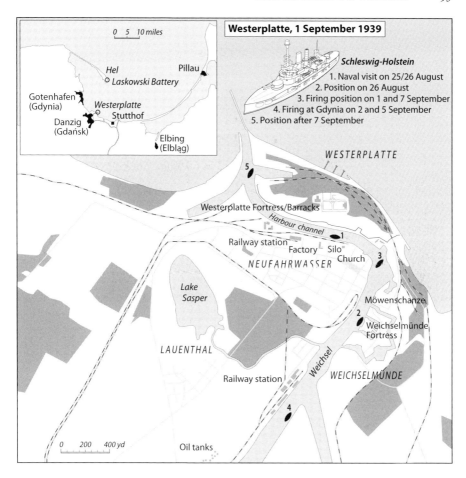

was a small *Marine Stosstrupp* (naval infantry unit), Group Henningsen,[2] of 225 men who were to attack immediately after the initial bombardment and capture the fort. The bombardment lasted for six minutes, during which the attack force took up position to make a surprise attack. The Polish garrison was prepared and the naval infantry unit from *Schleswig-Holstein* was forced back with heavy losses. A renewed bombardment was followed by another attack, which was also repulsed. In the first two attack attempts, eighty-three men from the force were killed or wounded. After this, land-based artillery were deployed, supported by an SS unit, Heimwehr Danzig (Danzig Home Defence), engineering troops and bombers. The 3in/75mm gun was disabled by a direct hit from *Schleswig-Holstein*. The

---

2   Named after the commanding officer, Oberleutnant Wilhelm Henningsen, who was mortally wounded during the attack.

The German *Zerstörer* (destroyer) *Z1 Leberecht Maass*, which was hit on 3 September 1939 by a shell from the Laskowski Battery on the Hel Peninsula. One of the forward guns on the destroyer was hit, four men from the gun crew were killed and four others wounded.

fort's commanding officer, Major Henryk Sucharsky, had orders to hold out for twelve hours, but he and the garrison held out against superior forces for a week. He did not surrender until 7 September, and when he did, it was mainly because of the lack of dressings and the condition of the wounded. A total of 2,600 German soldiers had taken part in the attack: German losses were 300 dead and wounded;[3] Polish losses amounted to fourteen killed and fifty-three wounded. After the surrender, the Germans attempted to get information from the radio operator about the Polish cipher systems, but when he refused to speak, he was killed.

The German destroyer force departed from Pillau (now the Russian town of Baltiysk) on 1 September at 0322 and then operated off the coast near Hel and Danzig. The Polish submarine *Wilk* carried out an attack on the German destroyer *Z15 Erich Steinbrink*, without hitting it though. German reconnaissance flights early on 1 September showed that most of the remaining Polish navy was in the port of Gdynia. These were the last destroyer *Wicher*, the minelayer *Gryf*, torpedo boat *Mazur*, depot ship

3   At Westerplatte, figures of fifty killed and 121 wounded are given, but they could have been higher.

Baltyk, and the auxiliary ships *Gdańsk* and *Gdynia*. The Germans wanted to disable the Polish ships, but it was bad flying weather with poor visibility. Stukas from IV Group, Lehrgeschwader 1, sank *Mazur* and *Baltyk* in Oksywie harbour near Gdynia on 1 September at around 1400. The following day, the auxiliary ships were sunk by Stukas from the same unit.

On 3 September, a German destroyer force led by Konteradmiral Günther Lütjens[4] attacked the minelayer *Gryf* and the destroyer *Wicher*, which had now been made ready to sail and moved to the base and fort at Hel, at the end of a 33km-long strip of land in the northwestern part of Danzig Bay. The fort succeeded at 0657 in getting a direct hit on the German destroyer *Z1 Leberecht Maass* from the Laskowski Battery. Later that day, the Germans brought thirty-three Stukas into action from Trägergruppe 186 (Carrier Air Group 186),[5] which had been intended as the strike force on Germany's first aircraft carrier, *Graf Zeppelin*. The aircraft sank *Wicher*, *Gryf* and, two days later, the gunboat *General Haller* at Hel.

Much later, on 25 September, the Laskowski Battery scored a hit on *Schleswig-Holstein*. The fort held out until 2 October 1939, when Rear-Admiral Josef Unrug had to surrender along with more than two thousand men: 100 men had been killed in the fort.

The war on land

The city of Danzig had already been taken over by the SS Heimwehr Danzig unit on the first day of the war. At the main post office, Polish soldiers, together with a group of postal workers and customers, had taken up the fight. All of them were executed after surrendering many hours later. This was the beginning of the Germans' numerous war crimes during the Second World War.

The war changes character

With the expiry of the British-French ultimatum on 3 September 1939, the German war against Poland changed character. After the ultimatum expired at 1100 (British time), Britain was at war with Germany. France joined the war later the same day. Members of Hitler's entourage have apparently

---

4   Lütjens was later promoted to admiral and, in May 1941, was in charge of the naval force consisting of the battleship *Bismarck* and the heavy cruiser *Prinz Eugen*. He was probably killed on the bridge of *Bismarck* on 27 May 1941.
5   Trägergruppe 186 was dissolved in 1940 when thoughts of aircraft carriers were abandoned.

reported that the British and French declaration of war came as a complete surprise to him. As mentioned earlier, Grossadmiral Raeder had asked Hitler at least twice in 1939 about the timing of a possible future war against Britain and received the response that it would not happen until 1944 at the earliest. Neither Hitler nor Raeder was prepared on 1 September for anything else but a war against Poland, and now – two days later – they were at war with Poland, France and Britain. The Kriegsmarine's operational plans had taken very little account of this situation but, as a precaution, on 19 August Raeder had ordered the pocket battleship *Deutschland*, *Admiral Graf Spee* and sixteen submarines to go out on patrol in the Atlantic. In the afternoon of 3 September, Lütjens received instructions to go to the German North Sea port of Wilhelmshaven, where the destroyer force was preparing to lay mines along the east coast of England. The large German submarines in the Baltic Sea were also diverted to the North Sea.

The five Polish submarines

The remainder of the Polish navy now consisted essentially of the five submarines, but on the other hand, they had great fighting potential and now their worst adversaries, the German destroyers, were gone. As early as 24 August 1939, the commander-in-chief of the Polish submarine squadron, Captain Aleksander Mochuczu, launched Operation Worek (Sack) and the submarines left their base at around midnight between 31 August and 1 September. Operation Worek was an anti-invasion plan, but the invasion of Poland did not come from the sea. *Orzel* and *Wilk* were to operate off Danzig, while the other three were to operate north of the Hel Isthmus. The submarines would not be able to change the immediate result of the war, but could possibly inflict noticeable losses on the Germans. In the initial stage, they had to be defensive and very unobtrusive. France and Britain had asked the Poles not to do anything provocative in the tense situation, but from 4 September, these restrictions were lifted. Three of the Polish submarines were exposed to depth-charge attacks and damaged; the Germans thought they had sunk all the Polish submarines in the first days of the war.

To comply with the London Treaty with regard to German merchant ships, the Polish submarines had to warn the crews of such ships before they were sunk. They therefore preferred to attack German cruisers and destroyers. On the night of 3/4 September, the submarines *Rys*, *Wilk* and *Zbik* laid fifty mines north of the mouth of the River Vistula. Most of their mines were swept relatively quickly by German minesweepers. However, one of the

German minesweepers, *M85*, struck one of these mines as late as 1 October 1939, causing the death of twenty-four men. The Kriegsmarine had initially sent ten submarines to Danzig Bay, particularly with a view to combating the Polish submarines, but they were not suited to this task.

At first the Polish submarines took part in defensive operations against the attackers at the Vistula estuary. *Orzeł* was specifically ordered to take care of *Schleswig-Holstein* if it were to leave Danzig harbour. The submarine lay there for a whole week and was subjected to a number of attacks, but the target never showed up. After 4 September, the other submarines were deployed as defence against invasion, partly near Hel, but the invasion from the sea did not materialise. The Germans came over land instead and thereafter, from 8 September, all five submarines were ordered to patrol between Bornholm and Danzig Bay, but no rewarding targets for the Polish submarine torpedoes appeared here, either. The submarines were to patrol as long as possible. They were then ordered to sail to the UK or to a neutral country, though not the Soviet Union. *Sęp* and *Rys* had been damaged during the Germans' hunt for the submarines and the two of them, along with the undamaged *Żbik*, sought haven at a Swedish port where the fifteen officers and 120 other crew members were interned.

Wilk found its way to the southern entrance to the Sound during the night of 14/15 September and here met a group of Swedish ships. The submarine

The damaged Polish submarine *Sęp* in Sweden after internment in September 1939. Alongside is the Swedish patrol vessel *Pollux*. (Krigsarkivet, Sweden)

'pretended it was Swedish' and followed them up through Flinterenden, past the German destroyer *Z4 Richard Beitzen* and the torpedo boat *T107*, which were guarding the entrance. Once up in the Kattegat, the submarine's commanding officer, Lieutenant Bogusław Krawczyk, sent a signal to navy headquarters: 'Have passed the Sound. Met two German destroyers. Now on our way to England. Long live Poland.' The submarine arrived at the Scottish port city and naval base of Rosyth on 20 September 1939.

The commanding officer of *Orzeł*, Lieutenant-Commander Henryk Kłoczkowski, became ill. Some sources say that he had typhoid-like symptoms, but there is a lot to suggest that he had a nervous breakdown. The submarine's second-in-command looked for a neutral or friendly port where the lieutenant-commander could be put ashore for treatment, and chose Tallinn in Estonia where the submarine arrived on 14 September 1939. The lieutenant-commander was admitted to a local hospital and handed over command of the submarine to its second-in-command, Lieutenant Jan Grudziński.

The German consul put heavy political pressure on the Estonian government for the submarine not to leave the port again. According to international law, a belligerent warship was not allowed to leave a neutral port if a ship from the other party had left the port less than twenty-four hours before and, according to the consul, a German merchant ship had just left Tallinn. After the expiry of the twenty-four hours, the Estonian authorities wanted to intern the submarine and began disarming it, but the Estonians' sympathies were clearly with the Poles. The breech-block with the firing mechanism for the deck gun was removed and the crew started to take the torpedoes ashore. This is a relatively complicated process and when they had removed fourteen of the ship's twenty torpedoes, the submarine's new second-in-command, Sub-Lieutenant Piasecki, saw to it that the wire on the torpedo windlass broke. The Estonians did not discover that it was sabotage and therefore finished work for the day.

Although the submarine was bathed in spotlights, an escape was organised at two in the morning, in which the two guards 'were overpowered'. During its departure, the submarine toppled a statue on a pier and briefly went aground on a sandbank, but soon came free again unaided. 'Very considerate' fire came from land without hitting the submarine. All the charts had been taken off the vessel, so navigation was left to the navigators' memories. The submarine still had six torpedoes on board, so the commanding officer began patrolling for German targets. On 22 September, the previously overpowered Estonian guards were put ashore on Gotland by raft, armed with cigarettes and a bottle of whisky. They could thus refute the German propaganda messages that they had been murdered by the brutal Polish submarine crew. *Orzeł* patrolled for more than two weeks, but since there were no rewarding targets, the submarine sailed through the Sound on the night of 8 October and rounded the Scaw on 11 October, after which the home-made Swedish flag was taken down. Unfortunately, *Orzeł* arrived at Scotland the day after Kapitänleutnant Günther Prien, the commanding officer of *U-47*, had sunk the battleship *Royal Oak* in Scapa Flow, so the British were initially somewhat distrustful when the Poles tried to establish radio contact on 14 October. They succeeded, though, without any misunderstandings and the submarine was escorted to Rosyth by a British destroyer. This was twenty-seven days after the flight from Tallinn and forty-four days after the departure from Gdańsk shortly before the outbreak of war.

Lieutenant Grudziński had three wishes when he went ashore: he wanted a sick crew member admitted to hospital; he would like to have a new breech-block for the deck gun; and finally he would like to receive orders for a new war patrol. The submarine first had to have various modifications carried out, among other things, to be able to use British torpedoes, which were of the same calibre of 21in (53.3cm) as the Polish. After two and a half months in port, the submarine was ready again. It was now included in the Royal Navy's 2nd Submarine Flotilla.

The end of the fighting

On 19 September 1939, Hitler came to Danzig and was hailed as the liberator of the city. He already considered the war against Poland to be over and he gave a speech that was broadcast on the radio. British intelligence also listened to the broadcast. Hitler referred to the Germans developing new breakthrough weapons that could not be defended against. This would keep the British intelligence services engaged in the coming six years or so, not knowing what weapons they would have to face in the future.

The war on land went relatively quickly for the Germans. The Polish forces could not put up any resistance against the combination of greater troop numbers, mobility, and modern tanks and aircraft. Poland's allies, France and Britain, had no military means to counteract a German attack so far from their own territory. On 8 September, German forces were close to Warsaw, but the next day the Polish forces organised an unexpected counter-attack. When Warsaw did not fall, the Luftwaffe and the army's artillery initiated a bombardment of the city.

On the morning of 17 September, the head of Polish intelligence, Colonel Jozef Smolenski, was able to notify the Polish commander-in-chief,

Marshal Edward Smigly-Rydz, that Soviet forces had now entered eastern Poland. For a very brief moment, the Polish forces thought that the Soviets had come to their rescue, but the consequences of the conspiracy were suddenly clear to them. The Soviet advance made a final Polish defence impossible. Soviet propaganda advised that 'the Belarusian and Ukrainian populations would now be freed from the Polish yoke'. Germany and the Soviet Union had now in their own eyes 'resolved the Polish problem'. With the Molotov–Ribbentrop Pact, Hitler had ensured peace to the east and he could therefore concentrate on military action against France and Britain. Stalin could begin to insure his 'glacis' (buffer zone) against a German attack in the long term. His thoughts were focused on the Baltic states and Finland in particular.

It is noteworthy that the German attack on Poland triggered the participation of Britain and France in the war. When the Soviet Union also attacked Poland sixteen days later, it did not trigger a war with Britain and France. The Polish agreement with the two countries was restricted to Germany as the aggressor.

After the end of the campaign, Generalfeldmarschall Gerd von Rundstedt praised the heroic efforts of the Polish troops. The German army and air forces now had combat experience, but naval warfare had not offered the Kriegsmarine any challenges. The German victory soon became clear. On the other hand, the German forces suffered a significantly larger number of killed and wounded during the campaign than the military leadership had anticipated.

German losses totalled approximately 13,500 killed or missing, and just under 30,000 injured. Polish losses were approximately 66,300 troops killed and 26,000 civilian deaths. The Soviet Union had 996 killed and 2,002 wounded in the fight against Poland in 1939.

Poles make their way to France and England

The forces in Warsaw did not capitulate until 28 September and military resistance continued until 6 October. Britain and France had not come to the rescue: now there was nothing else to do but to leave Poland. About 100,000 Polish soldiers fled to Romania and Hungary. On 30 September 1939, the Poles established an exile government in Paris; it later moved to London, where a Polish army was organised by General Władysław Eugeniusz Sikorski.

Rear-Admiral Jerzy Świrski succeeded in escaping from Poland via Romania and reached London, where he became head of the Free Polish Navy, which became a part of the Royal Navy. The Poles acquired a reputation for being tenacious, stubborn and competent fighters. Świrski's personal tenacity and foresight guaranteed the usable Polish destroyers and submarines to the ongoing struggle. The tonnage of the Polish merchant fleet when the war started was more than 135,000 tonnes; 10,000 tonnes had been sunk during the German attack, but a large part of the remaining ships, around 125,000 tonnes, reached British ports and were thus available to the Allies from the outbreak of war.

5

The Baltic Region After the Polish Campaign

October 1939 – June 1941

Poland's broader fate

As a result of the Molotov–Ribbentrop Pact, Poland was completely wiped off the map, just like in 1795. Former German territories were annexed to Germany, while other areas were managed as a *Generalgouvernement* (General Government). The Soviet territories were annexed into the Soviet republics of Belarus and Ukraine. The River Bug (a tributary of the Narev) was now the border between Hitler's Germany and Stalin's Soviet Union, with troops from the two countries guarding the new border. Co-operation between the Soviet and German forces in the border area went very well and gave the Germans an insight into the Soviet forces.

After a while, Hitler became aware of a growing number of reports – including those from the German officers in the General Government – which suggested that Soviet equipment and the training of Soviet officers and soldiers simply did not match with the equivalent German equipment and training. The Soviet Union, therefore, must be significantly weaker than previously thought.

Autumn 1939: an aftermath with the Polish submarine Orzeł, developments in the Baltic states, and the background to the Winter War 1939/40

As mentioned earlier, the Polish submarine *Orzeł* briefly came to Tallinn in September 1939 to put the submarine's sick commanding officer ashore. This episode had a very strange aftermath. In Moscow, Foreign Minister Molotov used the occasion to explain to an Estonian delegation: 'that your country's amateurish handling of the Polish submarine incident had in fact led to a serious loss for the Soviet government. On 26 September at 1800, an unidentified submarine sank the Soviet freighter *Metallist* off Narva.'

It was made clear to the participants at the meeting that the submarine could not be other than the Polish *Orzeł*. The Polish submarine was, however,

The Soviet submarine *Shch-303* was unable to sink the Soviet freighter *Metallist* off Narva on 26 September 1939. (Old Ship Picture Galleries)

at this time in reality near Gotland. During interrogations of prisoners of war two years later, the Germans discovered that the Russians themselves had staged this scene: the submarine *Shch-303* fired first one torpedo and then another, but neither of them worked nor struck *Metallist*. So the ship was sunk by the destroyer *Tucha* (Thundercloud). Using this fictional episode, Molotov procured an argument to garrison 25,000 men from the Red Army in Estonia and to acquire bases on Saaremaa, Hiiumaa and near Paldiski. On 2 October and 11 October 1939 respectively, Latvia and Lithuania were made the same 'offer' about Soviet garrisons. Both countries agreed.

From 5 October 1939, Finland was subjected to similar political pressure. This was intended to lead to Finland offering the Soviet Union some Finnish islands in the eastern Gulf of Finland, land districts on the Karelian Isthmus (the area between Lake Ladoga and the Gulf of Finland) and base rights on the peninsula of Hanko (in Russian: Gangut) at Finland's southwest point. These measures were intended to protect Leningrad. In return, Finland would be offered some forest areas in Karelia. The Soviet Union also claimed a small area at Rybachy Peninsula (Fisher Peninsula), which represented Finland's only access to the Barents Sea and the North Atlantic. While these negotiations were under way, the Soviet Union had already started deploying warships to Riga and Tallinn.

The looming prospects led to the Finnish navy moving to a war footing from 12 October 1939. The minelayers had taken wartime mines on board and the mining of internal territorial waters had already been authorised. With Soviet bases outside the Gulf of Finland, the Finnish navy was now in a weakened position, just as its ally, Estonia, had been outmanoeuvred. The whole basis of 'an inverted Peter the Great Naval Fortress' with Finnish and Estonian fortresses, submarines and mines had crumbled. The Finnish navy could no longer blockade the Soviet Baltic Fleet within the eastern end of the Gulf of Finland.

German use of the Baltic Sea in 1939/40

The Baltic Sea was a high priority for the Germans. They needed a lack of activity there (and literally peace, too) to be able to train submarine crews for the Battle of the Atlantic. The Baltic Sea was also very important as a route for supplies from the Soviet Union, first and foremost raw materials, particularly oil and grain. Germany could maintain trade with the other Baltic countries and Norway, but could no longer freely import and export via the oceans, since Britain was still the world's largest naval power.

German/Soviet co-operation 1939–41

Stalin thought that there would be war with Germany, but he needed time and a larger buffer zone so that he could keep the Germans away from the most important Soviet industrial regions. Some of the Soviet industrial production was moved to cities east of the Urals. During the period of waiting until the big clash, Stalin tried to optimise deliveries of military technology from Germany. He was very interested in obtaining German construction drawings for submarines, naval artillery and fire control systems for naval artillery. The Soviet Union succeeded in buying the unfinished heavy cruiser *Lützow* (*Prinz Eugen* class) with armament and ammunition, but without the fire-control system. The machinery had never been tested. The cruiser was renamed *Petropavlovsk*, which later in the war was changed to *Tallinn*. Furthermore, the Soviet Union took possession of German drawings for battleships and other ship's equipment, but Hitler refused an offer to buy Soviet submarines and to acquire the two Estonian submarines *Lembit* and *Kalev*, which came into the possession of the Soviet Union in 1940.

Stalin did not get the technical assistance from Germany which he had been hoping for. Soviet naval assistance to the Kriegsmarine took place mainly outside the Baltic Sea. The German auxiliary cruiser *Komet* was piloted through the Northeast Passage, that is, north of Russia and Siberia out to the Pacific Ocean, where she sank seven British merchant ships. The Soviet Union demanded one million reichsmarks in piloting fees. The Kriegsmarine was allowed to create Basis Nord in a bay near Murmansk, just east of the Finnish port city of Petsamo. This was Zapadnaya Litsa near Polyarnoye, which was an anchorage without any shore installations. During the attack on Narvik on 9 April 1940, German submarines and destroyers received fuel and ammunition from here, including from the supply ship *Jan Wellem*, which was a converted mother ship for whalers. When Denmark was occupied, Foreign Minister Molotov suggested to his German colleague – to Hitler's consternation – that the Soviet Union should participate in the control of the Danish straits.

Blockades and closures

It was in Germany's interest to keep the Allies out of the Baltic Sea, in particular because of the iron ore transports from Sweden, but also because of the other trade with the surrounding countries. This could be done, not because of the strength of the German navy, but because of the weakness of the Allies. If the area could be closed off to foreign influence, the Baltic Sea region could also be used as an exercise and training area, including for the growing submarine fleet. Moreover, new weapons could be developed free from prying eyes.

It was important for Germany that the Baltic Sea remained a peaceful inland sea, which could be used for import-export – especially from the Soviet Union. With control of the minefields, it would also be possible to regulate a substantial part of the neutral Scandinavian countries' shipping to and from Britain. Immediately after the outbreak of war, Germany also needed to prevent Polish warships escaping to Britain. By initiating a war against the world's greatest sea power, Germany had at the same time procured itself a serious problem. It had now cut itself off from trading with the rest of the world by sea, because Britain established a blockade of Germany. At the same time, Germany established a blockade of the island kingdom of Great Britain, which in the next two years would almost bring the British to their knees.

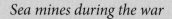

Sea mines during the war

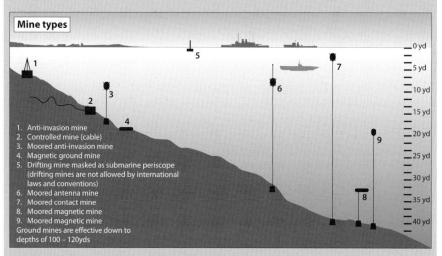

Mine types

1. Anti-invasion mine
2. Controlled mine (cable)
3. Moored anti-invasion mine
4. Magnetic ground mine
5. Drifting mine masked as submarine periscope
   (drifting mines are not allowed by international
   laws and conventions)
6. Moored antenna mine
7. Moored contact mine
8. Moored magnetic mine
9. Moored magnetic mine
Ground mines are effective down to
depths of 100 – 120yds

Sea mines: Types, placement and mode of operation

At the outbreak of the war, the various warring parties had large stockpiles of mines at their disposal, part of which were relatively simple mines from the First World War. Sea mines underwent major technological developments during the war and in some respects, the war evolved into a technology war between the engineers, technicians and mine-clearance experts on the two sides. When mines are laid, the aim is that the mines are made as difficult to 'sweep' (disarm) as possible. The mines are optimised for specific targets or specific types of ships.

Mines can be divided in different ways. There are bottom mines, anchored mines and drifting mines, according to where they are laid. Drifting mines are prohibited by the Hague Conventions. Mines can also be classified according to their mode of operation. Contact mines must be touched for them to detonate. It may, for example, be a Hertz horn that gets broken, after which the acid flows down into an element which provides current to the ignition cartridge. It could also be a mechanical contact. Some mine types, for example, anti-submarine mines laid by the Germans and Finns in the Gulf of Finland, just had to be touched by something metallic to detonate. This applied both to the mine casing and to the anchor cable, along with a possible 'antenna' with floats, which could thereby extend the operational area of the mine vertically.

Anchored mines are laid at a certain depth. All mines in such a minefield will then be at the same distance from the surface of the water, for example, at a depth of 6.5ft/2m, even if the depth of the water varies greatly in the area. This is done using a specific device that reels off the mine cable from the mine anchor on the seabed until a float with a cord of 6.5ft/2m in length reaches the surface. Then the float stops pulling on the reel and the unreeling will stop. The little float is provided with a very small hole, so that it slowly fills with water and then sinks. Now all the mine casings in the area will be floating at a depth of 6.5ft/2m measured from the surface of the water. The active range of the mines can be increased if they can be brought to detonate due to a 'distance effect', for example, merely from the passage of a ship. One way this can be done is with a magnetic ignition system. With a large explosive device, about 550lb/250kg trinitrotoluene (TNT), a ship can be sunk or severely damaged at a distance of up to approximately 328ft/100m.

Sea mines should not be laid too close to each other because of problems with 'countermining', where a mine causes the next in line to explode, so that a single detonation could wipe out an entire minefield. Mines are therefore normally laid at least 328ft/100m apart.

Sea mines can be laid from both ships and aircraft. From aircraft, it can be with or without a parachute; submarines can also lay mines. Some types of submarine can have a number of mines hanging on the outside of the pressure hull. Others have mines on board which fit into the torpedo tubes; that is to say, usually with a diameter of 21in/53.3cm. There can be two or three mines in each torpedo tube and they are ejected with compressed air, one at a time. The advantage of having submarines carry out minelaying is that their presence in the area will not normally be noticed. The mines can be laid with reasonable accuracy.

If a mined area can be kept under observation, it is possible to ensure that the other party does not sweep the mines. If the area has not been monitored, the mines may have been swept.

Minefields can be self-activating. Then the mines will typically work from about one hour after they have been laid, so that one's own minelayers and escorts have enough time to get out of the minefield. Controlled minefields can also be laid. In these, the minefield can be switched on and switched off. Such a minefield will typically be placed in a through-passage waterway – in the Danish straits, for example – where control of passage is sought. The mines are operated from a sea-mine control station on land to which cables are laid from the various mines. If the sea-mine control station is in danger of being captured, the minefield can often be armed with a special switch which removes the possibility of being able to disarm the mines later.

To make it difficult to sweep them, mines can be equipped with a counter which is activated according to ships sailing by. Some of the British air-dropped mines could be set with up to fourteen sailing passes, which meant that the mine would only detonate when the fourteenth ship to register a satisfactory profile sailed past. Once the Germans had acquired this knowledge of enemy mines, German minesweepers had to sail through a route more than fourteen times in order to declare the route swept.[*]

The mines could, moreover, be provided with an arming delay and a disarm function. The first activates the mine some time after it has been laid. An enemy minesweeper crew can thereby be led to believe that a route is safe. Then the mine is activated. Similarly, a disarm function can ensure that the mine is not active after a certain date; for example, if the minelaying party wishes to use the area after that date.

Surface ships and submarines normally lay mines in rows, so that bends or stops can be incorporated into the laying. Aircraft drop mines in a planned area so the relative positions of the mines and their position in relation to the planned area is dependent on the accuracy of the navigation system. Mines dropped from aircraft during the Second World War were often spread over much larger areas than were intended, especially during night operations. All the RAF's minelaying operations in the Baltic Sea were conducted at night.

Special minesweeping obstacles can be laid among the mines to damage the minesweeping equipment and complicate the operation for the enemy.

In Danish waters, about 20,500 mines were disarmed during and after the war and it took about thirty years before free passage was allowed outside the mineswept routes.

---

[*] It was probably such a mine that, on 11 June 1948, sank the DFDS passenger ship *København* in the northern Kattegat sixteen nautical miles east of Hals, when forty-eight people died. Some of the passengers were rescued by the DFDS freighter *Frigga*, which was itself sunk on 27 November 1950 by a similar mine in the same area.

Minefields laid out before the German occupation of Denmark on 9 April 1940

The German minelayers *Tannenberg* and *Hansestadt Danzig* laid a minefield between Trelleborg and Møn, which claimed its first victim, the Greek cargo ship *Kosti*, as early as 4 September 1939. This was the Undine minefield with about eight hundred anchored magnetic mines. The field was laid out on 4 and 5 September 1939 in international waters, partly in order to channel maritime traffic and partly to keep British submarines out of the Baltic Sea. German guard ships were in place and there was talk in general terms on the radio about minefields being laid. *Kosti* did not respond to signals from the German guard ships.

On 4 September, the Germans also laid the fields of Grosser Bär and Jade, south of the Danish islands of Langeland and Lolland; 300 mines directed at shipping and 700 anti-submarine mines were laid here. The latter were anchored contact mines where the mine casing was held down at a greater depth so that surface ships would not touch the mines. On 6 September, the Little Belt was blocked by a German minefield south of Als and Ærø. These fields were also laid in international waters.

In connection with the outbreak of war, Denmark also laid minefields. Among other places, Copenhagen harbour and the main naval base at

The Danish minelayer *Lossen* (Lynx).

Holmen were protected. The Danish naval ministry announced through
'Notices to Mariners' on 4 September 1939 that 'sea mines had been laid
at the entrances to Kongedybet, Hollænderdybet and Drogden'. Drogden
is the channel in the western part of the Sound off Dragør. In addition,
barrages were laid in the Great Belt and the Little Belt and directions given
to shipping on pilots, passage and the like. In the Great Belt, 180 mines
were laid and in the Little Belt, 264 – almost all of which were laid by the
minelayer *Lossen* (Lynx). Danish warships guarded the minefields and a
lightship was stationed north of each minefield from which the convoys
or pilotage could begin. After the initial minelaying in September 1939,
the Danish navy established a defence force in Aarhus Bay. The artillery
ship *Niels Iuel* was sent to the Kattegat with some torpedo boats to take
care of any violations of neutrality in connection with the German trade
war, which also affected Scandinavian shipping. In October, *Niels Iuel* was
replaced by the armour-plated ship *Peder Skram*.

Stalin's preparations in the Katyn Forest and in the Baltic countries in 1939 and 1940

When the Soviet military presence had begun in the Baltic states, the
Estonians sent a secret offer to Germany to take over their two submarines.
Grossadmiral Raeder presented it to Hitler, who recommended accepting it,
but required the Soviet Union to accept the sale and thus nothing came of the
matter. While the world was watching Britain's fight for survival during the
Battle of Britain the following year, all three countries were incorporated into
the Soviet Union as independent Soviet republics.

   The annexation of the three Baltic countries happened during the summer
of 1940, but shortly before, a mysterious incident happened that the Soviet
archives have not yet been able to shed light on. A Finnish airliner from
Tallinn to Helsinki was shot down over the Gulf of Finland on 14 June 1940.
On board were seven passengers and two pilots, all of whom were killed.
Among the passengers were two French diplomats on their way home from
talks in Moscow.[1]

---

1   The Finnish airliner Kaleva (a Junkers Ju 52) from the airline Aero O/Y was shot down
    on 14 June 1940 at 1405 Finnish time. It was en route from Tallinn to Helsinki, and it is
    suspected that Stalin ordered the shooting down because of the presence of two French
    diplomats. They had been negotiating in Moscow up until 11 June, but rapid developments
    on the front in France led to a French collapse and Stalin probably did not want the two
    diplomats' reports to reach the Quai d'Orsay (French foreign ministry) after the latest
    developments. The scheduled flight was shot down by two Soviet Ilyushin DB-3T torpedo
    aircraft from the Soviet Baltic Fleet. There was also an American courier and a diplomatic

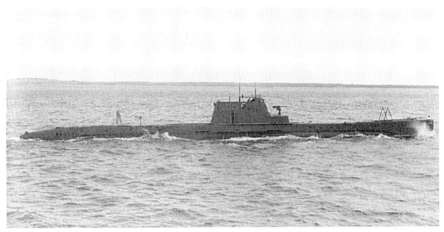

The Kaleva incident: the Soviet submarine *Shch-301* was at the scene at 1447 (Finnish time) to collect important courier mail and other sensitive material when the Finnish airliner Kaleva (a Junkers Ju 52) from the airline Aero O/Y was shot down on 14 June 1940 at 1405 Finnish time. (WIO)

Soviet naval bases were established at Tallinn, Riga, Liepāja and Ventspils. The last two ports were important because they are normally free of ice in winter. On 13 August 1940, the Soviet Union took over the Estonian submarines, which were given Soviet crews, but four Estonian engine-room officers remained in each submarine as the machinery was complicated. Four more Estonians in each submarine were given the task of training the new Soviet crews. The commanding officer of the submarine *Kalev* retained his position. In 1941, *Lembit* and *Kalev*, together with *L-3*, joined a minelayer division which was part of the First Submarine Brigade of the Soviet Baltic Fleet. In the summer of 1940, the Soviet Union also took over the two Latvian submarines, *Ronis* and *Spidola*.

The Baltic peoples were subjected to harassment by Stalin's secret police, the NKVD,[2] which imprisoned or deported 'anti-Soviet elements', ie possible political opponents, capitalists, intellectuals, priests and other shapers of public opinion. In the new Soviet part of Poland, the prisoners of war of

---

bag weighing over 220lb/100kg on board. The Soviet submarine *Shch-301* was at the scene at 1447 (Finnish time). Three Estonian fishing boats had salvaged the diplomatic bag and other things, but everything was taken from the fishermen and the whole 'loot' was sent to Kronstadt on the frigate *Sneg* (Snow). Two days later, Estonia was occupied by Soviet forces.

2   The NKVD was the secret police, the forerunner of the KGB. The acronym stands for Народный Коммиссариат Внутренних Дел (Narodnyi Komissariat Vnutrennikh Del), which means People's Commissariat for Internal Affairs. In 1946, the organisation changed its name to the KGB (Committee for State Security).

the Red Army were handed over to the NKVD and an exchange between Germany and the Soviet Union was begun. The Russians received the Polish prisoners of war who came from the eastern areas and the Germans took those from the west. At the same time, the NKVD began arresting the intelligentsia in the area. They were specifically interested in military and police officers, landowners, factory owners, lawyers, civil servants, priests, school teachers, intelligence agents and saboteurs. Just as in the Baltic countries, potential shapers of opinion were eliminated. The purpose was to ensure that no form of resistance against the Soviet regime developed in the occupied territories. In March 1940 in the Kremlin, Stalin and three other Politburo members, Foreign Minister Molotov, Defence Minister Kliment Voroshilov and the later minister Anastas Mikoyan put their signatures to a prepared list, which amounted to a death sentence for 25,700 interned Poles.[3] During the spring of 1940, these mass killings were carried out in Soviet camps. Since none of the documents found on the bodies were dated later than 1940, this indicates the time of death and who carried out the atrocities.[4] It is estimated that half of the Polish officer corps was executed in this operation, including fourteen generals, and the Polish navy lost one admiral and seventeen captains, among others. These events have been uncovered in several stages. Shortly after the Soviet Union had entered the war, the Polish government-in-exile tried to obtain an agreement that Poles interned in the Soviet Union should be released and organised to fight against Germany. Stalin gave an evasive answer that they were somewhere far away in Manchuria.

During 1942, the Germans received information about a large number of executions in the area. In the spring of 1943, German forces discovered a mass grave and the propaganda minister Goebbels arranged filming and Red Cross input, summoned international forensic experts and much more in order to use this obvious opportunity to tell the world about Communist atrocities. His ulterior motive was to sow discord between Germany's enemies; that is, between 'the cultured opponents of Britain and the USA' and 'the uncultured opponents from the Soviet Union'. The NKVD camp had been in Koselsk and about 4,500 Polish bodies from here were buried in the nearby Katyn Forest. The whole matter is now known as the Katyn Massacre,[5] but similar

---

3   After the Soviet collapse, the document with the four signatures was published and the responsibility for the atrocities has thereby finally been confirmed.

4   According to the latest Polish history research, the NKVD murdered 21,857 Poles during the massacres from 3 April to 2 May 1940. Among the victims were about eight thousand from the Polish armed forces and about six thousand from the police.

5   The Katyn Massacre has been a problem for the Polish relationship with the Soviet Union and Russia since 1943. During a reconciliation arrangement on 10 April 2010, the Polish president's plane crashed with the whole Polish delegation. The president, the country's top politicians, top civil servants and the aircrew, a total of ninety-six people, all died.

activities were carried out in at least two similar camps. As soon as they had reconquered the Katyn region, the Soviet Union tried to 'twist the case' in order to prove that the murders had taken place during a period when the Germans had been in the area, that is, after 22 June 1941.[6] The Americans had received intelligence that the Russians were behind the massacre, but President Roosevelt did not want to put too much unnecessary pressure on Stalin in the final year of the war. During the Nuremberg trials, the Soviet Union presented 'witnesses' who were pressurised into giving testimony that was fabricated by the NKVD.

The situation in Sweden between 1 September 1939 and 9 April 1940

What course did Sweden take? Put simplistically, Swedish sympathies at the beginning of the Second World War lay with Germany and, at the end, with the Allies. Sweden's situation – both politically and militarily – was extremely complex, however, and a large number of central circumstances have thus far been inaccessible to the public, but new light is now being shed on this period.

The Swedish policy being followed was neither glorious nor heroic but was, in fact, mainly pragmatic. In recent years, many books have been published on this subject, including ones from former Swedish intelligence officers and the circle of researchers who can be found at the Militärhögskolan (Defence Academy) in Stockholm. It appears from these sources that neither the political nor the military leadership was up to dealing with such complex and delicate issues as those that arose between 1939 and 1945.

Sweden had to quickly adapt to the harsh realities of war, which at times would necessarily cause some scratches on the moral paintwork. The Swedes could not just take morally correct decisions and act as if the outside world did not exist: political positions and decisions had inevitable consequences.

In November 1939, Sweden had a coalition government under Social Democrat Prime Minister Per Albin Hansson. This government had the following overall goals: to keep Sweden out of the war; to safeguard the population and Swedish property against the horrors of war; to keep Swedish production facilities intact; and to preserve the Swedish welfare state.

This required adapting to what was happening around them. Sweden declared itself neutral in the conflict but, as will emerge, neutrality is a very

---

6   A confounding fact was that the Soviet executioners preferred German firearms as they were of better quality and more reliable than the Soviet ones. So the executioners used German Walther 7.65mm PPK pistols, which Soviet propaganda could make use of in this 'information war'.

In November 1939, Sweden had a new coalition government under Social Democrat Prime Minister Per Albin Hansson. His primary objective was to keep Sweden out of the war. (SMB Arkiv)

elastic concept. Viewed from Sweden, the war shifted between a number of different phases in which the following events each marked the transition to a new phase of altered circumstances in the Baltic region:

- the German attack on Poland in 1939;
- the Soviet attack on Finland in 1939;
- the German occupation of Denmark and Norway on 9 April 1940;
- the German attack on the Soviet Union on 22 June 1941;
- the Soviet submarine war against Sweden in the Baltic Sea beginning in 1942;
- Germany's transition from offensive to defensive warfare after its defeats in 1943 at Stalingrad and Kursk, in North Africa and on Sicily;
- the Soviet breakout from the besieged city of Leningrad in January 1944;
- the peace treaty between Finland and the Soviet Union in 1944;
- and finally, the Soviet conquest of the Baltic states at the end of 1944/ beginning of 1945 and the collapse of Germany.

The sudden war situation in September 1939 led to Sweden quickly having to organise a modern intelligence service, a radio signals interception service and a security service. The intelligence service was given approval to hire foreign agents and in 1939 received the then huge sum of 100,000 Swedish crowns for the purpose. The entire civil service had to be organised so that foreign policy, security policy, military measures and the protection of the civilian population were co-ordinated. In the following years, Stockholm developed into an international spy nest where numerous intelligence organisations operated. The Swedish intelligence service succeeded in hiring a trusted female employee from the German embassy, who was able to provide crucially important information.

When the Soviet Union attacked Finland on 30 November 1939, Sweden wanted to go to great lengths to come to Finland's assistance, though without actively entering the war itself. Assistance was to be discreet and take place via volunteers. There was great popular support in Sweden for Finland, and Finland received large amounts of Swedish weapons and Swedish munitions, including a number of Swedish fighter aircraft, which meant that the Swedish defence forces' own stockpiles became seriously depleted. Hitler was worried that German imports of iron ore would be interrupted and German diplomats warned Sweden that Germany 'would carry out decisive action' if the Allies (then Great Britain and France) intervened.

In December 1939, the Soviet Baltic Fleet was ready to neutralise the Swedish navy if Sweden entered the war. Five Soviet submarines were sent on patrol off the Swedish navy's ports. They reported back quickly that there were no war preparations under way. At this point, Sweden mined South Kvarken, the narrow strait between Finnish Åland and Sweden, which meant that Soviet submarines were unable to sail into the Gulf of Bothnia, which is part of the open sea but into which passage takes place through Swedish territorial waters. Supply lines to Finland went first and foremost via Sweden.

In November 1939, Germany put pressure on Sweden and laid out a minefield up to three nautical miles from the coast of Sweden, that is, within Swedish territorial waters. The Swedish response was to initiate excavation work on the Falsterbo canal as early as December 1939. The canal was opened on 1 August 1941 and could be navigated by ships with a draught of up to 22ft/6.7m and a displacement of approximately 15,000 tonnes. Sweden had four-mile territorial waters and at Trelleborg it was therefore possible for a ship to follow the Swedish coast inside the German minefields and go east of Kogrund (the Kogrund channel is approximately four nautical miles north of Falsterbo). From here, it was possible to remain within Swedish territorial waters until the Scaw was passed and then come out into open waters.

Meanwhile, Sweden continued its exports of iron ore from northern Sweden to Germany. Both the new British First Lord of the Admiralty Winston Churchill and the German Grossadmiral Erich Raeder thought at the turn of 1939/40 that German war production would grind to a halt if Swedish iron ore exports were stopped and Germany would then have to withdraw from the war. In 1938, Germany had imported 22 million tonnes of iron ore, half of which came from France and Belgium. Of the remaining 11 million tonnes, 9 million tonnes came from Sweden. When the war began in 1939, deliveries from France stopped, which made Sweden an important partner for Germany. Now Sweden was delivering more than 80 per cent of German iron ore imports and the ore from Kiruna was of a much higher quality than that which Germany had been used to receiving. The other ore had an iron content of 30 per cent, while the Swedish ore had an iron content of 60 per cent and a low phosphorus content. Every day from the start of the war until the autumn of 1944, between four and six ships left Sweden with iron ore for Germany. In summer, they sailed from Luleå in the Gulf of Bothnia, but when the gulf froze between December and May, the ore was

A Finnish fighter donated by Sweden and operated by Swedish personnel organised in the Swedish squadron F19. The swastika was used by the national Finnish Air Force from independence in 1918 and was not used as a Nazi symbol. (Krigsarkivet, Sweden)

Winston Churchill, First Lord of the Admiralty from September 1939 to May 1940, then prime minister. (Museum of Danish Resistance, Copenhagen)

transported by rail to the nearby Norwegian port town of Narvik, which is always ice-free because of the Gulf Stream. In the first winter of the war, the Royal Navy was a threat to all ore transports from Narvik to Germany's ports in the North Sea and the Baltic Sea. The transports sailed down the Norwegian coast and could be attacked here by the British fleet inside or outside Norwegian territorial waters.

A major incentive for a British/French intervention in the Winter War in Finland, which Winston Churchill, then First Lord of the Admiralty, advocated, was to destroy the Swedish iron mines in Kiruna on the way to Finland, but Finland's capitulation in March 1940 put an end to this project. The Soviet Union was regarded at that time as an ally of Germany and a joint French/British attack directed towards Finland could have had serious consequences for the later British co-operation with the Soviet Union after Hitler attacked the Soviet Union on 22 June 1941. The ore exports were precarious for Sweden. If exports of iron ore to Germany were stopped, Hitler would seek to secure the ore deposits in northern Sweden by military force. The Swedish army may have been big, but it was not so big that it could stave off an attack by German forces. Sweden also exported ball bearings, high-grade steel, copper, sulphur and timber to Germany. Around the start of the war, 10 per cent of German ball-bearing requirements were covered from Sweden. Svenska Kullagerfabrikken AB (SKF) also produced ball bearings under licence in both Germany and Britain.

In November 1939, the two influential brothers from the Wallenberg dynasty, Marcus and Jacob Wallenberg, who dominated Swedish banks and industry, took the initiative to safeguard Swedish industry's requirements for supplies and exports. This was a consequence of experience from the end of the First World War, when Swedish industry, as well as imports and exports, stalled because of German submarine warfare. Marcus Wallenberg went to London and Jacob Wallenberg to Berlin. Here they negotiated an agreement on the possibilities of Swedish merchant ships sailing out to and returning from the high seas in spite of the war between Germany and Britain which was raging in the North Atlantic and the North Sea. The agreement was slow to come into effect and it is referred to in the sections which follow about Sweden.[7]

In December 1940, the Swedish explorer and writer Sven Hedin had an audience with Hitler. Hedin was very highly regarded in Germany and he was equally enthusiastic about the German regime. He very much wanted to plead Finland's cause, which was very close to his heart, but this was flatly rejected by Hitler. Foreign Minister Molotov had just been on a visit to Berlin the previous month and, during this visit, Hitler had refused a Soviet wish to occupy the whole of Finland, and so it was to be.

How could Stalin safeguard the Soviet Union?

In Stalin's view, fraternisation with Hitler would not be forever, but it gave him a useful respite, which among other things could be used to safeguard Leningrad, which was an important industrial city with a population of approximately 2.8 million people at the beginning of the war. Before the Winter War, it was only 19 miles/30km in a northwesterly direction to the Finnish border at Sestroretsk,[8] while the border with Estonia was at Narva, about 93 miles/150km southwest of Leningrad. Finland and the Baltic states could be used as 'a buffer zone' against an advancing enemy, which could be delayed here while mobilisation and defence was organised.

---

7 For each period in the book, there are one or more special sections on the situation with regard to Sweden.
8 Sestroretsk means 'sister creek'. The Finnish name is Siestarjoki or Rajajoki; the latter means 'border river'. In English, it is known as the Sestra river. This was the old border river between Russia and Sweden after the Treaty of Nystad in 1721. It is a small river, 53 miles/85km long, between Lake Ladoga and the Gulf of Finland.

The classic way to prevent an attack is to attack first. Historians have recently shown that Stalin had certain thoughts or plans for an attack on Germany, but it has never been entirely clear whether it was rough sketches or troop exercises or if real, detailed war plans had been made.

The Winter War 1939/40

The war on land and in the air

The Soviet public was not told directly what the developments in the Baltic states, Finland and eastern Poland were really about, but Stalin was preparing for war. A strong naval power with a large fleet and the possibility of transporting large forces of troops by sea would be able to fight its way through the Gulf of Finland and reach all the way to Leningrad at the gulf's eastern end. If an enemy was allied with Finland, there was, as mentioned, only 19 miles/30km from the Finnish-Soviet border at Systerbäck (Sestroretsk) to Leningrad. Stalin therefore wanted to keep an enemy at a longer distance from the city. The Soviet negotiators wanted Finland to cede land areas and give permission for their bases to be used. But if the Finns yielded to Soviet territorial demands, a later defence of Finnish territory would be impossible. The Karelian Isthmus constituted a natural buffer zone against a Soviet attack, so, viewed from a Finnish security policy viewpoint, it would not be possible for exchanges to lead to better security. For the Soviet Union, on the other hand, it would be possible. Finland was facing an existential struggle, while the Soviet Union had a territorial problem.

The Soviet Union could count on German goodwill after the Molotov–Ribbentrop Pact – or at least it could be expected that the Germans would not intervene against a Soviet attack on Finland. The last negotiations between the Soviet Union and Finland were held in Moscow on 15 November 1939, but the Finns would not make concessions. Soviet propaganda accused Finland of having fired on the Soviet village of Mainila with artillery on 26 November. Finland was within the Soviet sphere of influence, and it ought to go without saying that a nation of 4 million people does not wage a war of aggression on a nation of 180 million. The Soviet Union cut off diplomatic relations with Finland on 29 November. The next morning, troops from five Soviet armies crossed the Finnish-Soviet border – listed from north to south: the 14th Army attacked the Petsamo area; the 9th Army attacked in the central area between Salla and Kuhmo; the 8th Army attacked north of Lake Ladoga; and the 7th and 13th armies attacked Vyborg (at that time the Finnish city of Viipuri) via the Karelian Isthmus. At the same time, major Finnish cities were subjected to Soviet air attacks – the Soviet aircraft partly operated from their new bases in Estonia. The Finns acquired information about the 8th Army through an unusual collaboration.[9]

On the first day of the war, a new commander-in-chief was appointed in Finland. This was the hero of the civil war in 1918, Baron Carl Gustaf Emil Mannerheim, who was a Russian-trained officer. He had fought with great bravery during the Russo-Japanese War of 1904/5 and during the First World War, when he was promoted to lieutenant-general.

The Soviet leadership had counted on Finland, like the three Baltic states, giving in to Soviet political pressure, so they had not carried out any kind of military preparation, including war-related training of personnel. Nor did they send in their most modern fighter aircraft. What should have been a relatively modest military operation with a predictable outcome rapidly developed into a disaster for the Soviet forces, even though the Finns could not deal with Soviet numerical superiority in the long run. Minister for Defence Voroshilov had counted on the war being won by Stalin's sixtieth birthday on 21 December.

The Soviets sent 900 – not totally modern – aircraft into battle. They came from four bomber wings and two fighter wings. The Finns only had 150 aircraft and, of them, only about a third were modern: thirty-six Dutch Fokker D.XXI fighters and sixteen British Bristol Blenheim bombers. The air war periodically came to a standstill for days because of bad weather. Whereas the air war in western Europe was characterised by modern technology, including radar, the air war here, right up until the end of the war in 1944, took place without significant use of advanced electronics.

In the northern area, the 14th Army succeeded in capturing Petsamo. On the central front, the Soviets worked on advancing towards the Gulf of Bothnia towards Oulu, but the Soviet 9th Army's advance was stopped at Suomussalmi, where its two divisions, first the 163rd Division and then the 44th Division were wiped out.[10]

---

9   Since 1932, the Latvian army had been able to decipher some of the Red Army's signals and during the Winter War it could follow the 8th Army's operations from Latvia. The Latvian army's commander-in-chief was married to a Finnish woman and, through the couple's contacts, the Latvian information reached the Finnish forces along convoluted channels. The Finns could thus use this material directly, but there is nothing in writing after the war about this somewhat delicate collaboration, only the memories of those involved. See *Northern European Overtures to War, 1939–1941*, Michael H Clemmesen and Marcus S Falkner (Brill, 2013).

10 The 9th Army comprised a total of 93,610 men. The two divisions, the 44th and the 163rd, had between 45,000 and 55,000 men engaged in battle. Of those, 13,536 were killed and 32,573 injured. Source: Colonel-General Grigoriy Fedotovich Krivosheyev, who is the official historian of the Russian Ministry of Defence.

The Finnish defence in this area was in the hands of Colonel Hjalmar Fridolf Siilasvuo. When Stalin heard about the 9th Army's defeat, he sent the deputy commander of the Red Army's political administration, Lev Zakharovich Mekhlis, and his personal executioner, Vasily Mikhailovich Blokhin[11] from the NKVD, to the area. After a short trial in which the main accusation was to the effect that the army had lost fifty-seven field kitchens to the enemy, the army leadership was executed at a parade in front of the woeful remains of the army staff and the soldiers, and a new leadership was installed.[12] The Finns learned to appreciate the conquered Soviet field kitchens and they also captured large amounts of artillery and small arms with ammunition that were immediately put to use against the Soviets.

The Finnish forces in this area were outnumbered, but they were under excellent leadership[13] and they were well-motivated, resilient and tough, and had a high fighting morale. Their method of conducting warfare was unorthodox. They were highly mobile on skis, had good winter clothing and winter camouflage, and they took advantage of their knowledge of the terrain. The Finns used a kind of 'hit and run' tactic, and they could deliver a relatively large firepower. They often attacked the field kitchens in particular, because hot food was very important for the maintenance of morale on the Soviet side. On the desolate forest roads, the long Soviet columns were divided into groups and destroyed individually. The soldiers' favourite weapon was the Suomi sub-machine gun. Finnish marksmen developed a special technique and killed many Soviet officers and soldiers with scope-mounted rifles. The rifles, incidentally, were from the Russian manufacturer Mosin-Nagant from the tsar's time. The Finns also threw bottles containing petrol at Soviet tanks; this was found to be very effective and the bottles got the name Molotov cocktails.[14] The Soviet forces got a lot of combat experience here which they could later use in the war against Germany, but their training, equipment and leadership was initially very poor.

The 8th Army north of Lake Ladoga was nearly wiped out by the Finns, but it was saved by supplies dropped by the Soviet air force. In early February,

---

11 Some months later, Blokhin was sent to the NKVD's operation to liquidate large numbers of Poles and it is estimated that, in the spring of 1940, he personally killed about seven thousand people in the course of twenty-eight nights. (See the Katyn Massacre above).

12 The commanding officer of the 44th Division, Alexei Vinogradov, was among those killed.

13 The tactics and leadership from Suomussalmi are still used as a teaching example at West Point, the United States Military Academy.

14 The Finnish company Alko, which had a monopoly on the production and sale of alcohol, produced 450,000 Molotov cocktails during the Winter War at its factory in Rajamäki. They were not a Finnish invention, but the use of them was systematised and exploited tactically. The nickname 'Molotov cocktail' was, however, Finnish and Foreign Minister Molotov did not care for the appellation.

the Soviets realised the need for a more focused and professional effort, and they assembled a total of 1,500 fighter planes, which now included some of the more modern ones.

In the long run, the Finnish forces could not cope with the intense Soviet pressure and on 12 March 1940 had to sign a truce with the Soviets with effect from 13 March. This meant that Soviet troops moved into those areas that the Soviet Union had claimed. The Winter War thus lasted from 30 November 1939 to 13 March 1940. It had cost Finnish society dearly: 22,849 military personnel and 826 civilians killed. Approximately 43,557 were injured, of whom around ten thousand were disabled. Soviet losses have been kept secret for years, but following the collapse of the Soviet Union, the official toll has been revealed to be 126,875 deaths and 264,908 wounded.[15]

Two weeks after the Winter War ended, the Soviet People's Commissar of Defence (Defence Minister), Marshal Voroshilov, presented a report on the Soviet war effort. It was a large catalogue of military mistakes, partly as a result of Stalin's great purges in the military ranks in 1937/38. The most notable aspect was the complete lack of military initiative in the Soviet armed forces. The Soviet air force lost a total of approximately nine hundred aircraft to Finnish fighters and air defences, as well as to accidents and bad weather. The Finns lost sixty-two aircraft in combat and another sixty-nine due to accidents, bad weather and the like. When Stalin became furious and berated Voroshilov for the poor planning and leadership, Voroshilov apologised with the excuse that the generals did not know that there were forests in Finland, which hampered operations. The generals' incompetence and ignorance made Stalin even more furious and he railed at Voroshilov. The latter became furious in response and replied, 'You have yourself to blame for all of this. You're the one who annihilated the old guard of our army, you had our best generals killed.'[16] The First Secretary in the Ukraine, Nikita Sergeyevich Khrushchev, overheard the argument and said later that Voroshilov was the only one who could ever have got away with such criticism of Stalin with his life intact.

The Finns also undertook an analysis of their efforts immediately after the Winter War ended. The conclusion was clear. The defence of Finland had become more difficult now that the Russians were closer to the Finnish cities. An improved defence effort required modernisation and that was immediately started. By the next summer, the army had over sixteen well-armed divisions at its disposal and the Finnish air force had received supplies

---

15 The figures are from a statistical summary originally conducted in 1993, but not published until 2001. It has been edited by Colonel-General Grigoriy Fedotovich Krivosheyev.

16 Quotation from *Stalin: The Court of the Red Tsar* by Simon Sebag Montefiore (Weidenfeld & Nicholson, 2003).

from the USA, France and Britain. These countries regarded the Soviet Union as an ally of Germany and Finland's struggle had been looked on with sympathy and goodwill.

By the peace treaty, Finland had to cede areas on the Karelian Isthmus and Vyborg would be expanded as a naval base. The peninsula of Hanko at the opening of the Gulf of Finland was blocked off and a naval base was established here, along with an airbase and a garrison of the Red Army. Under the treaty, the Soviet Union also got hold of a number of important islands in the eastern end of the Gulf of Finland, which later came to play a role in the war. These were the large island of Suursaari (now Hogland or Gogland in Russian) and the smaller islands around Tytärsaari, as well as Lavansaari, Penisaari and Seiskaari. The poor relationship with the Soviet Union pushed Finland towards Germany, which, however, still had a collaboration agreement with the Soviet Union. From April 1940, Germany needed to supply German troops in northern Norway via Finland. In return, Finland was able to equip itself from the German arms industry. From September 1940, German-Finnish talks on military co-operation were expanded.

The Winter War at sea

The war was mainly pursued on land, but there were some skirmishes at sea. Soviet submarines from bases in the Baltic states sank five merchant ships, while Soviet naval aircraft sank four merchant ships. However, only four of these nine ships were flying the Finnish flag. Among the ships sunk were *Bolheim* and *Reinbeck* from Germany, which was neutral in this conflict.

The war at sea was of a very modest scope, because it was not long before the ice prevented navigation in the Gulf of Finland. Before the ice closed the routes, the coastal monitors *Väinämöinen* and *Ilmarinen* had supported military transfers to the Åland Islands, which had hitherto been demilitarised. Subsequently, the two coastal monitors were painted white (for winter camouflage) and based in Turku as support for the local air defence.

The Soviet Baltic Fleet was under the command of Admiral Vladimir Filippovich Tributs, who was assigned to the Leningrad military district. The fleet had its largest base in the port of Kronstadt on Kotlin Island, about 19 miles/30km west of Leningrad. Many units were transferred in 1939/40 to the newly acquired bases in the Baltic states. The largest combat units consisted of the two older battleships *Oktyabrskaya Revolyutsiya* (October Revolution) and *Marat*,[17] which had been modernised in the 1930s, the two modern cruisers *Kirov* and *Maxim Gorky* and the two large destroyers (destroyer leaders) *Leningrad* and *Minsk*. In addition, there were five modern, smaller

---

17 Named after the French revolutionary Jean-Paul Marat, who was murdered in 1793 by Charlotte Corday. Before the revolution, the ship had been called *Petropavlovsk*.

The battleship *Oktyabrskaya Revolyutsiya* (ex-*Gangut*) from the Soviet Baltic Fleet. (Old Ship Picture Galleries)

destroyers, seven older destroyers and a number of minelayers, torpedo boats and other vessels. The Soviet Baltic Fleet had about fifty-two submarines at its disposal, of which twenty-nine were operational at the end of 1939.

After some minelaying operations along the Estonian coast, the three large Finnish submarines were sent on patrols down the Baltic coast to find suitable Soviet targets outside the new Soviet bases. They had to return without results. Finnish submarines sank no ships with torpedoes during this war, but a German ship in Estonian waters was sunk by one of the submarines' mines. Finnish mines sank two Soviet patrol boats and a submarine. Soviet mines were less important, since Finnish minesweepers could sweep them relatively easily at this point in the war.

Finnish coastal batteries sank the Soviet destroyer *Stremitelnyi* (Impetuous) on 1 December. The cruiser *Kirov* and a destroyer were chased away by the 9in/234mm guns on Russarö which recorded hits on both vessels. Two weeks later, another coastal battery hit a Soviet destroyer. The major Soviet artillery units were being kept in readiness in the naval base of Kronstadt, in case there should be a need for artillery support for the Soviet forces on the Karelian Isthmus. This situation arose on 18 and 19 December 1939, when the battleships and four destroyers participated in the shelling of the Finnish battery on the island of Koivisto (now the Russian island of Beryozovye Ostrova). The Finnish islands west of the Karelian Isthmus were subjected to landing operations from Soviet marines. From the middle of January 1940, the ice conditions made it impossible for further naval operations.

The naval war prior to the occupation of Denmark and Norway

In the autumn of 1939, the Kriegsmarine deployed a couple of submarines against merchant shipping traffic in the Skagerrak, but after they had sunk Danish, Swedish, Norwegian and Finnish ships bound for Britain, there was such a commotion about it that the Kriegsmarine chose to pull them out, so that instead they would be able to concentrate on what was most important, namely the sea war in the Atlantic.

Right from the start of the war, the Danish merchant and fishing fleets suffered heavy losses. From the outbreak of war on 1 September until 9 April 1940, 378 Danish sailors and fishermen lost their lives at sea. From 1 January 1940 until 9 April 1940, 250 Danish sailors were killed. Over four days around Easter 1940, ninety-seven Danish seamen alone died in seven shipwrecks. The ships were sunk by submarines, mines and bombers. Even fishermen in the North Sea were attacked.

In 1939, the First Lord of the Admiralty Winston Churchill began work on Plan Catherine, without getting any particular support from the First Sea Lord, Admiral Sir Dudley Pound. The plan was named after Tsarina Catherine the Great, Empress of Russia from 1762 to 1796. It was a whole complex of schemes, in which the Royal Navy was to intervene in the Baltic Sea region and support Finland. Other simultaneous plans were concerned with the destruction of the Swedish ore mines and the infrastructure for the transportation of ore. The plan was abandoned on 20 January 1940. A British historian has since called Plan Catherine 'the Second World War's most ill-conceived plan'.

On the night of 16/17 February 1940, Commodore Vian RN arrived in Norwegian territorial waters with a force of three British destroyers. Two of them blocked the mouth of Jøssingfjorden[18] while Vian on board *Cossack* entered the fjord and went alongside the anchored German tanker *Altmark*. After some shooting with handguns, some of the British crew boarded the German ship. An examination of the ship's tanks revealed about three hundred prisoners, whom the Norwegian warship crews had not located – despite repeated inspections on board. They were the surviving crew from nine merchant ships sunk by the pocket battleship *Admiral Graf Spee* in the South Atlantic in the autumn. The liberation action was a violation of Norway's neutrality, but so was *Altmark*'s presence. Propaganda-wise, the Germans made a great deal out of the incident and the 'murder' of the seven crew members from *Altmark*, each of whom received a hero's funeral. Similarly, Vian and his men received a heroes' welcome when they returned home to a British port with the liberated prisoners. *Altmark* had been sailing under the

---

18 Jøssingfjord is about midway between Stavanger and Kristiansand.

The German tanker *Altmark* in Jøssingfjord on 17 February 1940, the morning after the Royal Navy's liberation action for the 300 British prisoners on board. The flag is at half-mast after the loss of seven crew during the action. (Old Ship Picture Galleries)

Reichsdienstflagge, that is, the governmental flag, and it had been a supply ship for an active warship. The armed crew had resisted with small arms.

The *Altmark* incident[19] was the real reason for the decision to occupy Denmark and Norway. The incident had shown Germany that Norway could not even ensure its own neutrality and that the British did not respect that neutrality. On 21 February 1940, Hitler summoned General der Infanterie Nikolaus von Falkenhorst, who had been appointed commanding officer of the invasion forces in Norway. The Norwegian internment of the German submarine *U-21* on 27 March 1940 reinforced the German view.[20]

On 22 February 1940, a German Heinkel He 111 bomber over the North Sea attacked two destroyers and dropped a number of bombs on them. This was due to faulty identification because both ships were German; the increased patrols were owing to the *Altmark* incident, but co-ordination between the Luftwaffe and the Kriegsmarine had broken down. The ships

---

19 *Altmark* had a strange destiny. Immediately after returning to Germany in late March 1940, the ship was renamed *Uckermark*. It came to Japan later during the war and was destroyed on 30 November 1942 by a violent explosion among the four German ships that were anchored at Yokohama. The explosion helped to put pressure on the already not particularly good relationship between Japanese and German crews in Japan. It probably occurred during tank cleaning, and fifty-three of those on board perished.

20 The German submarine *U-21* ran aground southeast of Mandal on 27 March 1940. The submarine and its crew were released in connection with the German occupation of Norway thirteen days later.

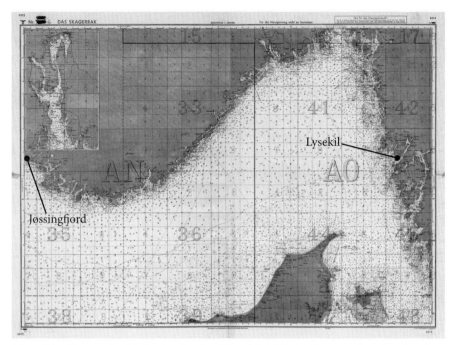

Map of the Skagerrak with Jøssingfjord and Lysekil. (Official German planning chart)

attacked were the destroyers *Z1 Leberecht Maass* and *Z3 Max Schultz*. They had to undertake vigorous evasive manoeuvres which carried them outside the mineswept channel they found themselves in; both of them were wrecked by mine detonations and 590 of the total crews of 650 men perished.

Hitler and the OKW could not agree on which operation should be launched first. Should it be Fall Gelb (Operation Yellow) or Weserübung (Exercise Weser)? These were the attacks on northern France, Belgium and Holland, and the invasion of Denmark and Norway, respectively. Generaloberst Jodl went straight to work planning both operations independently, so that either of them could be put into operation if a favourable opportunity presented itself. When it came down to it, Weserübung was launched first. The decision was made on 3 March 1940 and the actual invasion date was decided on 2 April. The invasion was to be carried out on 9 April at 0515. The conquest of northern Norway dragged on, so the Germans delayed the launching of Fall Gelb until the progress of the war in that area began to look a little brighter. When the Germans launched Fall Gelb, the French and the British began to phase out their operations in northern Norway. After Weserübung, Hitler was very proud of himself and regarded himself as a military genius. His daring operation had succeeded.

In the week up to 9 April 1940, the British had been planning to lay mines in Norwegian territorial waters (Operation Wilfred) to force the winter traffic with Swedish iron ore from Narvik out into international waters, where British submarines and surface vessels would find it easier to attack the ships. In support of these operations, nineteen submarines were sent to Norwegian and Danish waters, especially the Skagerrak, where there was suddenly an abundance of shipping targets for the submarines. When the purpose of the German ship movements dawned on the British, first priority was given to sinking troopships and second priority to warships. Four of the nineteen British submarines in the Skagerrak and along the Norwegian coast were sunk in April, May and June.

Operation Weserübung: the German occupation of Denmark and Norway

Operation Weserübung was divided into two sets of plans. Weserübung Süd was a modest operation directed against Denmark, while Weserübung Nord was quite extensive because of the great distances and the possibility of British intervention, primarily by the Royal Navy. Distances in Norway are great and the German supply lines from Germany to Norway were both long and vulnerable.

The purpose of Weserübung was partly to safeguard the important ore transport for Germany and partly to provide naval and air bases for the continuing battles against Britain: German submarines could have direct access to the North Atlantic from bases in Norway. German contractors immediately started building submarine bases with large submarine bunkers along the Norwegian coast. By a supreme irony, this requirement disappeared by and large a few months later, by which time German forces had occupied half of France, including acquiring bases in Brittany on the French Atlantic coast. From the coast of Norway – at Stavanger – German bombers could also carry out attacks against the northern part of the British Isles, primarily against Scotland.

The operation against Norway was exceedingly daring and could have gone very wrong for Germany. At one point, the Germans were about to lose the initiative in northern Norway but, thanks to transit permits obtained from Sweden, the situation was rectified, and when the Germans launched Fall Gelb on 10 May 1940, the Allies pulled back from Norway.

Denmark was just a stepping stone on the way from Germany to Norway. In the initial German plan, only German use of bases on 'Jutland's northernmost point' were featured, but with a stroke of the pen it was later corrected to

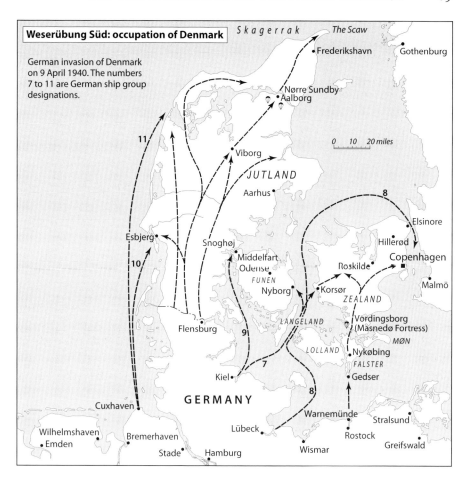

Weserübung Süd: occupation of Denmark

German invasion of Denmark on 9 April 1940. The numbers 7 to 11 are German ship group designations.

'Denmark', which led to an occupation of the whole country. Denmark was not particularly interesting from a German military point of view, as long as Britain did not occupy the country or operate in Danish waters.

Weserübung Süd

A crucial factor for Weserübung Nord was the German conquest of the two airfields at Aalborg/Nørre Sundby[21] in north Jutland. Without them, they could not provide air support during the critical early battles in Norway or send reinforcements with the Luftwaffe's Ju 52 transport aircraft.

Denmark had not entered into any alliances in 1940. Neither the country's leading politicians nor its senior officers were thinking along anything other

---

21 The current airfield was designated 'West' while the airfield at Rørdal was designated 'East'.

than national lines on the morning of 9 April. There were no illusions about a Danish existential struggle. If any of them had organised just a bit of resistance to the Germans, sought to delay them, or in any way at all sought to support Britain and France, the outcome of the battles could have taken an entirely different course. Hitler's big gamble could have gone totally wrong for him. If the Aalborg airfields had been held in Danish hands for a few hours, or days even, the German campaign in Norway could have collapsed. That did not happen. These are the hypothetical considerations and rationalisations due to hindsight which have nagged at Danes and the Allies, and made them ponder since 9 April 1940.

There had been many indications of impending military activity, but there was no interest in reacting to them. Among other things, a few days before the German occupation, DSB, the Danish railway network, had received a notification in advance of a large number of freight trains along the Jutland railway lines from Germany to Aalborg on 9 April 1940. It was a message from their good colleagues in the Reichsbahn (the German railways) and there was no reason to pass on the information outside the circle of railway people. Aalborg Airport ('West') was so important that the Luftwaffe dropped some of its elite troops from the newly created paratroopers on to the airfield, so that they could secure it until the troops from down at the border reached it by road. The German paratroopers came under Göring's Luftwaffe and it was an historic first deployment of parachute units. They established that the airport was not defended.

Similarly, they dropped some reserve units from the Luftwaffe paratroopers over the fort on Masnedø in Storstrømmen (the channel near Vordingborg in southern Zealand, Denmark) to neutralise this fort. It was probably somewhat excessive, because the fort's garrison consisted of only two conscript sailors who spent their time looking after hens. It took some time before the agitated German parachutists discovered that there was no additional complement at the fort at all.

The immediate invasion force on 9 April in Denmark consisted of approximately 38,000 men. One division and a brigade were to travel up through Jutland and one division to Zealand. About half drove across the border in southern Jutland and the other half came by ship. Around five thousand men were the first to be put ashore early in the morning and the others came in during the day. Ships sailed in suddenly in the morning at Copenhagen, Korsør, Nyborg, Esbjerg and Middelfart/Snoghøj.

The ship *Hansestadt Danzig* had sailed up through the Great Belt during the night of 8/9 April, gone north around Zealand and then south through the Sound. Early in the morning, she passed the fortress at Middelgrund, where most of the garrison had been demobilised a few days earlier. The

The German ship *Hansestadt Danzig*, which brought a German battalion from the 308th Infantry Regiment to Langelinie in Copenhagen early on the morning of 9 April 1940. From the beginning of the war in 1939, the ship had been used as a minelayer. (Museum of Danish Resistance, Copenhagen)

fortress asked for the ship's name via a flash signal, but otherwise nothing happened. Outside Copenhagen harbour, a German icebreaker 'by chance' lay at anchor to provide ice-breaking services if the ice in the harbour area had been excessive. *Hansestadt Danzig* had a battalion on board and her assignment was to capture Amalienborg (the Royal Palace) and Kastellet (the star-shaped fortress at the harbour entrance). If the operation had gone wrong in any way, it would not have mattered. From the German side, they had been willing to risk the battalion on a favourable chance of a surprise attack: it was a gamble which succeeded. If the battalion had been wiped out or put out of action in one way or another, the task would simply have been taken over by the division which had been put ashore in Korsør on the morning of 9 April and was heading across Zealand towards Copenhagen. Kastellet was captured without problems because there were no combat troops. At Amalienborg Palace, the Royal Life Guards put up a resistance and the Germans failed to get in.

In southern Jutland, the commanding officer of the Danish general staff's intelligence section, Ritmester (Captain of Horse) Hans M Lunding, a former warrant officer in a German Uhlan regiment[22] during the First World War,

---

22 The Uhlans were originally cavalry soldiers with lances from Poland in the sixteenth century. The word comes from the Turkish. During the First World War, there were Uhlan regiments in Russia and Germany.

had acquired the necessary information about German intentions and when they would cross the border. Some of the Danish Jutland division's personnel from the barracks near the border took up position with their weapons early in the morning of 9 April 1940. They were supposed to delay the German advance long enough for the other forces to establish a line of defence across Jutland at the River Vejle.

The soldiers near the border were particularly pleased with two weapon systems with great firepower: the Madsen light machine gun (0.32in/8mm) and the Madsen machine gun (0.75in/20mm). Both weapons systems were produced by DISA (Danish Industry Syndicate A/S, colloquially called *Riffelsyndikatet* – the Rifle Syndicate). The 0.75in/20mm guns were used by reconnaissance units who had them on their motorcycles with sidecars. The Danish soldiers at the border put up a stronger resistance than is generally acknowledged: a historian has found unconfirmed information in DISA's archives that German losses that morning in South Jutland amounted to 203 killed.[23] After 9 April, the company had the Germans as customers and they therefore requested information from the Wehrmacht on the effectiveness of the weapons. The Germans made sure that German casualties were not otherwise revealed to either the German or Danish public. Recent studies indicate that the figure of 203 deaths is not correct. There are no other accounts from German archives of the overall losses in Denmark. Some of the relevant archives were later lost during Allied bombing raids.

The Danish army's total losses in southern Jutland amounted to eleven men. In addition, three men from the Grænsegendarmeriet (border patrols) were killed. Finally, the Danish army air corps lost two officers through the shooting-down of a plane during the German air attack on the air base at Værløse, northwest of Copenhagen.

The same historian has discovered that the staff at Haderslev Hospital in south Jutland made the hospital ready on 8 April. Fifty patients were sent home, so that a large number of wounded could be admitted and the doctors spent the night at the hospital. This could be interpreted in different ways: partly, that it was well-known that something violent was going to happen, and partly that they were backing up the Danish army's expected action. Finally, it can be interpreted in the way that someone in Jutland could obtain information which the government in Copenhagen might not want to be made privy to. Similarly, the shipowner A P Møller (of the Maersk Company) could acquire sufficient information that, on the night of 8/9 April 1940, he could send instructions to the shipping company's captains to sail to a British or a neutral port if Denmark was occupied.

---

23 See Kay Søren Nielsen's *Soldaterne den 9. april 1940* (*The Soldiers on 9 April 1940*) (Cultours, 2010).

The Danish navy did nothing on 9 April 1940 for the simple reason that the navy's commander-in-chief, Viceadmiral Hjalmar Rechnitzer, knew Grossadmiral Erich Raeder personally. Rechnitzer was convinced that Raeder, whom he knew as a good colleague and a gentleman, would certainly approach him if he had a problem relating to Denmark and that they would be able to find a solution to whatever it was. The Danish naval attaché in Berlin, Kommandørkaptajn F H Kjølsen had been home in early April and was able to report on an impending occupation of Denmark, which Oberst Oster from the Abwehr had leaked, in the expectation 'that someone would do something about it'. When the naval officers in the

Viceadmiral Hjalmar Rechnitzer (1872–1953), commander-in-chief of the Danish navy in 1940.

Danish naval ministry and at the naval staff briefed Viceadmiral Rechnitzer about the many northbound German ships in the Great Belt and the North Sea, and suggested reconnaissance with naval aircraft and torpedo boats, the advice was rejected. All the aircraft in the Danish naval air service were grounded. The vice-admiral's attitude was 'that Denmark should not provoke the big neighbour to the south.'

This is, though, a slightly simplified presentation of the problem. Rechnitzer was loyal to the ruling Danish government and was continuing its policy both logically and consistently. He did not have the imagination, though, to conceive of a total occupation of the country and he probably shared this attitude with the politicians, the military leadership, and the majority of the Danish population. After almost a month of occupation, it was reported in the Danish navy that Rechnitzer had accepted a German demand for Danish mine clearance and a handover of Danish equipment. On 8 May 1940, the four most senior Danish naval officers presented themselves at his office in full dress, swords and medals, and informed him that the naval personnel no longer had confidence in him. Two days later, he chose to resign. When the country had been in need, his judgement had left something to be desired and his legacy has not been positive, particularly in the Danish navy. He was questioned by the Danish parliamentary commission after the occupation ended, but was neither charged nor convicted of withholding anything. However, the statement about mine clearance and handover of equipment to the Germans, which caused him to be overthrown a month after the beginning of the occupation, was apparently never uttered by him.

The German division which had been landed at Korsør reached Copenhagen in the afternoon. Reinforcements arrived later via the ferry from Warnemünde to Gedser on the Danish island of Falster. The following day, a landing force arrived at Thyborøn in northwest Jutland and another at Rønne on the island of Bornholm. From the beginning, the Germans wanted to gain control of the Danish-controlled minefields and, on 9 April, 100 men deployed in sixteen ships began the process of locating and capturing the four control stations from where the controlled minefields in the Great Belt and the Little Belt could be activated and deactivated. (See the text box on sea mines above.)

The Kriegsmarine sent their latest vessels to Norway and the old ones to Denmark. *Schlesien* (sister ship of *Schleswig-Holstein*), which was a veteran of the Battle of Jutland on 31 May 1916, was kept ready in the Great Belt, where it covered the landing at Korsør. It went aground near Halskov Reef lightship and was aground here all day. From May/June 1940, Vizeadmiral Raul Mewis was appointed Marinebefehlshaber Dänemark (naval commander-in-chief, Denmark). He set himself up with his staff in the Hotel Phoenix in Copenhagen.[24]

Weserübung Nord

Grossadmiral Raeder was worried about Weserübung, which he feared could cost the Kriegsmarine up to half of its large vessels. While the German vessels sailed north, they met the British minelaying destroyer *Glowworm*, which was on its way to lay mines along the Norwegian coast. When the two German destroyers *Z11 Bernd von Arnim* and *Z18 Hans Lüdemann* observed *Glowworm*, they sought assistance from the heavy German cruiser *Admiral Hipper*, which was sailing off Trondheim. The battle between the German cruiser and the British destroyer was uneven, but the commanding officer of *Glowworm* succeeded in ramming *Admiral Hipper* before the British destroyer sank. The commanding officer of the destroyer, Lieutenant-Commander Gerald B Roope RN, was just about to be rescued, when his

---

24 On 18 March 1943, he was replaced by the 51-year-old Vizeadmiral Hans-Heinrich Wurmbach, who had been chief of staff of the Black Sea region, and before that commanding officer of the pocket battleship *Admiral Scheer*.

The German destroyer *Z11 Bernd von Arnim* photographed from the Danish fisheries patrol vessel *Ingolf* in the Great Belt on 7 April 1940. Each of the German destroyers brought 200 men from the *Gebirgstruppen* (mountain troops). Some can be seen on the deck. Six days later, the destroyer was scuttled by its own crew in Rombak Fjord near Narvik after exhausting all its ammunition. The crew then took part in the fighting on land to support the German army units until the Allies withdrew from northern Norway. (Kai Aage Nolsøe Bang)

strength gave out as he lay in the water, having taken hold of a rope from the cruiser. He was awarded the Victoria Cross posthumously, partly because of an honourable mention from the commanding officer of *Admiral Hipper*. The cruiser had had some of its side-armour split and took quite a lot of water in, which led to two months in dry dock. That Raeder's concern for the surface ships was not entirely unfounded is shown by the loss statistics after Weserübung. The force at Narvik lost all ten of its modern destroyers; the light cruiser *Königsberg* was sunk by British naval aircraft near Bergen; the heavy cruiser *Blücher* (sister ship to *Admiral Hipper*) was sunk by the Norwegians at the fort of Oscarsborg near Drøbak in the Oslo fjord and the light cruiser *Karlsruhe* was sunk by the submarine HMS *Truant* in the Skagerrak. The pocket battleship *Lützow* had to be towed home from the Skagerrak to Kiel after being hit by a torpedo. The German minelayer and artillery training ship *Brummer* was sunk south of Oslo fjord on 14 April by the British submarine *Sterlet*. In the week after 9 April, British submarines also sank many troopships in the Skagerrak.

The heavy German cruiser *Blücher* was sunk approximately twenty miles south of Oslo by the torpedo battery and the old guns on the Oscarsborg Fortress. The delaying of the German troops made it possible for the Norwegian king and the government to escape to the north. (Old Ship Picture Galleries)

The delayed disembarkation of German troops in Oslo after the sinking of the heavy cruiser *Blücher* off Oscarsborg Fortress early in the morning of 9 April 1940. (SMB arkiv)

Torpedoes

The most widely used German torpedo during the Second World War was the G7A: it was a hot air type and had a large air flask with a pressure of approximately 2,845lb/sq in (200kg/cm²) and a petroleum burner. High-pressure air is mixed with the hot petroleum fumes from the burner and used in a steam engine which drove two propellers, each rotating in opposite directions so that the torpedo was kept stable in the water. The bubbles from the exhaust could sometimes be seen well aft of the torpedo if the weather was good and the sea calm, but it took some time before they came to the surface, depending on the torpedo depth which had been set.

The important thing with torpedo firings is the understanding of vector calculations. During its course towards the target, the torpedo has to maintain a preset speed, for example 30 knots, very accurately. The commanding officer in the firing vessel calculates, estimates or guesses the target vessel's target angle and speed. The target angle is the angle between the line of sight and the target's course. As the commanding officer knows the torpedo's speed, the target's speed and the target angle, he can then use vector calculations to calculate the angle the torpedo

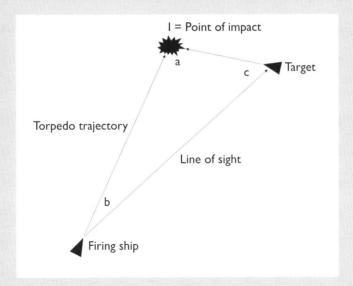

The angle 'c' is the target angle. Distance from 'Target' to 'Point of Impact' is the target vector. The distance from 'Firing ship' to 'Point of impact' is the torpedo vector.

should have from the line of sight to hit the target ship at the point of impact. An expert in vector calculation will note that it is not necessary to know the distance to the target. Using equilateral triangles, all distances to the target in this vector calculation will provide exactly the same course for the torpedo towards its target. The assumptions are that the target angle and the target's speed are correctly assessed.

Most torpedoes were of a calibre of 21in/53.3cm. The German G7A torpedo was approximately 24ft/7.2m long and weighed 3,391lb/1,538kg. From the front, it was divided into warhead, air tank, engine, a rear space with elevation and lateral rudders and various devices, and two propellers. A gyro maintained a constant course via the lateral rudders. The gyro was driven by air from the air tank. The depth could be set before firing. The warhead contained approximately 600lb/275kg of the high-explosive TNT (trinitrotoluene). Furthest forward on the warhead was an impact pistol that upon impact against the ship's hull detonated the TNT charge.

Immediately after the torpedo was fired, a small propeller in the nose of the torpedo used the forward propulsion through the water to screw the detonator into the explosive charge and arm the torpedo. If the air in the flask was not used up, the residual quantity of compressed air would increase the explosive effect inside the target. Usually, the same types of torpedoes were used by destroyers, torpedo boats, motor torpedo boats and submarines. If firing took place from longer distances, an array of torpedoes would often be fired – that is, with different angles – from surface ships. A submarine will typically fire from a distance of around 3,280ft/1,000m and fire two torpedoes with a small angle between the two courses in order to obtain a bit of spread. This is done to compensate for the uncertainties surrounding the target's course and speed. If the spread is set too wide, there is a risk that one torpedo will have a course in front of the target and the other will have a course behind it. A submarine could instead fire from different torpedo tubes with the same angle but with a fixed time lag between firings.

Some LUT torpedoes could begin a search programme along the ship's course if they did not hit the target close to the calculated point of impact. The German torpedoes could be set to 30 knots, which was the normal setting, or to 40 or 44 knots, but then the range of the torpedo was significantly shorter. Late in the war, the Germans succeeded in constructing a torpedo that sought out the propeller noise of the target ship.

Soviet submarine *Shch-320* loading torpedoes. (Old Ship Picture Galleries)

A torpedo is considered a 'battle-decisive weapon': a single torpedo hit is not usually something that a ship can recover from. Even if the target ship does not sink after a hit, it will usually have serious limitations in speed, seaworthiness and fighting ability.

Torpedoes are fired from a torpedo tube; the gyroscope and the engine start up while the torpedo is still in the tube. The firing is usually done with compressed air or with a gunpowder cartridge. Large surface vessels have torpedo tubes on the aft deck. They can be rotated and are usually fired laterally over the side of the ship. There are maybe three or four torpedo tubes mounted together. Motor torpedo boats are usually equipped with two torpedo tubes in the bow or on the foredeck, so aiming can more or less be done with the ship. Submarines have a number of bow tubes, maybe two to eight, to fire forwards, and during the war it was also common for submarines to have two torpedo tubes in the stern which fired directly aft. These tubes were sometimes used for minelaying.

Torpedo bombers were developed to be a battle-decisive weapon during the Second World War. The torpedoes were often relatively small and firing distances were quite short. They were usually dropped 1,970–2,625ft/600–800 m from the target. Torpedo planes suffered heavy losses as, while dropping the torpedo, they had to fly in very low (at a height of 82–98ft/25–30m) and very slowly, and immediately after the drop necessarily had to come quite close to the target and were therefore in danger of being hit by flak from the target ship.

The Kriegsmarine's torpedoes were hit by technical problems in the spring of 1940. There was a high failure rate which took several months to overcome and that weakened the German submarine campaign in the Atlantic, as well as Weserübung Nord.

The Polish submarine *Orzeł* accounted for one of the major triumphs at a time of meagre results. On 8 April 1940, the submarine sank a German troopship, *Rio de Janeiro*, off Lillesand on the Norwegian coast. About 150 German soldiers are suspected to have gone down with the ship. The commanding officer on that occasion was awarded the British Distinguished Service Order (DSO) and the highest Polish distinction, the order of *Virtuti Militari*. The submarine achieved a total of seven war patrols, but in May (probably 23 May) or in June 1940 the submarine was presumed lost with all sixty-three crew on board. One source mentions that the submarine was lost in a newly established minefield south of Norway.[25]

Regardless of the danger of mines, on the night of 24 April, the three French destroyers *Indomptable*, *Malin* and *Triomphant* attacked some German VP-boats (patrol boats) in the Skagerrak, about fifty nautical miles northwest of the Scaw. The purpose of this operation was to attack the German anti-submarine vessels and, in so doing, to support the ongoing British submarine campaign. Two small vessels from the Kriegsmarine were sunk.

When the Allies pulled out of the fighting in northern Norway in May/June 1940, they destroyed Narvik's modern shipping facilities for iron ore. After this, only 15 per cent of German supplies of iron ore from Sweden came via Norwegian ports.

---

25 Shortly after the war, Danish submarine officers at the submarine school HMS *Dolphin* near Portsmouth heard rumours that one of the school's instructors, while a British submarine commander in the Skagerrak in 1940, had sunk a Polish submarine by mistake in the belief that it was German. Further details about this have not been forthcoming. Source: Kommandørkaptajn N F Stegmann, a student at the submarine school in 1946/47.

Minefields laid out after 9 April 1940

On 9 April, four German minelayers laid about 1,600 mines in the Skaggerak between Hanstholm in Denmark and Kristiansand in Norway, and three days later supplemented the field with another 1,000 mines. The purpose of the barrage was to prevent passage between Jutland and the Norwegian coast. If any ship was to sail by, it had to stick close to one of the coasts and in both areas German VP-boats were on patrol and temporary artillery batteries were set up by the German army.

Twelve days after the occupation, the Germans began to lay a net barrier in the Kattegat between Sjællands Odde and Djursland (ie between northwest Zealand and east Jutland). It was approximately seventeen nautical miles long with an opening about one mile wide and it was intended to prevent submarines from penetrating the Great Belt. The laying of the barrier was completed in May 1940. In the same month, the Germans established a 4in/105mm gun emplacement at Hornbæk, which was to cover the northern entrance to the Sound.

On 12 May 1940, Germany demanded that Sweden lay mines on the Swedish side of the Sound, and the Swedes bowed to this demand. Germany

To the left is shown the net barrier between Sjællands Odde and Djursland blocking the northern entrance to the Great Belt. To the right is the German net barrier with mines blocking the Sound. Two miles north of Helsingborg, the Djuramåsa Fortress was established in 1940 (see page 109). (Official German planning chart)

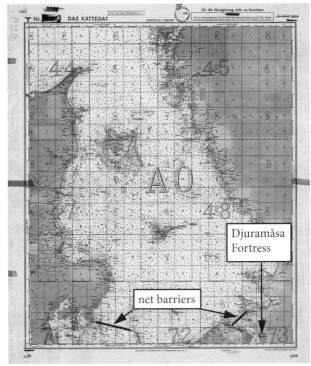

During the heavy fighting in Rombaksfjord in the vicinity of Narvik, ORP *Grom* was hit by a bomb from a Heinkel He 111 on 4 May 1940. The bomb detonated close to the torpedoes on deck. The Polish destroyer broke in two and went down, taking fifty-nine men with her. (Old Ship Picture Galleries)

One of the many German *Vorpostenboote* or *VP-Boote* (patrol cutters). They were often requisitioned fishing vessels armed with a variety of guns. (SMB arkiv)

also pressurised Sweden into creating an effective barrier for submarines. The Swedes claimed that it was Swedish policy to ensure free passage, but the Germans were eager to block off the Sound to British submarines, which had been a major problem during the First World War. The Swedes perceived the submarine net as a violation of their neutrality, but submitted to it anyway. Germany was to lay the net while Sweden was supposed to take care of security and control on the Swedish side. On 10 June 1940, the German ship *Genua* laid a submarine net between Viken in Sweden and Hornbæk in Denmark. The net was ready the following day and later hydrophone stations were installed on both sides so that they could listen for submerged submarines. In April 1941, the Germans laid another minefield with 1,000 anti-submarine mines between the east coast of Jutland and the Swedish west coast. Sweden laid a north–south minefield from Lysekil to Varberg in the spring of 1941. The purpose here was primarily to force German ships into international waters. The inshore waters could continue to be used with a Swedish pilot on board.

Collaboration with the Germans and the situation with the merchant navy

Collaboration with the German authorities was taking place in all the German-occupied countries, but this has been a taboo subject for decades. In many of the countries, collaboration was also far more extensive than the people immediately became aware of. As Denmark lost the British market when the war broke out, Danish agriculture was faced with a problem. At the same time, there arose instead a huge need for food production in Germany, part of which Denmark very quickly came to cover. The Germans could absorb a large part of Danish agricultural production, but they were even more interested in industrial production and shipping. Without collaboration, there would not have been any deliveries of raw materials to Denmark – particularly of oil and coal – and it was the Germans who set the conditions. Industry leaders were generally positive about collaboration with the Germans.

Danish assistance to the Germans by way of, for example, the construction of airports, bunker construction, shipbuilding, shipping, and industrial or agricultural exports was partly conditioned by the social circumstances of that time. The 1930s had been a very hard time for many working-class families. Unemployment had been very high and possibilities of welfare benefits were slim, so people took whatever work was available.

German construction projects constituted a dilemma for trade unions, politicians and individual jobseekers, but there was nothing that was considered odious about seeking employment at these. The alternative would be to find work in Germany. The Danish Communists came to terms with this state of affairs until 22 June 1941, but after that date, they accounted for a large part of the strikes, work stoppages, sabotage and information collection which took place at businesses, not least at the many Danish shipyards.

When the occupation took place on 9 April 1940, the Danish merchant fleet had been divided in two: the domestic fleet and the overseas fleet. The first consisted of the merchant ships which were in Danish waters or 'within the Scaw' at the start of the occupation. The second came to represent Denmark's most important contribution to the Allies during the war. Some of the ships went directly to British ports, where the captain and crew made themselves available along with their ship, while others sought haven in a neutral port – in the USA, for example. Most of these sooner or later came to sail for the Allies. Shipping tonnage was a critical shortage during the war on both sides. Britain, in particular, was very hard-pressed until the United States entered the war in December 1941. The initial contribution from Denmark was therefore particularly welcome.

Part of the domestic fleet sailed with cargo for the Germans and the owners could not decline. The freight was distributed by the Freight Board (a state institution), which of course also helped to keep the companies going and create satisfaction among the shipowners. The latter wanted to ensure that their assets – ie their ships – came through the war unscathed. Ore, fertiliser, copper, nickel, aluminium and zinc were collected in Norway and Sweden and shipped to Germany, and agricultural, fishery and industrial products were exported from Denmark. Coal, coke, steel, fertiliser and oil were brought from Germany. Much of the transport between the regions which today goes by road was at that time sent by short voyages, often in small wooden ketches. At Rasmussen's shipyard[26] in Svendborg, twelve minesweepers were built for the Kriegsmarine, but otherwise it was the German merchant vessels to which Danish shipyards rendered service. Shortly after the occupation of Norway and Denmark, as well as that of the Netherlands, Belgium and northern France, Germany took a general decision on the use of national shipbuilding capacities. For security reasons, Germany preferred to build its warships at its own shipyards and use the yards in the occupied countries as repair and building yards for merchant vessels.

The 'military collaboration' with the Germans collapsed just one week after the beginning of the occupation, and it was in itself a somewhat artificial situation to maintain an army and a navy in an occupied country. In April 1940, the Germans demanded that some of the Danish army's anti-aircraft guns were given up and, later the same year, they demanded the rest of them. In January 1941, the Germans demanded that some of the Danish navy's ships were handed over, and this resulted in six Danish torpedo boats being transferred to the Kriegsmarine on 5 February 1941. The Danish King Christian X was against it and he ordered Rigets Flag (the national flag) at

---

26 Rasmussen was a German citizen and owner of several shipyards in Germany, just south of the Danish border.

German minesweeper with the gear streamed aft and minesweeping equipment on the quarterdeck. The equipment can both cut anchor cables to anchored mines and simulate the magnetic, acoustic and pressure conditions in the water so that the mine thinks it is a target ship passing. This makes it detonate. Note that the minesweeper itself has to get past the mine first. It must therefore be silent, non-magnetic and move at a low speed, to minimise the water pressure.

Batteri Sixtus on the naval base on Holmen to be put at half-mast in protest.[27] This handing-over was sharply criticised by Britain and it was later made clear by the British government via contacts in Stockholm with both the royal family and the Danish government that if Denmark also handed over its submarines to Germany, Denmark would not be regarded very kindly after the war.

One of the areas where the Germans had to make a choice was in regard to the Danish navy. Should they go for confrontation and demand equipment be handed over or work carried out, and thus be met with negative attitudes, or should they try to co-operate and make the best out of the situation? The Germans wanted as much help as possible, and the Danish navy could, for example, perform minesweeping tasks, but this would have been active support for the German war effort. The compromise was that Denmark

27 This flag is normally only set at half-mast on Good Friday and at the death of the reigning monarch, but it can also be set at half-mast according to a decision from the royal family, which King Christian X took advantage of.

took care of the minesweeping in the east–west routes in order to maintain connections between the different parts of the country, while the Germans themselves took care of the north–south routes, which were connected with the war in Norway. It was not long, though, before the Germans tightened up on their demands. As soon as the minesweeping partnership began, there were problems with the crews, who started grumbling.

Sweden between 9 April 1940 and 22 June 1941

Sweden's situation was dramatically changed on 9 April 1940 when Hitler occupied Denmark and Norway. The war had now moved even closer. At that time, the country was quite exposed and, because of the situation in Finland, there were virtually no defences in southern Sweden. German troops now stood all along the Norwegian border and just on the other side of the Sound.

The collaboration between Germany and the Soviet Union helped to complicate the situation in Sweden. In the summer of 1940, the Soviet Union had secured bases in Finland and incorporated the three Baltic countries as Soviet republics, and the Soviets now regarded the Baltic Sea in a broader perspective.

The Germans were busy elsewhere. German troops were positioned in Norway and Denmark, the German army was on a victorious advance through Holland, Belgium and France, and Britain was under threat of invasion.

It was precisely at this moment, the summer of 1940, that Swedish cryptanalysts succeeded in breaking the Soviet naval ciphers. It became clear from this signals traffic that the Soviet Union had offensive plans in the Baltic Sea. Soviet submarines and naval aircraft were, among other things, going to lay mines off some Swedish ports. In the middle of August, units from the Soviet Baltic Fleet's air force received maps and aerial photographs of 'target no. 55621c', which was Stockholm. The Soviet ciphers could only be read for a period of three months. During this period, the Soviet Baltic Fleet also busied itself with plans to capture the Åland Islands. This is evident from Soviet archives, which were briefly available for Swedish researchers immediately after the Soviet collapse in 1991. In addition to the military threat from Germany, there was thus also a regular Soviet military threat directed against Sweden to be taken into account.

It was not only the Soviet signals traffic which was tapped by the Swedes. In April 1940, following the occupation of Denmark and Norway, the Germans rented some cables from the Swedish Telegraph Agency. The cables ran along the Swedish west coast and telex communications were being sent to and

Arne Beurling broke the encryption of the German *Geheimschreiber* (ie secret teletype). He was a professor at the University of Uppsala and later at Princeton, USA. (SMB arkiv)

A T-52 *Geheimschreiber* (secret writer) developed by Siemens & Halske in the 1930s. It was an electromechanic teletypewriter, mainly used for communication via land lines and, rarely, by radio. It had ten cipher wheels visible on top, and was a rather bulky machine weighing more than 220lb/100kg.

from the German forces in Norway. These communications were tapped by the Swedes, who also tapped other traffic on telephone and telegraph cables to and from Berlin, Oslo and later also Helsinki. It was mostly military traffic, but on the Berlin–Stockholm connection it was also possible to intercept diplomatic communications. Responsibility for the tapping of radio and telecommunications traffic lay with Försvarets Radioanstalt (FRA – the Military Radio Agency). A large part of the radio traffic was carried out by the Germans' *Geheimschreiber*, a teleprinter/telex machine with a scrambler.[28] The telegraph agency gave copies of the radio traffic to the FRA,

---

28 It was used for enciphered telex messages and produced by a company called Siemens und Halske (model T52). In the British cryptanalysis centre at Bletchley Park (Government Code and Cipher school) enciphered telex systems were named after fish and this version was called Sturgeon. Between 1940 and 1942, the FRA deciphered 350,000 German messages.

but they could not read the enciphered messages. A mathematics professor in Uppsala, Arne Beurling, had offered his assistance and he asked for all signals traffic for a single day; within two weeks, he had cracked the cipher. After this, a teleprinter was ordered according to Beurling's specification from the phone manufacturer L M Ericsson, and then the FRA could read the essential parts of the German signal traffic through Sweden, though with periodic exceptions.

The Swedish government was very keen to stay out of the war and therefore gradually increased its concessions to Germany when the war started. Hitler had demanded that Sweden remain strictly neutral in April 1940; neutrality should in this context be understood as support for Germany and lack of support for the Allies. From the German point of view, Sweden could supply Germany with raw materials and industrial products, and Sweden also had an extensive shipping capacity at its disposal. On the other hand, the Swedish military forces represented a threat to the German occupation of Norway. For Konteradmiral Dönitz, commander-in-chief of the German submarine forces, Sweden could pose a threat to submarine exercises in the Baltic Sea, and to the sea trials and work-up of newly built submarines. Personally, Hitler assessed the German occupation of Norway and Denmark as a stark challenge to Sweden to continue its iron ore exports.

The first serious Swedish concession came when the Germans were subjected to heavy fighting in northern Norway. The battles in Narvik were about to develop into a German defeat. After pressure from Germany, Sweden allowed the transit of unarmed 'medics', who were to take care of the wounded Germans in northern Norway. It turned out later that they were elite troops. The Luftwaffe dropped arms and ammunition to them on the Norwegian side of the border. The first group of 'medics', consisting of forty men, skied towards Bjørnfjell, which was the Norwegian station on the Narvik–Kiruna railway line which was closest to the border. They changed their Red Cross armbands for yellow armbands marked 'DW', which stood for Deutsche Wehrmacht (the German armed forces), and used the weapons dropped to them to capture Bjørnfjell station. It cost the lives of six Norwegian soldiers, while sixteen were seriously wounded. For a while, the German propaganda machine had been preparing itself for the Allies winning at Narvik, but thanks to the Swedish assistance, things went differently.

Immediately after 9 April 1940, the Swedish defence forces resorted to many panicky measures, and it was difficult for them to prioritise individual actions. One of the military wishes was to be able to cover the northern entrance to the Sound and this proposal enjoyed rapid prioritisation. A reconnaissance unit was sent off to identify appropriate positions and by 17 April a complete proposal was ready on the commander-in-chief's desk.

The German pocket battleship *Lützow* on its way north in the Great Belt on 8 April 1940. The ship was sailing immediately astern of the heavy cruiser *Blücher*, which was sunk near Drøbak in the Oslo Fjord the following day. *Lützow* was hit by three 11in/280mm shells from the Norwegian fort at Drøbak. On 11 April 1940 in the Skagerrak, on its way home to the shipyard in Kiel, *Lützow* was hit by a torpedo from the British submarine *Spearfish*. The stern was on the point of breaking off and the damage cost the pocket battleship a one-year stay in the shipyard. (Charles Nielsen)

A fort should be established north of Hälsingborg. It was to be located 1.9 miles/3km from the coast at Djuramåsa and it was to be equipped with four 6in/152mm guns. Poland had previously ordered four 6in/152mm guns from Bofors for delivery in 1940, but when Poland was defeated, the Swedish government could immediately take over these pieces of ordnance. The new fort – Batteri Hälsingborg – was reported operational as early as 7 June. On 23/24 August 1940, the final inspection and approval took place. The battery could cover an area that stretched from Gilleleje and Nivå in northeast Zealand to the northern tip of the island of Ven. If a German attack against Sweden came from Elsinore, Sweden would regard the whole stretch of railway line near Elsinore as a very important target for the battery. Close by was the submarine barrier which the Germans had laid between Viken and Hornbæk.

The so-called *permittentavtal* (furlough agreement) covered German soldiers supposedly on their way to Germany on leave. It was reached between the Swedish foreign minister, Christian Günther, and the German foreign minister, Joachim von Ribbentrop, on 22 June 1940. It allowed German soldiers to travel by train through Sweden. At first, it was only to Norway, but later the agreement was extended to include traffic to Finland. The Swedish rationale for their co-operation with the German army was that the Swedish measures did not support any warring party, since the fighting in Norway was finished. That argument was not sustainable, as it would have been much more demanding on resources for the Germans to find other solutions, and transport capacity, in particular, was one of the biggest problems for a belligerent Germany. One year after the treaty was signed, the trains through Sweden were bringing fresh troops to the Eastern Front and wounded soldiers back to Germany. The treaty was revoked by Sweden in July 1943.

Torgny Segersted, chief editor of the *Göteborgs Handels och Sjöfartstidning* (*Gothenburg Trade and Shipping Journal*), had angered Hitler several times around the outbreak of the war with his articles and editorials. The Swedish government banned some of the newspaper's editions in the autumn of 1940, as well as introducing special legislation with reduced freedom of the press in June 1941.

When Germany occupied Norway, the British destroyed the shipping facilities for ore in Narvik harbour. Some of the ore was then directed by rail to the ice-free port of Oxelösund, south of Stockholm, and from there shipped to Germany. SOE had at one point planned to destroy the facilities in Oxelösund.

The Swedish iron ore carrier *Vollrath Tham*. The ship struck a mine in the river Ems estuary on the German North Sea coast and sank on 11 November 1941 without any casualties. (SMB arkiv)

In February 1941, the Swedish army attaché in Berlin had a discussion with German army's chief of staff, Generaloberst Franz Halder. Oberst Curt Julin-Dannfelt asked Halder about what Germany's view would be were Sweden to allow Allied forces transit if the Soviet Union attacked Finland once more. 'In such a case,' said Halder, 'Sweden would be reduced to a pile of rubble.'

On 23 January 1941, five Norwegian merchant ships which were berthed at Lysekil succeeded in taking advantage of the bad weather and escaping to Scotland. Lysekil is in the outer reaches of the Swedish archipelago, about 47 miles/75km northwest of Gothenburg. This was the British Operation Rubble, conducted under the leadership of the British industrialist George Binney, who was based in Sweden, involving four cargo ships (*Elisabeth Bakke*, *John Bakke*, *Tai-Shan* and *Taurus*) and the motor tanker *Ranja*, with a total of 25,000 tonnes of Swedish ball bearings and 147 Norwegian sailors on board. The ships had been chartered earlier by Britain and had British captains. Without knowing it, they sailed quite close to the two German battleships *Scharnhorst* and *Gneisenau*, which at that time lay at anchor eight nautical miles north of the Danish island of Læsø in the Kattegat.

In the spring of 1941, the Swedish defence chief informed the Swedish government that the country would not be able to defend itself in the event of a German attack, and would therefore have to use all its powers to avoid involvement in the war. At this point, German forces were in position along the Norwegian-Swedish border, as well as in Denmark. Later in the war, when Sweden had to assess the threat from Germany, there were also German forces in Finland, the three Baltic states and along all the other coastlines in the Baltic.

Acts of war in the Skagerrak between 14 April and 10 June 1940 resulted in Sweden losing thirteen merchant ships and a number of fishing boats. To avoid further losses, Swedish imports and exports were concentrated on the Finnish port of Petsamo out to the Barents Sea. From here, 1,000 tonnes of Swedish goods on average could be dispatched every day. It only lasted until the Continuation War in Finland began in the summer of 1941.

The Wallenberg brothers' negotiations had led to Sweden being allowed to have individual merchant ships with supplies – mainly from South America – sailing into Gothenburg. Two tankers were allowed to pass through the barriers in the Skagerrak in October 1940. Later this traffic became more systematic.[29] Apart from these few ships, Sweden was reduced to importing and exporting solely via Germany and German-occupied territories. Germany was the largest export market for Sweden and the

---

29 This traffic has been called the 'Gothenburg traffic' or 'safe passage traffic'.

The German battleship *Gneisenau*, which during the night of 26/27 February 1942 was so badly damaged during an RAF attack on Kiel that it never became operational again. On 23 March 1945, it was sunk as a blockship in Gotenhafen harbour during the Soviet advance. Two of the ship's twin 6in/150mm guns were placed at Grådyb at Esbjerg before the war ended. Ten years later, they were moved to the new Stevns Fort and are now part of an exhibition about the Cold War.

The Swedish commander-in-chief from 8 December 1939 to 31 March 1944, General O G Thörnell. (SMB arkiv)

iron ore was important for Germany, which meant that Sweden could get something in return.

The British naval attaché in Stockholm, Henry Denham,[30] emphasised in his reports that the Swedish navy, in particular, was extremely pro-German. He also underlined that the Swedish secret police (Säpo) worked very closely with their German counterpart, and that his own movements were closely followed. In some Swedish circles, Säpo was referred to as 'Swestapo'. The defence chief,

---

30 On 9 April 1940, he was the British naval attaché in Denmark.

General Thörnell, was also regarded as very pro-German and there is evidence that, in April 1941, Thörnell suggested to the Swedish government that Sweden should join a possible future German war against the Soviet Union. The Germans tried to get Swedish assistance during the planning of Operation Barbarossa, the attack on the Soviet Union. Hitler declared that he could probably get Sweden into the war if he handed over the Åland Islands to them. The OKW was considering as late as May 1941 how the Swedish forces might be used if Sweden joined the war against the Soviet Union.

The Royal Air Force over the Baltic Sea

The Royal Air Force came to play a crucial role in the Baltic Sea. A very large proportion of the mines in Danish waters and across the southern part of the Baltic Sea were dropped by bombers from the RAF. The British mining of Danish territorial waters from the air was launched on 11 April 1941. At that point in the war, each bomber could only carry a single mine. One of the first targets was the Great Belt. The British wanted to hit the north–south traffic from Germany to Norway, but for a period in the middle of April 1941, the mines also paralysed the east–west Danish ferry traffic.

 A number of German ships were converted to floating flak batteries. In this photograph, FLAK-Schiff *Arkona* is seen in 1944 with Würzburg radar (top parabolic radar antenna) for both detection and fighter control, an optical rangefinder and a floodlight for illuminating aircraft. The ship was equipped with 4in/105mm, 1.5in/37mm and 0.75in/20 mm anti-aircraft guns.

On 25 April 1941, the Germans succeeded in salvaging a British mine that had recently been dropped from a plane. It was found west of Samsø in shallow water. It was possibly a faulty mine, but German sappers succeeded in defusing it and taking it to the Kriegsmarine's experimental plant in Kiel, where it was found to be a magnetic mine, and that knowledge was used to take effective measures against British mines.

The Baltic Sea in the spring of 1941: Bismarck and Prinz Eugen leave the Baltic

On 2 April 1941, the German naval staff issued instructions concerning an operation directed against British convoys in the North Atlantic using *Bismarck*, *Prinz Eugen* and *Gneisenau*. *Scharnhorst* should also have joined them, but the ship had problems with her boilers and was lying in Brest, together with her sister ship. Before departure, *Gneisenau* was damaged in an RAF bomb raid, so neither of the two battleships participated. The other two ships, *Bismarck* and *Prinz Eugen*, were in the Baltic. On 24 April 1941, however, *Prinz Eugen* struck a magnetic mine – a British bottom mine – south of Gedser (the southernmost harbour in Denmark) and had to go into the shipyard for fourteen days. The operation bore the code name Rheinübung and was to begin on 18 May 1941. Admiral Günther Lütjens went on board *Bismarck* in Gotenhafen with his staff at the beginning of May. The escort on the way out of Danish waters consisted of the destroyers *Z10 Hans Lody*, *Z16 Fritz Eckoldt* and *Z23*, plus the 5th Minesweeper Flotilla and three flak ships.[31] There were sixteen German submarines in the area of operations in the North Atlantic. In addition, twenty tankers, supply ships and weather ships were spread out over the central part of the Atlantic and up to the Arctic. At first, the force was to go to Kors Fjord in Norway, as the cruiser's tank capacity was low and its fuel consumption high, and it needed to be topped up.

On 19 May at 1400, the vessels left Gotenhafen, passed Cape Arkona on the island of Rügen at 2300 and then, on 20 May 1941 at around 0200, sailed up through the Great Belt. *Bismarck* and *Prinz Eugen* passed Kalundborg at sunrise on 20 May 1941.[32] The passage of the Great Belt should have taken place in the dark, but the fleet had been delayed. *Sperrbrecher 13* and *Sperrbrecher*

---

31 Flak is a German acronym for anti-aircraft guns: *Fl.ieger Abwehr Kanonen.*

32 On 24 May 1941, *Bismarck* and *Prinz Eugen* met His Majesty's Ships *Hood* and *Prince of Wales* in a short battle in the Denmark Strait between Greenland and Iceland, where the battlecruiser *Hood* was sunk. After this, the entire British navy chased the German ships. *Prinz Eugen* escaped to Brest, but *Bismarck* was sunk about three hundred miles west of Brest on 27 May 1941.

The ship *Sperrbrecher 13*: a *Sperrbrecher* (barrier breaker) was the German name for a cargo ship which had some large cables wrapped around its hull. A strong current in the cables created a magnetic field which could cause a magnetic mine to detonate at long distances. *Sperrbrecher 13* and *Sperrbrecher 31* went ahead of *Bismarck* and *Prinz Eugen* during their exit passage through the Great Belt in May 1941, to cause any British magnetic mines to detonate outside the critical distance. (SMB arkiv)

31 sailed in front of the force, which had apparently not been reported to the British – via Stockholm – by Danish observers. An observation by the Swedish cruiser *Gotland* around 20 May at 1300 in the northern Kattegat was passed on the same evening to the British naval attaché Henry Denham in Stockholm. Before *Bismarck* exited the Baltic, the German intelligence service had been very worried that Danish agents would report significant movement of ships in Danish waters to the British. When *Bismarck*'s sister ship, the battleship *Tirpitz*, was to be transferred to Norwegian waters in January 1942, it was therefore decided to have the ship travel through the Kiel Canal and then sail north through the North Sea.

A British submarine brought in to Frederikshavn by the Germans

On 5 May 1941, the British submarine *Seal* had to surrender to a German Arado 196 seaplane and was later towed to Frederikshavn, where the crew were interned. The submarine should have been scuttled by its own crew but, against all odds, it stayed afloat until the Germans came on board. The submarine was repaired and began to operate in the Baltic Sea, even though

The German Arado 196 used by the heavy ships in Kriegsmarine. (SMB arkiv)

the Kriegsmarine's experts had explicitly stated that there was 'nothing to be gained' by inspecting it more closely.

In the North Atlantic, the submarine war was raging on and Britain was hard-pressed. More merchant ships were being sunk in the Atlantic than could be built. The number of enemy submarines was increasing. Large German surface vessels were operating in the Atlantic, but the sinking of *Bismarck* on 27 May 1941 had made an impression, and Germany now focused on submarine warfare, with the aim of starving Britain and forcing the country to surrender. After twelve months of war, Dönitz had lost twenty-nine of the fifty-seven submarines which he had had at his disposal at the outbreak of the war. War production during the same period had delivered twenty-nine new submarines to the Kriegsmarine, so that in the autumn of 1940, Dönitz still had fifty-seven submarines, but thereafter the number rose sharply. So many German net barriers and mine barrages had now been laid, that penetration into the Baltic Sea by hostile submarines was unlikely. The building of the new submarine forces took place in the Baltic Sea, which the Kriegsmarine could now regard as a secure area.

The progress of the war: the Baltic Sea
viewed in the broader perspective

Since the attack on Poland, it had been peaceful in the Baltic Sea, apart from the Winter War and individual acts of war. The period up to the attack on the Soviet Union saw German victories in Denmark, Norway, Holland, Belgium, France and the Balkans. According to Hitler, the Battle of Britain was as good as won. He had identified the Soviet Union as his next target. When Foreign Minister Molotov visited Berlin in November 1940, they had to go in the air-raid shelters one evening because of a British air attack. 'If Britain is defeated, why are we sitting here?' Molotov asked his German hosts.

The year after the conquest of Norway and Denmark, greater depth had been introduced into the German defence of the Baltic through artillery positions in North Jutland and on the southern coast of Norway. In the Skagerrak, large minefields had been laid, and in the Kattegat there were ordinary minefields, anti-submarine minefields, and special anti-submarine nets with mines. The mines and the net barriers prevented submarines and surface ships from entering, and the large numbers of aircraft from the Luftwaffe ruled out an offensive attack from the sea.

Submarine warfare

The submarines of the past should really be described as 'dive boats', because they could dive but not operate submerged for very long. They had to resurface, start their diesel engines and charge their batteries, and in this situation they were very vulnerable. In the Atlantic, German submarines often operated on the surface during convoy attacks, just like a torpedo boat. They presented a small target as they approached, they could do 17 knots, and they could dive if they were noticed. A typical dive depth was 328ft/100m, but they were built with a safety factor of 1.2 – meaning that the submarine hull would only collapse at about 328ft/100m + 394ft/120m = 722ft/220m.

The main armament was torpedoes, which could be fired out of torpedo tubes in the bow or stern. In the Baltic Sea and around the British Isles, submarines were also used for minelaying. A deck gun could be used to sink unarmed merchant ships, so that the submarine could save on torpedoes. Submarines were suitable for the landing and picking-up of commandos and agents.

The latest German submarines in 1944/45 (Types XVII, XVIII, XXI and XXIII) represented a technical breakthrough that could have caused the Western Allies major problems in the North Atlantic. The Allies could not do much against these submarines, which could outrun the convoys when submerged. However, they did not get to be deployed to a significant degree before the war was brought to an end, but in the last days of the war, completed submarines of these types were hurrying up through Danish waters towards submarine bases in Norway.

At the beginning of the war, submarines were hampered in their operations by the rules of the time, which demanded that unarmed merchant ships should be warned before being sunk, so that the crew could get into the lifeboats. This was stated in Article 22 of the London Naval Treaty, signed on 22 April 1930. Here, submarines were put on the same footing as surface ships, which were not allowed to sink merchant ships without the crew and passengers first having the opportunity to get into the lifeboats ('delivered to a place of safety'). Warships, on the other hand, could be sunk without warning. Germany had not actually signed this treaty, because the country was forbidden from possessing submarines at the time it came into being.

The many layers of water in the Baltic Sea – with the differences in salinity and temperature – make submarine hunting with modern sensor and weapon systems very complicated. The water has a low salt content, as much of the water supply is composed of rain and meltwater from the many rivers in the area. Around the Scaw, there is a surface current on the way out with fresh water, while there is an underlying inflow of salt water. During the Second World War, the warring parties in the Baltic Sea preferred to use hydrophones (passive underwater microphones) as Asdic/sonar with active audio transmissions were not available. The average depth of the Baltic Sea is said to be somewhere between 180ft/55m and 213ft/65m. The greatest depth can found northeast of Gotland at Landsort Deep where the depth is 1,506ft/459m.*

---

* It is precisely because of this that the requirement for the Swedish submarine rescue service has so far been that it must be able to salvage a submarine crew from a wrecked submarine at a depth of 1,506ft/459m.

6

Attack on the Soviet Union

22 June 1941 – Spring 1942

Operation Barbarossa

Hitler believed that the Soviet Union could be defeated in a campaign characterised by swift manoeuvres with modern tanks, supported by tactical air forces. His decision to conquer the western part of the Soviet Union was not a sudden impulse, but the opportunity apparently emerged earlier than anticipated. It fitted into his somewhat outdated geopolitical views, and he was supported by OKW, OKH and the general staff, as well as by the political leadership of the country. The assessment was that it was better to have a trial of strength now, while the Soviet Union was weak, rather than wait a few years and give the Soviet Union the opportunity to rearm in the meantime. On 18 December 1940, Hitler put his signature to Führer directive no. 21 concerning Operation Barbarossa, ie the attack on the Soviet Union. At that time, Hitler believed that it was simply a matter of time before Britain realised the logic of giving up. This would mean that the problems of the First World War with a war on two fronts could be avoided. The attack was originally scheduled to take place on 15 May 1941, but Italy's war with Greece demanded German intervention, which delayed the operation by five to six weeks. This postponement probably had disastrous consequences for the German war effort. The planning of Operation Barbarossa was not put in the hands of OKW or the general staff, but of OKH.

Barbarossa: the overall plan

The invading German forces were divided into three army groups: Army Group North, Army Group Centre and Army Group South. The total strike force numbered about three million German troops and about two hundred thousand foreign allies with a total of 162 divisions. Behind the lines, there were a further million or more German troops. The operation was planned to last four months. The troops had supplies with them for about twenty days, and thereafter they would partly have to 'live off the land'. The main objective was to occupy the European part of the Soviet Union from Arkhangelsk on the White Sea in the north, to Kuybyshev in the east and onwards down to Astrakhan on the Caspian Sea. Seen in a very large perspective, it was to be an army operation with support from the Luftwaffe. The Kriegsmarine was putting its main efforts into the fight against Britain and only participated to a limited extent in the attack on the Soviet Union.

The German army had excellent support from the Luftwaffe, which in many ways could be regarded as the army's tactical air force. The Luftwaffe was trained to support the advancing army as a sort of extended artillery, but it only had a few long-range bombers that could destroy an opponent's industrial capacity. It also lacked long-range fighters as escorts. This was demonstrated over Britain in 1940 and a year later over Moscow.

As mentioned earlier, the Kriegsmarine did not have its own independent air force, but large parts of the Luftwaffe carried out naval tasks such as attacking shipping, minelaying, reconnaissance, search and rescue services and so on. German naval warfare in the Baltic Sea was characterised by the use of smaller vessels, older ships, requisitioned ferries used as minelayers, etc. Mines were meant to help keep the Soviet naval units bottled up in their bases, and mines dropped by aircraft were to play a critical role from the start of the war.

The invading force

The main force was Army Group Centre under Generalfeldmarschall Fedor von Bock, who in addition to two army corps had two armoured groups under General Heinz Guderian and General Hermann Hoth respectively. Like Napoleon's invading force in 1812, it was to advance north of the Pripet (Pinsk) marshes and attack in the direction of Minsk, Smolensk and Moscow.

South of this, Army Group South under Generalfeldmarschall Gerd von Rundstedt attacked with three German army corps and one Romanian. This force was to advance against Kiev and the entire Dnieper Valley (the area between Kiev and the Black Sea coast) and destroy all Soviet forces between the Pripet Marshes and the Black Sea coast.

Army Group North consisted of two army corps and an armoured group. It was commanded by Generalfeldmarschall Wilhelm Ritter von Leeb, who had at his disposal twenty infantry divisions, three tank divisions and three motorised infantry divisions. In addition, there were the Finnish forces. Its overall strength was significantly less than Army Group Centre which had over forty-seven divisions at its disposal. Army Group North's responsibilities stretched from the North Cape to East Prussia, in a difficult terrain with poor infrastructure. In the northernmost area, General der Infanterie Nikolaus von Falkenhorst's forces moved from northern Norway towards the railway line from Murmansk to Leningrad, which was to be cut off. The Finnish forces further south primarily had to take over the area from the Karelian Isthmus to Lake Onega. The army group moved from East Prussia into Lithuania, Latvia and Estonia. The commanding officer had already received his instructions on 31 January 1941 from the OKH: 'Army Group North shall destroy the enemy forces in the Baltic Sea region and, by occupying the Baltic ports, including Leningrad and Kronstadt, deprive the Soviet Baltic Fleet of its bases. Co-ordination and co-operation with Army Group Centre will be the responsibility of the OKH.'

One of von Leeb's problems was that there was more depth in the Soviet defences in his sector than in the others. The Soviet Union had established itself in the three Baltic states in 1940 and it would be preferable to circumvent the forces here if possible. He decided to use all his armoured forces to move against Leningrad via the towns of Daugavpils in Latvia, and Ostrov, Pskov

and Novgorod in western Russia. The German command had thought about making an amphibious thrust directly against Leningrad and taking the city and the naval base of Kronstadt with the marines during a surprise attack, but the plan was abandoned as too risky.[1] In the original plan, it was intended that Leningrad and Kronstadt would be reached within a month.

Warnings to the Soviet Union about the attack

The German High Command attached great importance to the secrecy of the attack plans. It has since emerged that numerous reports of very different kinds and at many different levels had reached Stalin and his intelligence services. The top Soviet agent at the German embassy in Tokyo, Richard Sorge, had said that the attack would come on 20 June 1941. A Communist typographer in Berlin had informed the Soviets that the German army was in the process of printing a very large supply of a small Russian language guide for their soldiers, containing such useful phrases as 'Hands up' and 'Follow me'. In addition, the number of German reconnaissance flights and violations of Soviet airspace was increasing and troop movements had been detected in the border areas.

For the attentive Soviet observer, there had been a long series of incidents in the Baltic region alone that should have alerted them to the fact that there was something brewing. Around the end of May, Germany decided to close the office in Leningrad where Admiral Feige and about seventy engineers and technicians were working to make the heavy cruiser *Petropavlovsk* (ex-*Lützow*) ready for the Soviet Union. The first German minelayers, minesweepers, torpedo boats and ships departed from German ports as early as 12 June on their way towards the Finnish archipelago, where they hid under camouflage nets until the outbreak of war. On the same day, Germany established patrols in the central part of the Baltic Sea. From 16 June, Soviet ships were no longer allowed to leave German ports, and twenty-five German merchant ships had left Riga without being unloaded. Despite all this, the German attack came as a shock to the Soviet forces.

---

1   An analysis carried out after the war showed that the plan would probably have succeeded when the lack of Soviet war preparations and the chaos which broke out at the beginning of the war are taken into consideration, but that is with the benefit of hindsight.

Radio detection and code-breaking

Normally, a military organisation is structured around a central command authority with subordinate units. In order to make full use of such an organisation, a radio network is built with the same levels. With the help of radio monitoring, an enemy radio detection unit can thus obtain information on the organisation itself and can locate the respective transmitters using direction-finding from several receivers. These can also be used to determine whether the transmitters are stationary or moving. The operation requires radio listeners or telegraphists who master the particular languages and special Morse alphabets. Radio stations use call signals that are often encrypted and if this encryption can be cracked, the units that have been prioritised can continue to be followed. Transmission from a high-frequency radio transmitter can also be located; the radar type or manufacturer can be identified by analysing the radar signal, and sometimes the individual radar can also be identified.

Signal texts or telegram texts are normally enciphered, and if the cipher can be deciphered or 'broken', the 'plain text' will also become available. The cipher can be obtained by cryptanalysis, in which a mathematician can calculate the mathematical basis for the cipher using knowledge of the particular language, the word frequency and the character frequency. If the texts are long or there are many of them, the cryptanalysis is made easier for the other party. Frequent changes in the basis of the cipher make it harder.

Another method is to steal the cipher without the knowledge of the 'proprietor'. During the Second World War, all the warring parties put large resources into intercepting and deciphering signals. The best known is probably the British success in deciphering signals from the German Enigma cipher machine, which was used by the foreign ministry, the three armed services, the SS, the Abwehr and the police forces. From 1940, Swedish intelligence was also able to follow some of the German teleprinter traffic which went through leased Swedish cables. Finland achieved great success in locating and identifying Soviet units and in deciphering their signals. The terms 'code' and 'cipher' are often used interchangeably, but there is a crucial difference. A code is a kind of secret, agreed language. A cipher* consists of the use of an algorithm to calculate an enciphered text; the algorithm can then correspondingly be used for deciphering. This requires the use of a 'key'. The texts from the

---

* Comes from the Arabic word *sifr*, meaning 'zero'.

Enigma machines were deciphered by British codebreakers at Bletchley Park who, on a daily basis, procured the missing key mathematically.

Strategic radio detection is usually carried out from an establishment on land, but tactical radio detection units can operate near the front, in the hinterland, on ships and in aircraft.

In 1940, a co-operative effort between escaped Polish intelligence specialists and British mathematicians succeeded in initiating the deciphering of the German so-called Enigma ciphers. This took place in the newly established Government Code and Cipher School at Bletchley Park, between Oxford and Cambridge, northwest of London. Those who had the worst 'signal discipline' were the most sought after when looking at users of the Enigma machines. This was the Luftwaffe, so it was here that the effort was concentrated, and the results soon began to show.

Prime Minister Winston Churchill himself read some of the signal texts, from which he could see that the Luftwaffe's aircraft, personnel and logistics were moving away from their bases near the English Channel towards Romania and German-occupied Poland. This eased the threat to Britain and, although Churchill did not have a high opinion of Stalin, he could become a useful ally, so Churchill saw to it that Stalin was informed of the impending attack, without the source being revealed.

The German invasion of the Soviet Union on 22 June 1941 came as a shock to the entire Soviet population, including the country's leadership but, as mentioned, there had been plenty of warnings. The situation is a classic example from the intelligence world, where a dictator does not trust the intelligence reports, because they do not fit into his own personal view – which thereby creates a demand for the head of intelligence to modify them.

Stalin had blind faith in the falsity of the many intelligence reports and warnings that he received up to the German attack on the Soviet Union on 22 June 1941. His intelligence chief, Lavrentiy Beria, customised his intelligence reports up to midnight between 21 and 22 June 1941, so it would appear as if all the German troop movements on the border were provocations that were intended to trigger more favourable trading conditions for Germany. If his intelligence agents indicated something else, they were thrown in prison at best. Prime Minister Churchill had never sympathised much with Stalin and, in his memoirs, he gave a description of Stalin's lack of action against the German build-up in June 1941. He outlined the situation very succinctly and straightforwardly:

War is mainly a catalogue of blunders, but it may be doubted whether any mistake in history has equalled that of which Stalin and the Communist chiefs were guilty when they cast away all possibilities in the Balkans and supinely awaited, or were incapable of realising, the fearful onslaught which impended upon Russia. We have hitherto rated them as selfish calculators. In this period they were proved simpletons as well.

Hardly anyone would have predicted before the war that Stalin and Churchill would become allies, and they were strange bedfellows, but there is an old adage that says that my enemy's enemy is my friend.

The war on land

From spring 1941, the German forces established a readiness in northern Norway, so that they could – if necessary – quickly secure the large nickel deposits in northern Finland. The area was also an excellent base for an

General C G E Mannerheim (with binoculars) meeting with generals (from left) Paavo Talvela, Erik Heinrichs and Vilho Nenonen in Punkasali on 26 June 1941, four days into the Continuation War. General Nenonen was the brain behind the very efficient indirect fire from Finnish field artillery batteries. (SA-Kuva)

Generaloberst N von Falkenhorst and Major-General H F Siilasvuo meeting in northern Finland in summer 1941. (SA-Kuva)

attack directed at Murmansk. In May 1941, the Finnish government, as mentioned, agreed to go along with the attack on the Soviet Union. Before the start of the war, during May and up until 15 June, 43,000 German troops were transported by sea to Finland, 32,000 were sent to the Soviet Union's border with Finland, and 11,000 were moved on to northern Norway. In the north of Finland, the attack did not begin until 28 June, that is, one week into the war. That did not prevent the Soviets from taking the initiative and one of the few successful Soviet operations took place precisely here, where, as early as 25 June 1941, the Soviets sent 236 bombers escorted by 224 fighters against nineteen airfields in northern Norway and northern Finland. The Soviets claimed that they destroyed forty-one enemy aircraft with this action. The German attack against Murmansk quickly lost momentum, and the troops had to dig in for the winter relatively quickly. Warfare in the northernmost area proved to be very difficult right up until the end of the war.

The war in the Arctic: Operation EF

In order to show support for his new Soviet ally, Prime Minister Winston Churchill ordered an attack to be carried out in the Arctic. On 30 July 1941, a total of thirty-eight carrier-borne aircraft from the Fleet Air Arm attacked shipping and harbour installations in the Kirkenes and Petsamo area. The targets were mainly German and Finnish merchant vessels, but surprise was difficult to achieve in the summer, north of the Arctic Circle, so Luftwaffe fighters were waiting for them on their arrival. Sixteen of the attacking aircraft were shot down, and thirteen airmen lost their lives. The attacking force from the Royal Navy consisted of two cruisers, six destroyers, and the aircraft carriers *Victorious* and *Furious*. The damage inflicted was modest. What is interesting about this attack is the fact that it was carried out by Britain on a Finnish harbour, more than four months before the formal British declaration of war against Finland on 6 December 1941.

The attack on Leningrad

Leningrad had symbolic value for Hitler. He had instructed the commander-in-chief of Army Group North, Generalfeldmarschall Wilhelm Ritter von Leeb, that the city should be razed to the ground as soon as it had been captured, because it had been 'the cradle of Bolshevism'. General Mannerheim's Karelian army attacked on 10 July 1941. The Finnish forces had a superiority of two to one and they were able to advance, while the Soviet forces were on a fast and chaotic retreat. The German command wanted the Finnish forces to move quickly towards Leningrad, so that they could meet the German forces as they advanced towards the city from the south and west. Mannerheim declined. The Finnish government had no desire to participate in an attack on Leningrad, and Finland also lacked the necessary dive-bombers and heavy artillery to carry out such an operation. If Finland had agreed, Leningrad would undoubtedly have fallen around the middle of September. Finland's situation had changed since the Winter War. Now it was Finland which could improve its territorial relationship, and the Soviet Union that found itself in a struggle for existence. The pendulum swung back again in 1944.

In addition to Hanko, which was evacuated between 30 October and 3 December 1941, the Soviet presence in the Baltic Sea was quickly limited to three small islands, Lavansaari, Penisaari and Seiskari, at the eastern end of the Gulf of Finland; Kotlin Island with the Kronstadt base; a small, isolated area around the actual city of Leningrad; and an isolated coastal area at Oranienbaum (see map on page 135).

The coastal area at Oranienbaum was about 18 miles/30km east–west and 12 miles/20km north–south. The rest of the coastline of the Gulf of Finland was in German and Finnish hands. Leningrad was very close to falling in the autumn of 1941, but General Mannerheim would not give permission for the Finnish troops to advance further than to Sestroretsk, which represented the old border before the Winter War. Mannerheim knew that Finland's fate would be sealed if Germany lost the war and he had helped them take Leningrad. At the time around the American entry into the Second World War, diplomatic pressure, among other things, was put on Finland by the United States, with the message that if Finland actively participated in the capture of Leningrad or of the railway line between Murmansk and Leningrad, then Finnish wishes would not be taken into account after the war. Unlike Great Britain, the United States did not declare war on Finland.

In his Führer directive no. 34 of 30 July 1941, Hitler changed the task from capturing Leningrad to laying siege to it. Although the German forces moved quickly towards Leningrad from the south and west, they were forced to regroup, recover and refurbish their equipment around 8 August, but by then they had reached right up into the vicinity of Lake Ilmen and Novgorod. The German armies were already beginning to have problems with their long supply lines. On 16 August, they captured Novgorod and, on 27 August, they stood just 50 miles/80km from Leningrad.

The first artillery shells fell on Leningrad on 4 September 1941. The attack was extended on 8 September with an air strike which started 178 fires. From this point on, the situation deteriorated steadily for the inhabitants of the city. From 8 September to 31 December 1941, the Luftwaffe carried out 100 bombing raids and dropped 3,000 bombs and 65,000 small incendiary bombs on the city.[2] Throughout the nearly nine-hundred-day siege, 4,638 explosive bombs and 102,500 incendiary bombs were dropped, but it was the hunger and the shelling from the German artillery which came to pose the greatest problems for the city's population.

Hunger in the city was worst in the first winter, and it was disastrous from 20 November until 25 December 1941. Then some modest supplies arrived via the 'Road of Life' which crossed the frozen Lake Ladoga, but in January and February 1942, the death toll rose once more, when approximately two hundred thousand people in total died of starvation. It is estimated that about four hundred thousand children remained in the city during the siege.

Field artillery during the war

Army artillery can engage targets either by direct or indirect fire. For direct fire, the target is visible and aim can be taken using the gun's own sights. For indirect fire, the position of the gun or howitzer is marked on a map. The target is similarly marked, and then the direction, distance, and any height difference between the two positions is calculated.

Artillery observers hidden much further forward in the terrain can correct the fire via field telephones or radio. A gun normally fires with elevations between 0 and 45 degrees. A howitzer fires with a curved trajectory, ie with elevations between 45 and 90 degrees. If soldiers take cover behind an earth bank, it will not provide significant protection against fire from the curved trajectory weapons (howitzers and mortars), because the shells come down vertically.

Mortars in the form that was used during the Second World War date from the First World War, when they were introduced as a much cheaper option for shelling than from ordinary guns. These are curved trajectory weapons, and light mortars can be dismantled and carried by infantrymen. This means that 'firepower' (means of shelling) can be carried. Heavy mortars require vehicles for transporting arms and ammunition.

---

2   The German command found out that if a city was to be destroyed, it would be better effected by dropping a large number of 7.7lb/3.5kg incendiary bombs, instead of dropping a small number of 550lb/250kg or 1,100lb/500kg explosive bombs. The Western Allies later reached the same conclusion regarding the destruction of German cities.

Anti-tank guns usually have a long gun barrel and fire with high muzzle velocity. This increases both precision and penetration. The higher the speed, the longer will be the close, horizontal part of the trajectory of the projectile (the initial trajectory). Anti-tank guns fire directly at tanks using optical sights such as binoculars, foresights, cross-hairs or similar. At the beginning of the war, some of the anti-tank guns being used were of such a small calibre that their shells could not penetrate the newest enemy tanks.

Anti-aircraft artillery consists of guns that can often rotate 360 degrees (laterally) and fire with high elevations. Heavy calibre anti-aircraft guns can fire with timed shells, which means that they can be set to explode at a certain distance or height after firing. They have been used for defence of, for example, urban areas and factories, and one of the purposes has been to keep bombers away from their target. If the aircraft comes within a short distance, they can also be shot down with machine guns with calibres from 2in/57mm down to 0.75in/20mm. Machine guns with a calibre of less than 20 mm are not normally regarded as artillery. They and other hand guns are effective against low-flying aircraft.

One of the German anti-aircraft guns, the 3.5in/88mm gun, was also found to be an excellent anti-tank weapon, because the muzzle velocity was very high. This meant that the trajectory of the shell was almost horizontal for the first few miles, which gave a high hit probability, and the weight and speed of the shell was sufficient to destroy armoured vehicles of almost any kind.

When firing, there are a large number of things which have to be corrected for: air temperature, barometric pressure, wind, altitude differences in the terrain between the firing gun and the target, humidity, the gun's own temperature, the wear and tear of the gun, the particular batch of ammunition, and much more.

On the Soviet side, the prevalence of radios was extremely limited right up to the end of the war. Radios were common among the higher ranks and at headquarters, but they were rare in tactical units, which therefore were dependent on field telephones connected by cables. So operating with advanced artillery observers who had to communicate corrections to the fall of shots was not without its problems.

The official version of the history of the city up until now is as follows: Leningrad's city council had been so careless as to let all the city's food supplies be stored at a single, central location. This was at the Badayev warehouses – thirty-eight wooden warehouses, with food reserves for the city for thirty days. Whether or not the German forces had this information, or whether it was just pure luck (for them), is not known, but the warehouses were set on fire during the first major air attack on 8 September and everything went up in flames. At that time, there were probably about 2.5 million residents of the city left and, added to this, there were about a hundred thousand refugees from outside. The siege lasted for 871 days.

The latest research reveals some important nuances.[3] Despite warnings, the city council had not spread the food stocks around the city. They were concentrated in the Badayev warehouses, but on the other hand, there was only food for a few days here. There were probably a mere 3,000 tonnes of flour and 2,500 tonnes of sugar. Since the Molotov–Ribbentrop Pact of 1939, the Soviet Union had been exporting large quantities of food to Germany, so stocks were small. When the attack came in 1941, Stalin had furthermore demanded food from across the nation be sent to Moscow, which was under threat. This had a very negative affect on the Leningrad supplies too. When the Badayev warehouses burned down, the party used it in propaganda to convey the message of German wickedness: now everyone could see that they went directly after the city's food stocks, and it was their fault that there was nothing to eat. This was an easy response for the party to make in response to criticism of the catastrophic lack of leadership and planning.

When the German attack on Moscow stalled, Hitler commanded that some of the tank units and VIII Fliegerkorps (8th Air Corps) should be transferred from the Leningrad front to Moscow. Hitler made his decision on 6 September and Soviet intelligence units quickly registered the move. This slightly relieved the pressure on the defenders of the city and made it difficult for the German forces to capture it. The winter of 1941 was harder than normal and began a month earlier than expected. This was also a contributing factor to the German attack losing momentum everywhere on the Eastern Front. The German army had no special winter clothing, so the German population was put into action with Operation Winterhilfe (Operation Winter Help), collecting coats and other warm clothing for the soldiers. It was, furthermore, an irony of fate that the then chief of staff of the German army had suggested in the late summer of 1941 that the troops be issued with winter clothing. This had been rejected by Hitler personally, because the campaign was supposed to be completed before winter arrived. The chief of staff at that time was Generalleutnant Friedrich Paulus, who a year later found himself surrounded at Stalingrad, where he and his troops were to suffer so terribly from their lack of winter equipment. The Soviet personnel and equipment were better fitted to performing in extreme winter

3   See *The Leningrad Blockade 1941–1944* (2012) by Richard Bidlack and Nikita Lomagin.

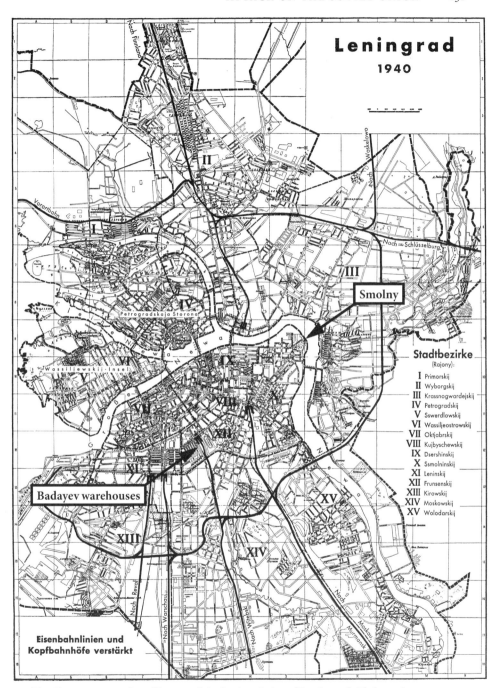

The German general staff's map of the besieged city of Leningrad. Zhdanov's party headquarters were in Smolny, and the city's food stocks were in the Badayev warehouses. The front line is just outside the southwest corner of the map, where tram line 9 terminates. (German planning map from 1940)

conditions. The Soviet soldiers were hardier and, after the failure during the Winter War, a number of improvements to clothing and equipment had been introduced.

The Baltic Fleet air force had been gradually expanded. The aircraft were, technologically speaking, not very sophisticated, and the pilots were not as skilled as their German counterparts, but German air superiority was gradually reduced in line with the German command being in need of offensive and defensive aircraft on the other sections of the front. The air defences in Leningrad had already in 1941 subjected the Luftwaffe to unacceptably high losses.

Stalin and his inner circle in Moscow expected Leningrad to fall, and Stalin followed developments with mixed feelings. He was reluctant to lose the city's industrial complex, but on the other hand, he was not enthusiastic about the local party secretary, Andrei Alexandrovich Zhdanov,[4] who could easily have become a political rival. In Leningrad, pictures of Stalin were replaced by ones of Zhdanov. He was a ruthless leader who had implemented Stalin's purges in the city from 1937 to 1939. Around 28 August 1941, Stalin sent a political commission to Leningrad so he could get a sober account of what was actually happening. The commission consisted of Foreign Minister Vyacheslav Mikhailovich Molotov, Party Secretary Georgy Maximilianovich Malenkov, Commissar for Naval Affairs (Admiralty Minister) Admiral Nikolay Gerasimovich Kuznetsov, Air Vice-Marshal Pavel Fedorovich Zhigarev, Marshal of Artillery Nikolay Nikolayevich Voronov, and the young head of evacuation planning Alexei Nikolayevich Kosygin.[5]

Malenkov was one of the most obsequious and malevolent members of the Communist Party, and he hated Zhdanov intensely, presumably because of the latter's superior position in the hierarchy.

German forces captured a small nearby train station called Mga a few days after the commission's arrival. The town was relatively unknown and insignificant, but since the Germans had already captured the main line between Moscow and Leningrad, the only alternative rail service went via Mga, and now the German army had also taken that. From now on, it was going to be extremely difficult to bring supplies to the city. It speaks volumes for Soviet planning that the plan for the evacuation of the city was being drawn up while German forces were capturing the last rail link out of town.

Leningrad's defenders 'forgot' to tell Stalin about Mga because they hoped they could quickly recapture the town. Things panned out very differently; Stalin got his information from many different sources, so it was impossible

---

4   Andrei Zhdanov was number two in the Soviet Communist Party and his son later married
    Stalin's daughter Svetlana Iosifovna Alliluyeva.
5   Alexei Kosygin was later Soviet prime minister for a long period.

to withhold information from him. He was furious with the two locally responsible officers, Party Secretary Zhdanov and People's Commissar (Defence Minister) Voroshilov,[6] whom he accused of being 'specialists in retreat'. Stalin had just taken the decision to appoint a man who was principled and correct in command of a new army in the area; he chose Marshal Grigory Ivanovich Kulik, who was one of his most ruthless and stupid officers, as commanding officer of this 54th Army. The loss of Mga can probably be attributed to Kulik. He managed well in the beginning, but later on he too was blamed for the failed initiatives and he had a somewhat unusual fall from grace.[7]

On 10 September, Stalin sent General Georgy Konstantinovich Zhukov to Leningrad to organise the city's defence. Voroshilov had been fired and sent to Moscow. At this time, the ships of the Soviet Baltic Fleet and the main installations of the city were being made ready for demolition under the supervision of the NKVD. It was thought that the city could not be held much longer, but that assessment was quickly overturned by Zhukov, who, however, enjoyed only a brief command here because when Moscow also came under threat, Stalin wanted him home again.

On 8 November 1941, German forces captured the important railway town of Tikhvin, which was 108 miles/175km east of Leningrad. The distance from Leningrad to a rail link thus became even longer. If the city was now to be supplied, then it would have to be from the nearest Soviet train station east of Tikhvin, from there through the rugged forest terrain of about 125 miles/200km to the ice on Lake Ladoga at Zaborie, and then across the ice towards Shlisselburg Bay and onwards to Leningrad. There was also a small airfield near Tikhvin, which had also supplied the city on a smaller scale. The Soviet Air Force's Lisunov Li-2 transport aircraft, which was an American Douglas DC-3 aircraft built under licence in the Soviet Union, operated from here. The airfield was now in German hands too. The city of Shlisselburg (in German, Schlüsselburg) was itself captured by German forces on 8 September 1941. The city is located on Lake Ladoga where the River Neva

---

6   Voroshilov had been fired by Stalin after the Winter War, but came into favour again within a year. Churchill's Chief of the Imperial General Staff, General Alan Brooke, sat next to Voroshilov at table in Moscow in August 1942 and refers to him as 'nice and friendly, but with the military insight of a child'.

7   In the Winter War, Kulik was responsible for the initial Soviet artillery attack. His achievements here were a catastrophe. In 1941, Kulik was blamed for the discouraging results on the front south and east of Leningrad. Most high-ranking Soviet officers would then have been shot. However, Kulik had belonged to Stalin's inner circles for a long time. He was court-martialled and demoted to major-general. During the purges following the war, he was arrested in 1947 and liquidated in 1950 for high treason. He was rehabilitated by Khrushchev in 1956 and posthumously restored to the rank of marshal of the USSR.

begins. The thickness and strength of the ice on Lake Ladoga was measured under the leadership of a glaciologist from the Baltic Fleet. On 21 November, the Leningrad Military Council received a report over the radio that the ice was now strong enough to bear the weight of supply lines. Ten light trucks were sent out: two disappeared in a snowstorm and went through the ice; eight of them returned with a total of 33 tonnes of food, but this accounted for only 1 per cent of the city's daily supply needs.

On 9 December 1941, Soviet forces recaptured Tikhvin, but then the railway line could not be used immediately because of damage. The railway line was repaired again around the turn of the year, after which bread rations to the inhabitants of Leningrad were raised slightly. In November 1941, the number of civilians killed was 11,000; in December, the total losses rose to 50,000 – these figures cover victims of bombs and shells as well as people who died of starvation. The loss of Tikhvin cost the German army 7,000 killed.

It gradually became clear to the Soviet leadership that Hitler's plan was now to starve the citizens of Leningrad, while German forces were concentrated on the capture of Moscow. The depleted German forces around Leningrad were exposed to gradually increasing Soviet counter-attacks. At first, the scale of them was modest, but they inflicted unacceptable losses on the German forces. Increasing numbers of a new type of 28-tonne tank, the T-34, joined the attacks. This type had been produced since 1940, being built at many different factories in the Soviet Union, including in Moscow, Stalingrad and Leningrad. The Soviet Union classed it as a medium-heavy tank, and it proved to be significant for the outcome of the war.

In December, a Soviet peace overture to Finland offering a separate peace treaty came via the Soviet ambassador in Stockholm. According to Mannerheim, the Finnish refusal was because of Finland's dependence on food supplies from Germany, but Germany's military strength had probably also been part of their deliberations.

Naval warfare in the Baltic Sea

In the planning phase, Grossadmiral Raeder was against the launching of an attack on the Soviet Union. In his view, it should not take place until Britain had been defeated, because the Baltic Sea was very important for the Kriegsmarine. The German submarine exercise areas were here and the entire Baltic Sea needed to remain outside the war so long as the submarine war in the North Atlantic was raging. When the war against the Soviet Union was nevertheless a reality, Hitler and the leadership of the German navy agreed that the Soviet Baltic Fleet should not under any circumstances be allowed

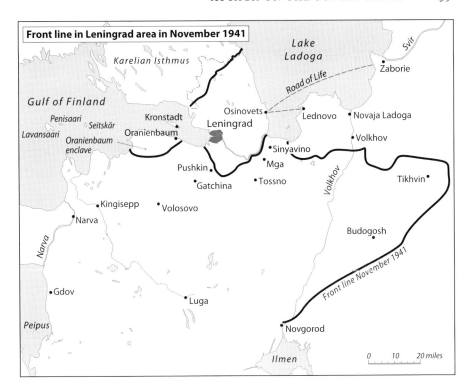

Front line in Leningrad area in November 1941

to slip out of the Gulf of Finland. It could put paid to submarine training, as well as interrupting iron ore shipments.

In the summer of 1941, the Kriegsmarine had major problems. The battleship *Bismarck* had just been sunk and her sister ship, *Tirpitz*, was not yet ready for operations. The battleships *Scharnhorst* and *Gneisenau* and the heavy cruiser *Prinz Eugen* were blockaded at Brest, and the pocket battleship *Lützow* was still in the shipyard after being hit by a torpedo. The heavy cruiser *Admiral Hipper* and the pocket battleship *Admiral Scheer* were also in dry dock, and only two of the four remaining light cruisers were ready for operation. All ocean-going submarines had to be used in the Atlantic.

There were therefore few naval forces available in the Baltic Sea. These were mainly focused on the *S-Boote* (S-boats, or motor torpedo boats), minesweepers, small coastal submarines and various auxiliary warships. As a result, the Kriegsmarine attached great importance to capturing Leningrad and the naval base at Kronstadt swiftly so that the Soviet Baltic Fleet was sidelined. This would quickly free up the Kriegsmarine's vessels for the ongoing battle against Britain. In the absence of battle-decisive German ships, sea mines in large numbers would come to play a crucial role in the battle for the Baltic Sea. The plan was to capture all the Soviet Baltic ports quickly, whereby the

The pocket battleship *Admiral Scheer* photographed in 1942. It was the second of the three German Panzerschiffe from the early 1930s to be built. The ship visited Copenhagen from 4–10 August 1943.

A German *S-Boot* (motor torpedo boat). Several hundred of them were built in many variations and their armaments were constantly being changed. They would typically have two bow tubes, each containing one torpedo. On the aft deck, there were two more torpedoes for reloading. They could be equipped with mines instead and used as offensive minelayers. There were a number of machine guns (20–40mm) on board and the crew was about twenty-five men.

important German traffic across the Baltic Sea from Germany to Finland would be secured. At the same time, the German naval command made its own ports in Memel, Pillau and Koldberg safe with defensive minefields. Finally, the ore transports between Sweden and Germany had to be secured.

German U-boats had already been authorised from 14 June 1941 to sink Soviet submarines south of a line through the Åland Islands, as long as there

The German minelayer *Brummer* (ex-Norwegian *Olav Tryggvason*) from minelayer Group North participated in laying the Apolda minefield in June 1941. Her capacity was 280 mines. (SMB arkiv)

were no survivors. If they were to be caught in the act, the explanation was to be that they thought it was an invading British submarine.

On the night of 18/19 June 1941, ie more than three days before the outbreak of the war, the German minelayers *Preussen*, *Grille*, *Skagerrak* and *Versailles*, and six minesweepers from the 6th Minesweeper Flotilla began laying mines between Memel and Öland. It was an operation that lasted three days, and on the first night the German forces observed the Soviet cruiser *Kirov* in the distance, but she did not intervene in the operation. This was the Wartburg minefield containing 1,500 mines and 1,800 so-called explosive buoys, which were minesweeping obstacles. In October 1941, these mines sank the Soviet submarine *S-8* off Öland's south coast.[8]

The German minelayers in Finnish waters consisted of requisitioned merchant ships. They were divided into two groups which hid in the Finnish archipelago from 14 June 1941. At Turku lay minelayer Group North with *Tannenberg*, *Brummer*[9] and *Hansestadt Danzig*[10] with an escort of motor

---

8   *S-8* was found by Swedish divers in 1999.

9   This ship was the seized Norwegian minelayer *Olav Tryggvason*, which was now named after the ship which was sunk in the Skagerrak on 14 April 1940 by the British submarine *Sterlet*.

10 The same ship that had sailed in to the Langelinie quay in Copenhagen harbour on 9 April 1940 with a battalion of German troops.

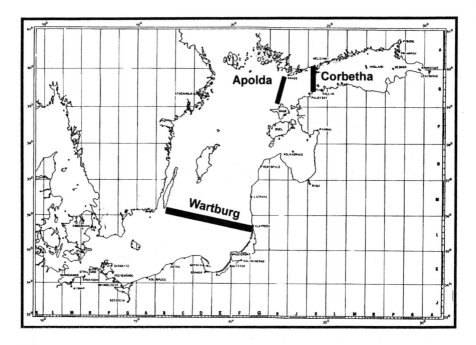

torpedo boats and minesweepers. At Porkkala Peninsula, minelayer Group Cobra lay camouflaged. This consisted of the minelayers *Cobra*, *Königin Luise* and *Kaiser* with a similar escort. They received their minelaying orders on 19 June, which ordered them to start laying their mines on 21 June at 2330. Group North was to lay the Apolda minefield between Hiumaa and Hanko, while Group Cobra was to lay the Corbetha minefield between Kallbådagrund and Pakerort, that is, across the Gulf of Finland just north of Baltischport (now Paldiski in Estonia).

On the evening of 21 June 1941, all shipping traffic east of Gedser in the south of Denmark was stopped and German ships at sea were ordered to seek haven in Finnish, German or Swedish ports. At the start of the German attack, the Kriegsmarine was concerned that the large Soviet battleships would try to break out of the Baltic Sea. At Gedser, an additional minefield was laid in connection with the net barrier, and three minelayers, each with 200 mines on board, were being kept ready to close the Danish straits. The armour-plated ship *Schlesien* was stationed at Sjællands Odde, a peninsula at the northwest tip of Zealand. Her sister ship, *Schleswig-Holstein*, was stationed at Drogden, and the light cruiser *Nürnberg* arrived in Copenhagen harbour. The armour-plated ships were the last to return to their German base on 29 August 1941.

Minelaying from the Finnish minelayer *Ruotsinsalmi*. The ship is named after the fortress at Ruotsinsalmi (Svensksund or Swedish Sound) on the island of Kotka where two naval battles between Sweden and Russia took place in 1789 and 1790. (SA-Kuva)

German motor torpedo boats from the 6th Schnellbootflotille at Elsinore in Denmark during Operation Barbarossa. A number of S-boats, along with the depot ship *Tanga*, lay at anchor in Elsinore along with three submarines, *U-56*, *U-83* and *U-125*. The German forces reduced their preparedness gradually from 1 July 1941 as the Soviet forces retreated towards Leningrad and no longer threatened to break out from the area. (CCB Vognsen)

Senior Finnish officers had already been participating in the planning of Operation Barbarossa from May 1941. The three large Finnish submarines would participate in the opening actions of the war and would each lay a minefield along the Estonian coast. The mines were German and imported for the purpose. Each submarine brought four torpedoes and twenty new magnetic mines, the targets being primarily the Soviet battleships *Marat* and *Oktyabrskaya Revolyutsiya*. The commander-in-chief of the Finnish submarine squadron, Lieutenant-Commander Arti Kivikuru, had some problems explaining the situation to the commanding officers of the submarines. The submarine crews were put in 'a kind of quarantine' until 26 June, when Finland officially joined the war, but by then the submarines had long since laid their mines. These mines sank a Latvian ship of 3,000 tonnes and damaged the Soviet destroyer *Steregushchy* (Vigilant) and the passenger ship *Vyacheslav Molotov* (named after the Soviet foreign minister), which was

Two of the German submarines at Elsinore in the summer of 1941. The Swedish coastline at Hälsingborg is faintly visible in the background. (CCB Vognsen)

evacuating the wounded. On 27 August, the submarine *Shch-301* was also sunk by one of the mines.

From the start of Operation Barbarossa, the following small vessels of the Kriegsmarine were part of the war in the Baltic Sea: five submarines (*U-140, U-142, U-144, U-145* and *U-149*), twenty-eight torpedo boats and motor torpedo boats, ten minelayers, three flotillas of minesweepers (*Räumboote*)[11] and three large minesweepers. In addition, two large minesweeping vessels with motorboats on board for sweeping mines in coastal waters took part. The Luftwaffe handled a lot of the reconnaissance and other maritime tasks for the Kriegsmarine. German Ju 88 bombers from Küstenfliegergruppe 806 (Coastal Air Group 806) dropped twenty-seven mines near the Soviet naval base at Kronstadt and attacked shipping targets in the area on the night of 22/23 June. During the advance, these aircraft, along with aircraft from Aufklärungsgruppe 125 (Reconnaissance Group 125), undertook coastal reconnaissance. Later, the Ju 88s dropped mines in Leningrad harbour, the River Neva and at locks on the White Sea–Baltic Canal and in Lake Onega.

---

11   The German *Räumboote* (R-boats, or mine-clearing vessels) had much success. They were wooden constructions with a relatively high speed (maximum speed 22–25 knots), well suited for minesweeping, capable of carrying twelve mines and useful as patrol vessels, for escort of submarines to patrol areas, etc.

The passenger ship *Vyacheslav Molotov* was evacuating wounded personnel at the start of the war when it struck a mine laid by one of the Finnish submarines. (Old Ship Picture Galleries)

Three of the German minelayers, *Tannenberg, Preussen* and *Hansestadt Danzig*, sailed from Turku on 8 July, and the following day they all three ran into mines at the southern tip of Öland, where a Swedish minesweeper tried in vain to warn them. The mines had been laid by Sweden – at the request of Germany – to supplement the German Wartburg minefield in Swedish territorial waters. All three ships sank with a loss of a total of twenty-three crew members. Seekriegsleitung (the naval operations staff) had received information about the Swedish minefield, but forgot to pass it on to subordinate authorities. The German staff officer responsible was sentenced to a year in prison.

Since the end of the Winter War, the Soviet Union had had army, air and naval forces totalling 27,000 men stationed at Hanko, and with the rapid German advance in Estonia, it became difficult to evacuate these forces. German mining operations hindered an evacuation, and after just such an operation, on 25 September 1941, the German minelayer *Königin Luise* ran into a mine off Helsinki's harbour – the mine had been laid by a Soviet submarine, and the ship went down with seventy-seven men. The main German minelaying operations ended in early November when the minelayers were sent back to German ports. An exception was the Luftwaffe's efforts to drop a total of twenty-nine mines in the approaches to Kronstadt, as well as some attempts to drop individual mines from 'storm boats' (pioneer dinghies) in the sea channel that led from Leningrad out into the Gulf of Finland. Finally, the German forces also laid fifteen mines in the sea channel during the winter by having soldiers pull the heavy mines on sleds across the ice in the bay. When they reached the sea channel, they cut holes in the ice and dropped the mines, so they would be ready when the ice disappeared and passage was opened again in the spring. It cost the Soviet Baltic Fleet a submarine in the spring of 1942, so they had to reroute the exit passage from the base to go north of Kronstadt and Kotlin Island.

Because of the rapid German advance, the Soviet Baltic Fleet was soon concentrated in the Leningrad region. During the Leningrad siege, the Baltic Fleet and the city thus shared a common destiny. Germany had not expected any major naval campaign in the Baltic Sea. The operations of the German army and the Luftwaffe were intended to make use of rapid advances to deprive the Soviet Union of all naval bases in the Baltic region. The mines proved to be a considerable help by keeping the Soviet warships trapped in ports, or sinking them, until the naval bases were captured by the advancing German armies.

Up to October 1941, the Kriegsmarine lost one minelayer, two motor torpedo boats, ten minesweepers, four other smaller warships and six merchant ships to Soviet mines and aircraft. A Soviet submarine sank the steamer *Baltenland*. From December 1941, the Soviet Baltic Fleet no longer offered a serious threat to German shipping in the Baltic Sea and Germany could resupply its military units in northern Russia via convoys.

The Soviet Baltic Fleet around the beginning of the Great Patriotic War in 1941

The first post-war sources did not quite agree on the numbers in the Soviet naval forces, but that has gradually been remedied. The uncertainty had many causes, primarily Soviet secrecy around military production, but also additions to and departures from other fleets via canals and rivers. Some deliveries, new shipbuilding and projects were never completed. Although the Soviet Union had a relatively large fleet in the Baltic Sea – which in principle could have taken up the fight against the German fleet – no major confrontations of this kind took place. At the outbreak of the war, the Baltic Fleet had two battleships, two heavy cruisers, twenty-three destroyers, about seventy-five submarines, forty-eight torpedo boats, thirty-nine minelayers and 707 fleet aircraft[12] at its disposal.

The Baltic Fleet's inventory of submarines consisted of approximately twenty-five each of large, medium and small vessels. Among the operational

---

12 The sources mention between 656 and 707 naval aircraft.

submarines, the Soviet Union had lost twenty-nine[13] by the end of 1941, including fourteen by mines.

Four submarines were transferred to the Caspian Sea and fifteen to the White Sea via inner waterways. A few newly built submarines were delivered by the shipyards in the area.

The Baltic Fleet could do little during the attacks by German forces on 22 June 1941. It did not have air forces of its own at sea, only the support of land-based naval air forces, and their airfields were soon captured by the German armies. Luftwaffe attacks inflicted heavy losses. Mines in the Gulf of Finland – laid by Finland and Germany – also took their toll: two new cruisers were damaged and nine destroyers were sunk.

The initial Soviet response in the Baltic Sea

It is noteworthy that the Soviet Baltic Fleet was already at war from a little before midnight on 21 June, but the history of the war should not be rewritten because of it. German minelaying had started more than two days earlier. The Commissar of Naval Affairs (Admiralty Minister), Admiral Nikolay Gerasimovich Kuznetsov, who two years earlier had become commander-in-chief of the Soviet Navy at only thirty-four years of age, defied various orders not to provoke Germany unnecessarily. He put the fleets on the alert and the new commander-in-chief of the Baltic Fleet, the forty-year-old Admiral Vladimir Filippovich Tributs, made his fleet ready for battle. Two of the Baltic Fleet's aircraft therefore attacked minelayer Group North with machine guns at 0221 on the night of 22 June. It was possible because it was midsummer with light nights in the northern latitudes; the 'white nights' of Leningrad are famous. At that point, there were still two hours and twenty-four minutes to go to the 'official German attack time', when German troops crossed the Soviet border.

At the outbreak of war, the Soviet battleship *Marat* was in Leningrad, while the other battleship, *Oktyabrskaya Revolyutsiya*, lay at anchor off the port of Tallinn, but immediately went back to Leningrad without problems. The cruiser *Kirov* lay at anchor in Riga with three destroyers and three submarines. Muhu (Moon) Sound lies between Muhu Island and the Estonian mainland, and by a skilful act of navigation, the Soviets succeeded in sailing all these vessels without loss through this strait to Tallinn. The passage is narrow, and normally a cruiser would not take the risk of going through here, because of the water depth.

---

13 Some sources mention between fifty-six and sixty-eight Soviet submarines in the Baltic Sea on 22 June 1941. There are also minor disagreements regarding losses: probably from twenty-seven to twenty-nine submarines were lost.

Soviet minelaying operations began on the night of 23 June, when Soviet minelayers laid minefields in the western Gulf of Finland, covered by a cruiser and some destroyers. The Soviet Baltic Fleet lost a destroyer, *Gnevny* (Indignant), to a German mine, while another destroyer, *Gordy* (Proud) and the cruiser *Maxim Gorky* were damaged by mines near Saaremaa, but these two reached Tallinn. The cruiser was able to proceed to Kronstadt under its own power, even though its bow had been blown away. On 26 June, German motor torpedo boats sank the frigates *Tucha* (Thundercloud) and *Taifun* (Typhoon) in Irben Strait, which is the western exit from the Gulf of Riga. Initially, the Soviet Baltic Fleet was defensive and did not use its destroyers for offensive mining of German ports or supply lines.

Of the approximately seventy-five Soviet submarines in the Baltic Sea, thirty-five were operational at the outbreak of the war. Fifteen of them were in the Latvian port of Liepāja (which the Germans called Libau), along with a destroyer. Those which could sail tried to get back to the Gulf of Finland. Among them were the two former Estonian submarines *Kalev* and *Lembit*, which reached Tallinn where they each took twenty mines on board. The Soviet submarine *S-3* tried to sail undetected from Libau on the night of 24 June. It sailed on the surface with some shipyard workers on board, a total of a hundred men including the crew. It was spotted and sunk by two German S-boats (*Schnellboote*), *S-35* and *S-60*, which took up a few survivors from the submarine, which in the end tried to dive. By the time Liepāja was captured by the advancing German armies on 29 June 1941, the Soviets had themselves scuttled the two older destroyers *Desna* (named after a tributary of the River Dnieper) and *Karl Marx*, and the five submarines which lay at anchor in the harbour, among them the two former Latvian submarines. In a matter of days, the Soviet Baltic Fleet lost almost all its twenty airbases that had just been established in the new Baltic Soviet republics. The small Soviet submarine *M-78* was sunk by the German submarine *U-144* off Ventspils (known in German as Windau), but on 28 July, *U-144* was itself sunk by a torpedo from the Soviet submarine *Shch-307* in the western Gulf of Finland. This was Germany's first submarine loss in the Baltic Sea. On 18 July, the Soviet destroyer *Serdity* (Irascible) was sunk in Muhu Sound during a German air raid.

In early August, the submarines *Lembit* and *Kalev* left Tallinn again. *Kalev* laid its twenty mines southwest of Ventspils and they sank two German ships. *Lembit* passed west of Bornholm and laid mines off one of the German ports. On 25 August 1941, both submarines were back in Tallinn to take more mines on board, but this was during the evacuation of the city.[14]

---

14 *Kalev* did not return from a later patrol and was assumed to have been sunk by a mine near the Estonian island of Keri, directly south of Helsinki, around 28 October 1941 – *Kalev* has never been found. *Lembit* sailed under the Soviet Baltic Fleet's flag for the remainder of

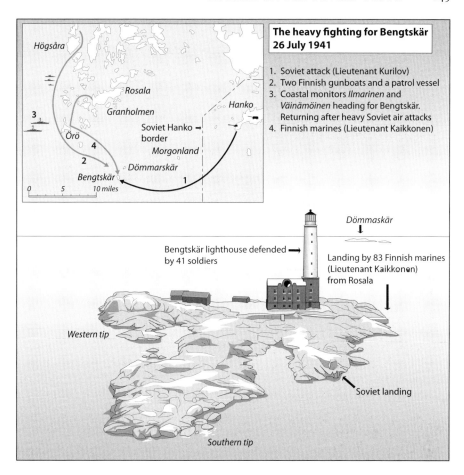

The heavy fighting for Bengtskär
26 July 1941

1. Soviet attack (Lieutenant Kurilov)
2. Two Finnish gunboats and a patrol vessel
3. Coastal monitors *Ilmarinen* and *Väinämöinen* heading for Bengtskär. Returning after heavy Soviet air attacks
4. Finnish marines (Lieutenant Kaikkonen)

Bengtskär lighthouse defended by 41 soldiers

Dömmaskär

Landing by 83 Finnish marines (Lieutenant Kaikkonen) from Rosala

Western tip

Soviet landing

Southern tip

The opening skirmishes in the Baltic Sea: Morgonland and Bengtskär

One of the Soviet demands on Finland in connection with the peace treaty after the Winter War in 1940 was a base near Finland's most southwesterly point on the peninsula of Hanko. When the war suddenly started in 1941, the Soviet forces at Hanko were very isolated and far from their own units. That the intended outpost of a total of 27,000 men on Hanko suddenly found themselves in enemy territory, far behind the actual front line, was an unexpected situation. The Soviet units on Hanko were exposed to fire from both the Finnish coastal artillery and the two Finnish coastal monitors, *Väinämöinen* and *Ilmarinen*. The Soviets therefore wanted to deprive the

the war and is now a museum submarine in Tallinn. On 6 March 1945, the Supreme Soviet decided to award *Lembit* the Order of the Red Banner. This was one of the Soviet Union's highest honours for military action.

The Finnish monitor *Väinämöinen* shelling Soviet troops at Hanko early in July 1941.
The heavy 10in/254mm guns could fire a 496lb/225kg projectile at an effective range of
19 miles/30km. Each gun could fire two to three rounds per minute. (SA-Kuva)

Finnish forces of the possibility of observing targets and correcting artillery
fire from the two islands of Morgonland and Bengtskär. Morgonland was
captured by Soviet troops from Hanko on 16 July 1941. On 26 July, the fighting
started for Bengtskär, which has a tall lighthouse in granite, from which
there is a great view over Hanko. The Russians landed barely a hundred men
from the border troops under Lieutenant Kurilov, but the forty-one Finnish
soldiers – and four men who were the lighthouse staff – under Lieutenant
Luther prepared themselves to give stiff resistance. The next morning they
were relieved by soldiers from the nearby Finnish islands. The Russians
had sixty dead and twenty-eight were taken prisoner, most of whom were
seriously wounded. Finland lost a total of thirty-one men during the fighting,
and forty-five were injured, but Bengtskär remained in Finnish hands.

Naval artillery during the war

Naval artillery normally has longer gun barrels than equivalent guns
in the army. This is because naval artillery fires precision shots at point
targets at great distances, whereas field artillery is often used for shelling
areas. All naval artillery, except for anti-aircraft guns, fires with elevations
from 0 to 45 degrees. High-angle artillery is not used here.

If a ship under way fires on another ship under way, the fire-control
equipment will continuously calculate changes in bearing and distance,

and translate them into changes in the elevation and lateral direction of the guns. When firing, adjustments will be made for air temperature, barometric pressure, wind direction, wind speed, humidity, the gun's own temperature, gun wear and tear, and the particular batch of ammunition. Compensation will also be made for the ship's movement on all three axes (X, Y and Z).

Up to the beginning of the Second World War, battleships were the battle-decisive warships, but after the performance of aircraft carriers in the early days of the war, battleships suddenly became outdated. The Allies thereafter used the warships' heavy artillery against targets on land. The firing distance could be up to about 25 miles/40km. This is known as shore bombardment. It is usually battleships, cruisers and destroyers that carry out shore bombardments, but smaller vessels have also participated. If a warship fires at a target on land, observers will often be sent out. Artillery observers can be on board the ships, put ashore with the troops being supported, or on board an aircraft. Observations on where shots fall are usually given by radio. The observers report where the shell falls in relation to the target, and recalculations are made on board the vessel doing the firing for changes in elevation and lateral direction.

Soviet artillery units from the Baltic Fleet supported Red Army operations during the siege of Leningrad from 8 September 1941 to 27 January 1944. German commanders copied this practice by firing from their large ships in the Baltic Sea in 1944/45 during the big retreat operations in coastal areas.

Even though a ship's gun can fire a long distance, it is not always the maximum range which is decisive. The probability of a hit is important, because of the finite amount of ammunition in the ship. Even the largest warships have limited amounts of ammunition on board. A destroyer will typically carry enough ammunition for approximately ten minutes' continuous firing with the main battery. The range when opening fire is usually the distance where a 1 per cent hit probability for the particular target is expected. The Soviets have operated with opening fire at a range with 0.5 per cent hit probability. Big targets are easier to hit than small targets. The nearer the target, the greater the hit probability, and if one has speed superiority over an opponent, this can be used to increase hit probability. Firing therefore takes place at greater distances for large targets than for small targets. If the bigger guns are used against air targets, the range when opening fire at an aircraft is therefore considerably shorter than at a ship, because of the size of the aircraft.

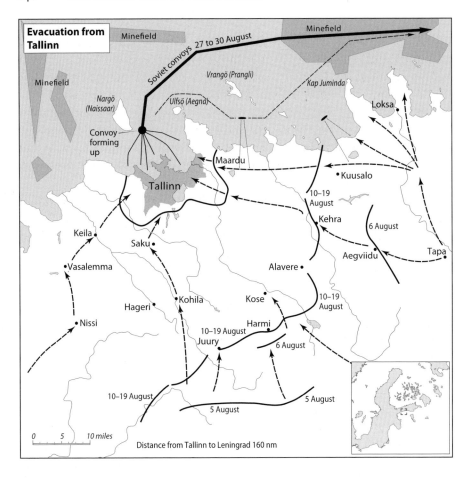

*The evacuation of Tallinn: the 'Soviet Dunkirk',
or the mine battle at Tallinn*

On 7 August, German troops reached the city of Kunda on the Estonian north coast, 50 miles/80km east of Tallinn. This meant that Soviet units in Tallinn were then unable to retreat over land. They could now only be evacuated by sea. This applied to those remaining from three divisions, the 10th Division, the 16th Division and the 22nd Division, and units from the Marine Corps. The attackers knew immediately how to exploit the situation. During the next fourteen days, German and Finnish forces laid a large number of mines in the Juminda minefield, which in reality consisted of nineteen separate minefields. Cape Juminda is one of the northernmost points on the Estonian coast and the German army set up a 6.5in/170mm coastal battery here. Initially, the minefield consisted of 1,370 mines and a similar number of explosive buoys laid as minesweeping obstacles, but in the following days, further mines were laid. The minefield went across the Gulf of Finland from the Estonian coast to Söderskär, off the Finnish coast. The operation was intended to prevent the Soviet units in Tallinn harbour from escaping back to Leningrad.

The Soviet Union decided to evacuate Tallinn, and sent two hospital ships eastward on 10 August with the injured from previous battles. There were a total of 6,500 people on board the two ships. One of the ships hit a mine, but managed to reach Kronstadt under its own power. The other was sunk with almost no survivors.

German forces launched the attack on the city on 19 August. The Soviet naval forces sought to hide behind a heavy smokescreen, but German air raids and artillery fire became fiercer by the day. The cruiser *Kirov* and the Soviet destroyers used their artillery fire to keep the German forces at bay, so that the large number of merchant ships and warships could be made ready for departure from the harbour. The commander-in-chief of the Soviet Baltic Fleet, Admiral Tributs, had informed Stalin just a few days earlier that Tallinn would not fall to the advancing German troops. Now he was forced to take a flight to Leningrad to explain himself, and Vice-Admiral Valentin Petrovich Drozd[15] on board the destroyer *Stoikiy* (Steadfast) took command of the overall forces.

The decision-making process under Stalin was dangerous. Few dared to make decisions themselves because of reprisals. As a rule, they had to be either taken or approved in Moscow, so decisions on withdrawals and evacuations were often delayed for such a long time that they could not be implemented as originally proposed. Local commanders often had a better understanding of the situation, but the Soviet leadership was racked with suspicion and indecision. Furthermore, the local commanders sometimes had to embellish the situation a little, in order not to fall out of favour.

On 27 August, the Soviet units were finally ready to evacuate Tallinn in about 170 ships divided into four convoys, of which twenty-nine ships were over 6,000 tonnes. The relatively concentrated air defence on the ships in the harbour area could keep the German aircraft at a distance, but as soon as the convoys were formed up out to sea, they were subjected to threats from

---

15 Vice-Admiral Valentin Petrovich Drozd's fate has been quite difficult to investigate. One source said that he died in a car crash, and it is always necessary to be sceptical when people are reported dead in traffic accidents under Stalin's regime. Another source said that he had fallen in battle. After numerous investigations, it was discovered that both sources were correct. On 29 January 1943, Vice-Admiral Drozd was on his way across the ice in a staff car from Kronstadt to Leningrad, when German forces opened fire with artillery from the coast near Petrodvorets. The car fell into a hole in the ice caused by a shell falling in front of it and everyone in the car died.

Close-up picture of the Soviet cruiser *Kirov* with bridge and 'B' turret (7in/180mm).
(Old Ship Picture Galleries)

mines, submarines, aircraft, torpedo boats and shore batteries. The distance
to Leningrad was about 160 nautical miles (300km). The weather was bad
and the minesweepers in the force could not immediately set out their
minesweeping equipment because of the heavy seas.

When the convoys reached Cape Juminda, the fighting began in earnest.
When the first mine detonated, the progress of the entire Soviet force was
stopped. At the same time, the German coastal battery opened fire and seven
Junkers Ju 88s launched a bombing raid. The cruiser *Kirov* fired some very
precise counter-battery shelling with her 7in/180mm guns at the German
coastal battery on Cape Juminda, which was destroyed. Some ships in the
convoy tried to force their way through the minefields, while others dropped
anchor for the night and prepared themselves to continue the next morning.
Five of the nine Soviet destroyers were sunk. Four of them were older Soviet
destroyers from 1915, now named after political VIPs (*Yakov Sverdlov*, *Kalinin*,
Artem and *Volodarsky*). The fifth was the brand new *Skoryi* (Rapid), built in
1941. In addition, two of the three frigates, *Sneg* and *Tsiklon* (Cyclone), were
sunk. Of the twelve submarines, *S-5* and *Shch-301* were sunk. Twenty-five of

the twenty-nine larger merchant ships were sunk, three were put aground, and only one of them reached Leningrad. Approximately two-thirds of the convoy's ships reached Leningrad, but it was mainly the small vessels that successfully negotiated the voyage. The two largest of the sunken merchant ships, *Ivan Papanin* and *Vtoraya Pyatiletka* (Second Five-year Plan), each had more than three thousand soldiers on board. In the Stalinist system, the rule was that in the case of failure, some scapegoats were required. Among the few rescued persons were individual ship's captains who had been fished out of the water and brought to Leningrad. Most of them had behaved very heroically in the situation, but they were nevertheless put on trial and executed. They were rehabilitated in 1962.

Germany called the subsequent battle *Die Minenschlacht von Reval* (the mine battle at Tallinn), and regards this as the most successful mining operation in the history of naval warfare. Altogether, 2,828 mines and 1,487 explosive buoys were laid. The official number of Soviet casualties during the voyage of the convoy from Tallinn to Leningrad was set at 10,000 immediately after the war, but is now estimated to be 14,000 people. Sixty-five ships went down, but about 28,000 people and 60,000 tonnes of equipment reached their destination.

The Soviet defence was not very well organised in 1941, but the forces, and not least the Baltic Fleet, fought fiercely and succeeded in inflicting a number of losses on the German forces. Their inferiority in equipment was often offset by personal heroism, patriotism, fighting spirit and tenacity. The regime had also ensured, primarily with the help of Communist Party functionaries and NKVD units (the secret police, which also included border troops), a reduction in the possibilities for desertion, speaking out in defeatist terms, and similar. Soviet historiography during and just after the war painted a rosy picture of a united people who were behind all the decisions of the Party and fought against hunger, cold and superior power. A somewhat more nuanced picture of the abuses of the system against its own citizens, criminality, cannibalism, and much more, is slowly becoming available to historians, but a number of Soviet archives are still inaccessible. The more recent statistics show, for example, that starvation did not take nearly as many victims among members of the Communist Party elite, NKVD personnel and employees of the food industry as in the general population. The general picture of the city's leadership, like so many other places in the Soviet Union at that time, is characterised by incredibly bad leadership, lack of sense of responsibility, poor, slow planning, corruption and nepotism. For example, there is anecdotal evidence that Party Secretary Zhdanov, in the middle of the worst of the famine in 1942, had fresh peaches flown in by courier plane.

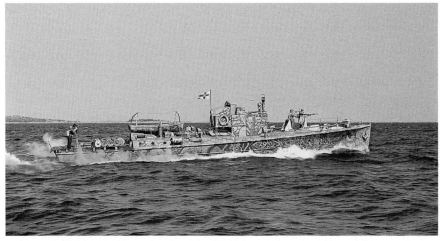

One of the four VMV boats escorting *Ilmarinen* which picked up a total of 132 men from
the sinking coastal monitor. (SA-Kuva)

The Finnish navy's greatest loss

At the beginning of the Continuation War in 1941, the Finnish navy totalled two
monitors, five submarines, seven torpedo boats and various minesweepers,
auxiliary ships, etc. On 13 September 1941, both the Finnish coastal monitors
took part in Operation Nordwind (Operation North Wind), which was a
German landing on the Estonian islands of Saaremaa and Hiiumaa. Some
Finnish and German ships took part as a diversion, transmitting a series of
long, dummy enciphered signals on the radio to lure any Soviet attackers
to the wrong place. Three German light cruisers were ready a little further
away if any large Soviet vessels happened to show up. During a turning
manoeuvre twenty-five nautical miles south of the outermost Finnish skerry
Utö, *Ilmarinen* got in a tangle with its minesweeping wires and paravanes,[16]
which were supposed to make sure that anchored mines were moved away
from the hull and the anchor cables cut. Two Soviet anchored mines, just laid
by a submarine from Hanko, had probably taken hold of the minesweeping
wires and, during the turning manoeuvre, the two mine casings collided with
the side of the ship and exploded on either side of a watertight bulkhead that
separated the ship's two largest spaces, the engine rooms. *Ilmarinen* rolled

16 A paravane is a float giving buoyancy to the minesweeping gear that is dragged on wires
    behind the ship. The wires are equipped with kites which get the sweep to spread out away
    from the ship and provide a certain width in the minesweeping. Furthermore, the wires
    can be equipped with explosive knives, or mechanical knives that can cut the anchored
    mines' mooring cables.

Hit probability, accuracy and standard deviation for artillery shells

Hit probability is especially important in regard to ammunition consumption. The greater the firing distance, the less probability there is of a hit and the greater the deviation there is between the shells. The ballistic trajectory which a shell delineates starts out as almost linear and at this point the speed is high. The speed decreases during the trajectory, which becomes more curved. When firing at the maximum range, the gun's elevation will be close to 45 degrees and the projectile will come down on the target almost vertically.

The hit probability is high on the horizontal part of the trajectory, technically known as point-blank trajectory, but less on the curved part of the trajectory. For example, if the target is a ship at an assumed distance of about 20,000ft/6,000m, and there are only 16,400ft/5,000m to the ship, then the ship will still be struck, just a little higher up. On the other hand, if the target is a ship at an assumed distance of 52,500ft/16,000m, and there are only 49,200ft/15,000m to the ship, then the shells will fall from on high, 3,300ft/1,000m beyond the target.

The deviation between shells can be specified with a distance. If the spread is specified at 500m (about 1,640ft) towards a point at a given distance, it means mathematically that if 100 shots are fired at the point, fifty of the shells will fall within a radius of 500m from the point. It is relatively easy to calculate the lateral training of the gun, but it is difficult to calculate the elevation. If the exact distance to the target is known, a range table can be used. The greater the distance, the more difficult it becomes to achieve a hit on the target.

over and sank in just seven minutes. Only 132 of the 403-man crew were rescued. It was the Finnish navy's largest loss.[17]

The evacuation from Hanko

In the period between 30 October and 3 December 1941, the Soviet Union carried out the evacuation of its forces on Hanko. Soviet minesweeper crews showed great courage and, despite countless mines, succeeded in

---

17 *Ilmarinen* lies upside down as a listed warriors' tomb in 230ft/70m of water, just about eight nautical miles (15km) from the wreck of the ferry *Estonia* which sank on 28 September 1994.

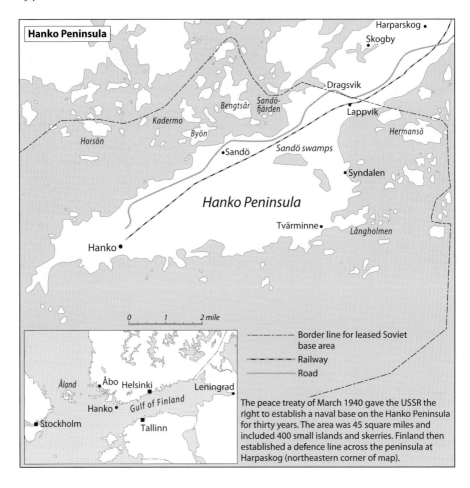

The peace treaty of March 1940 gave the USSR the right to establish a naval base on the Hanko Peninsula for thirty years. The area was 45 square miles and included 400 small islands and skerries. Finland then established a defence line across the peninsula at Harpaskog (northeastern corner of map).

getting large vessels in for the evacuation of Hanko, but when it came to the return journey, things went wrong. A Soviet destroyer with 500 soldiers on board hit a mine, was brought to a halt, drifted further into the minefield and detonated another mine – and then yet another. They succeeded saving about half of those on board. With the last transport from Hanko, about 5,600 soldiers came on board the liner *Josef Stalin*, a ship of 7,500 tonnes. Two mines brought the ship to a halt. Towing was attempted, but meanwhile the ship was fired on by a Finnish coastal battery and a hit caused an explosion in ammunition stores on board the ship; 1,740 men were transferred to other Soviet vessels. The wreck now drifted towards the Estonian coast with about 3,800 men on board, many of whom had been killed or wounded. In this extreme situation, the soldiers threw the officers and *zampolits* (commissars/political officers)

The Soviet destroyer *Opytnyy* (Experienced) shelling German positions with her 5in/130mm guns from the Leningrad area. (SMB arkiv)

overboard. The ship drifted aground and the survivors, about 1,500 men, were captured by the Kriegsmarine. It is believed that at least six thousand Soviet troops died during the evacuation from Hanko. After the evacuation, there was no longer any threat to the Finnish coast and shipping traffic in this area. The Soviet Union now only had troops in the eastern end of the Gulf of Finland.

The Soviet Baltic Fleet is trapped

After the initial chaos and the panic that followed immediately after the German surprise attack, the Soviet forces just about managed to become entrenched in the vicinity of the city before Leningrad was invaded. Naval artillery units had a total of 360 guns with barrels between 4in/100mm and 12in/305mm. They were subsequently used as bombardment units in support of army operations, as well as for the air defence of Leningrad and Kronstadt. Naval air defence had, in addition, more than 350 land-based heavy anti-aircraft guns. The change in the situation for the Baltic Fleet meant that several thousand men could be transferred to the fighting on land.

In addition to the base areas in Kronstadt and Leningrad, about 17 miles/28km of berths and channels on the inland waterways could be used by smaller vessels, so the ships did not represent stationary targets for

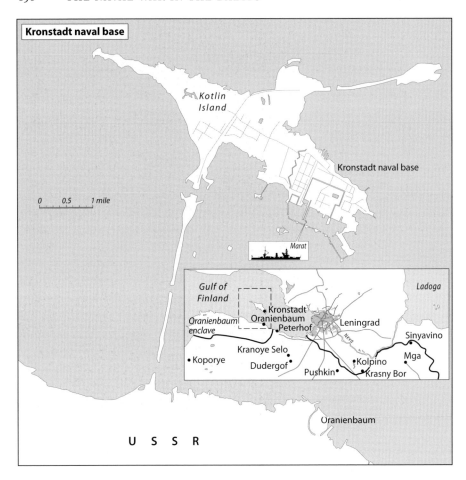

The heavy Soviet cruiser *Kirov* on the Neva river in Leningrad. (Old Ship Picture Galleries)

The German air offensive against the big ships began on 21 September and lasted for three days. On 23 September 1941, a Stuka pilot, Oberleutnant Hans-Ulrich Rudel, succeeded in striking the bow of *Marat* with a 2,200lb/1,000kg bomb. This put the forward turret ('A' turret) out of play and damaged the bow to such an extent that the ship sank, but she stood stable on the harbour bottom and 'B' turret soon resumed the artillery defence of Leningrad. During the same period, *Oktyabrskaya Revolyutsiya* was hit by six bombs without suffering damage. (Krigsarkivet, Sweden)

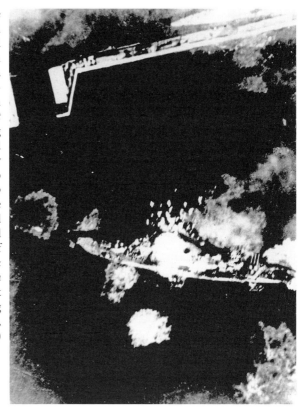

German artillery and air strikes, and they were constantly being moved. Soviet forces made considerable use of secrecy, deception, camouflage, and the specific concept of *maskirovka*, a word which is difficult to translate, but contains elements of the first three terms. A little way up the Neva, three destroyers and three gunboats were camouflaged. In the area between Leningrad and the White Sea–Baltic Canal lay the cruiser *Maxim Gorky* (with a blown-up bow since 23 June), the cruiser *Petropavlovsk* (the former German *Lützow*) and six destroyers. The battleships *Oktyabrskaya Revolyutsiya*[18] and *Marat*, the cruiser *Kirov*, the large destroyer *Minsk* and six smaller destroyers were berthed in Kronstadt. From 7 September 1941, the German advance across the country was impeded partly by the heavy artillery from the battleships' 12in/305mm guns. The bombardment took place at Oranienbaum, Krasnoye Selo (the Red Village) and Peterhof (in Russian, Petrodvorets). Even though the battleships were hit by German

---

18 Before the revolution, *Oktyabrskaya Revolyutsiya* was called *Gangut*, the Russian name for Hanko. Peter the Great defeated the Swedish navy here during a galley battle in 1714.

6in/150mm shells, they were not damaged because of their superior armour. The German command was thus presented with a problem that it had to solve. The threat from the Baltic Fleet's heavy artillery had to be eliminated, and this was a job for the Luftwaffe.

The German air offensive against the big ships began on 21 September and lasted for three days. On 23 September 1941, a Stuka pilot, Oberleutnant Hans-Ulrich Rudel,[19] succeeded in striking *Marat* with a 2,200lb/1,000kg bomb. This put the front turret ('A' turret) out of play and damaged the bow to such an extent that the ship sank, but she stood stable on the harbour bottom, and 'B' turret soon resumed the artillery defence of Leningrad. During the same period, *Oktyabrskaya Revolyutsiya* was hit by six bombs without suffering damage.

The destroyer *Steregushchy* (Vigilant) capsized after a direct hit, but was raised again. The cruisers *Kirov* and *Maxim Gorky*, the destroyers *Gordy* (Proud), *Grozyashchi* (Menacing) and *Silnyi* (Strong), the submarine depot ship *Smolny* (named after the monastery),[20] and the submarines *Shch-302* and *Shch-306* were all damaged. A submarine was destroyed in a dock, and the large destroyer *Minsk* was sunk, but later raised again. The attack on *Kirov* cost one of the two Stuka group commanders his life.

The week before, Hitler, however, had been concerned that the two Soviet battleships, supported by the other artillery units, would try to break out of Leningrad and threaten German operations. Grossadmiral Raeder informed Hitler that this would not be possible, but Hitler still ordered Vizeadmiral Ciliax, with a force consisting of the battleship *Tirpitz*, the pocket battleship *Admiral Scheer*, the cruisers *Köln* and *Nürnberg*, three destroyers and a number of torpedo boats and motor torpedo boats to an anchorage at Mariehamn in the Åland Islands. The cruisers *Leipzig* and *Emden* were in reserve at Libau. The comprehensive German air attack some days later on the naval base of Kronstadt and the port of Leningrad resulted in major damage to the Soviet ships. After assessing the damage to the Soviet ships, the German fleet returned to Gotenhafen (Gdynia) and Kiel on 29 September 1941. Germany's air superiority was gradually

19 Rudel was not very highly rated by his superiors prior to the war, but he proved to be an excellent Stuka pilot in wartime, and he ended up as a colonel in the Luftwaffe, and as the most decorated Luftwaffe officer. He was a convinced Nazi. He received the *Ritterkreutz mit dem Eichenlaub mit Schwertern und Brillanten* (Knight's Cross with Oak Leaves with Swords and Diamonds) from Hitler in January 1945, and completed a total of 2,530 wartime missions. Among other achievements, he is noted for having destroyed 519 Soviet tanks. He was shot down or crash-landed a total of thirty-two times.

20 The Smolny monastery was Lenin's headquarters during the October Revolution. It was situated where Peter the Great's tar stocks for the fleet originally lay. *Smola* means 'tar' in Russian.

The German light cruiser *Leipzig* in Copenhagen Freeport. (Simon Bang)

reduced in line with the improvements in the Soviet air defence and the subsequent decreasing number of German aircraft.

During the German-Soviet collaboration between 1939 and 1941, the Soviet Union had ordered some 15in/380mm battleship guns from Germany. When the war against the Soviet Union broke out in the summer of 1941, it was instead decided to put these guns in a German position at Dueodde on the south coast of the occupied Danish island of Bornholm, which would then be able to fire on large Soviet vessels which were either trying to break out of the Baltic Sea or wanted to fight the Kriegsmarine in the western Baltic Sea. Since the Soviet Baltic Fleet no longer constituted a threat, the guns were instead set up in two gun positions at Arendal, near Kristiansand in Norway, and at Hanstholm in northern Jutland, respectively. From here, they could block the Skagerrak, except for about four nautical miles in the middle which was blocked by mines.

The air war in 1941: Moscow and Berlin attacked

When the war on the Eastern Front was only a month old, the few German long-range bombers struck Moscow for the first time. Many of the initial Soviet efforts were directed at evacuating cities, populations and particularly manufacturing to places that were so far east that they remained outside the range of German bomber aircraft.

Soviet air forces were now going to bomb Berlin as retaliation for the attack on Moscow. The only type of aircraft in the vicinity which had

A Soviet Petlyakov Pe-8 four-engine heavy bomber. This type participated in the long-range bombings of Berlin in August and September 1941. (Krigsarkivet, Sweden)

sufficient operational radius was the Ilyushin Il-4 (DB-3F) from the Soviet Baltic Fleet's 1st Mine and Torpedo Air Corps. The aircraft were at the bases on the Estonian islands of Hiiumaa and Saaremaa. On 7 August, the regiment carried out the first attack with five aircraft: two were shot down on the outward journey and two did not reach the target; the last aircraft dropped its bombs on a Berlin suburb. Despite heavy losses, Soviet air forces continued these attacks until 4 September, when the German armies moved closer. In later attacks, some four-engined Petlyakov Pe-8 bombers from the army air forces, which had been sent to the Leningrad area, also took part. All in all, 311 bombs of 550lb/250kg and 1,100lb/500kg and 324 fire bombs were dropped on Berlin during ten attacks. The air attacks were primarily intended to destroy the confidence of the people of Berlin in the German leadership and propaganda. The military significance of the attacks was slight and they ended when the islands came under threat. The four islands at the northwest point of Estonia – Hiiumaa, Saaremaa, Vormsi and Muhu – were captured by German forces between 14 September and 21 October 1941.

The Luftwaffe redirected its tactical units at the end of August 1941. Two Stuka groups were based near Lake Ilmen, from where they were mainly going to be used against the supply lines between Moscow and Leningrad. The winter weather, however, quickly became a problem, since neither personnel nor equipment could withstand the freezing temperatures. The pace of the advance towards Moscow slowed considerably.

Sweden between 22 June 1941 and the spring of 1942

Because of Professor Beurling's breakthrough in deciphering texts from the German *Geheimschreiber* ('secret writer' cipher machine), the Swedish prime minister received notification of the impending German attack on the Soviet Union in good time. Sweden's relationship with Britain was, to put it mildly, somewhat strained because of the extensive Swedish support for the German war effort, so Sweden gained a diplomatic reward and thanks from Prime Minister Churchill, when the British government was surreptitiously informed of the impending German attack. The Swedish assessment mentioned that this attack was going to take place between 21 and 25 June 1941. Churchill had, of course, been well informed about it from his people at Bletchley Park, but he could not, for good reason, inform Sweden that he was also reading deciphered German cipher telegrams. The German signals could also be used in other ways in Sweden, in that Sweden got a head start in negotiations with Germany about politics and economics, because they knew the German negotiating position in advance and how much flexibility Germany would have.

The 'furlough agreement' had already been reached between the relatively pro-German Swedish foreign minister Christian Günther[21] and the German foreign minister Joachim von Ribbentrop on 22 June 1940. Günther was the foreign minister for the coalition government, but he was actually a civil servant and a diplomat, not a politician. The coalition government preferred a professional diplomat in the post of foreign minister. He saw it as his primary task to keep Sweden out of the war, and he was therefore willing to go to great lengths to keep Germany happy. The agreement was not so important when it was signed, but exactly a year later, it acquired very great significance, because it meant Sweden was now effectively supporting Germany's war against the Soviet Union. Initially, Germany tried to get a division moved from southern Norway to northern Finland. This was the 163rd Division (Division Engelbrecht, after its commanding officer). In late June and early July 1941, the division was transferred and deployed on the Eastern Front, north of Lake Ladoga. Germany also demanded transit permits for the rail transport of military equipment, supplies and troops to Finland and northern Norway. In July 1941, Sweden refused permission

---

21 Foreign Minister Christian Günther was named as Sweden's ambassador to Denmark after the war, but that appointment was rejected from the Danish side. Instead, he became the Swedish ambassador in Rome. He is regarded as a controversial person, but it was largely his professional efforts that kept Sweden out of the war. His 'German-friendliness' could instead be construed as an understanding of the potential consequences from Germany in the case of conflict.

for the next division, but later gave permission for an SS battalion to pass through. The agreement allowed German soldiers to go by train through Sweden to either Finland or Norway. In all, it was used by 2.1 million German soldiers until the agreement was terminated on 5 August 1943. The 'furlough agreement' referred to soldiers on leave, and Sweden had probably yielded rather too much, when the rail traffic indicates that we are talking about 2.1 million soldiers 'on leave'. These were actually fresh troops – with equipment in sealed wagons – one way, and wounded soldiers the other way. The Soviet Union, the US and Britain would not have seen this as an ordinary gesture from a neutral country.

On 25 September 1941, Princess Sibylla of Sweden visited wounded German soldiers during a stopover at the railway station in Krylbo, northwest of Stockholm. She served them coffee and chocolate. On 13 November 1941, she repeated this support for the German troops. She was married to Prince Gustav Adolf, then heir to the Swedish throne, and was the mother of the current Swedish King Carl XVI Gustaf. Her father was Archduke Carl Eduard of Saxe-Coburg and Gotha.[22] The Swedish government tried to give the impression that the rail transports through Sweden were a purely humanitarian activity organised by the Red Cross, but in reality the transports had been organised by the German military attaché in Stockholm.

In the autumn of 1941, Germany demanded that Swedish naval vessels protect German convoys. After this, Swedish warships escorted German merchant ships with supplies for Finland. German ships were allowed to sail in Swedish territorial waters, provided that they sailed under the merchant navy flag and did not carry troops – Germany interpreted this in its own way. The German army had troops on board, of course, but they were ordered below deck. The danger to the troops could be reduced if they sailed to Sweden on the connections between Sassnitz and Trelleborg or Elsinore and Helsingborg and then travelled by train across Sweden. In mid-1942, the SOE considered sabotaging the ferries on the Elsinore–Helsingborg crossing (Operation Barholme), but this was abandoned, partly because of the fear of German reprisals and partly because of the Danish resistance movement's use of the crossing.

---

22 Archduke Carl Eduard of Saxe-Coburg and Gotha was appointed General der Infanterie during the First World War, but this was a formality for a prince. He did not lead any troops. He was one of Hitler's early supporters and, in 1933, was appointed Reich leader of the German Red Cross, which was a full-blown Nazi-controlled organisation. He joined the SS the same year. In 1933, he became a member of the Nazi Party and was later appointed Obergruppenführer. He was interned by American forces after the war and was fined DM 5,000 as a collaborator. His son, Prince Hubertus, fell on the Eastern Front on 26 November 1943.

In Luleå in northern Sweden, with approval from the Swedish authorities, Germany established huge stocks of German food and ammunition intended for the Eastern Front. Swedish haulage contractors were responsible for transportation and a large service facility carried out maintenance on all kinds of vehicles from the German army units in northern Norway and Finland. This reduced German transportation requirements and gave them savings in time, manpower and fuel.

The Swedish commander-in-chief of defence forces, General Olof Thörnell, without government permission, had arranged that more than forty Swedish officers could serve in the German army from July 1941. In the following month, the Swedish press revealed that the Waffen-SS had also set up a recruitment office with approval from the Swedish military authorities. Both actions were stopped by the government. As winter approached, the German army command tried to buy winter uniforms in Sweden for the troops outside Moscow. This too was opposed by the government and to prevent the purchases being made illicitly by frontmen instead, textile rationing was established from 1 January 1942.

The fuel situation in Sweden was quite another story. Throughout the war, the Western Allies were very much in favour of Sweden having a strong navy and air force that could prevent a German military action in Sweden. Sweden did not have its own oil deposits, so apart from the fifty tankers that entered Gothenburg during the war, fuel supplies, paradoxically, had to come from Germany. Oil was a critical commodity for Germany and it was therefore allotted a relatively high price in relation to the exchange of goods, but – in addition to the iron ore – Sweden had something that Germany lacked: a large merchant fleet. Many ships from the Swedish merchant fleet lay idle in the Baltic Sea because of the war. They carried supplies over the Baltic Sea for Germany from 1941. Fuel supplies to the northern half of the Eastern Front were almost exclusively transported by Swedish tankers – the Swedish government had given its tacit approval to this traffic. The shipowners did incredibly well out of it, and payment often came in oil, petrol and coal. There was also an opportunity here to increase revenue, but the shipping transports cost the lives of many Swedish sailors. Germany paid war reparations if the ships were sunk because of acts of war; the standard marine insurance was no longer valid, but the Germans were good payers, solely because of their need for shipping tonnage.

One event in Finland might have been related to Sweden. On 14 September 1941, a fierce explosion occurred in Helsinki harbour. Some German minesweepers (*Räumboote*) were lying side by side when a depth charge on an aft deck detonated. A total of ten German crew members were killed, while fifty-six were wounded and three of the minesweepers sank.

Three days later, on 17 September 1941, the Swedish navy was hit by a similar explosion accident in the 1st Destroyer Division at their base in the Hårsfjärden Fjord outside Stockholm. It is food for thought that there were just three days between these events, and both explosions occurred precisely where the concentration of explosives in the ships was highest: namely, near the depth charges and torpedoes respectively. Under normal circumstances, explosives are stable and susceptible to neither shock nor heat. A detonator is required to initiate an explosion. Whether someone placed a detonator and a modest 'pre-charge' at the two accident sites is not known: neither of the two explosions has ever been solved. There are different theories that either a 'flying squad' from SOE or local Communist sympathisers were behind them.

Hitler was extremely concerned about Sweden. At the end of 1941, he feared a British invasion of Norway in particular. He noted the growing hostility from Sweden, and the Swedes could be suspected of wanting to support an Allied landing in Scandinavia. If the Allies achieved supremacy in Sweden, Germany would lose its freedom of movement in the Baltic Sea. In April 1942, Hitler therefore decided to strengthen German forces in Norway by 70,000 men. The new 25th Panzer Division was stationed near Oslo. OKH was against this arrangement, but it was Hitler's way of getting his message across to the Swedish government. On 28 January 1942, the German propaganda minister Joseph Goebbels reflected on the Swedish contribution so far in his diary: 'Sweden has done more for the German war effort than is known publicly. Above all, they have ... given us valuable support in the war against the Soviet Union.'[23]

Some months earlier, the King of Sweden had tried to contact Hitler on a personal matter. The king had consulted with Foreign Minister Günther, who had no objections to a letter, as long as it appeared that it was sent directly and thus bypassed the Swedish government. When Prime Minister Per Albin Hansson got to know about it, he felt that he had to take action: the king should not be writing letters to Hitler. The king did so, anyway, by slightly circuitous means. He summoned the German ambassador, the Prince of Wied, and read the letter out loud to him. That same evening at 2345, the Auswärtiges Amt (Ministry of Foreign Affairs) received the text from the embassy in Stockholm and it was thereafter forwarded to Hitler's headquarters in Wolf's Lair. In the letter to Hitler in October 1941, King Gustav V wrote, among other things:

---

23 Quoted from the book *Min kære Reichskanzler* (*My Dear Reich Chancellor*) by Staffan Thorsell (Borgen, 2007).

My Dear Reich Chancellor

I need to personally write quite openly to you about a matter that is close to my heart and which has the greatest impact on me and my country. It is about the Russian question. I think that it is of great importance for the future that you are aware of my opinion on the matter. Already after the last World War, I understood what a great danger Bolshevism was, and still is, not just for us in the Nordic countries, but for the whole of Europe. I would therefore like to express my sincere thanks to you for deciding to strike at this plague wherever possible. I congratulate you on the results you have already achieved, great successes ...

With my warmest regards, I remain, dear Chancellor, Your devoted Gustav R[24]

Hitler did not reply immediately, but on 7 December he wrote a response that was delivered three days later by a representative from the Auswärtiges Amt, the diplomat Karl Schnurre, who had previously sounded out the terrain of useful options in Finland and Sweden before Operation Barbarossa was launched. Hitler wrote that he had received the letter from the Swedish king with sincere joy. He had been happy for Swedish assistance in the German battle in the east and ended the letter by expressing that:

... the messenger Schnurre, who has the honour of bringing this letter to Your Majesty, will in connection with his visit to Stockholm endeavour to strengthen the interest of the Swedish government in this matter.

With best wishes, I remain Your Majesty's devoted
Adolf Hitler[25]

The foreign minister was present during the meeting between the king and Schnurre and, earlier in the day, he had held a meeting with Schnurre. At this meeting, Foreign Minister Günther had argued that the help that Germany was already receiving would have to suffice. The foreign minister did not know that the German leadership was worried about the 83-year-old king. If he suddenly died, they would be left with a new king who was more modern and democratically minded and, what was worse, whose late wife had been English.

The Danish navy and merchant navy

In accordance with Danish government regulations, the Danish navy assisted the Kriegsmarine with minesweeping, the marking of mineswept routes, the destruction of mines discovered and drifting mines, etc. The Kriegsmarine had adopted the Danish navy's patented and efficient system

---

24 Quoted from the book *Min kære Reichskanzler* (*My Dear Reich Chancellor*) by Staffan Thorsell (Borgen, 2007).
25 Ibid.

of minesweeping magnets developed by Orlogskaptajn Bahnsen from the Sea Mine Service. Icebreaker assistance was given to German warships and merchant ships. The Danish naval police carried out surveillance operations in the Sound.

A shipping agreement was included in the Danish-German collaboration from April 1940. Shipowners could not refuse to take freight, but they were generally interested in all the earnings that were possible, anyway. Despite German promises, the Danish Freight Board had already been asked to make tonnage available for ore transportation from the end of 1940. In 1941, Danish ships transported about 670,000 tonnes of iron ore, and probably a similar amount in 1942. These transports normally began from Luleå in northern Sweden and went to North German ports. In 1943, about 30 per cent of the Danish domestic fleet – by German 'request' – was being made available for these transports. In 1940, it was only the larger ships in the Danish domestic fleet which interested Germany, but from August 1942, all the small ships also came under the Freight Board's control. Danish merchant ships were also involved in transport via the North Sea, where they fetched, among other things, coal and coke for Denmark in Rotterdam and in the German North Sea ports. There were usually German personnel on board the ships in the North Sea. Navigation was particularly dangerous in the North Sea because of the large numbers of mines, submarines, torpedo boats and aircraft.

From 1942, Germany introduced a ship as a standard type that would be mass-produced in three sizes. This was the so-called Hansa type, which was the German response to the Allied Liberty ships. The shipbuilding programme was introduced in Germany, Holland, Belgium, France, Denmark, and to some extent also in Sweden, but the French part of it never materialised because of the invasion of Normandy. Thirty-seven of these ships should have been built in Denmark, but the Danish government ensured that eighteen of these were assigned to Denmark. They were administered by a state shipping company set up for the purpose, the Steamship Company of 6 February 1943, which would hereafter be required to hand over the operation of each ship to the shipping companies. Denmark thereby got something out of the expenses on the National Bank's so-called clearing account with Germany. Production was much delayed and some of the ships were sabotaged in Danish ports or Danish shipyards. The Hansa-class ships did not manage to achieve any significance during the war, but some of the ships were finished after the end of the war and became absorbed into the Danish merchant fleet.

Aircraft navigation during the war

At the start of the war, the RAF did not have navigation systems at its disposal which could be used with accuracy at night over Germany, and the large numbers of German fighters were not exactly an invitation to make bombing raids during the day. Initially, British bombs fell very far away from their targets, and work began developing various navigation systems which could be used by both ships and aircraft. Most of them were based on radio waves and, after the war, they developed further into what became known as Decca and Loran. The first usable system was Gee, which was the forerunner of Loran.

In 1941, British scientists invented the magnetron, which enabled them to produce high-frequency radar systems with a wavelength from 10cm down to 3cm (corresponding to a frequency of 3–10GHz), while Germany could only produce radar systems with a wavelength of about 100cm to 50cm. Such British high-frequency radar – type H2S – was installed in selected bombers, and with an airborne radar system, the contours of a coastline could be seen and, in this way, towns along the coast could be located and large formations could be directed. Gee was used together with radar during the first major attack against a German city. The RAF received a directive that authorised the bombing of urban areas on 14 February 1942. The first attack against a coastal city was launched on the night of 28/29 March (Palm Sunday) 1942. Out of all the possible targets on the coast, Lübeck was selected.

Norwegian merchant ships flee from Swedish ports

On 31 March 1942, another ten Norwegian merchant ships on the Swedish west coast tried to sail to Scotland undetected (Operation Performance). In addition to the crews of about 330 men, there were seventy sailors from the Royal Navy who had served in the British destroyers that were sunk during the battles at Narvik in April 1940. They had fled across the border to Sweden. The breakout attempt across Skagerrak was detected by the Kriegsmarine, who for the same reason had a fairly high level of preparedness with a large number of patrol vessels, torpedo boats, motor torpedo boats and submarines, along with aircraft ready at the air bases at Aalborg and Stavanger. Two ships reached Scotland, two turned back to Swedish territorial waters, and six ships were sunk by German forces; 235 men were taken prisoner. Six men succeeded in reaching the Norwegian coast in a lifeboat and escaping to Sweden – once more. The remainder died in the fighting on the ships.

Radar

Radar (RAdio Detection And Ranging) was an American name for what the British had for some years known as RDF (Radio Direction-Finding). Radar played only a very small role in the war around the Baltic Sea. Some of the German ships had navigational radar, which could be used to find the bearing and distance of a target at sea. The large German ships had artillery radar mounted high on a central sight, from where a bearing and a more accurate range could be taken; this could be used directly as a gun fire-control system (GFCS) on board, but the low German radar frequencies led to inaccuracies.

In the late 1930s, Britain developed a primitive, low-frequency, early-warning radar system which was vital during the Battle of Britain in the late summer of 1940. The stations in the radar chain were together called Chain Home. The use of this type of radar, along with their excellent organisation on the ground, enabled the RAF to deal with the attacks from the numerically superior German Luftwaffe. The invention of the magnetron in 1941 formed the basis for high-frequency radar systems, which were then mass-produced by the US electronics industry.

The H2S radar system was installed in many destroyers, frigates and corvettes, as well as Coastal Command's anti-submarine aircraft. This could be used for scanning large areas of the sea for submarine periscopes, as well as submarines which had surfaced at night. The same radar type was installed in a number of selected four-engined RAF bombers. The radar could, in fact, be used for navigation, in that it was possible to see the contours of coasts, harbour areas, estuaries, lakes, etc, from the air. After a crash near Rotterdam in 1943, Germany acquired knowledge of H2S radar from the aircraft wreckage, and thereby the magnetron, but it did not have time to utilise this knowledge in radar production before the war ended.[*] In the final days of the war, British and US anti-submarine aircraft with radar chased a large number of German submarines in Danish waters heading for Norway from German ports.

In 1944, the German forces brought air-raid warning radar systems to the Karelian Isthmus, where they supported the Finnish and German air defences with information about the direction and distance to Soviet air targets. This gave them time to organise a fighter defence and not send the aircraft up until they needed them and, not least, to send them in the right direction.

---

[*]   The Germans hereafter described this radar type as 'Rotterdam'.

RAF bombing of the Baltic ports

The RAF was gradually increasing its operations over the Baltic Sea. More mines were being dropped, in line with the acquisition of larger bombers with increased operational radius. Until early 1942, the RAF had conducted nightly bombing of German cities, but since the navigation systems at this time were very inadequate, hit probability and results had not matched the losses of aircrew and aircraft. The RAF still wished to bomb German cities at night, one by one, but there were two problems. The first was to locate the city, and the other was to achieve an increased impact from the bomb load in the target area.

Lübeck was chosen for the trial run, because the long-range navigation systems for the RAF had not yet been fully developed, but with the H2S radar, it was easily possible to find and identify a coastal city from a bomber. Many of the explosive bombs in the aircrafts' bomb loads were replaced by incendiary bombs. Incendiary bombs do not weigh very much, so there could be a lot of them on board the bombers, and the idea was to start a large number of fires in the city. On the night of 28/29 March 1942, the city was attacked by 234 aircraft. Goebbels was very concerned about this development, and counted himself lucky that on this occasion he could control the news to the German population. Lübeck was destroyed, and this had immediate consequences in Peenemünde army weapons research centre. Werner von Braun's rocket project had lost its funding when Poland was invaded, but Hitler was so enraged after the bombing of Lübeck that he again allocated money to the development of the A-4 rocket, which later became better known as the V-2.

Britain was generally concerned about support for Germany from Danish industry. B&W's shipyard at Refshale Island in Copenhagen harbour carried out maintenance on German ships. On 16 April 1942, two Mosquito aircraft attacked the floating dock containing the German minelayer *Skagerrak*, but some of the bombs did not explode and the damage was minor. B&W's engine plant in Christianshavn in Copenhagen produced diesel engines for German ships and production of submarine engines for the Kriegsmarine had begun, but this was stopped. The plant later came on the RAF's target list. Collaboration between the SOE and the Danish resistance movement led to an agreement that Danish industry targets would primarily be disabled by the resistance movement, and not by air strikes carried out by the RAF.

The situation around Leningrad and the rest of the Eastern Front in the first half of 1942

Hitler's dissatisfaction over the lack of progress at Leningrad led to the replacement of Generalfeldmarschall Wilhelm Ritter von Leeb as commander of Army Group North. On 17 January 1942, he was replaced by Generaloberst Georg von Küchler.[26] Hitler had already given von Leeb a written order on 22 September 1941, which stated:

- The Führer orders that Petersburg[27] be removed from the surface of the Earth.
- After the defeat of the Soviet Union, there will no longer be a requirement for this large residential area.
- A blockade of the city is proposed, along with the bombardment of it with artillery of all calibres and bombing it from the air until it is levelled.
- If the city offers to surrender, it shall be refused.

The army commander-in-chief Generalfeldmarschall Walther von Brauchitsch was dismissed on 19 December 1941, and the two other commanders on the Eastern Front, the commanding officers of Army Group Centre and Army Group South, were also replaced. Hitler thereafter took over the post of head of OKH, which was responsible for prosecuting the war on the Eastern Front. Strategy for the other fronts was put in the hands of OKW. This meant that two wars were being fought from each set of staff. Hitler was in charge of OKH and, as head of state, was commander-in-chief of both staffs.

Prompted by the order for the destruction of Leningrad, the city was shelled by artillery for 252 days during 1942.[28] It is remarkable that, after the war, no German documents have been found addressing the moral and ethical issues surrounding the siege of a city with more than a million inhabitants and the starvation of the population. The Nuremberg trials also found no material on these issues. In the West, there was – and still is – discussion about the moral and ethical issues in relation to the bombing of German cities.

As mentioned, the Luftwaffe should also have participated in the attack on Leningrad, but the situation was beginning to go wrong for Germany. First, it could not allocate very many aircraft to the Leningrad sector and, secondly, the Soviet land-based air defence began to be effective. The fighter defence of the Red Army air force and the Baltic Fleet air force was also

---

26 Hitler promoted von Küchler to Generalfeldmarschall on 30 June 1942.

27 Note that the name 'Leningrad' is not used in the wording.

28 According to official Soviet sources, 148,478 artillery shells, 102,500 incendiary bombs and 4,638 explosive bombs fell during the whole siege; 16,747 were killed and about 33,000 wounded during the artillery attacks, which took the most victims.

more effective, as the pilots and the aircraft improved. The Soviet Union had received Curtiss P-40 and Bell P-39 Airacobra fighters from the US and Hawker Hurricanes from Britain, via the ports of Murmansk and Arkhangelsk. The Soviet Union now began slowly to establish production of the Ilyushin Il-2 Sturmovik. This aircraft later played a key role as the Soviet Union's air-to-ground fighter, that is, a fighter bomber which could provide close tactical support during army operations.

When Leningrad was surrounded in September 1941, the Kriegsmarine's leadership was happy. The Soviet Baltic Fleet was locked in and everyone was expecting the city to fall. When the city had not been captured by spring 1942, and the ice began to melt, the Seekriegsleitung (naval operations staff) began to get worried. In order to prevent a Soviet breakout into the Baltic Sea, the Seekriegsleitung requested the Luftwaffe to direct air attacks against the most important ships. The attacks in April 1942 resulted in hits on the battleship *Oktyabrskaya Revolyutsiya*, the cruiser *Maxim Gorky*, and several smaller vessels.

Subsequently, the Kriegsmarine's requests became more straightforward. They just wanted the army to capture Leningrad. If the army could not get their act together for this, then it would at least be an operational advantage if the army captured the Soviet enclave of Oranienbaum and the three small islands of Lavansaari, Penisaari and Seiskari. Then it would be easier to keep the Baltic Fleet trapped in the easternmost part of the Gulf of Finland using coastal batteries and mines. The result, however, was that the Soviet Union retained both the three islands and the Oranienbaum enclave. From the point that the ice began to break up until 10 May 1942, the Kriegsmarine and the Finnish navy laid the Hogland minefield from Vigrund to the southeast of Hogland to the skerry of Haapasaari in the north; 4,569 mines were laid here, including 700 magnetic and acoustic bottom mines. The water depth was up to 240ft/73m. The minefield was covered from the south by German coastal batteries and from the north by Finnish coastal batteries. After this the Porkkala minefield was extended, stretching from Porkkala in the north to Naisaar in the south; 1,825 contact mines were laid here. Even though Germany and Finland had laid more than 13,000 mines in all in the Gulf of Finland, a number of Soviet submarines still succeeded in slipping out of the Gulf between June and September 1942.

Autumn 1941 to spring 1942: the major war fronts

General Zhukov was appointed commander of the defence of Leningrad on 10 September 1941, but since Moscow also came under threat shortly afterwards, Stalin called him back to the capital on 6 October. On 2 October, Germany

General Georgy Konstantinovich Zhukov was promoted to chief of the general staff in February 1941. In March 1943 he was promoted to field marshal. He was the brain behind all offensive Soviet operations and was finally the marshal who took Berlin. (SMB arkiv)

had launched Operation Typhoon, which was the storming of Moscow. In early December, the leading German units, which were about 18 miles/30km northwest of the centre of Moscow, could see the gold gleaming in the domes of the Kremlin. On 14 September 1941, the Soviet agent Richard Sorge in Tokyo had informed the Red Army that Japan would not embark on a war with the Soviet Union. Without the knowledge of the German forces, Zhukov had twenty-seven divisions transported from the Siberian armies to Moscow. They were battle-trained and able to operate under difficult conditions in the Russian winter. Zhukov organised a counter-attack based on the exploitation of the winter weather, which favoured the Soviet forces because the German troops lacked winter clothing and their equipment was not designed for the extremely low temperatures. Nor was the German equipment suitable for the mud, which was typical of the Soviet Union before and after the frost period, known as *rasputitsa* (the time with bad roads) in Russian. One of the Soviet T-34 tank's advantages was its wide tracks, which ensured that it could move in terrain which was muddy and difficult to negotiate. General Zhukov launched a counter-attack on 6 December 1941. After this, the Red Army counter-attacked across a broad front, including in the Leningrad region. In some places west of Moscow, they managed to reclaim 155 miles/250km of terrain before the spring's *rasputitsa* once again put an end to all offensive warfare. There was only one area where the Soviet Union had no success in the winter of 1942: that was the Finnish front – the Finnish troops were well prepared for winter warfare.

Southeast of Lake Ilmen (just south of the town of Novgorod), 100,000 German troops from six divisions were surrounded in February 1942 in an area that was called the Demyansk Pocket.[29] On 20 February, seventy-five Junkers Ju 52 transport aircraft were sent in for a rescue operation. During the next three months, the Luftwaffe flew 24,000 tonnes of supplies in, and in May, the surrounded troops were finally rescued by German forces, but it had cost a total loss of 265 aircraft. A similar but smaller pocket had occurred at Kholm, about 62 miles/100km further southwest. There were only 3,500 men to be relieved here, but the German airfield was within the range of Soviet artillery, so after a few weeks they had to abandon any ideas about landing, and drop supplies from the aircraft instead. These troops were also rescued in May after heavy German losses. Göring's conclusion after these two operations was that it was possible to relieve large surrounded armies by deploying transport aircraft – a somewhat ill-fated presumption as it proved during the following winter at Stalingrad.

When reviewing the first months of Operation Barbarossa, some interesting observations can be drawn and guesswork performed. Hitler was very near to gaining victory over the Soviet Union in 1941. If the operation had begun as planned on 15 May instead of 22 June, much could have looked very different. Leningrad was very close to falling to the Germans, as was Moscow. If they had been attacked individually instead, Stalin would probably have lost both cities. Hitler's campaign partly came to a standstill because of the winter arriving early, just as Napoleon had experienced in 1812.

The Soviet casualty figures were enormous, but Stalin could replace the losses. During 1941, approximately 3.3 million people from the armed forces had been killed and 2.4 million men taken prisoner. Most of those taken prisoner from 1941 died in captivity. The Soviet Union had 'exchanged space for time'. The 'space', the wide expanses and the long supply lines, wore out the German armies, and Germany did not have time. German losses on the Eastern Front in 1941 were significantly higher than the German public imagined. The army's key personnel could see the losses in an undisclosed assessment made by OKH: on 1 December 1941, the number of dead, missing,

---

29 'Pocket' is the English term. Both the warring parties used the expression 'cauldron' about encircled forces (*Kessel* in German and котёл in Russian).

captured and wounded amounted to 767,415 men; that is, 24 per cent of the original strike force of 3.2 million men.

For the German planners, the Soviet infrastructure proved to be worse than anticipated. Only a few of the towns had paved roads. Long stretches of road were of gravel and mud. The two annual *rasputitsa* seasons with mud and slush, floods, thaws, etc, made it impossible to transport anything for months. The road network was not nearly as developed as it was in Western Europe. Roads were few and far between, and they were of poor quality. The German commanders were aware that accurate maps were a precondition for operating in the area: just behind the front line, German land surveyors and cartographers worked on surveying and producing maps for the German army and the Luftwaffe. When the fortunes of war turned, the Soviets used the same captured maps in their advance on Germany.

In December, there had been a significant change in the war. After the Japanese attack on Pearl Harbor on 7 December, the United States had entered the war and, four days later, Hitler declared war on the US. Since 6 November 1941, the Soviet Union had already been part of the lend-lease agreement which President Franklin D Roosevelt had got through the US Congress in March 1941, and this provided the Soviet Union with further supplies. After the US entry into the war, US supplies to the Soviet Union increased.

In the Baltic Sea, the battleship *Tirpitz* had completed its initial training and acceptance tests. The ship had left Gotenhafen and sailed through the Kiel Canal on 14 January 1942 on its way to Norwegian waters, from which it never returned. The ship was not attacked en route by British forces, as Bletchley Park was at this time taking ten days to decipher German signals.

On 8 February 1942, the German armaments minister, Fritz Todt, died in an aircraft accident and the next morning, Hitler asked his 'court architect' Albert Speer to take over this important post. Even though German industry performed miracles under Albert Speer, Germany could not compete with the industrial production of the United States, Britain and the Soviet Union.

7

The War Between Spring 1942 and Spring 1944

The progress of the war

In 1941, many people regarded it as a matter of course that Germany would be victorious in the war. After 1941 this image slowly began to shatter. The German losses in Poland in 1939 and in the Soviet Union from 1941 had been greater than anticipated, but the German population had been kept in ignorance. Instead of co-operating with the local inhabitants in Ukraine and other parts of the Soviet Union to overthrow Stalin's regime, Hitler chose to exterminate the Jewish population and commit further comprehensive war crimes against other groups of people who in his eyes were 'inferior'. This reinforced widespread partisan activity, which came to plague the German war effort all the way to the moment of defeat. In 1941, Stalin was very reluctant to support partisan activities, because he was worried that the partisans could not be controlled. In 1942, the Soviet leadership managed to establish a partisan movement with strong party control from Moscow under the leadership of Panteleimon Kondratyevich Ponomarenko. His organisation was responsible for command leadership, communications and resources. The vast distances in the Soviet Union gave the German forces some long supply lines that were highly vulnerable to partisan activity. The road network was not suitable for large transports, so these had to be conducted by rail instead. The extensive partisan activities against German supply lines created a shortage of railway rolling stock with the broad Soviet gauge of 1520mm. Maritime transport across the Baltic Sea was supposed to help reduce the need for railways on the Eastern Front, but for geographical reasons, the options were limited.

Even though the Soviet Union had suffered huge losses in 1941, the country had not been defeated. The United States had finally entered the war. It was outside the war zone and had a large industrial capacity and a solid economy. Britain and the United States supported Soviet war efforts with substantial supplies, partly through what was then known as Persia (Iran) and partly via convoys north of Norway to Murmansk and Arkhangelsk. For political reasons, the assistance from the Western Allies received very little publicity in the Soviet Union after the war. In the United States and Britain, there was concern throughout 1942 about whether the Soviet defences would collapse. Stalin harboured a desperate wish for the opening of a second front to provide relief. However, the Allies were a long way from having built up a large enough invasion force to open a new front on the European continent, so they had to operate with a contingency plan, Operation Sledgehammer, which was a panic landing on the Channel coast to relieve the German pressure on the Eastern Front. This operation could very easily have turned into a disaster if it had been launched. On 19 August 1942, the Western Allies carried out a small raid – mainly with Canadian forces – on the French town of Dieppe on the English Channel. None of the operational aims was achieved and the jury is still out on whether the experience gained with the raid measured up to the costs in human life. Out of a landing force of about six thousand men, about four thousand were killed, wounded or taken prisoner. Even though Stalin's military needs were conspicuous, his desire for a new front was difficult to fulfil, because in 1942, US industrial production and the entire workforce were still in transition and the large amounts of tanks, ships and aircraft required would just have to wait a while.

In Finland, there was strong support for the resistance against the Soviet Union which had violated the country's borders both during and after the Winter War. Now the Finnish forces were a little way into Soviet territory in

Hitler receives Field Marshal Mannerheim in Wolf's Lair, Rastenburg, on 27 June 1942. Mannerheim carries the marshal's baton which he had received on his appointment in Finland twenty-two days earlier. (SMB arkiv)

the Continuation War. On 5 June 1942, the Finnish government promoted the country's commander-in-chief, Baron Carl Gustaf Emil Mannerheim, to field marshal, or Marshal of Finland.

Soviet submarines and the undeclared war between Sweden and the Soviet Union

In the summer of 1942, the Soviet Union considered Sweden to be a capitalist country which was actively supporting the German war effort. The Soviet Union thus regarded itself as at war with Sweden, and Swedish ships were therefore seen as legitimate targets for Soviet submarines and other Soviet forces. There was no official declaration of war, but the Soviet Union did not need one. When spring arrived in 1942, it was impossible to bring the major surface vessels from the Soviet Baltic Fleet into the fight against the Finnish and German forces. Instead, they relied on their large number of submarines, which could operate without regard to the threat from the air. The Baltic Fleet had carried out intensive submarine training during the winter, and had also demagnetised its submarines and otherwise sought to reduce the risk from mines. Thirty submarines from those in the beleaguered city of Leningrad were chosen to be prepared for operations during 1942. The sea ice had been 35–40in/90–100cm thick that winter, but in spite of the large number of anchored mines in the Gulf of Finland that had been destroyed by the powerful drifting ice, the mine threat was still very great. The iron ore transports from Swedish ports to Germany were natural targets for the Soviet submarines, and merchant ships from Denmark, Norway, Sweden and Finland in particular were involved in this activity.

The prepared Soviet submarines had been given a thick coat of paint and provided with a line of heavy timber around the hull and fins in order to prevent metallic contact between submarine and mine. Most anti-submarine mines were designed in such a way that if some foreign metal came in contact with the mine casing, the anchor wire or the mine's antenna, it would detonate the mine.

Hydrophones and Asdic/sonar

Around 1941, British scientists succeeded in producing an apparatus which was known as Asdic. It was named after the committee that had worked on the project: Anti-Submarine Detection Investigation Committee. The

Americans called it sonar (Sound Navigation And Ranging) and, since the war, this has become the most frequently used term.

During the war in the Baltic Sea, submarines and submarine hunters mostly used hydrophones. Asdic/sonar did not reach the same importance as in the Atlantic. In the Baltic Sea, the salt water is mixed with large amounts of fresh water from streams and rivers. This leads to stratification, and a hydrophone or sonar preferably needs to be in the same layer of water as a submarine to hear it.

Hydrophones are passive listening equipment – underwater microphones, which surface ships can use to listen for submarines. A bearing will often be given: that is, a direction to the sound source. Submarines can similarly use hydrophones to listen for activity on or under the surface. The noise from propellers and engines can be heard underwater. This means that approaching torpedoes can also be heard. If a submarine turns its engines off, it will not give out sound itself, and can therefore not be heard by hydrophones. During the Second World War, the hydrophones were rather basic and inaccurate.

An Asdic/sonar sends a strong sound (called a 'ping') through the water, which is reflected when it hits a submarine. This reflection can be detected by the sender, which thereby provides an indication of the presence of a submarine, along with its direction and distance. If the ping is returned with a changed tone, it indicates that the submarine is either approaching or receding (the Doppler effect).

The difference between the use of hydrophones and Asdic/sonar is that an active sound output reveals one's own presence and which direction one is coming from. If a ping is sent, the submarine crew can hear the sound and thereby know that they are being chased and have been discovered. If only hydrophones are used, this will not reveal one's presence.

Between 12 and 19 June 1942, five Soviet submarines were sent out, of which *M-95* was sunk by a mine east of Hogland. The others slipped out and sank about twelve merchant ships, including three Swedish; *S-7* and *Shch-317* each sank four. The submarines also laid mines along the Swedish east coast. One of the first ships to be struck by Soviet torpedoes was the Danish steamer *Orion*, which was west of Gotska Sandön, between Stockholm and Gotland, on 17 June 1942. One man from the Danish crew was killed. The ship was towed into Visby on Gotland and the remains of a Soviet torpedo were found on board. Five days later, the Swedish ship *Ada Gordon*, loaded with 4,000 tonnes of iron ore to Germany, was torpedoed and sunk east of Öland. Both ships had been hit by torpedoes from the Soviet submarine *Shch-317*, which then went on patrol north of Bornholm. When the Soviet ambassador in Stockholm, Madame Alexandra Kollontai,[1] was confronted by the Swedish Prime Minister Per Albin Hansson with the remains of the Soviet torpedoes from *Orion* and some Swedish ships, she claimed that it was a German provocation. Subsequently, it was impressed upon the Soviet submarine commanders that Swedish shipping was not to be attacked, nor were they to operate within Swedish territorial waters. At night, though, it could be impossible for submarine commanders to determine the nationality of their targets. On 28 June 1942, a German ship off Rixhöft (now Polish Rozewie) near Danzig Bay was sunk by a Soviet submarine. In August and September, two more Soviet submarines slipped out and sank five ships totalling approximately 10,000 tonnes.

Some operational duties were shared between Finland and Germany. Finnish forces retook Hogland and Tytärsaari (now called Bolshoy Tyuters) from the Russians between 27 and 29 March 1942. Hogland was later fortified, partly with German assistance. At the behest of the Kriegsmarine, German troops were to capture the small island of Lavansaari (now Moshchny Ostrov), but the attack was repulsed by the Russians. This small island is located sixty nautical miles (about 110km) west of Kronstadt. It has an excellent harbour, which provided the springboard for the breakout of the Soviet submarines from the Gulf of Finland in 1942. The submarines were able to sneak out from Leningrad at night, charge their batteries at Lavansaari the next day and then try to force the Finnish-German minefields the following night.

Sweden was urged by Germany to close the gaps in the German minefield near the Swedish coast between Öland and the Baltic coast, which Sweden agreed to do. Furthermore, during the summer of 1942, a Swedish minefield was supposed to prevent Soviet submarines from entering the Gulf of Bothnia, but as Finland had not yet completed its part of the minefield, a single Soviet submarine was able to penetrate.

Soviet submarine efforts were now concentrated in the Åland Sea, through which Finland received its supplies from Sweden and Germany. So in the autumn of 1942, the Finnish navy deployed its three big 500-tonne submarines, *Vetehinen*, *Vesihiisi* and *Iku-Turso*, in the Åland Sea as part of the fight against the Soviet submarine threat. The small 250-tonne submarine *Vesikko* was deployed on patrol between Helsinki and Tallinn. They were all

---

1   Madame Alexandra Mikhailovna Kollontai was a particularly eccentric and colourful women's activist who belonged to the Soviet Communist Party's original inner circle. She also belonged to Stalin's close circle of friends and is supposed to have survived only because she was a diplomat abroad when the purges gathered pace.

The Soviet submarine *Shch-317* sank four ships on her patrol starting in June 1942. *Shch-317* was sunk on 15 July 1942, southeast of Helsinki, by the Finnish minelayer *Ruotsinsalmi* and the Finnish patrol vessel *VMV16*. (SMB arkiv)

The Soviet ambassador in Stockholm, Madame Alexandra Mikhailovna Kollontai (1872–1952). She was the ambassador of the USSR in Stockholm from 1930 to 1945. She played an important role from Stockholm in the negotiations between the USSR and Finland from 1939 to 1944. (SMB arkiv)

The Swedish iron ore freighter *Bengt Sture* was sunk by the Soviet submarine *Shch-406* in October 1942 on her return from Danzig. The survivors were taken to Leningrad, handed over to the NKVD for interrogation and then shot. (SMB arkiv)

equipped with a depth-charge rack astern. On 21 October 1942, *Iku-Turso* sank the Soviet submarine *S-7*[2] at Lågskär in the Åland Sea with a torpedo shot at 3,300yds/3,000m. The submarine commander, Captain Sergei Lisin, was taken prisoner: he had been thrown into the water from the conning tower when the torpedo exploded. After being interrogated by the Finns, he was temporarily 'loaned out for interrogation by the Kriegsmarine'. On 5 November 1942, *Vetehinen* sank the Soviet submarine *Shch-305*. All Finnish patrol aircraft operating over the sea in this period were equipped with a standard depth charge of 440lb/200kg set to detonate at a depth of 65ft/20m.

As a curiosity, it should be mentioned that on the night of 28/29 October 1942, the Soviet submarine *Shch-406* sank the small Swedish ore freighter *Bengt Sture*, on her way back to a Swedish port with fifteen crew members on board after unloading in Danzig. In 1963, it was stated in a Soviet book that *Shch-406* sank the ship and took the five survivors on board: the captain, the first mate, an engineer, a cook and a cabin stewardess. They were brought to Leningrad, where all traces of them have disappeared. Much later, Western historians have discovered that some aspects concerning *Shch-406* in that book, an official historical work, have been replaced by a circulated correction – in the case of all 11,000 copies – while the equivalent page reference in the book's index has, in error, not been deleted. In 2005, Swedish naval historians found evidence in the archives in Moscow that the five survivors were handed over to the NKVD on 10 November 1942 for interrogation, and then shot.

---

2   *S-7* was found by divers in 1998.

The Finnish submarine *Vesihiisi*. On 21 October 1942 a torpedo from *Vesihiisi* sank the Soviet submarine *S-7* at Lågskär in the Åland Sea. (SMB arkiv)

Two Finnish submarines of the *Vetehinen* class. During the campaign against Soviet submarines in 1942, the three *Vetehinen*-class submarines were fitted with depth-charge racks. Each submarine sank a Soviet submarine in October – November 1942. (SA-Kuva)

The German destroyer *Z31* with 6in/150mm guns in Rønne harbour on Bornholm in September 1942. (Maritime Museum of Denmark, Elsinore)

When Prime Minister Nikita Khrushchev came on an official visit to Sweden in 1964, the questions surrounding the fate of the diplomat Raoul Wallenberg and the lost crew of the *Bengt Sture* were the two biggest stumbling blocks. Studies by Western historians in Soviet archives have not yet been able to answer all of the questions. It is believed that the five crew members were killed in Leningrad for two reasons: partly because the Soviet authorities were reluctant to reveal that they sank neutral shipping, and also because there would be five fewer mouths to feed in the famine-stricken city.

The German and Finnish minefields were reinforced, but despite that, Soviet submarines continued to break through and convoying became necessary. Between 18 September and early November 1942, the Baltic Fleet sent eighteen submarines out. Four of them were sunk by mines on the way out. The remaining fourteen submarines sank only six cargo vessels totalling 12,000 tonnes, but Germany found it unacceptable that there were enemy submarines lurking in the waters. It was, after all, also using the Baltic Sea as a transport route for fresh troops to the Eastern Front, and 400,000 troops passed through annually. Finally, there were tankers with fuel travelling to the northern part of the Eastern Front. This was almost exclusively handled by Swedish tankers. On 14 and 19 October 1942, Soviet submarine attacks were reported southeast of Trelleborg. On 6 November 1942, there was a submarine attack about twenty-five nautical miles east of Bornholm.

The Kriegsmarine did not really have enough vessels to send out escorts for the convoys, and an escort would, even so, only have very limited possibilities of locating and sinking attacking submarines. The Kriegsmarine command found a solution to this during the autumn and winter of 1942: it was decided to block the Gulf of Finland completely when the ice broke up in the spring of 1943. The aim was that no Soviet submarines should slip out in 1943. It was to be an operation carried out by the Kriegsmarine, assisted by the Finnish navy.

The Soviet submarine campaign in the Baltic Sea in 1942 cost the Soviet Union a total of twelve submarines and thereby more

Karl Dönitz here as Vizeadmiral betwen September 1940 and March 1942. (Museum of Danish Resistance, Copenhagen)

than four hundred of their specialists. They sank – so they claimed – fifty-one ships totalling 400,000 tonnes, but the real figure was probably eighteen ships totalling 45,000 tonnes. A further four vessels were sunk by mines laid by the submarines. The casualty numbers were compiled long after the war ended, and speak volumes about the difference between 'estimated casualties in the heat of battle' and the sober facts.

At the Führer conference on 26 August 1942, the commander-in-chief of the Kriegsmarine had underestimated the threat from the Soviet submarines. He said to Hitler, 'to date, only two or three submarines have slipped out during the summer of 1942. Twenty submarines had been sunk in or near their bases in Leningrad'. At the Führer conference on 22 December 1942, Grossadmiral Erich Raeder was much more concerned. He noted that the Kriegsmarine had too few vessels for escorting convoys, and that the Soviet submarine threat could be reduced if the German army could allocate the forces to capture the three small islands and the coastal stretch, the so-called 'cauldron', at Oranienbaum. The army, meanwhile, could not afford to allocate troops to these operations. He concluded by saying that, 'all the submarines that slip out are a threat to our transports, which are already insufficient.'

The situation in the besieged city of Leningrad

The first winter of the siege was the worst for the Leningrad population, which had almost been starved to death. The winter was the coldest for fifty years and on 24 January 1942, the temperature dropped to minus forty degrees Celsius. When the famine was at its peak in the first winter of the war, more than eight thousand people a day were dying. In November 1941, a route was established over the ice on Lake Ladoga which could be used for supplies one way, and evacuation the other. The ice held up until 24 April 1942. When the ice broke up, supplies had to be brought in by boat. The route over the ice and the lake was known as the Road of Life. The navy took part in these supply operations to the dwindling population and the Baltic Fleet air force constituted the primary fighter defence against German air raids. The young Alexei Nikolayevich Kosygin, vice-chairman of the National Evacuation Council, wrote in a report to the Kremlin: 'More than 500,000 people have been evacuated via Ladoga during the winter. 800,000 fewer ration cards have been issued than when the siege began. The city has received 270,000 tonnes of food over the ice.' A pipeline was then laid on the bottom of the lake to supply the city with fuel.

In 1942, Italy also began to take part in the fighting in the area. Germany had requested that assistance be sent to Lake Ladoga by the Italian navy and four small torpedo boats with Italian crews, *MAS 526, 527, 528* and *529*, were participating alongside the Finns in the fighting against Soviet vessels. The Italian boats had been transferred to Tallinn in the winter of 1942/43 and subsequently bought by Finland. They were given the names *Jylhä, Jyry, Jyske* and *Jymy* (which mean Robust, Thunder, Storm and Rumble respectively). In 1943, the Finnish navy also had five newly-acquired motor torpedo boats

One of the four Italian torpedo boats, *MAS 526,* on Lake Ladoga in 1942. They had Italian crews and each carried two torpedoes. The following year five more boats were purchased in Italy. They were used in the Gulf of Finland by Finnish crews. (SMB arkiv)

The Finnish fast patrol boat *Hirmu* (Horrible) of the Baglietto class, built in Italy, leaving on a patrol. Behind the helmsman is Commander Peuranheimo (Squadron Commander) with Lieutenant-Commander Siivonen and Lieutenant Wikberg. (SA-Kuva)

of the Italian Baglietto class delivered. They were given the names *Hyöky*, *Hirmu*, *Hurja*, *Hyrsky* and *Häijy* (meaning Tidal Wave, Horrible, Wild, Spray and Vicious respectively). Another six small torpedo boats were delivered from Finnish shipyards and three captured Soviet vessels were reconditioned.

Under a new Führer directive (no. 45), dated 5 April 1942, Hitler had ordered the new commander of Army Group North, Generalfeldmarschall Georg von Küchler, to capture Leningrad during September 1942 at the latest. If Germany had been expecting the city's population to be broken by the siege, the opposite had actually happened. The siege had created feelings of solidarity and defiance that Germany had not counted on. Germany was aware that the March Revolution in Petrograd in 1917 was due to the reaction of the women to the bread shortage, and they counted on something similar happening in the winter of 1941/42, but the population had not been crushed. Later Soviet propaganda would like to give the impression that solidarity was strengthened and that cultural life was flourishing. The libraries had large numbers of visitors and doctoral dissertations were still being submitted and defended. For the intellectual part of the population, morale and intellect were paramount. The crowning glory was the world premiere of Dmitri Dmitriyevich Shostakovich's Symphony No. 7, which was broadcast to the entire Soviet Union and overseas on 9 August 1942. This also gave the Germans a sense that the city was still alive. Thanks among other things to an iron discipline, the city's population succeeded in getting through all the adversity, but behind the facade lurked the wretched leadership and abuses of power of the Communist Party, and not least the brutal behaviour of the NKVD. Despite death, starvation, suffering and deprivation, the citizens of the city supported the regime – or to put it another way, they did not challenge the regime. In the spring of 1942, all the green areas of Leningrad were planted with vegetables, thus giving the people a form of self-support through their own production. Small sorties from the city were intended to improve the defence situation.[3]

Sweden between spring 1942 and spring 1944

Between June 1940 and August 1943, the Swedish railways had transported 2.1 million German troops and 700,000 tonnes of German supplies. More than sixty thousand wounded German soldiers, mainly from battles in Finland, were transported home by train, often in Swedish hospital trains.

---

3   The future President Vladimir Putin's father was injured during a sortie from Leningrad in the winter of 1941/42. Vladimir Spiridonovich Putin was presumably part of a demolition party under the NKVD.

In 1942 alone, Swedish intelligence deciphered 1,305 miles/2,100km of encrypted German telex texts, but by the end of 1942, they could no longer understand large segments of the German signals traffic. The reason was that a Finnish officer had been left alone in an office during a visit to the Swedish defence staff, where he discovered that Swedish intelligence was apparently able to read some of the German ciphers. He warned the Germans, after which German security was tightened up somewhat, and the Swedes had to acquire their information from other sources.

Swedish support for Germany was at its strongest while Germany was marching forward victoriously. When the fortunes of war began to turn, Sweden reviewed the situation and its complicated balancing act continued. The Swedish defence forces had been strengthened considerably in the second half of 1943, after which they reined in German troop permits. In August 1943, the German transit traffic to northern Norway was halted and, at the same time, German ships were no longer allowed to sail in Swedish territorial waters.

As Germany went on the defensive, the Western Allies increased their pressure on the Swedish government. Now they were able to take the liberty of putting a stop to exports of ball bearings and iron ore to Germany. At the same time, ball-bearing imports from Sweden became even more vital to German war production, since the German factories which produced the SKF (Svenska Kullager Fabrikken, ie Swedish Ball-Bearing Factory) bearings under licence in Schweinfurt, were being subjected to heavy bombing raids. It was a daytime attack on 17 August 1943 which cost the United States Army Air Force (USAAF) heavy losses. It received wide American press coverage and in the eyes of US Congress members, there was a direct link between the US casualties in the attack on the factories in Schweinfurt and the Swedish contribution to ball-bearing production, whether they came from Sweden or from production under licence. After this, the Swedish government received a note with threats of bombing the SKF ball-bearing factory in Gothenburg if exports to Germany did not cease.

SKF had factories making ball bearings under licence in both Germany and Britain. Sweden was even exporting to Japan, another enemy of the Allies. The Japanese defence attaché in Stockholm was purchasing bearings and specialised steel, which were shipped to German submarine bases and from there sent on German submarines to Japanese-occupied territories in the Far East.

When the Swedish defence forces had consolidated after the first years of the war, one of their plans was to support an Allied landing by fighting their way out to a Norwegian port – Narvik, for example. In turn, they now felt more secure against the danger of German invasion, but in this they were

One of the fishing vessels built in Sweden for the Kriegsmarine in 1943. In Germany they were supplied with guns. The Kriegsmarine used them for a variety of purposes and called them KfKs (*Kriegsfischerkutter*, ie war fishing vessel). (SMB arkiv)

making a big mistake. Sweden generally perceived itself as most threatened by Germany in the first half of the war. Analyses long after the war show that the opposite was the case. German units in Norway, Finland, Denmark and the Baltic countries could be quickly transferred to Swedish territory if a political or operational need arose. When Hitler received intelligence reports that Sweden was impressed with the Allied landings in North Africa in November 1942, he used the opportunity to stress that 'German protection of Scandinavia' was more important than the offensive in Russia the following summer. He therefore ordered reinforcements for the 25th Panzer Division[4] in Norway. In December 1942, Generaloberst Nikolaus von Falkenhorst was planning Operation Polarfuchs (Operation Arctic Fox), which was a German invasion of Sweden. He calculated a need for ten German divisions for ten days.

In February 1943, a Swedish newspaper revealed that the building of forty-five wooden fishing boats at shipyards closely associated with Stockholms Enskilda Bank was, in fact, about a delivery of small minesweepers to the Kriegsmarine. This was an offshoot of the Wallenberg brothers' involvement in German industry.

In March 1943, Hitler ordered the German forces in Norway to research possible operations in Scandinavia if there were changes in the political or military situation. Generaloberst Jodl, the OKW's chief of staff, was ordered to reinforce German troops in Norway and make sure that the 25th Panzer

---

4   The 25th Panzer Division had a number of older French tanks and a few Panzer IV and Tiger tanks at its disposal.

Division near Oslo was equipped with the heaviest and most offensive weapons. Sweden had little to put up against them, but the division was transferred to the Eastern Front (via Denmark and France) in 1943.[5] At the same time, a further division from Norway was transferred to the Balkans, because of the deteriorating situation for Germany there. By the end of 1943, Generaloberst Jodl was of the opinion that an Allied landing in Norway would lead to Sweden's entry into the war on the Allied side, whereby the whole of Scandinavia would fall. This would put the power balance in the Baltic Sea in danger. The Kriegsmarine had had a number of plans for the conquest of Sweden since 1943. The Swedish navy would be a very appropriate addition to the German fleet, which was suffering from a considerable lack of escort units. If the army could capture the bases in a very short time, it would be an advantage. However, if it took a long time, the disadvantages would outweigh the benefits. Lengthy battles could lead to disruption of both submarine training and supply lines.

On 27 April 1943, a German fighter plane shot down a Swedish DC-3 aircraft called Gladan over the Skagerrak. It was an aircraft that was usually used as a courier plane. It had been sent to keep an eye on the Swedish fishing boats which two days earlier had been seriously obstructed by German vessels in a fishing area north of Hirtshals in northern Jutland. The episode culminated when German ships sank two Swedish fishing boats with twelve crew members during the night. None of the fishermen survived. There was great indignation in Sweden, especially when the crews of two nearby boats came home and reported the incident to the press. The shooting down of the aircraft cost the lives of a further seven men.

In the same period, the Swedish navy was looking for a missing submarine, *Ulven* (Wolf), which had run into a mine on 15 April 1943. The submarine had been submerged when the accident happened and all thirty-three on board had been lost. The submarine was first located in 170ft/52m of water after a twenty-one-day search. It was lying a few hundred metres within Swedish territorial waters. The minefield had been laid by Germany in 1940 to prevent British submarines from entering the Baltic Sea. It stretched from the Scaw to the skerry of Pater Noster, northwest of Gothenburg. These were anchored mines, which were so deep that they only posed a danger to submerged submarines. *Ulven* was salvaged and brought into Gothenburg in August, where the dead were buried in a joint ceremony. This accident created renewed resentment against Germany and brought Swedish-German relations to a low point. In the summer of 1943, the threat of invasion was again felt in Sweden. On 28 July 1943, which was just a few days before

---

5   The division received new artillery equipment in modest quantities. It was wiped out at the Dniester river in the spring of 1944.

The Swedish submarine *Ulven* (Wolf) was sunk by a German mine in Swedish territorial waters northwest of Gothenburg on 15 April 1943. All thirty-three men aboard perished. (Marine Museum, Karlskrona, Sweden/Krigsarkivet, Sweden)

Sweden cancelled all German transit through its territory, secret Swedish reconnaissance flights started between the Kalmar Strait and Bornholm. Mines were also laid around Sweden's threatened southeast coasts. During the first week of August, Swedish destroyers carried out patrols between Gotland and the Swedish east coast. At this time, Germany had troops all the way round Sweden.

At the start of the war, the Swedish government had declared that it remained neutral and that, for this reason, the warring parties would be treated equally and in accordance with the Hague Conventions of 1907. The conventions were concerned with land and naval warfare, but air warfare had not been foreseen, so the Swedish government interpreted the principles for this itself. The problems came to be about the release of emergency landed/errant aircraft; the release of crews to their home country; overflying by bombers; overflying by courier planes; and defecting/fleeing aircrew.

Sweden was partly playing with concealed cards, so Germany and Britain did not always know how Sweden would interpret a situation. In some cases, they returned crash-landed German crews to Germany. When that was done, they returned a corresponding number of Britons – sometimes ten times as many. Towards the end of the war, US aircrews were also returned. From

1944, Sweden was more open in its support of downed Allied aircrews, and regular traffic went from Stockholm to Britain by aircraft, taking advantage of bad weather when the German air defences in Denmark and Norway had to be passed. Swedish air defences were pre-advised not to shoot down this traffic.

Among the many people detained in Sweden were fifteen officers and 120 other crew members from the three Polish submarines which had been interned in September 1939. During 1943, twenty-nine of them had the opportunity of travelling with RAF aircraft from Sweden to Britain, so they could serve in submarines sailing under the Polish flag but equipped by the Royal Navy.

In July 1943, the Kriegsmarine gave German warships permission to fire on Swedish aircraft flying past. In August 1943, the Kriegsmarine complained that a Swedish aircraft had followed a German convoy in the Baltic; the Swedish authorities would almost certainly forward information to Germany's enemies about it. The worried admiral was Hubert Schmundt, commanding officer of the German naval forces in the Baltic Sea from March 1943 to February 1944. The Kriegsmarine was also concerned about the large Swedish merchant fleet, which they would be reluctant to see fall into the hands of the Allies. In August 1943, German vessels sank two Swedish fishing cutters in the Baltic Sea as revenge for the alleged sabotage of buoy lights in out-of-bounds German territorial waters by some other cutters.

Back in Brofjord, north of Lysekil on the Swedish west coast, sat the British industrialist George Binney, still with the two Norwegian ships *Lionel* and

The Norwegian merchant vessel *Dicto* in Lysekil was used by George Binney for storage of all the ball bearings he could obtain in Sweden and send towards Britain. (SMB arkiv)

Admiral Hubert Schmundt, commander-in-chief of German naval forces in the Baltic 1943/44. He was concerned about the large Swedish merchant fleet, which he was reluctant to see fall into the hands of the Allies as a result of an Allied action against Scandinavia. (SMB arkiv)

Dicto. It would now be impossible for him to send them to Britain, but their precious cargo of ball bearings could perhaps still be delivered. At first, he tried to do this via aircraft, but they could only carry a very small load and it was a hazardous journey, flying over the Skagerrak with all the fighter planes Germany had stationed in southern Norway and Jutland. The eventual solution was to convert five swift boats which could do around 22 knots. They had a displacement of about 200 tonnes and were fitted with anti-aircraft guns and machine guns. Officially, they sailed under the British Merchant Navy flag (the Red Ensign) and merchant ships sometimes carried anti-aircraft guns. The boats each had a twenty-man crew. They could go from Hull to Lysekil under cover of bad weather, passing the Skagerrak in the dark and reaching the Swedish coast before dawn. Then they could take the cargo of ball bearings on board and depart at nightfall the following evening. If all went well, it would take eighteen hours to sail from Hull to Lysekil. Some of the Norwegian sailors went to Hull with the boats. The route was plagued by numerous accidents and one ship's crew was captured during the crossings. Germany had put quite large forces out to detect and suppress the traffic from Lysekil, but on 5 March 1944, the Kriegsmarine ordered most of its destroyers, torpedo boats and VP-boats to the Gulf of Finland, where Finland and Germany were now hard-pressed. Around the same time the

Nonsuch, one of the British patrol vessels flying the Red Ensign, used for fast transports between Lysekil and Hull, initially with ball bearings and later with weapon supplies for the Danish and Norwegian resistance movements (Operation Moonshine). (SMB arkiv)

British cancelled their operations, but by then thirteen trips had procured 347 tonnes of ball bearings for Britain.

On 14 May 1944, a German fighter shot down a Swedish aircraft near Libau in Latvia. Admiral Kummetz, Admiral Schmundt's successor, had assumed it was a Soviet aircraft with Swedish markings, but he added in his report that if it really was Swedish, then it was a question of Swedish espionage against German submarine training, and that it thus had to have been commissioned by either the Soviet Union or Britain. Admiral Kummetz was informed that three Swedish airmen had been rescued shortly after from a 'dinghy' (a small inflatable life raft). The following day, the Germans shot down another Swedish aircraft, this time near Ventspils in Latvia. Admiral Kummetz declared that 'Sweden, as well as Germany's enemies, was aware of the importance of flight reconnaissance over this part of the Baltic Sea and that he had to interpret the very intense rescue efforts from the Swedish side as proof of the great importance it attached to this information.'

Sweden was probably genuinely concerned about the loss of life and it was also of great importance to the fighting morale of the Swedish aircrews, in particular, that great efforts were made to find the missing crews. In Germany, at this stage of the war people were accustomed to very large losses. As the situation between Finland and Germany deteriorated towards the end of March 1944, Sweden tried to act as broker between Finland and

Marshal Leonid Aleksandrovich Govorov (1897–1955). He had distinguished himself as the commander of the artillery under General Zhukov's defence of Moscow in 1941 and later as the liberator of Leningrad. (SMB arkiv)

the Soviet Union. This was taken very badly by Germany, which imposed an arms embargo on Finland.

The situation in Leningrad

In April 1942, Stalin sent one of his best officers to Leningrad. Major-General Leonid Aleksandrovich Govorov[6] had distinguished himself as the commander of the artillery under General Zhukov's defence of Moscow. He was now put in charge of the defence of Leningrad and of planning a breakout from the town. Govorov's direct opponent was Generaloberst Georg Lindemann, who ended up as the last German commander in Denmark. Govorov was a specialist in counter-battery firing: that is, locating and destroying enemy artillery. He launched an offensive at the turn of 1942/43 which brought an easing of the siege, but not an end to it.

---

6 Leonid Aleksandrovich Govorov (1897–1955) was one of the few Soviet officers who had a past in the tsarist army. He had become a lieutenant in 1916. He was a highly professional artillery officer and a competent planner, and it has been said of him that 'he is a man who has never been seen to smile'. He became a Marshal of the Soviet Union before the end of the war.

Soviet artillery during a massive attack

During the massive Soviet attacks at the end of the war, the following equipment played a part in the artillery preparations: mortars, guns, howitzers and rocket launchers (Stalin Organs, or Katyushas*). There could be more than 250 artillery pieces (guns) per continuous kilometre of front line; that is, only 13ft/4m between the guns. In practice, this is achieved by setting up the batteries (a company in an artillery unit) behind each other. In a Soviet massive attack, the enemy positions would typically be bombarded for an hour. The moment the shelling ceased, the Soviets' own units could begin advancing across the terrain. When the German forces had prior knowledge of such preparations for firing, they drew personnel back from the front lines and had the personnel run forward again when the bombardment ceased. At the end of the war, the German armies were typically operating with seven prepared defensive lines, where withdrawal could take place gradually from no. 1 to no. 7. This was a development of tactics from the First World War.

Soviet forces often used artillery in a mass action. After the war, it has been estimated that more than half of the German soldiers who fell on the Eastern Front were killed by Soviet artillery fire.

* The original Soviet designation was Бм-13 (BM-13).

The first breakout from Leningrad

The first, if modest, breakout from Leningrad, Operation Iskra (Spark), began on 2 January 1943 with a massive artillery bombardment. It came from the artillery under the command of General Govorov's 67th Army from the Leningrad Front and General Meretskov's 2nd Shock Army from the Volkhov Front, and it was directed towards the bulge in the front near Sinyavino and Schlisselberg. Until then, Leningrad had only been able to receive supplies via the Road of Life over the ice, or by boat across Lake Ladoga. However, these transports were exposed to German artillery and air strikes. Around 18 January 1943, Soviet forces captured about 6 miles/10km of territory and, behind the front, the engineer and railway corps immediately began to establish a rail link. General Zhukov had been sent to Leningrad a few days before the operation began in order to monitor the outcome. When its limited goal was achieved on 18 January 1943, Stalin promoted him to Marshal of the Soviet Union. The military follow-up included the construction of a railway bridge over the River

Neva. The 20-mile/33km-long railway line was completed in nineteen days. On 7 February 1943, the first train with supplies was able to roll in to Vitebsk railway station in Leningrad. Although the siege was not lifted, the supply situation was relieved and optimism thereby grew among the urban population, who five days earlier had received the news of the great victory at Stalingrad.

Lieutenant-General Govorov could also use the railway for transporting heavy equipment and supplies with fresh troops into the city. He was now planning the ultimate escape from the besieged city. It was going to take place when an overwhelming firepower had been built up and, if they could wait for winter, then they could once again use the darkness and the winter as allies.

The August uprising in Denmark and the sinking of the Danish fleet

The so-called August uprising in Denmark arose from an act of sabotage at Odense shipyard. On 28 July 1943, a ship's electrician at the shipyard succeeded in carrying a magnetic bomb provided by the SOE aboard a ship under repair. During the lunch break, the bomb was lowered below the waterline and detonated with a delayed fuse. The ship was the German freighter *Linz*, which was being converted into a minelayer for the Kriegsmarine. The German authorities had wanted to guard the vessel, but the workers at the shipyard refused to work under guard and this started the unrest which spread during August to many Danish cities. It started slowly, but by the end of August, it had become so violent that the Danish and German authorities had lost control of the situation.

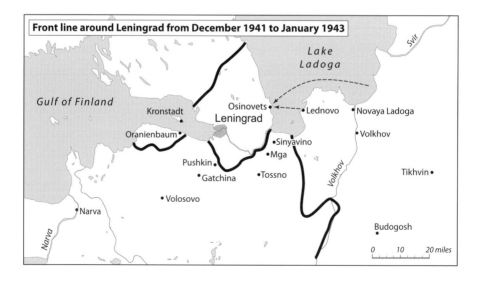

Front line around Leningrad from December 1941 to January 1943

Dr Werner Best on his arrival in Denmark in November 1942. The German plenipotentiary in Denmark, Dr Best had a dual role, in that he had been sent by the German foreign ministry as its formal leader in Denmark and, in addition, had the rank of general as an Obergruppenführer in the SS, in which function he was subordinate to Heinrich Himmler, Reichsführer SS.

The German plenipotentiary in Denmark, Dr Werner Best, had a dual role, in that he had been sent by the German foreign ministry as its formal leader in Denmark and, in addition, had the rank of general as an Obergruppenführer in the SS, in which function he was subordinate to Heinrich Himmler, Reichsführer SS. In the one role, he had to make sure of peace and quiet, so that Germany got the maximum benefit out of Danish agricultural and industrial production and also the support of as large a part of Danish society as possible. In the second role, in relation to the SS, he was responsible for the maintenance of order and discipline – by German standards – which at this time amounted to a very bloody crackdown, including the maintenance of production through coercion, threats and reprisals.

The pocket battleship *Admiral Scheer* came to Copenhagen on a naval visit from 4–10 August 1943. It had previously been stationed in northern Norway, but was now back in the Baltic Sea. At that time, the August revolt in Denmark was, as mentioned, slowly beginning to simmer. The German military commander in Denmark, General Hermann von Hanneken, would have liked to have had the visit postponed until calm had been restored, but Vizeadmiral Wurmbach was of the opposite view. The Danes would benefit from seeing such a show of force as the ship's presence would constitute – and besides, he wanted to see the ship himself, because he had been its commanding officer in the years immediately before the war. There was also a difference of basic perceptions between the general and the admiral. For Wurmbach, the collaboration was going extremely well and, all things considered, the Germans avoided a wide range of maritime roles that would otherwise cost resources and manpower.

On the other side stood General von Hanneken, who wanted the Danish army disarmed. If an Allied landing came on Danish territory, Danish units would be able to co-operate with the Allies and pose a threat to supplies and communications, thereby tying up large numbers of German forces, and he wanted that threat removed. This was the background for Operation Safari, the German operation, which was finally launched by Germany on 29 August 1943. The planning had already begun to take shape in June 1943 and detailed plans were laid in July – directed solely against the Danish army.

At a very late stage, the Germans decided to neutralise the Danish navy too. Vizeadmiral Wurmbach could not inform his subordinate commanders of the plans until 12 August 1943. This planning lasted until 26 August, but at that time the participating ships from Germany had not yet taken their mines on board. The ships at the Holmen base in Copenhagen were to be prevented from escaping to Sweden or Britain. Guns and spotlights were therefore installed on the Customs House and Langelinie Quay, as well as the artillery made ready on the ships moored at Langelinie and at the B&W shipyard opposite.

The Kriegsmarine was to commit troops to the capture of the Holmen base, as well as the ships in the provinces. The Danish army garrisons were to be caught unawares by units from the 166th Division. Operation Safari was going to be launched on 28 August at 0400, but if it could be postponed for twenty-four hours, units of the 25th Panzer Division, which was en route from Norway to northern France, could be deployed in Copenhagen. If these units were to break their journey in Copenhagen, they could reach the city to take part by the morning of 29 August. Torpedo boats would ensure that no ships escaped across the Sound to Sweden. Similarly, there were German torpedo boats in the Great Belt. Minesweepers would be used to mine the exit from Isefjord in north Zealand to prevent the artillery ship *Niels Iuel* escaping. Finally, a north–south chain of VP patrol boats was spread out between the Scaw and the Norwegian coast. They were to observe and report on ship movements. To the west, between Thyborøn in north Jutland and Stavanger in Norway, the submarines *U-309*, *U-643* and *U-841* were in a patrol line, ready to sink any ships bound for Britain. Only the old torpedo boat *Havkatten* (Sea Wolf) and some small minesweepers and naval cutters managed to sail to Sweden.

The commander-in-chief of the Danish navy, Viceadmiral A H Vedel, ordered the sinking of the navy's vessels, so Germany could not use them in warfare. The navy's action was of great importance. This had decisive 'signal value' for Denmark, so that among the Western Allies the view spread that not only was Denmark in its particular situation not wholehearted in its support of the German war machine with its industrial and agricultural products, but active resistance was also being organised.

Danish army garrisons were also attacked and disarmed during 29 August. It resulted in fights at several barracks with deaths on both sides. Personnel from the two services were interned by German forces at Danish military installations until October 1943.

The Danish armour-plated ship *Peder Skram* sunk under the mast crane at Holmen naval base in Copenhagen – an iconic photograph that went round the world. The Danish navy's action was instrumental in Danish merchant ships in Allied service from 25 December 1943 being given permission to sail under the Danish flag.

After the resignation of the elected Danish government on 29 August 1943, Viceadmiral Vedel continued as director of the naval ministry and had a seat in the permanent secretaries' administration, which was a kind of caretaker government, until liberation in 1945.

Because of this work, he could not participate in resistance work, but on his behalf, Kommandørkaptajn Kaj Lundsteen organised some initial resistance activities for Danish navy personnel in an organisation that was called Elverhøj (Elf Hill). Some of the midshipmen were already organised in a resistance organisation called Holger Danske, and some of the regular personnel were part of the BOPA (civil partisans) resistance group. During the last eighteen months or so of the occupation, a very large part of the Danish navy's personnel were active with diverse tasks such as weapons smuggling from Sweden, sabotage, radio communications, liquidation of informers, refugee routes to Sweden, and much more. As the safety of individual members of the resistance eventually became compromised, they typically went to Sweden and became part of the Danish Flotilla, which was the Danish navy's equivalent of the Danish Brigade of military personnel and resistance people in Sweden. Eight naval officers were flown to Britain via Stockholm, where they quickly became part of the Royal Navy and the RAF.

Danish Jews and Communists deported to concentration camps

The German action directed against the Danish Jews took place on the night of 1/2 October 1943. Most of the approximately seven thousand Jews had been warned and were able, within a relatively short time frame, to make it over to Sweden via a network of routes, mainly over the Sound; 481 Jews were arrested and sent to the concentration camp at Theresienstadt in Czechoslovakia. The ship *Wartheland* left from Langelinie in Copenhagen as early as the morning of 2 October with the first 198 Danish Jews to Theresienstadt, and 150 Danish Communists to the concentration camp at Stutthof. In this situation, Germany did not lack shipping tonnage. Here was a German ship with a German crew being requisitioned to carry out one of the regime's less flattering tasks. As the German authorities had not been able to intern as many Jews as expected, the interned Communists from the Horserød internment camp just outside Elsinore were sent instead to help rectify the statistics.

German anti-invasion preparations in Denmark

Coastal batteries, anti-aircraft guns, sea mines, land mines and much more were installed along the whole west coast of Jutland, but there were also large installations on the east side of the Scaw. At Bangsbo in Frederikshavn, a fort was established with the guns from the artillery ship *Niels Iuel*. At Fynshoved on Funen, and Sjællands Odde and Gilleleje on Zealand, powerful coastal batteries were set up. On Nordstranden (North Beach) near Kronborg Castle in Elsinore, three torpedo batteries with wire-guided torpedoes were installed, and at Nivå on the east Zealand coast south of Elsinore, a small battery was established with four 3in/75mm PAK (Panzer Abwehr Kanonen) guns which could be useful in a limited way against targets at sea. Some of the forts around Copenhagen had been manned by German troops and primarily equipped with anti-aircraft guns. All these activities were aimed at a possible invasion by the Western Allies through Danish waters towards German coasts. The German Organisation Todt implemented these major construction projects, which were financed through a special clearing account in the National Bank.[7]

Peenemünde

The Baltic Sea as a firing range for ballistic missiles and pilotless aircraft

In 1936, the German army's missile test project had been moved from Berlin to a new area at Peenemünde on the German Baltic coast. The responsibility for building the facility had been delegated to the Luftwaffe and Organisation Todt. They had built an airfield, laboratories, accommodation and a test rig for rockets. The total area was about 10 square miles/25 sq km. A factory that could produce large quantities of liquid oxygen had also been built and the military area had got its own huge power plant, which was particularly necessary for the production of oxygen; in addition, the whole area had been given its own railway network and then divided in two. To the west lay the Luftwaffe facility, Erprobungsstelle Karlshagen (Karlshagen Test Facility), with an airfield. To the east lay Heeresversuchanstalt Peenemünde (the German army's test facilities). The army wanted to use the 250-mile/400km-long Pomeranian coastline as a firing range, with triangulation stations along the coast. The head of the army's test project was the engineer-trained Major Walter Dornberger (later Generalmajor), who had been in charge of research into rocket technology since 1929, and in 1932, he had hired a young engineer named Werner von Braun. The development of von Braun's A-4 rocket (Aggregate Unit no. 4, later known as the V-2, Vergeltungswaffe 2 (retaliation weapon)) went slowly, and two months after the end of the German campaign in Poland in 1939, Hitler had halved the funding for von

---

7   Under the Danish judicial settlement after the occupation, participation in these projects as a Danish construction worker was not regarded as a criminal act.

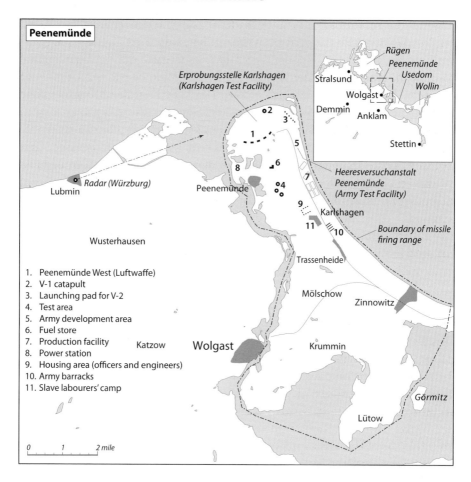

Braun's research because, after all, according to Hitler, the war was almost won now. After the British bombing of Lübeck at Easter 1942, Hitler gave orders to step up the trials with the new weapon. On 3 October 1942, von Braun and his team succeeded in conducting a successful test launch of a V-2 rocket, but the rocket design had not been finalised. On the other hand, both Hitler and Himmler became interested. British intelligence agencies had received sporadic information on the advanced rocket projects, but they did not quite know what they were looking for and where to look.

At the Luftwaffe base, one of the things they were developing was a pilotless aircraft developed by the Fieseler factory, which had been given the designation Fi 103, but it also had another name for the purpose of deception. This was FZG 76, which stood for Flak Ziel Gerät (target drone for anti-aircraft guns). Later, this weapon system became known as the V-1, or Vergeltungswaffe 1.

When Churchill's scientific adviser, Professor R V Jones, could not get all the information he wanted, the engineer in him was aroused: 'I'll just have to count backwards,' he thought. His reasoning was that if the Germans wanted to track these rockets in their trajectory, then it would be carried out by their technical elite. No one else would be able to do it. So he instructed the security agencies to keep an eye on the 14th and 15th companies from the Luftwaffe's experimental signals regiment. After six months of waiting, there was a reward. Some of the units were traced to the island of Rügen, and to Dueodde and Svaneke on the occupied Danish island of Bornholm, and these units had just received the latest version of the Würzburg radar. Germany had a wide range of different monitoring stations on Bornholm. Some were related to the extensive submarine construction and others related to activities in Peenemünde. On 3 and 4 April 1942, Werner von Braun was on the island with two technicians, Dr Ernst Steinhoff, and the engineer Gerhard Reisig.[8] They were going to set up radar stations which could follow the V-2 launches from Peenemünde.

Professor R V Jones also instructed other British organisations to keep an eye out for anything that was related to Peenemünde. One day he received one of the deciphered signals from Bletchley Park analysed by a skilled intelligence officer, who attached great importance to details. It was a fairly insignificant signal on the distribution of petrol rations to authorities subordinate to the Luftwaffe, but the officer had found out that all the Luftwaffe authorities were listed in order of priority. The Luftwaffe's experimental facility in Rechlin, 93 miles/150km north of Berlin stood at no. 1 – and the unknown Peenemünde was listed as no. 2. This was a breakthrough in the argument for looking more closely at Peenemünde – and perhaps for bombing the facilities. Photo-reconnaissance flights were conducted between 22 April and 13 June 1943, and the images revealed large, rocket-like objects.

In the summer of 1943, the RAF prepared to carry out a bombing raid on Peenemünde, but it could not be implemented during the light nights. There had to be a full moon and the darkness had to be so advanced that the bombers could get there and back in the dark. These conditions were met on 17 August 1943, the same day as the USAAF attacked the SKF ball-bearing factories in Schweinfurt in southern Germany.

The bombing raid, Operation Hydra, was organised by the commander-in-chief of Bomber Command, Air Chief Marshal Arthur 'Bomber' Harris RAF: 597 bombers took part in the attack on Peenemünde. The main objective was to kill as many of the rocket specialists as possible. It was the first major operation with a 'master bomber'. This was the mere 29-year-old Group Captain John Henry Searby from 83 Squadron, Pathfinder Force. The master bomber's task

---

8   All three of the engineers later became key figures in the US space programme.

was to stay on the edge of the area throughout the attack – for more than an hour – and direct the target indicator aircraft from the Pathfinder Force towards the target. He had an H2S radar system in his own aircraft and Pathfinder Force dropped some marker flares over the designated target. One of the aircrews from the force, which was also equipped with radar, mistook the small island of Ruden and the north coast of the island of Usedom for the target. Because of this, the aircraft dropped a target indicator flare 1–2 miles/2–3km too far south over some barracks where some of the slave labour lived. Between five and six hundred of these slave labourers, mainly Poles, were unfortunately killed by the bombs from the following attack aircraft. The master bomber had a new flare dropped over the right target and 180 German specialists were killed here. All in all, about 1,800 tonnes of bombs were dropped during the first raid on Peenemünde.

The RAF had developed a deception plan for the attack, Operation Whitebait: that is, a plan for misleading the enemy. Seventy-five minutes before the main force came in over Peenemünde, eight Mosquito fighter-bombers from 139 Squadron carried out a raid on Berlin. Germany knew that a major attack was under way, but the target was unknown and the Mosquitoes were supposed to attract all the German fighter strength. In July and August, Bomber Harris had had a number of Mosquitoes carry out nightly raids against Berlin, but their path always came in over Peenemünde, so air alarms were not something the people there reacted to.

When the Mosquitoes flew in over Berlin, there were 158 German night-fighters over the area, and fifty-five day-fighters were on their way. They were, moreover, the same day-fighters that had been involved in the fighting earlier in the day over the SKF ball-bearing factory in Schweinfurt. Just as they were running out of fuel and would have to land, the RAF began the raid on Peenemünde. The German air defence summoned extra fighters from Jagel in Schleswig and from Kastrup in Copenhagen. On the outward journey, the RAF did not lose many aircraft because of the deception plan, but on the trip home, the force suffered greatly, losing a total of forty aircraft, each with a crew of about seven men.

Bornholm lay close to the test firings, and on 18 July 1943, the German anti-aircraft guns in Svaneke had shot down an unidentified aircraft. The search for the aircraft was stopped on the orders of Suchleitung Swinemünde (the search headquarters at Swinemünde – now Polish Świnoujście). It had been a stray V-1 rocket.

Five days after the bombing raid, the commanding officer of Bornholm's naval district, Kaptajnløjtnant Christian W T Hasager Christiansen, was called out to something that looked like a crashed aircraft. He managed to photograph the object before German troops arrived at the scene. On 22 August 1943, an early prototype of the V-1 had crashed at Bodilsker and Hasager Christiansen's photographs and report reached Professor R V Jones. Five copies of the report and photographs were made: Professor Jones received three sets via different channels. He noted drily that someone must have been determined that the information should reach the British. This episode is thus later than Operation Hydra, but the target in the latter was von Braun and his V-2 rockets. The bombing raid had not struck the Luftwaffe's V-1 production. Both the RAF and the USAAF thereafter bombed Peenemünde several times, but it did not stop the production of the retaliatory weapon, which was now mostly being carried out in mountain mines, such as those at Nordhausen south of Harzen.

Spring 1943: Gulf of Finland blocked

The background to the Nashorn minefield and the Walross anti-submarine net

Now the Gulf of Finland was to be blocked. Germany and Finland had earlier laid a minefield across the Gulf of Finland. It had the code name Seeigel (Sea Urchin) and went from the Finnish archipelago east of Hogland and the Tytärsaari islands down to Cape Kurgalovo, but it had proved to be insufficient. In the spring of 1943, this minefield was supplemented by an additional 1,737 mines, including 482 magnetic and acoustic mines.

This new combined barrage would keep Soviet submarines trapped east of a line between Porkkala and Naisaar off Tallinn, and consisted of a combination of nets and mines. The net barrier went under the code name Walross (Walrus). It consisted of two parallel submarine nets, 330ft/100m apart, with a mesh of 13ft x 13ft (4m x 4m), where the net stretched from the surface to the seabed. The maximum depth of the barrier was 302ft/92m and there was an underwater ridge in the middle of the barrier. East of the nets, Germany and Finland laid the Nashorn (Rhinoceros) minefield with around seven thousand German mines, of which 3,120 were magnetic mines. There were large horn mines, anchored magnetic mines and magnetic ground mines in the minefield, which was constantly guarded by between fifteen and twenty *Kriegsfischerkutter* (KFK), which were armed trawlers.

The minefield had to be established as soon as the ice broke up in the spring of 1943, and the work had already started on 28 March 1943. The anti-submarine nets across the Gulf of Finland would have to be towed back before the ice covered the waters once more in the coming winter. The minefield was 30 nautical miles (about 55km) long and proved to be effective. Soviet forces did nothing to prevent the laying and three Soviet submarines are known to have been lost while attempting to force the barrier. No submarines slipped through it, but there were probably three submarines which instead slipped outside it and into the Baltic Sea in 1943. They sneaked along the seabed outside the northern end of the minefield, but they were all sunk in a relatively short space of time. At this time, the Swedish government was no longer allowing German rail transports through Sweden, so Germany had to carry out these transports by ship, which meant they would now be more vulnerable to submarine attack. With the Nashorn and Walross barrage, the maritime traffic and supply lines in the Baltic were made more secure for Germany and Finland, but otherwise time was not on their side.

Two Soviet POWs informed the Finns about the way Soviet submarines had tried to force the submarine minefields. One of them had been in the conning tower when his submarine dived and he was fished out by the Finns. The second man was a petty officer called Galkin on board *Shch-303*. He performed a consummate – and spectacular – defection in May 1943 by locking the crew inside the submarine, bringing the submarine to the surface, jumping into the water and swimming over to the nearby guard vessels. The Soviet submarine had dived again before an attack on it could be implemented. Galkin, in particular, was very willing to answer questions about Soviet attempts to get past the minefield. The prisoners stated that the submarines were equipped with wooden fenders which were supposed to insulate them from contact mines. The wooden fenders were screwed into the hull of the submarines. An additional wooden beam was screwed onto the outside of the fenders with short screws into the wood – without touching the metal hull. The screw heads were countersunk to avoid completely any metallic contact with anchored mines, their antennae and anchor cables. When breaking out, the submarines sneaked along the bottom at 2 knots (3–4kph). When the Soviet submarines launched a breakout attempt, diversions were undertaken, such as torpedo boat raids or air raids with as many as seventy naval aircraft.

From the autumn of 1943, Germany and Finland were faced with an unexpected problem. They lost air superiority to the Soviet Union, which could then send minesweepers in to sweep the minefields at the eastern end of the Gulf of Finland. Defending the minefields thereby became very costly for the Finnish and German patrol boats. Among other things, the Finnish gunboat *Turunmaa* was damaged, and the increased Soviet activity with torpedo boats led to the loss of the Finnish minesweeper *Riilahti*, in which twenty-four crew members were killed. In the spring of 1944, this problem became even more intense. From the spring of 1944, Germany therefore introduced a system whereby German submarines guarded the minefields by day and surface ships guarded them by night. Because of the rivalry between forces and differences in operational priority – and not least the lack of aviation fuel – the Luftwaffe's aircraft were not deployed.

The River Narva runs between the Estonian town Narva with Hermann Castle (left) and the Russian Ivangorod Fortress on the other side. The first castle on the Estonian side was founded by the Danish king in 1256 and the first castle on the Russian side by Tsar Ivan III in 1492. In the border town of Narva in spring 1944, the stubborn German defence and the many Soviet attacks resulted in severe damage to the built-up area, including the two castles. (SMB arkiv)

The Soviet Baltic Fleet air force

The Baltic Fleet air force was expanded to 940 aircraft in 1943, and in March 1943 it began to receive numerous American-produced Douglas A-20 Boston aircraft that could be armed with bombs or mines.[9] Some of the aircraft were converted to carry two Soviet 36AN torpedoes with a diameter of 17in/45cm. They were a threat to German shipping all the way down to Libau. Losses among the torpedo-carrying aircraft were very great. German shipping was a profitable target in the economic warfare against the country: by sinking merchant ships in the Baltic Sea, industrial production could be put under strain, fuel supplies and personnel transports impeded, and other logistical resources hindered. In this way, the Soviet Union could now also directly participate in the destruction of the German production facilities which had been subjected to raids by Allied bombers for some time. The lack of supplies and resources began to place restrictions on the German war machine.

Finland's complicated situation

Finland had been following the German defeats in the Soviet Union during 1943, first at Stalingrad and later at Kursk, with some concern. In the autumn

---

9   This was a twin-engine US-built aircraft which the Russians received more of than the Americans. In the US, the aircraft was usually referred to as the Havoc, but the Russians used the British name 'Boston'.

of 1943, a Finnish delegation sought an audience with the Soviet ambassador in Stockholm, Madame Alexandra Kollontai, to discuss the possibilities of peace. Finland was worried, among other things, that German forces would leave Leningrad because of Soviet pressure and pull back to the Panther Line, which was a defensive line that followed the Narva river from the south coast of the Gulf of Finland all the way down to a point approximately 100 miles/175km south of Lake Peipsi. If the German forces were to do that, then Finland could have a problem holding its defensive lines on the Karelian Isthmus.

Soviet forces break the siege of Leningrad

The Soviet forces were organised in fronts. They continually changed name and number during the war. A front could include forces from the Red Army and the navy. There was no independent air force and the army and the navy each possessed its own air force: a front thus included two or more armies with their air forces, and possibly also naval forces. Around the turn of the year 1943/44, the forces in and around Leningrad were organised in the Leningrad Front. South of that were the forces of the Volkhov Front and still further south, the 2nd Baltic Front. Against them was the German Army Group North.

Detailed plans for the breakout from Leningrad were ready in September 1943. Govorov was now appointed Colonel-General of Artillery and Party Secretary Zhdanov contacted Stalin to help him procure battle-decisive equipment for the operation. Colonel-General Govorov was given 1,240,000 men at his disposal. During the Leningrad siege, Soviet forces had control of a small area southwest of Leningrad. The front was not further away than could be reached by tram, line 9, out to the front – that is, when there was electric power for the tramways. Approximately 18 miles/30km west of here, on the southern shore of the Gulf, the German forces had a headquarters at Peterhof, the old tsar's palace. Here they had control over a stretch of the coast. West of this lay the Oranienbaum pocket (Oranienbaum is also referred to as Lomonosov in Russian), which was the name of the coastal area the German forces had never managed to capture. It was an isolated area on the south coast of the Gulf of Finland, where the bay is very narrow on the last stretch towards Leningrad. Unseen by the Germans, there was now a build-up of Soviet forces in this area. Between 5 November 1943 and 14 January 1944, Colonel-General Govorov built up a force here from the 2nd Shock Army[10] of 44,000 men. Supplies arrived at night and the ships had to be gone again

---

10 The 2nd Shock Army had been recreated after being wiped out in June 1942 on the Volkhov/Leningrad Front. The commanding officer at that time, Lieutenant-General

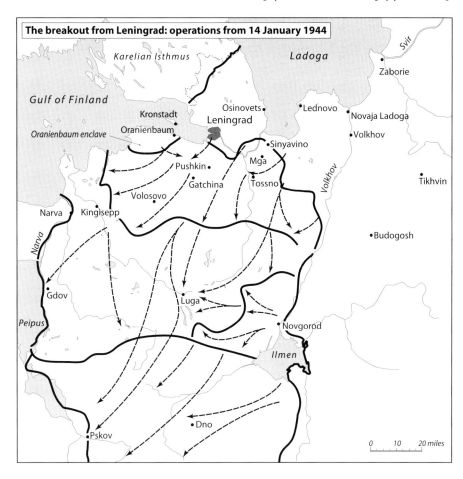

before dawn. The Baltic Fleet was responsible for these transports. Over 200 tanks, 650 artillery pieces, 2,400 vehicles, 6,000 horses and 30,000 tonnes of ammunition and other supplies for the army were delivered. Later, the troops could walk over the ice.

When the final breakout from Leningrad came on 14 January 1944, it started with an artillery bombardment and a breakout from the Oranienbaum pocket that was primarily directed towards Narva in the southwest. The following day, the breakout from Leningrad itself began. The Soviet Baltic Fleet supported the breakout with artillery fire from the ships in Kronstadt harbour and along the Neva river within the city. The vessels fired a total of 24,000 shells. The total Soviet ammunition consumption on 15 January was

---

Andrei Andreyevich Vlasov went into service for Germany and led the units manned by Soviet prisoners. He was hanged in the Lubyanka gaol in Moscow on 2 August 1946.

200,000 shells. The old battleship *Marat*, which stood on the harbour bottom at Kronstadt, had managed to fire 1,971 12in/305mm shells between 1942 and the breakout in January 1944. Officially, the Leningrad siege ended on 27 January 1944 after 871 days. The embattled and under-equipped German forces retreated to positions around Narva. The Soviet Union had now also wrested air superiority from the Luftwaffe over the land-based battlefields. Now the Soviet forces could muster 1,200 aircraft belonging to the 13th Air Army, the 14th Air Army, the 2nd Guards Fighter Corps and the Baltic Fleet Air Force.

The 13th Air Army under Colonel-General Stepan Dmitriyevich Rybalchenko offered close air support to two armies of the Leningrad Front: the 2nd Shock Army and the 42nd Army. Their first task was to try to encircle the German forces in Krasnoye Selo, Ropsha and Strelna. Afterwards, they had to move on towards Gatchina, about 28 miles/45km south of Leningrad and Kingisepp, east of Narva. The German forces had military headquarters in both of the two old tsar's palaces in Tsarskoye Selo and Gatchina.[11] Both palaces suffered massive damage during the Soviet advance.[12]

The 14th Air Army under Lieutenant-General Ivan Petrovich Zhuravlev provided close air support to the 59th Army of the Volkov Front, which was to advance against Novgorod and Luga. In the beginning, the Soviet attack went well, but bad flying weather delayed the destruction of the German artillery, which was the main target. When Mga was recaptured, the normal rail link between Leningrad and Moscow could be restored. In addition to lifting the siege of Leningrad, the overall Soviet plan was to encircle the northern of the two German armies, the 18th Army, so that the Leningrad Front and the Volkhov Front could push the German forces back over the Narva river. After this, the Volkhov Front was to push westwards from Novgorod and wedge itself between the 16th and 18th armies, which were the two German armies which formed Army Group North's forces south of Leningrad. Together they had over forty infantry divisions at their disposal, but no tank divisions. Some fierce fighting arose; the 18th Army alone suffered more than fifty thousand dead and wounded within two weeks. The commander-in-chief of Army Group North had visited Hitler several times prior to the attack and he was well aware that Hitler wanted counter-attacks and offensive warfare, not retreats. Von Küchler tried to

---

11 Following the assassination of Tsar Alexander II in 1883, the new tsar's family (Alexander III and his Danish-born tsarina) moved to Gatchina, where they would be more secure than in St Petersburg.

12 The panels in the Amber Room at the imperial Catherine Palace were removed by the German forces and brought to Königsberg, but from here, all trace of them has been lost. The castle has been rebuilt and a new Amber Room has been installed. Gatchina is slowly being brought back to its former glory, but it will take a few more years.

persuade his chief of staff, General der Infanterie Eberhard Kinzel, to make a number of counter-attacks, but instead the chief of staff explained to the commander-in-chief that if they did not retreat to the Panther Line, the 18th Army would be wiped out. After this, von Küchler visited Hitler again. On 30 January 1944, Hitler lost patience and replaced him with Generalfeldmarschall Walter Model.

On the night of 13/14 February 1944, the Soviet 260th Marine Infantry Brigade undertook a landing operation on a beach about 12 miles/20km west of Narva, near Mereküla. The operation was part of other Soviet operations in the Narva area. The German commanders had prior knowledge of the action from the interrogation of prisoners and it ended with the annihilation of almost the entire 517-man force. Only a few managed to escape into the cover of a small nearby forest. Danish Waffen-SS units took part in this action on the German side. The commanding officer of the SS-Kampfgruppe Küste by the Estonian coast was the Danish Oberstløjtnant Christian Peder Kryssing,[13] who was now an SS Brigadeführer.

The Kriegsmarine in the Baltic Sea

In the spring of 1943, the aircraft carrier *Graf Zeppelin* returned to Stettin. It had been in Kiel in 1942 when work on it had been resumed, but now it had again been stopped again due to lack of shipbuilding materials.

In September 1943, Grossadmiral Dönitz discussed with Hitler whether to have the damaged battleship *Tirpitz* come in to a shipyard in the Baltic Sea, but it remained in northern Norway. The heavy cruiser *Prinz Eugen* was supposed to have replaced *Tirpitz*. Dönitz was summoned by Hitler on 13 February 1944 and questioned about whether the navy could support the army's defensive battle in Estonia. The next day, the Kriegsmarine sent the pocket battleship *Admiral Scheer*, the heavy cruiser *Prinz Eugen*, two destroyers and six torpedo boats to the Gulf of Finland. Army Group North had advised that there was no need for larger German warships, unless similar Soviet warships showed up to support the Red Army operations. In mid-March 1944, the Kriegsmarine sent three destroyers, Z25, Z28 and Z39 a long way into the Gulf. Their task was to support the withdrawal operations of the German army units near Hungerburg (Narva-Joesuu, 8 miles/13km northwest of Narva) by firing on the advancing Soviet forces with their heavy ship's artillery.

---

13 Kryssing was Frikorps Danmark's first commander-in-chief in 1941 and, after the occupation, he was sentenced to four years in prison. He became the highest ranking SS officer in the Nordic countries. Both of his sons fell on the Eastern Front, in 1942 and 1944 respectively.

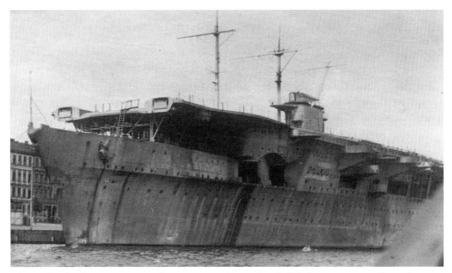

The unfinished German aircraft carrier *Graf Zeppelin*. (Old Ship Picture Galleries)

Fire support for the army from a German heavy cruiser of the *Admiral Hipper* class (*Admiral Hipper* or *Prinz Eugen*) in the final months of the war. *Admiral Hipper* was severely damaged on 9 April 1945 in Kiel by an RAF raid, and *Prinz Eugen* was berthed in Copenhagen Freeport at the end of the war.

German intelligence reports, which came from POW interrogations, among other sources, confirmed that the Soviet Union had increased the number of submarines in the Leningrad area, so that they would be able to send a large number of submarines into the Baltic Sea after the breakout. They had been brought in via the Ladoga Canal and the Volkhov river.

Army Group North's fear of further landing operations resulted in a heightened readiness from the Kriegsmarine, which also included the German submarines under training in the Baltic Sea. Dönitz took the opportunity to warn that if the army withdrew from Narva, then it would be difficult to keep the Soviet Baltic Fleet trapped in Kronstadt and Leningrad. The German marshals and generals were well aware of the problem that Dönitz was outlining for them. If the Soviet ships came out into the Baltic Sea, the army's operations in the coastal areas would be threatened by the Soviet ships' artillery. Grossadmiral Dönitz promised the army that the Finnish-German minefields would be supplemented as soon as the ice disappeared from the Gulf of Finland. Soviet submarines posed a particular problem for supply lines at sea. Finland would be difficult to supply and thereby maintained as a combatant. Supplies of iron ore from Sweden would be interrupted, and ultimately the assembling of the new German submarine forces would be delayed. The Kriegsmarine now had a noticeable lack of escort vessels and fuel.

The Soviet offensive

The battles in the Narva region surged back and forth for long periods and, while Hitler was putting pressure on his marshals and generals, Stalin was putting pressure on Colonel-General Govorov. From a political and military point of view, it was important to capture Narva no later than 17 February 1944, said Stalin.[14] The Soviets made numerous unsuccessful attempts to capture Narva in both February and March. As the winter went over to thaw and mud – *rasputitsa* season – the fighting throughout the area ground to a halt. It could not be resumed until late May. Hitler had already designated Narva as a 'stronghold', or 'fortress town', on 23 March 1944. This meant that it should be kept in German hands at all costs. The German forces now dug themselves into their Panther Line and, as far as possible, provided replacements for the lost forces. Generalfeldmarschall Model was now sent further south and, on 31 March 1944, Generaloberst Lindemann took command of Army Group North.

---

14 Stalin became very displeased if his commanders did not meet the deadlines he had assigned them and this is one of the reasons why the Soviet military commanders sacrificed large forces to senseless attacks, just to try to comply with the deadlines.

Colonel-General Georg Lindemann was commanding the 18th Army south of Leningrad and from 31 March 1944 was commander-in-chief of Army Group North and later Wehrmachtsbefehlshaber Dänemark, the last supreme commander of German forces in Denmark. (SMB arkiv)

A significant part of the German resistance consisted of Waffen-SS units under Obergruppenführer Felix Steiner, who was one of Germany's most legendary, dynamic and talented commanders. The force was concentrated in III SS Panzer Corps, which had a large element of enlisted foreigners from occupied countries. They were supported by the German 5th SS Artillery Regiment. Even though the soldiers came from many different Waffen-SS units, the troops constituted an elite among the German forces. The Soviet attack was naturally directed at the corps' weakest link, made up of two infantry divisions from the Luftwaffe,[15] and they were unable to withstand the Soviet pressure. Army Group North then had to implement a rapid retreat towards the Narva river, which was the old border river between Russia and Estonia.[16] The Soviet forces managed to cross the river with significant forces,

---

15 The infantry divisions from the Luftwaffe were far from being professionals, and when the Waffen-SS units saw their defensive, dug-in installations, called them '*Luftwaffe Ferienwohnungen*' (the Luftwaffe's holiday apartments).

16 The Narva river was the original boundary marker between the Catholic Church and the Russian Orthodox Church in the Middle Ages. To the east is the Russian fortress of Ivangorod and, opposite it, a Swedish fortress was built in the sixteenth century, but

but on 29 February 1944, the newly established Estonian 20th Waffen-SS Grenadier Division was among those which counter-attacked. However, the Russians held the bridgehead.

Between 7 June and 12 June 1944, the Danish Waffen-SS units were among those which were exposed to fierce attacks. Steiner was aware that his staffing resources were constantly being thinned out and therefore began an extension of Tannenbergstellung (the Tannenberg defence line), while the Dutch, Estonian and Danish SS forces around Narva held out. On 23 July, Steiner, despite Hitler's orders 'to hold Narva or die', decided to fall back to his newly established Tannenbergstellung. Otherwise, he risked being surrounded by the numerous, and now very mobile, Soviet forces.

Colonel-General Govorov followed up with an attack on Steiner's retreating forces the very next day, 24 July, during which he was able to deploy 800 tactical aircraft from the 13th Air Army, while the German commanders could only scrape together 137 aircraft from Luftflotte 1 (Air Fleet 1). The Dutch Waffen-SS forces had to cover the crossing at the Narva Bridge. The bridge was subsequently blown up by the retreating Germans. The Soviet forces had used large resources and suffered heavy losses without encircling Steiner's forces. He had certainly retreated, but his forces were not wiped out.

The top German military leadership

During the Allied advance in Italy in 1943, Hitler frequently conferred with Generalfeldmarschall Albert Kesselring, the German military commander of the Mediterranean, and with Grossadmiral Karl Dönitz. The discussions were concerned with where the Allies would strike next. Would it be the Balkans, southern France, the Channel coast or Norway? Hitler listened to the advice of these two, while being extremely sceptical about advice from his other military commanders. Dönitz had replaced Grossadmiral Erich Raeder on 30 January 1943, as a result of Hitler's outbreak of rage after the battle in the Barents Sea over the New Year 1942/43. Hitler's instructions had been that the large ships were not to expose themselves to danger – and thus the aggressive British force commander, Captain Robert St Vincent Sherbrooke RN succeeded in reaching Murmansk with his convoy and an inferior escort.

---

hegemony over the west bank has changed, with Danish, Polish and German armies also being in the ascendancy at different times.

The Royal Air Force steps up operations in the Baltic Sea

In the autumn of 1942, Germany demanded that Danish merchant ships in the North Sea were armed with anti-aircraft guns. This resulted in a crisis between the Danish sailors on the one side, and the German authorities on the other. The sailors did not want to contribute actively to shooting down RAF aircraft. They were angry enough at being singled out as targets by the RAF. The German demand was then dropped.

On 27 January 1943, the RAF attacked the B&W engine factory in Copenhagen harbour. It also affected the nearby sugar factory and residential area, but extensive damage was inflicted on the production of diesel engines. A total of ten civilians were killed in the raid, which was one of the very few Allied air raids against a Danish industrial target.

In 1943, the RAF was mostly targeting German industrial cities, but a number of flights were assigned to dropping mines in the eastern part of the Baltic Sea. On the night of 20/21 April 1943, the port city of Stettin was subjected to an air raid by 339 bombers, twenty-one of which were lost.

With the introduction of the long-range Lancaster bomber, the RAF had been able to drop mines as far away as Danzig Bay since 1943. In 1943, they dropped a modest number of mines, but in 1944 the number was increased. The purpose of the minelaying was to prevent and delay German submarine training. German submarine production was reduced by extensive RAF raids targeting shipyards, especially in Kiel. Stettin was again subjected to attacks from the RAF on the night of 5/6 January 1944; 358 aircraft took part, of which sixteen were lost. On the night of 16/17 August 1944, there was a renewed attack with 461 bombers.

A major minelaying operation on 25 February 1944 consisted of ninety-four aircraft from Bomber Command, which were carrying a total of 376 mines. The British minelaying campaign was effective, and the target areas were continuously switched. Sometimes it was directed against German troop transports from Aarhus in Jutland to Norway. Then later it could be against shipping in the Sound and in the Fehmarn Belt. The mines were constantly being improved and modified, and the only effective weapons against the minelaying operations were night-fighters that could shoot down the heavy, four-engined bombers before they dropped their cargo. The Kriegsmarine used this argument to arrange for the injection of additional night-fighters into Danish airspace.

On 22 May 1944, the RAF carried out another major minelaying operation with eighty-eight aircraft. A smaller force of twenty-three aircraft dropped mines in the Kattegat, while the main force of sixty-five aircraft dropped their cargo in the Bay of Kiel. The mines were intended for German submarines which were going to be transferred from Kiel to bases in Norway after training. Towards the end of the war, there were about a hundred minesweepers working exclusively in the Bay of Kiel to keep a route open, primarily for the submarines.

Admiral Skagerrak

The organisation of the German navy in Denmark was changed on 15 April 1944. Admiral Wurmbach changed his title from Kommandierender Admiral Dänemark (Commanding Admiral for Denmark) to Admiral Skagerrak. In late May, his organisation moved with all its security flotillas – now combined under the 8th Security Division – to a newly built bunker facility in Havreballe forest near Marselisborg in Aarhus.[17]

The progress of the war in broad terms up until the summer of 1944

The Western Allies had won the Battle of the Atlantic against the German submarines in May 1943 and the submarine threat was now declining rapidly. Dönitz demanded that submarine production reached forty submarines per month and that it was to be placed under Armaments Minister Speer, which Hitler approved on 31 May 1943. Production should preferably be of the new Type XXI and Type XXIII submarines.

Around the time of the Battle of Stalingrad, Stalin changed the reference points surrounding the war for the Russian population. Now it was no longer a matter of purely Communist concern, but of national revival. The Russian Orthodox Church was given a freer hand and in Leningrad, the church repaid this by raising money for a large number of tanks and aircraft. The armed forces introduced uniforms that recalled the old tsarist uniforms, and the people were reminded of past national heroes such as Alexander Nevsky,[18] Kuzma Minin, Dmitry Pozharsky,[19] Alexander Suvorov[20] and Mikhail Kutuzov.[21] The officers in the Red Army wanted the role of the political

---

17 Since 1961, the bunker facility has served as the operations room of the Admiral Danish Fleet (the operationally supreme organisation of the Royal Danish Navy).

18 Russia's national hero and prince of Novgorod. Defeated the Swedish warrior Birger Jarl at Neva in 1240 and the Teutonic Order on the ice of Lake Peipus in 1242.

19 Kuzma Minin and Dmitry Pozharsky liberated Moscow in 1612 from the Polish-Lithuanian occupation since 1610.

20 Count Alexander Suvorov, a field marshal who never lost a battle. Captured Warsaw in 1795, died in 1800.

21 General Mikhail Kutuzov was Napoleon's opponent in 1812.

commissars trimmed and the latter now had less influence on operational matters. After a somewhat dubious start in 1941, since 1943 the Soviet forces had had extremely competent leaders in the heavy posts. Discipline in the Red Army was incredibly tough. Neither Stalin nor Marshal Zhukov pulled any punches when results were evaluated. If an order had been received to advance, unexpectedly tough resistance was not an argument for slowing down, and people thereby became concerned with the concept of 'cowardice'. It is reported that 251 Soviet generals were 'liquidated because of cowardice' during the war.

In January/February 1943, the German forces at Stalingrad surrendered. A quarter of a million men from the Wehrmacht had been killed or taken prisoner. Stalin had not mentioned anything to his allies about the offensive in November 1942, and did not do anything in the first days thereafter. The Western Allies – and Germany – could find out for themselves. In July and August 1943, the world's largest tank battle took place at Kursk, and although the German forces took some big risks and inflicted great losses on the Soviets, they did not win this battle. The German army suffered a severe blow at Kursk, from which it never recovered.

During the sailing of a convoy with supplies to Murmansk, the Royal Navy sank the German battleship *Scharnhorst* on 26 December 1943 and, apart from the battleship *Tirpitz*, most of the Kriegsmarine's large surface vessels were now to be found in the Baltic Sea.

With the breakout from Leningrad, Finland's situation began to be threatened, because if the German forces retreated too far in Estonia, Finland would be unable to defend itself. If air supremacy switched to the Soviet Union, it would not be possible to defend the minefields and barriers over the Gulf of Finland. Soviet naval forces would therefore be able to sweep routes through the minefields and send submarines and surface ships into the Baltic Sea to attack shipping from Germany, Finland and Sweden.

The people of the three Baltic countries had experienced a period under Stalin's rule up until 1941, and they were now dreading the Red Army's return to the area. Local people volunteered for the Waffen-SS, or were forcibly conscripted into the service or as labour in Germany.

In 1944, the Western Allies increased their supplies to the Soviet Union. In addition to outright arms assistance, the Russians received many other supplies, including trucks, locomotives and food.

The build-up of forces in southern England increased strongly from the second half of 1943 and during the spring of 1944, the United States and Britain built a mighty military capability here. Germany knew in the spring of 1944 that there were large forces ready in the south of England, but it did not know when and where they would strike.

Stalin had long pleaded for a second front, so the Eastern Front could be relieved. There is no doubt that the Soviet Union had borne the greatest burden in this war. In June 1944, the German army was able to muster 360 divisions and, of them, 212 were on the Eastern Front. On the other hand, Stalin at this time felt safe in the saddle. He had not been able to do that for good reason in 1941 and 1942, but Germany was now on the retreat everywhere. Germany had suffered particularly heavy losses on the Eastern Front. The Red Army had called up not only many millions of young men, but also many millions of middle-aged men, and now there were also large numbers of soldiers coming from the non-European Soviet states. These were people who did not have Russian as their mother tongue – or maybe did not speak Russian at all.

Stalin had planned an ambitious campaign, which in many respects exceeded the planned invasion of the continent by the Western Allies, and the consequence was another disaster for the German forces.

8

Towards the End

Spring 1944 – New Year 1944/45

The war in a broader perspective

June 1944 was a rather turbulent month for the German military leadership. If the Western Allies implemented an invasion on the Channel coast, Germany would try to defeat the invasion force *in situ*, which would not by any means be an impossible task for them. After such a defeat, the Western Allies would not be able to implement a new invasion for a considerable period of time – maybe a few years – and Germany could then transfer large military forces to the Eastern Front and regain the initiative there. The great invasion of Normandy took place on 6 June 1944. At a meeting on 10 June, it had already become clear to the Germans that the Allies had gained a foothold on the Channel coast and the chances of driving them into the sea were now minimal. Generalfeldmarschall Keitel believed that German forces could instead hold the Allies at bay at the Westwall (the western rampart of the Siegfried Line), but this view was not shared by his chief of staff, Generaloberst Jodl. Dönitz thought that if the Western Allies succeeded in extending their beachhead, Germany would lose the whole of France. Hitler was aware that Germany had plenty of 'room' (territory) on the Eastern Front to retreat into. The same did not apply to Western Europe, where retreat could directly threaten Germany's existence.

Hitler had long perceived Norway as a 'zone of destiny' and Britain had realised this from reading German signals traffic. In the big deception plan, Operation Fortitude, which was intended to make Germany think that the invasion would take place somewhere else and later than Operation Overlord, a fictitious plan for an Allied attack on Norway was included, and feelers were put out to the Swedish authorities for support and co-operation. Intelligence on this was received by Hitler.

The Eastern Front in the summer of 1944: Operation Bagration

Stalin had for some time been planning an operation of unprecedented magnitude in the central part of the Eastern Front. The ambitious goal of

Operation Bagration[1] was nothing less than the destruction of Army Group Centre (Heeresgruppe Mitte), that is, the central one of the three German army groups which represented the German Eastern Front. This was the Soviet Union's major offensive of 1944 and it was scheduled to start on 20 June 1944. It started with two days' delay on 22 June 1944, the third anniversary precisely of the German attack on the Soviet Union.

Army Group Centre was centred on Minsk in Belarus and was at that time under the command of Generalfeldmarschall Walter Model. At his disposal, he had the 2nd, 4th and 9th armies and the III Panzer Army, with 1,200,000

---

1   Named after the Georgian prince and national hero Pyotr Bagration. He was a general and was badly wounded during the fighting against Napoleon in 1812 at Borodino, west of Moscow. He later died of his wounds.

men and 1,000 tanks divided into fifty divisions. The Luftwaffe could support the army units with 1,400 fighters. Model was faced by four Soviet fronts (listed from north to south): the 1st Baltic Front, the 3rd Belarusian Front, the 2nd Belarusian Front and the 1st Belarusian Front. When the Red Army carried out major attacks at the end of the war, it would typically take three to four months to organise an attack and move the logistics forward, at the same time as using *maskirovka* to carry out deception and camouflage. The reason was that railways, bridges and roads did not exist in the area. The infrastructure had to be established or re-established. The actual attack often died out after about three weeks and then the building of logistics began for the next attack. On the other hand, the German armies were subjected to an overwhelmingly superior force in the actual attack phase. This was often with fierce 'preparatory fire' where everything in the Soviet artillery was deployed, according to a detailed plan for mortars, guns, howitzers and rocket launchers.

Despite huge Soviet losses, Operation Bagration went largely according to plan and, by 13 July 1944, it was difficult to say that Army Group Centre still existed. The remnants of the German forces were driven into the former Baltic states and on to former Polish territory, and the Soviet forces were soon at the German border in East Prussia. During that summer, the Soviet Union sent hundreds of thousands of German prisoners of war on foot through Minsk and Moscow, so that the people could have confirmation of the success of the Red Army. After the large numbers of Germans had been marched past the urban populations, the streets – in a symbolic act by the regime – were flushed clean by large water trucks.

Finland finds itself hard-pressed in the summer of 1944

At the beginning of June, before launching Operation Bagration, the Soviet Union had launched an offensive against the Finnish forces on the Karelian Isthmus. Here Finland had over six divisions, 300 Finnish aircraft and a small number of German planes from Luftflotte 1 (Air Fleet 1) at its disposal. Its defensive line was strongest around Viipuri (now Vyborg). The Soviet attack was probably started at precisely that point in time in order to blur the picture for the German command before the large-scale offensive further south on 22 June. The Soviet Union had prepared well and flown 610 reconnaissance missions to establish an overview of the Finnish defence preparations. After this, 215 bombers and 155 close air support fighters attacked, followed by the 21st Army led by General Dmitry Nikolayevich Gusev. This attack ran along an approximately 9-mile/15km-wide zone in the western part of the isthmus, where the large vessels from the Baltic Fleet could support the Red Army operations with long-range artillery. Further east, the 23rd Army under Lieutenant-General Alexander Ivanovich Cherepanov advanced towards Lake Suvanto and Lake Vuoksi (now Russian, Sukhodolskoye Ozero and Vuoksa Ozero). Both these generals were under Colonel-General Govorov's Leningrad Front. In less than a week, the Russians had captured two of the three Finnish defensive lines. The Finnish forces were hard-pressed and, on 12 June 1944, they asked Germany for help. Germany had intercepted the Finnish peace overtures to the Soviet Union in April 1944 and from that point had stopped arms exports. Germany immediately repealed its arms embargo, but with the proviso that if Finland should again seek to make contact with the Russians on a separate peace treaty, then deliveries would cease once more. For the same reason, the German Foreign Minister Joachim von Ribbentrop came to Helsinki on 22 June 1944 to tie Finland closer to Germany and President Ryti promised on 26 June that Finland would not begin separate peace negotiations without German consent.

The goal for the 21st Army was Viipuri. When the Soviet offensive began, the Germans deployed Jagdgeschwader 54, a fighter wing of the Luftwaffe, with new Focke-Wulf Fw 190 fighters and some Ju 87 Stukas from Schlachtgeschwader 1 ground attack wing to the area. From 23 June until 3

When the Soviet offensive towards Viipuri began, the Germans deployed Jagdgeschwader 54 (fighter wing) with new Focke-Wulf Fw 190 fighters and some Stuka Ju 87s from Schlachtgeswader 1 (ground attack wing 1) to the area. It was named the Kuhlmeyer Group after the commanding officer (Oberstleutnant Kurt Kuhlmey, Luftwaffe). (SA-Kuva)

September 1944, German equipment aid came to Finland: forty-seven tanks and self-propelled artillery pieces, fifty anti-tank guns, eighty-eight artillery pieces with 184,000 shells, eighty-eight anti-aircraft guns, 24,112 Panzerfaust and 16,602 Panzerschreck. The last two were portable anti-tank weapons (of the Bazooka type). In addition, the Finnish forces received 4 million bullets for small arms ammunition. In the light of Germany's beleaguered military situation in the summer and autumn of 1944, the delivery was a rather generous gesture to Finland. Marshal Mannerheim had asked Hitler for six divisions. Hitler however could only afford a single division, which was ordered to Finland from Army Group North's area on 20 June. When Viipuri fell to the Russians on 21 June 1944, it was a severe blow for Finnish morale. In the following weeks, the Finns stopped the Soviet onslaught with a tremendous effort in the battles at Tali-Ihantala, which represented the fiercest fighting ever in the Nordic region. The Finnish forces were now concentrated west of Viipuri with half of the available Finnish artillery. In early July, the Finnish army intercepted a Soviet signal indicating an impending Soviet attack to be carried out by the 63rd Division and the 30th Tank Brigade. The attack was to be launched on 3 July at 0400, and at 0358, the Finnish forces launched a massive artillery bombardment of the Soviet deployment areas.

In support of that, forty German Stuka Ju 87s and about forty Finnish bombers were deployed. The operation was sufficient for the Soviet attack to stall and on 7 July, the Finnish intelligence service ascertained that some of the best Soviet units were being transferred to Estonia and even more remote combat areas. Finland also noted that the German situation in the central part of the Eastern Front was serious, now that Army Group Centre had virtually been wiped out, and in Normandy, the Western Allies had apparently gained a foothold. The newly added German division from Army Group North was ordered away from Finland again at the end of July.

In this situation, President Ryti of Finland chose to resign on 31 July 1944 and the Finnish Parliament appointed Marshal Mannerheim as the new president on 4 August. Parliament placed the responsibility for ending the war on Mannerheim. He was the most respected figure in Finland. Marshal Mannerheim had repeatedly informed Germany that if it withdrew from Estonia, then Finland would be forced to pull out of the war. If Estonia fell into Soviet hands, the Finnish coast would lie open to a Soviet invasion and air attacks from the south, and the Finnish lines of communication across the sea to the outside world would be cut off.

Hitler was uneasy about the development and sent Generaloberst Schörner from Army Group North to Finland. He had to assure Mannerheim that German forces would hold their positions at Narva, but it was at a point in time when the German positions were seriously under threat. Afterwards,

Generalfeldmarschall Keitel himself turned up to visit Mannerheim on 17 August 1944. He was told that Mannerheim and his government did not feel bound by Ryti's earlier declaration on German acceptance of peace overtures. On 25 August, the Finnish legation in Stockholm re-established contact with the Soviet legation and, the following day, Finland declared that Ryti's declaration was no longer valid. On 2 September, the Finnish parliament voted to cut contact with Germany, and at the same time ordered all German troops to leave Finnish territory by 15 September. These demands were part of the Soviet preconditions for concluding a peace treaty. A cessation of hostilities was established on 4 September with effect from the following day and, on 19 September 1944, Finland signed the ceasefire agreement.

It was a tough peace treaty from a Finnish point of view. The war had obviously resulted in very heavy losses for the armed forces. It had also severely impacted the Finnish economy, but the civilian population had – relatively speaking – been spared in comparison to what many other European countries had been exposed to. Two thousand civilians had been killed during the fighting. The fiercest fighting did not take place in urban areas, but in the vast forests. The Soviet Union demanded the borders returned to their 1940 positions. Moreover, it took the Petsamo region in the north, where there were rich nickel deposits, and demanded base rights on the Porkkala Peninsula near Helsinki for fifty years.[2] On the Karelian Isthmus, Finland lost its second largest city, Viipuri (which now became Vyborg again), as well as ports, hydroelectric plants, paper mills, sawmills, farming areas, and the important industrial complex at Vuoksi.

Finland had to oust the German forces from the country on its own. Finland thus became involved in its third war since 1939, and the Soviet Union could now concentrate on Germany. The first war was called the Winter War (1939/40), the next, the Continuation War (1941–44), and now came the Lapland War (1944/45). Some German forces could immediately be pulled out via Finnish ports and sailed back to Germany or transferred to Estonia. This was a matter of 4,049 combat-ready soldiers and 3,336 wounded soldiers. A lot of German military equipment had to be left behind, because it was not immediately possible to take it on board ship and sail it away. The other German troops had to fight their way back across land to the north, on the way to German-occupied northern Norway. All the German troops that could be, were sailed away from Finland before the deadline, but there were large troop forces which had to be deployed northwards – often on foot – to join up with the German troops in northern Norway. Since the German forces did not want to leave Finland voluntarily and quickly enough, the

---

2   The Soviet Union did, however, give this area back to Finland as early as 1956.

Finns had to use force of arms. At first the former brothers-in-arms made a little show of it, but it said in the peace agreement that if Finland did not chase the German forces out, then Soviet forces would come and do it for them. As it was going a little too slowly, the Soviet Union threatened again. This war was, in turn, felt very strongly by the Finnish civil population, because the German forces burned down village after village during their retreat northwards. In the Soviet war propaganda, Finland featured side by side with the Nazis, but the Soviet Union has never been in any doubt that Finland had only gone along with Germany because of the Soviet assault in 1939, and only to regain the ground lost in the Winter War.[3]

Naval warfare around Finland's withdrawal from the war

On 13 March 1944, the Kriegsmarine began strengthening the Seeigel minefield with 8,499 mines and 2,795 minesweeping obstacles. The minelaying fleet was subjected to fierce Soviet air attacks. On 21 April 1944, the German minelayer *Roland* detonated two mines and went down with 235 men. Soviet naval aircraft had dropped mines near the buoys that marked the end of the fields where the new minelayer should take over, but *Roland* had presumably hit two German mines. In late July 1944, Soviet minesweepers succeeded in breaking through the minefield between Narva and Tytärsaari in the Gulf of Finland. The Kriegsmarine sent three submarines to cover the gap. Dönitz requested air support from the Luftwaffe to attack the Soviet minesweepers and protect the German minelayers. Germany also sent motor torpedo boats in, without regard to the Soviet air threat. During a minelaying operation on 18 August 1944, three of the large German torpedo boats *T22*, *T30* and *T32* (they were small destroyers of 1,754 tonnes displacement) sailed into a German minefield, where they all sank. They were supposed to be strengthening the Seeigel 10B minefield in Narva Bay, but sailed into the neighbouring minefield, Seeigel 9B, which had probably been inaccurately laid by *Marinefährprähme* (landing craft). The Kriegsmarine never got round to investigating the exact circumstances because of the evacuation from Finland shortly after. A fourth torpedo boat, *T23*, sailed away from the area without providing help. Fifty-one men from the three crews of approximately

---

3   In the post-war period, there has been understanding for Finland's plight and the country was not put in the same box as the other Axis powers, Germany, Italy and Japan. Finland was at war with the UK but not the USA; Finnish troops did not become engaged in or contribute to the siege of Leningrad; Finnish Jews were never interned or deported, despite German wishes. However, there was strong German pressure on Finland regarding fleeing German Jews in the country, and eight of them were handed over via Estonia in 1942.

206 men each were rescued by minesweepers, ninety men were picked up by the Luftwaffe's *Seenotflieger* (rescue aircraft), and 106 men fell into Soviet captivity. The remaining crew members, about 371 men, perished.

On 30 July 1944, the German submarine *U-250* was on patrol near Koivisto, close to the Karelian Isthmus, where it sank a Soviet patrol boat. A nearby Soviet patrol boat saw the periscope and dropped a total of nine depth charges, one of which exploded just above the submarine's engine room. The submarine sank immediately, but the commander and five men managed to escape through the conning tower. The submarine was in shallow water, so the Soviet Baltic Fleet recovered it and brought it in to Kronstadt, where it was studied in detail. The Russians found an acoustic homing torpedo, classified documents, codes, ciphers and, not least, one of the Kriegsmarine's special versions of the cipher machine Enigma, with four sets of rotors instead of the normal three.

While Finnish forces were retreating on the Karelian Isthmus, the Soviet Baltic Fleet relieved the Red Army by carrying out a tactical landing close to Björksund at Vyborg. The Russians had great respect for the Finnish coastal monitor *Väinämöinen*, which now and then turned up and fired on the Soviet forces with its long-range and very precise 10in/254mm guns, and then disappeared again. In mid-July, Soviet aircraft from the Baltic Fleet successfully located the ship. It lay camouflaged in the archipelago near Kotka and a huge attack was planned: 132 Soviet naval aircraft – bombers as well as fighters – attacked it on 16 July 1944. The ship was hit by at least nine bombs and ended up as a wreck on the rocks at Kotka, partially visible, but it shot down nine of its attackers.

The Kriegsmarine's special version of the Enigma cipher machine, with four sets of rotors instead of the normal three. At Bletchley Park, that coding system was known as Shark. In the Kriegsmarine, it was called Triton.

German submarine *U-250* (Type VII C) salvaged by the Soviet Baltic Fleet and brought to Kronstadt. One of the forty-six perished German crew members can be seen on the stretcher on the gangway. The submarine contained a number of interesting finds, including a four-rotor naval Enigma machine and an acoustic torpedo. (SMB arkiv)

The Finnish monitor *Väinämöinen* camouflaged in the archipelago. (Old Ship Picture Galleries)

After returning, the Russians celebrated the victory by raining medals on the participants, including four Gold Stars, one of the highest honours in the Soviet system. The recipients also became Heroes of the Soviet Union. When some of the peace treaty papers were to be signed in September 1944, a Soviet delegation was invited on board a coastal monitor and the members were greatly astonished when it proved to be the undamaged *Väinämöinen*. The explanation was quite simply that the Soviet Union was not aware that Germany had sent a special flak ship to the area. It was the former Dutch cruiser *Gelderland* from 1898, which Germany had taken over from the Netherlands in 1940. It had been commissioned into the Kriegsmarine under the name of *Niobe*. So it was *Niobe* which the Soviet forces had discovered and sunk on 16 July 1944, when seventy men from the German crew died.

As mentioned earlier, on 15 September 1944 Finland was forced out of the war. Part of the agreement was that the country had to sweep passages through the net barriers and minefields in the Gulf of Finland. The Soviet Baltic Fleet had twenty-five operational submarines ready to be piloted out. The Baltic Fleet would then once more be able to threaten Germany's maritime lines

The old Dutch cruiser *Gelderland* from 1898 was requisitioned by the Kriegsmarine and renamed *Niobe* and used as a flak ship in the Finnish archipelago. (Old Ship Picture Galleries)

The wreck of the German flak cruiser *Niobe* (ex-Dutch *Gelderland*) off Kotka, sunk by more than one hundred attacking aircraft from the Baltic Fleet Air Force on 16 July 1944. Although well camouflaged, it was located and sunk. The target was believed by the attackers to be the Finnish coastal monitor *Väinämöinen*. (SMB arkiv)

of communication. The large Soviet warships were not brought into action, but submarines and naval aircraft were deployed in large numbers. Soviet motor torpedo boats and motor gunboats took part in the operations but with very modest results. The Baltic Fleet hereafter used Turku and Hanko as submarine bases.

Hitler got wind of the Finnish peace initiatives as early as February 1944, so two operations were planned which were given the code names Tanne East and Tanne West, being the capture by Germany of Hogland and the Åland Islands respectively. They were to be implemented at short notice if Finland withdrew from the war. Tanne East was important, as the coastal batteries on Hogland, along with the batteries on the German-occupied island of Tytärsaari (Tütters in German), were able to cover the Seeigel minefields between Estonia and Finland. If the whole Soviet Baltic Fleet slipped out, Germany's situation would be radically changed. The submarines would be able to attack German supply lines and artillery vessels would be able to support the Red Army. This would have insurmountable consequences for the German economy and industry, and it would also complicate the tactical situation for the German army, the Kriegsmarine and the Luftwaffe. The Kriegsmarine's possibilities for training new submarine crews would particularly be under threat. However, the circumstances under which Finland would come out of the war were not entirely clear. Germany had plans to keep parts of northern Finland occupied, so at least the nickel deposits around Petsamo would remain in German hands.

Tanne East was launched on Dönitz's initiative in September 1944, when the break with Finland was a fact. The German ships withdrew at midnight on the night of 14/15 September, mining the waters near Kotka as they left. The next morning, the Kriegsmarine arranged a landing on Hogland, which was carried out with troops from the German army. Germany had expected a sham resistance from its former Finnish allies, but they resisted very strongly and, during the afternoon, the Finnish forces called in Soviet air support. The landing turned into a total failure which cost the Germans 1,300 dead and wounded. During the summer, Tytärsaari had received sufficient supplies for the island to be able to hold out for six to twelve months, but on 19 September 1944, four days after the failure at Hogland, Germany evacuated Tytärsaari. The Tanne West plan was never activated.

On 16 September, the German heavy cruiser *Prinz Eugen* turned up at Utö in the southwestern Finnish archipelago, along with two destroyers. Finland had seized two German tugs and a German net-layer (for laying anti-submarine nets). If they were not released, the cruiser was going to open fire on Utö's fortifications. After some negotiations, the ships were handed back to Germany.

The Finnish minelayer *Louhi* was lost southeast of Hanko on 12 January 1945 with the loss of ten men. For many years the ship was believed to have struck a mine. New information indicates that *Louhi* was hit by an acoustic G7e torpedo fired from the German submarine *U-370*. (SA-Kuva)

During the Lapland War in the Gulf of Bothnia, the Finnish navy lost the minelayer *Louhi,* which went down with ten men on board. German dive-bombers sank two Finnish transport ships, *Bore IX* and *Mainiki* on 4 October 1944.

The Wellenbrecher doctrine and Dönitz as Hitler's key adviser

Hitler had let the entire slow retreat over land in the Baltic states take place partly on advice from Dönitz. The Germans called it the *Wellenbrecher-Doktrin* (the breakwater doctrine). The argument was that the Soviet forces would have to leave two or three men back to cover each German soldier left in the defended areas. With this doctrine, Hitler would ensure that he could beat the Red Army before an assault was launched against Berlin. Hitler, as well as Goebbels, did not count on the assessments of Fremde Heere Ost (Generalmajor Reinhard Gehlen's intelligence section of the Eastern Front) being correct. They regarded them as both exaggerated and pessimistic. But Gehlen had an extensive information network. His intelligence reports were generally accurate, and he often knew the times of the Soviet attacks, the size of the attacking force, Soviet deception tactics and much more, but his predictions were not popular in the top echelons of the leadership and he was fired in April 1945.[4] Hitler's personal assessment of the Red Army troops was to the effect that they were overworked; they were on the verge of collapse; their replacement system did not work; their resources were exhausted, and they had thrown their last reserves into a desperate struggle.

There was, however, something to the Wellenbrecher doctrine, because it was true that it tied up a lot of Soviet forces in the autumn of 1944. In Courland (western Latvia) alone, there were three or four Soviet divisions for each German one. The Courland forces had been isolated since Soviet troops had reached the coast in Latvia, southwest of Riga, after which they could only be supplied by sea and air. At the point in time that the Courland forces became isolated, there were plans that they would later break out and inflict unacceptable losses on the Soviet forces, thereby contributing to the final victory over the Red Army.

---

4 Reinhard Gehlen surrendered on 22 May 1945 to the Americans in southern Germany and he agreed to co-operate with them in exchange for getting some of his men released. They came to work for the OSS and later for the CIA. When West Germany got its own Federal Intelligence Service – the Bundesnachrichtendienst (BND) – in 1956, Gehlen became its director in Pullach near Munich. For years after the war, he had his own organisation of agents behind the Iron Curtain.

The large numbers of German 'strongholds' (fortified towns) were supposed to tie disproportionately many Russians down while trying to gain time, but the doctrine did not have the impact anticipated. Some of the fortified towns were those at Schneidemühl, Posen, Elbing, Thorn, Glogau and Breslau (now the Polish towns of Piła, Poznań, Elbląg, Toruń, Głogów and Wrocław respectively). Hitler had many troops tied up in the fortified towns, but the Soviet forces rarely engaged with them before they attacked Berlin. They often went around them and captured them or took them over in conjunction with the cessation of the war. In connection with the introduction of the doctrine, Hitler deployed some of the German army's toughest generals. They should be able to stand firm under attack. He trusted in their loyalty and that they embraced Nazi ideology. They were brutal types, such as Generaloberst Schörner and Generaloberst Rendulic, who, among other things, guarded against untimely retreats by cracking down hard on deserters.

Furthermore, Hitler, at least as an argument with his own generals, used the Courland forces as diplomatic pressure directed against Sweden, which at this point might have been tempted to align itself with the Western Allies. Hitler was skilful at emphasising foreign policy arguments with his generals, because they were not in fact allowed to get involved in foreign policy, only in military matters. Germany was worried about Sweden. The country had relatively large military forces and that could influence the situation in the Baltic Sea, where the Kriegsmarine were set on deploying the crucial new submarine force. Furthermore, Sweden had borders with Norway, which was to be used as a base area for the submarine force. This is seen as the reason why Hitler did not evacuate the approximately 380,000 German troops who remained in Norway until May 1945. They could have been thrown into the battle against the advancing Soviet troops.

The German forces withdrew as slowly as possible, partly to ensure the relocation and training of the new submarine crews and production of the new submarines of Type XXI and Type XXIII. Submarine training had to be moved from Memel and Gotenhafen. It was first moved to Bornholm, and from here most of it was transferred to Norway in the final phase of the war. Submarine production was centred on Kiel, but there were subcontractors throughout Germany. Dönitz assured Hitler that the new submarines would be able to regain the initiative for Germany in the Battle of the Atlantic, and Great Britain would thereby be forced out of the war. Dönitz claimed after the war that he had never had any influence on the war on land, not even in Courland (West Latvia), but he urged Hitler to defend some coastal areas long after they had any value to the army. This applied, for example, to Narva and Hogland. When the German army retreated from Estonia, Dönitz was aware that he must either

One of the new Type XXIII small submarines armed with only two torpedoes. (SMB arkiv)

lay a minefield across the Gulf of Finland or do battle with Soviet warships in their attempt to break the German blockade. The Seekriegsleitung considered that the Estonian islands were important in this regard.

Dönitz was a convinced Nazi and he believed in a final victory. In his memoirs, there is not much about Nazi ideology, but a number of leading historians agree that Dönitz showed real affection for Hitler and the ideology. In many respects, he was Hitler's favourite. He was respected because he dared to speak his mind and he was, according to Hitler, the only one who did not deceive him. He was one of the very few in Hitler's inner circle who was given an SS escort and an armoured Mercedes. Goebbels praised him for 'a correct ideological attitude, for his determination and for continuing the fight.' The admiration between Hitler and Dönitz was mutual. He supported Hitler to the last and was therefore appointed to be his successor. He continued Hitler's fight right up to 4 May 1945, when he realised that further fighting was pointless, but even on the morning of 4 May, there were German submarines being transferred from northern Germany to their war bases in Norway. On the other hand, Grossadmiral Raeder referred to his successor as 'Hitler Youth Boy Dönitz', with reference to a Nazi propaganda film from 1933 entitled *Hitler Youth Quex*.

Hitler's overall strategy in the last year of the war and the new wonder weapons

Many historians have emphasised Hitler's lack of strategy in the last years of the war, including the lack of logic and consistency in his deployments. American Professor Howard D Grier argues, however, in his book *Hitler, Dönitz and the Baltic Sea. The Third Reich's last hope, 1944–1945* that Hitler had a strategy, but the implementation of it was continually being delayed by the Allied bombing of urban areas, port areas, industries, railways and energy supplies. Mines laid by aircraft were also crucial in this respect. In 1944 and 1945, Germany therefore had the so-called Durchhalte strategy (hold-out strategy), which was effectively one of delaying and sticking it out[5] until the new 'wonder weapons' arrived and brought with them the long-awaited victory.

There were many 'wonder weapons'; German ingenuity was great and German engineers produced a number of pioneering projects. As soon as the United States joined the war against Germany and Japan, a meeting was held between President Franklin D Roosevelt, Prime Minister Winston Churchill and their military commanders, in which they established that the defeat of Germany had first priority as the country might have the ability to produce nuclear weapons. Although Germany did not succeed in this, many of its other weapons were technologically more advanced than the corresponding Allied weapons. This applied to the V-1 and V-2 systems in particular. Germany also produced various jet aircraft, missile air defence systems, and submarines that, even when submerged, could sail faster than the Allied convoys in the Atlantic. The Type XXI submarine, in particular, could have had an impact on the outcome of the war, but the project was delayed for so long that it did not come to play any role. During the spring of 1944, Britain intercepted some encrypted messages from the head of the Japanese naval delegation in Berlin, Rear-Admiral Katsuo Abe. At Bletchley Park, they could read the Japanese naval attaché's messages, a cipher system which the British referred to as Coral. It was evident from his signals to Tokyo that the new submarines with Walter engines could sail at 28 knots

---

5   The relationship between Hitler and Dönitz is described in Professor Howard D Grier's book *Hitler, Dönitz and the Baltic Sea. The Third Reich's last hope, 1944–1945*. After a study of Hitler's decision-making process in the last years of the war, Grier has reached the conclusion that Hitler was far more rational in his decisions than was previously thought. It is necessary to understand that Hitler himself believed that he could regain the initiative on both the Eastern and Western Fronts. The precondition was that the newest and most decisive weapons were developed and deployed. This could be managed if the retreats from the east, especially from the Baltic states, were delayed and carried out under control. This theory explains Hitler's and Dönitz's deployments in 1944/45. Internal rivalries and fragmentation in the German command structure have contributed to erasing the broader picture.

submerged (Type XVII and Type XVIII). He also told Tokyo in detail about Type XXI and Type XXIII, and that they had been delayed due to the heavy bombing, which meant that they would not be ready until the spring of 1945. This meant that the RAF intensified the bombing of submarine bases and shipyards, as well as increasing their minelaying.

Hitler's thinking regarding the new weapons was that Britain would be struck by thousands of V-1s and V-2s, so the losses in the civilian population and the material destruction would force the country out of the war. The attacks should also be seen as revenge for the Allied bombing of German cities. The Allied air raids would be stopped through the use of new superior German jet fighters, including the Messerschmidt Me 262 Sturmvogel, and the new anti-aircraft missile batteries Rheintochter and Wasserfall.[6] Large aircraft losses by the Western Allies could also force them out of the war. Finally, shipping between the US and the UK would be cut off by the new submarines, primarily of Type XXI and Type XXIII. Whereas all other contemporary submarines could really only be described as diving boats, the two new types were completely revolutionary, and genuine submarines. They could move fast and operate submerged for a long time.

On the other hand, the Allies had a head start in terms of production of radar and sonar systems, as well as numerical superiority in the production of aircraft, tanks and ships, and also all logistics, including fuel supplies. Finally, it was possible for the Allies to read large parts of the German signals traffic. In many cases, they could gain an insight into the enemy's assessment of a situation and respond accordingly. At an early stage of the war, it was clear to experts who had access to the relevant key statistics for German industry and the German forces that Hitler and Germany would not be able to win the war. When the United States threw its full potential in, including the political will, the economy, industrial production and military forces, Germany had no chance. Goebbels' propaganda made sure, however, that such information was not available to the German population. What kept the armed forces and the German population in the fight was the regime's threats, but also very much the propaganda about the secret, battle-decisive weapons that Hitler would have ready 'shortly'. The German population was disciplined, orthodox and did not ask questions of the authorities. These *Wunderwaffen* (wonder weapons) would turn the progress of the war, it was officially stated in Germany. In line with the Soviet Union's advance towards the Baltic coasts, two of Germany's new decisive war weapons were put in danger. The ambitious programme for the Type XXI and Type XXIII submarines required shipyards and training in the Baltic Sea.

---

6   The first Soviet and American air defence missile systems during the Cold War were in fact copies or further developments of German weapons systems from the Second World War.

German submarines and the German arms industry

In July 1943, two months after the Allied victory in the Battle of the Atlantic, Hitler received a very thorough briefing from Dönitz about the new German submarines and their capabilities. Because of their superior speed, the new submarines would be able to do what they wanted in the Atlantic. Convoys were not able to pick up speed to 10 knots swiftly and the submarines had a speed of 18 knots. The company IG Farben had promised to make a material to coat the outside of the boats so they did not reflect radar waves. At the same time, the Kriegsmarine was working on developing a special homing torpedo, which could home in on the propeller noise from anti-submarine vessels.

Speer and his staff were working tremendously hard to reduce production time and maintain production numbers. The Type XXI was now being made in eight hull sections of up to 150 tonnes and, instead of a production time of twenty-two months, they were now down to five to nine months by using the experience gained on assembly lines in the automobile industry. The time on the building slipway, which was the vulnerable part because submarines on the slipway were particularly exposed to air attack, had been reduced by half. In the autumn of 1943, Dönitz ordered 170 Type XXI and 140 Type XXIII. There were thirty-two subcontractors for the ship sections, which were delivered by river transport. There were eleven outfitting shipyards, where the submarines had propellers, engines, periscopes, cables and similar installed. This was now concentrated on three cities, Bremen, Hamburg and Danzig, instead. The Kriegsmarine's ship construction office calculated that the first three Type XXI submarines would be delivered in April 1944. A total of 152 should have been delivered by 31 October 1944. However, because of bombing raids and minelaying, all were continuously delayed. Britain knew from a deciphered signal at Bletchley Park that on 4 December 1944, there were a total of eighteen Type XXIII submarines in the Baltic Sea. On 1 January 1945, the Kriegsmarine had received sixty-two Type XXI and twenty-eight Type XXIII submarines, but the RAF's determined efforts against submarine construction and their bases made a dent in inventories. Up until May 1945, the number of operational submarines of these types was greatly reduced.

On 24 May 1943, Grossadmiral Dönitz issued an instruction to all submarines. In case of air raids, the submarines were to take up the fight on the surface against the attacking aircraft. The submarines had been armed with heavy anti-aircraft guns, but Dönitz, for very good reasons, could not assess during the next few months whether or not it had been the right decision, since he did not know what had happened to the submarines which did not return. According to analyses made by the Western Allies' air forces after the war, it turned out to be the wrong decision, one which

Type XXI submarines

Type XXI was an Atlantic submarine with a fifty-seven-man crew, a length of 256ft/78m, a displacement of 1,600 tonnes and a submerged speed of 18 knots* for ninety minutes or 12–14 knots for ten hours. The existing submarines could only sail at 6 knots for forty-five minutes on their batteries. Most Allied convoys sailed at 6–9 knots. The maximum diving depth was 394ft/120m (Type VII-C, the most commonly-used Atlantic submarine could dive to 328ft/100m). It carried twenty torpedoes which could be fired through six bow tubes. It could fire the first eighteen torpedoes within twenty to thirty minutes.

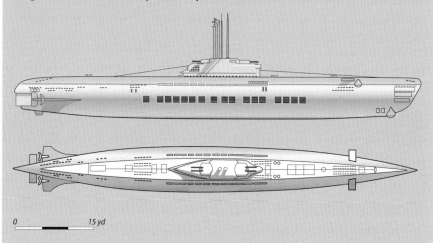

0   15 yd

* A ship's speed is measured in knots = nautical miles per hour: 1 knot = 1 nautical mile per hour = 1.15mph = 1.852kph.

resulted in the loss of many submarines. In the Baltic Sea, the order probably had limited significance. Most of the German submarines were submerged during daylight hours.

On 24 September 1943 and again on 26 February 1944, Hitler gave Dönitz assurances that he would do everything possible to boost submarine production significantly, but in April 1944 he suddenly issued an order that production of fighter planes now had priority instead. This gave rise to some confusion in the armaments industry. It should be added here that one of the reasons why Germany lost the war was its quite hopeless leadership structure. Power was divided between numerous agencies, which were played off against each other, and each of which sought to make the most

Type XXIII submarines

Type XXIII was specifically designed to operate in British waters, the Black Sea and the Mediterranean. It had a fourteen-man crew, was 124ft/37.7m, long with a displacement of 250 tonnes, and could navigate submerged for an hour at 12.5 knots. The maximum diving depth was 360ft/110m. One of the 'staff requirements' from Grossadmiral Dönitz was that this type of submarine should be transportable by rail, which in many respects was a great advantage. On the other hand, it meant that its armament was restricted to just two torpedoes.

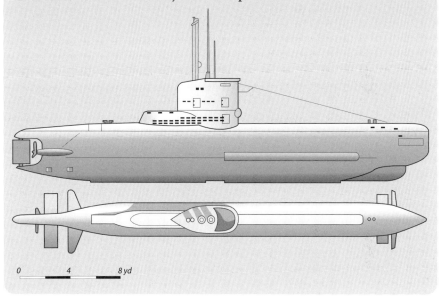

0   4   8 yd

out of the situation. Those in positions of leadership sought to promote the projects that they themselves got the most out of and that gave increased resource allocation, and, not least, increased prestige. If Hitler was presented with an interesting project, it became the first priority. If the Führer's next guest also presented an interesting project, it was also given first priority, and so on – until all projects had first priority. Before the war was over, German industry was drowning in a large number of projects with high technological and scientific standards, but there was no overriding authority which could cut through and say, for example, that there was a single fighter-plane project and a single submarine project which were now to be prioritised.

Two of the Type XXIII submarines were delivered in February 1944, and the plan was that all 140 submarines should be delivered no later than 31

October 1944, but in mid-April 1944, an engine factory in Augsburg was bombed and the engines for the Type XXI and Type XXIII submarines were delayed. Later, Dönitz demanded an expansion of the air defences over the three shipyards where the submarines were being assembled. In early October 1944, Dönitz, in private conversations with Hitler, had explained the plans for the next submarine campaign that would begin in the North Atlantic with the new Type XXI submarines in January 1945.

Wonder weapons and German morale

As a curiosity, it can be revealed that, since the landing at Anzio in Italy in January 1944 and right up to the final German collapse in May 1945, senior American officers in Europe had been puzzled by the results of interrogations of German prisoners of war. A very large proportion of the German prisoners, especially the younger officers, were totally convinced that, even though they were going through a tough time, Germany would certainly come out of the war victorious. They trusted the propaganda that Hitler and the German arms industry had some *Wunderwaffen* in reserve, and that the Durchhalte strategy would lead to a final victory for Germany.

The war in Estonia and Latvia

When the German forces were hard pressed around Narva, the army began to get restless regarding a total retreat from Estonia. Dönitz very much wanted to hold on to Estonia, because then it would be easier to keep the Baltic Fleet trapped and defend the minefields in the Gulf of Finland. It was also important for the Kriegsmarine to get oil from shale oil deposits in the area between Narva and Tallinn. The oil area stretched from Narva about 60 miles/100km west and about 25 miles/40km in a north–south direction. The centre for oil extraction was at Kohtla-Järve, 20 miles/32km west of Narva. It was primarily the Kriegsmarine that used the extracted oil, but German tanks also drove on oil extracted from these shale deposits. In February 1944, Hitler ordered the deployment of additional anti-aircraft artillery in the area around the shale oil production. From this point in time, Germany's fuel problems began to be very serious. Soviet forces were also about to reach the Romanian oil fields at Ploesti.

The Leningrad Front began its attack on Narva on 24 July 1944 and, two days later, the German commanders ordered the evacuation of the city. Steiner had now fallen back to his Tannenbergstellung, which was in a very flat terrain broken by three hills quite close to each other. The Estonians call them Sinimäed, the Blue Mountains. Going from east to west, there was Orphanage Hill, Grenadier Hill and Hill 69.9. Steiner's force here now consisted of Dutch, Norwegian and Danish Waffen-SS units, complemented by the 20th Waffengrenadier Division from Estonia and two Belgian Waffen-SS combat units, referred to as the 5th Volunteer Storm Brigade Wallonia and the 6th Volunteer Storm Brigade Langemarck. A few Tiger and Panther tanks, complemented by the force's anti-tank guns, destroyed 113 armoured Soviet vehicles, including a significant number of T-34 tanks. Within sight of the three hills, around 25,000 – perhaps even as many as 35,000 – Soviet soldiers fell in the summer of 1944.

The Valentin submarine production hall

Because of the bomb threat from the RAF, Germany planned to build the Type XXI submarines in the new bombproof Valentin factory on the Weser river near Bremen. It was a huge concrete building, but was not underground. It was about 1,400ft/426m long with 15ft/4.5m thick walls and a 23ft/7m thick roof. The hall was equipped for submarine production with thirteen stations, the last of which was in a 72ft/22m deep tank, from which it was possible to test-dive the submarine and sail out into the River Weser. Production of fourteen submarines per month was planned from August 1945, but the German collapse occurred before then. The hall had taken since 1943 to be built and its construction had cost the lives of somewhere between 2,000 and 6,000 forced labourers. Two bombing raids in March 1945 put an end to production.

Type XVII and Type XVIII submarines

On 4 January 1943, Dönitz ordered twenty-four small Walter Type XVII submarines. The somewhat larger Type XVIII was a submarine for the Atlantic, and was a result of thorough investigations and staff discussions following the construction of the Type XVII. Propulsion was supplied by Walter engines in which hydrogen peroxide drove the turbines. It could sail submerged at a speed of 28 knots over 270 miles. Type XVII was produced in single examples, but did not come into full operational service, and the type XVIII submarines were never finished.

On 27 July 1944, Steiner lost Orphanage Hill to the Soviet forces and a Norwegian Waffen-SS counter-attack failed. After this, Steiner's troops fell back towards Grenadier Hill. The Waffen-SS units were now getting isolated in Estonia because of events further afield. After the Soviet success further southeast with Operation Bagration, Soviet forces tried to advance towards the Gulf of Riga and thereby isolate the bulk of Army Group North in Courland, a region of West Latvia. The Soviet breakout from Leningrad had already split Army Group North's area into two and the situation was critical in both places. However, German tank forces managed to break the isolation and reconnect with the many scattered Waffen-SS units in Estonia.

The town of Tukums, 37 miles/60km west of Riga in Latvia, was captured by Soviet forces on 30 July. The German operations were supported by artillery fire from the heavy cruiser *Prinz Eugen*, which smashed forty-eight T-34 tanks with its 8in/203mm guns as they paraded in the town hall square in Tukums prior to a Soviet attack. In addition, the Kriegsmarine had sent the destroyers *Z25*, *Z28*, *Z35* and *Z36* and torpedo boats *T23* and *T28* to provide artillery support in the coastal areas. Despite this, the massive Soviet build-up continued. On 21 August 1944, fifteen Soviet divisions initiated an attack on Tartu, about 105 miles/170km southeast of Tallinn.

Further south on 28 July 1944, the 1st Baltic Front under Colonel-General Ivan Khristoforovich Bagramyan[7] succeeded in cutting the last railway line that Germany could use to supply its troops in the Baltic. Two days later, the Soviet forces also reached the coast in the Gulf of Riga. Army Group North was thereby cut off from Army Group Centre. In some fierce fighting between 16 and 20 August, SS Tank Group Strachwitz, under the colourful tank general, Generalmajor der Reserve, SS Brigadeführer und General der SS Hyazinth Graf Strachwitz von Gross-Zauche und Camminetz,[8] along with some of the Kriegsmarine's artillery units, succeeded in recapturing Tukums and establishing a supply corridor with a width of about 18 miles/30km.

On 14 September 1944, the 1st Baltic Front, 2nd Baltic Front and 3rd Baltic Front continued the wave of attacks. These attacks were intended partly to capture Riga and partly to resume the attempt to isolate the remnants of Army Group North in Courland. The German commanders now ordered a total evacuation of Estonia, and Steiner's forces withdrew to the south and

---

7   Bagramyan was Armenian and had two sets of names. His Russian name was Ivan Khristoforovich Bagramyan while his Armenian name was Hovhannes Khachaturi Baghramyan. He ended his career as Marshal of the Soviet Union and Deputy Minister of Defence.

8   Near the end of the war, he was appointed Generalleutnant der Reserven and thereby became Germany's highest ranking reserve officer.

west under pressure from the 2nd Shock Army. Tallinn was evacuated on 22 September, but part of the armed Estonian units, both from a local militia and from the 20th Waffen-SS Grenadier Division from Estonia, chose to remain in the area and initiate guerrilla warfare against the invading Russians. All these events should be seen in the light of the cessation of hostilities in Finland. The Germans had had the dilemma that, if Finland was abandoned, they might as well leave Estonia, as the country would be open to invasion across the Gulf of Finland. Similarly, if Estonia fell to the Russians, Finland would be open to invasion.

Many of the German armies on the Eastern Front had suffered great losses which were often not replaced. At the end of November 1944, Generaloberst Schörner had alerted the OKH to the fact that one of his divisions in Courland now consisted of only 315 men. When Hitler was reshuffling his divisions, he counted on there being 17,734 men, as at the beginning of the war.

Dönitz was aware that there was no point in retaining Estonia if the Soviet forces had reached the Baltic coast in Latvia and Lithuania. In that case, the result would also be that Germany lost naval supremacy in the Baltic Sea, because the Kriegsmarine would not be able to operate in the Baltic Sea with a large Soviet air threat if the Luftwaffe could not secure the airspace over the sea.

The battle for the Estonian islands

When Germany retreated from the Estonian mainland, a strong German minefield was laid in Muhu Sound. On the Estonian islands, Soviet forces carried out their largest amphibious operation in the Baltic Sea. Altogether 78,000 men were landed and the battle lasted for two months. The fight was for the islands of Vormsi, Muhu, Hiiumaa and Saaremaa, and the fighting ended at Sõrve, Saaremaa's southern tip. The German problem was that if these islands fell to the Soviet Union, Soviet aircraft and torpedo boats could be a threat from here both to iron ore transports and to submarine training. Originally, Germany had planned to defend the islands with artillery barges, minesweepers and motor torpedo boats. When this support did not arrive, Seekriegsleitung had to send 2. Kampfgruppe (2nd Battle Group).[9] The land fighting on the islands alone cost the Kriegsmarine 2,000 killed and wounded. The Soviet Baltic Fleet did not have enough transport capacity

9   2. Kampfgruppe was established on 17 July 1944 as a force of heavy naval artillery vessels, primarily with a view to co-ordinating and providing fire support for the German army's many operations. The group included pocket battleships, cruisers, destroyers, and a few other smaller artillery-bearing units.

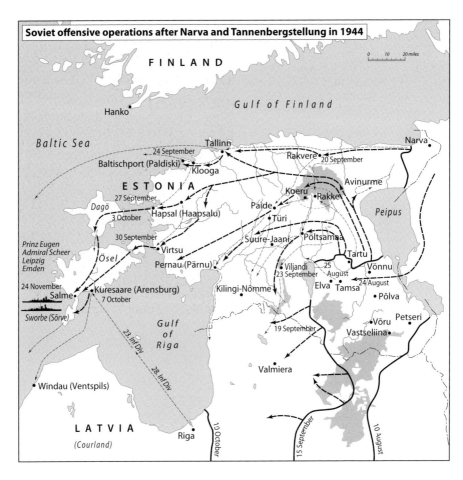

Soviet offensive operations after Narva and Tannenbergstellung in 1944

FINLAND

Gulf of Finland

Hanko

Baltic Sea

Narva

Tallinn

24 September

Rakvere 20 September

Baltischport (Paldiski)

Klooga

ESTONIA

Avinurme

Koeru

27 September

Rakke

Dagö

Paide

3 October

Hapsal (Haapsalu)

Türi

Peipus

30 September

Suure-Jaani

Põltsamaa

Prinz Eugen
Admiral Scheer
Leipzig
Emden

Ösel

Virtsu

Tartu

Pernau (Pärnu)

Viljandi

25

Võnnu

23 September

August

24 August

24 November

Elva

Tamsa

Salme

Kuresaare (Arensburg)

Kilingi-Nõmme

Põlva

7 October

Sworbe (Sõrve)

Gulf
of
Riga

19 September

Võru

Petseri

Vastseliina

Windau (Ventspils)

Valmiera

23. Inf Div

28. Inf Div

LATVIA

Riga

10 October

15 September

10 August

(Courland)

Soviet soldiers from the 109th Infantry Division landing on the Estonian island of Saaremaa. (SMB arkiv)

Sailors from the Baltic Fleet took part in the defence of Leningrad. Later they participated in the landing operations on the Estonian islands in 1944. Sergeant Granovsky in the front of the picture was later killed in action. (SMB arkiv)

for the attack on Saaremaa, so Finland had to supply the transport vessels in accordance with the peace treaty. The final German withdrawal from the island's southern tip took place during the night of 23/24 November 1944.

The war in the Baltic Sea in the autumn of 1944

On 11 July 1944, a meeting had taken place in the Seekriegsleitung, under the leadership of Admiral Meisel, in which the consequences of a Soviet thrust towards East Prussia and the Baltic states were discussed. Konteradmiral Eberhardt Godt, who was operational commander of the submarine forces, said that the Kriegsmarine had 25,000 men at the submarine training centres on the coast between the Hel Peninsula in Poland and Libau in Latvia; 50–60 per cent of all submarine training took place in the eastern Baltic Sea. In Danzig Bay, there were five shipyards and industries involved in submarine production. If the area were to be evacuated, the Kriegsmarine would only be able to finish the training for twelve to fifteen submarine crews per month.

The day before the attempted assassination of Hitler, Kapitän zur See Heinz Assmann, the head of naval operations in the OKW, was working on a plan to order the destroyers home from northern Norway and, if possible, also the battleship *Tirpitz*. Grossadmiral Dönitz was aware that getting the battleship back to the Baltic Sea was not without its problems, because even more American and British air strikes would be invoked. This would reduce production rates at the submarine yards. The large vessels were supposed to ensure naval supremacy and support the army's operations around Danzig Bay, where Soviet forces were advancing towards the coast. At that point in time, Germany did not know much about Soviet intentions. When the Baltic Fleet finally came out of the Gulf of Finland, it was mainly with a number of submarines followed thereafter by a number of motor torpedo boats and motor gunboats. The battleships, cruisers and destroyers only participated with fire support during the fighting in Karelia in June 1944. The material condition of the large vessels was poor after the Leningrad siege, and Stalin probably did not want to risk the ships if they were to be used in a subsequent showdown with the Western powers.

When Finland withdrew from the war in September 1944, the Kriegsmarine had twelve submarines in the Gulf of Finland – they now had to be based in Danzig and Gotenhafen. When the Germans evacuated Tallinn on 22 September 1944, the Baltic Fleet air force attacked a ship carrying refugees which had reached the coast off Ventspils. Seventeen Douglas A20G-Boston aircraft bombed the military hospital ship *Moero*, which was bringing 1,273 wounded soldiers and refugees, of whom 655 probably died. It was the first German ship with refugees and wounded which went down in the Baltic Sea, but over the next eight months many similar sinkings occurred. On 7 October, *Nordstern* was spotted moving away from Saaremaa with evacuees and was sunk by the Soviet submarine *Shch-407*; 529 people went down with *Nordstern*.

On 6 October 1944, Soviet forces forced their way out to the Baltic coast between Libau and Memel. A major Soviet goal was thereby reached: the remains of Army Group North were now isolated in the Courland pocket, and they could hereafter only be supplied by sea or air. On the morning of 14 October 1944, comprehensive artillery fire from 2. Kampfgruppe's units against Soviet troop concentrations was instrumental in repelling an attack on Memel.

From 22 October 1944, when Soviet forces forced their way into the German territory of East Prussia in earnest, a huge number of German refugees began streaming westward. As the situation developed and Soviet troops reached the Baltic Sea coast here and there, large populations became cut off from moving westward over land. Similarly, the Soviet advance into Estonia earlier in the year had led to a stream of Estonians fleeing by boat to Sweden.

The larger German naval vessels could be useful in different ways in the Baltic Sea. Since the Luftwaffe no longer had the resources to support the army's operations to a significant degree, the artillery on these ships could be used to support German army forces which were now fighting in the coastal areas in the Baltic states. At the same time, the Kriegsmarine could support the army with transports and supplies, but another problem began to make itself felt.

The heavy German losses after Operation Bagration had resulted in thousands of wounded soldiers. They were usually transported back to Germany in hospital trains, but railway operations were being made difficult by Soviet advances and air raids by the Western Allies. The Kriegsmarine now undertook the task of organising transport and helping to bring the injured home.

Even though, as mentioned earlier, Germany had been using artillery support from the heavy naval vessels, these operations were now intensified. This was owing to two factors: first, the large German naval vessels could no longer operate on the high seas without being sunk, and, secondly, Germany had experienced a very convincing demonstration of the use of naval artillery in Normandy. In August 1944, the British historian B H Liddell Hart was given the opportunity to interview all the German generals who had been captured in northern France during the summer of 1944. He was especially interested in finding out what had most surprised the generals about the Normandy landings. A common characteristic in their statements was their amazement at the effectiveness which the Allied naval forces had demonstrated with their artillery. They had fired very precisely over great distances, and there had apparently been perfect co-ordination between army and navy. In the autumn of 1944, Germany therefore deployed all the large warships they had in providing artillery support for the German army, which was now retreating towards German territory as slowly as the operational situation allowed. The difference between the operations in the Baltic Sea and those off Normandy was that the Western Allies had an uncontested air supremacy over the invasion coastline. In the Baltic Sea, the threat from the air had become serious and German warships had to bring heavy anti-aircraft fire to bear. The Luftwaffe lacked fuel and could not provide air cover.

The greatest threat to the Courland convoys was Soviet aircraft. Throughout 1944, mine warfare had only cost the Germans eight ships (warships and merchant ships) sunk and eleven ships damaged. Four ships had been sunk or damaged by Soviet submarines, of which two were merchant ships near Memel on 15 October, so the submarine threat was just beginning to manifest itself. By contrast, fifty-eight ships were sunk and 112 damaged by Soviet aircraft – this mainly happened around the end of the year when the air threat was very pronounced.

The forces in Courland were supported by 2. Kampfgruppe: the pocket battleship *Lützow*, the heavy cruiser *Prinz Eugen*, the destroyers *Z25*, *Z35* and *Z36*, and torpedo boats *T13*, *T16*, *T20* and *T21*. The large warships from 2. Kampfgruppe directed fierce artillery fire at Soviet troop concentrations near Memel on 11/12 October and 14/15 October. The submarine trainees took part in the defence of the city. On 23 October, the Seekriegsleitung decided to send the large ships in to provide support without fighter cover. Fortunately for them, the Soviet command system was so rigid that it was not possible to improvise an attack, even if such a good opportunity presented itself.

When the Russians began operating with motor torpedo boats along the Baltic coast, the Seekriegsleitung considered sending all the German motor torpedo boats from the Netherlands and Norway into the Baltic Sea, but the final order only included two of the six motor torpedo boat flotillas from there.

On 30 October, the troop transport ship *Bremerhaven* sailed with evacuees from Ventspils to Gotenhafen. Just before reaching Gotenhafen, the ship was attacked by five Soviet aircraft. The attack resulted in a fire which took the lives of 410 people. There were 3,216 people on board, of whom 1,515 were wounded combatants.

It was the Kriegsmarine, not the army, which demanded that Memel had to be defended and on 22 November 1944, OKH General Reinhardt declared that Memel had been designated as a 'stronghold'.

The Kriegsmarine lost two of its precious destroyers, *Z35* and *Z36*, due to their own mines on 11 December 1944. *Z36* is shown here. After these losses, the Kriegsmarine only had seventeen destroyers left. (SMB arkiv)

In the autumn of 1944, the Seekriegsleitung decided to lay a new minefield in the Gulf of Finland. It was given the name Nilhorn and it was supposed to have been laid west of Nashorn, to hold the Russians back in the Gulf of Finland. On the morning of 11 December 1944, three German destroyers and two German torpedo boats left Pillau to lay this field. Once again, the German vessels sailed into their own minefields and two of the destroyers, Z35 and Z36, sank. After this, the Kriegsmarine only had seventeen destroyers left.

Autumn 1944: fuel and transport problems

Fuel shortages in Germany had become more palpable. During 1944, Allied bombers had destroyed a large part of the German oil industry facilities, including the facility in Pölitz near Stettin, and the oil fields in Estonia and Romania had been lost. Production of diesel oil decreased by 30 per cent. From 1 July 1944, a kind of rationing of heavy fuel oil was introduced for the various German authorities, and a month later this was extended to diesel fuel. The coal-fired ships had another problem. In a way, there was a lot of coal available from different coal mines, but now there were great difficulties in getting it transported to the users in the ports. German rail traffic was greatly reduced because of Allied air raids, but they could still use large barges for coal transport via the German rivers.

The land war reaches Germany's borders

Since the defeat at Stalingrad in the winter of 1942/43, the German armies had been on the retreat in Russia. The retreats took place under fierce fighting, but they were generally well-organised from the German side. The pressure from the huge Soviet forces was, however, too great. By October 1944, Soviet forces had advanced so far that they were threatening German territory in what was then East Prussia. On 22 October 1944, units of the 2nd Guard Tank Corps under the 11th Guards Army, commanded by General Kuzma Nikitovich Galitsky, captured the first town on German soil, Nemmersdorf (now Mayakovskoye in Russia). The town is located a little more than 60 miles/100km east of Königsberg. The Soviet forces got an opportunity of bringing tank units over the River Angerepp as the German army had not blown up the bridge in time. Now the fight had been taken to German soil and it had a decisive effect on the attacking soldiers from the Red Army, as well as the German forces and the civilian population of Germany.

During the German presence on Soviet territory from 1941 to 1944, German forces had committed monstrous acts that defied all description and which had laid the ground for an understandable hatred of Germans. The well-known Russian writer Ilya Ehrenburg had stirred up hatred and wishes for revenge in the Soviet media, and the Soviet authorities did nothing to restrict their soldiers' activities. What happened in Nemmersdorf can be found in several versions, although some of the reports contain exaggerations and misinformation.

The capture of the town took place in a blood-frenzy. It was recaptured by units from the German 4th Army after a few days. The sight that met the German troops was said to be indescribable. It was alleged that women had been raped and nailed up on barn doors; that women, children and old people had been mowed down, and that the same fate had befallen liberated German Communists and French prisoners of war. The situation was a gift for the Propaganda Minister Joseph Goebbels. His role in the Third Reich's beleaguered moment was to encourage and motivate the population to mobilise all forces against the enemy and here there was a propaganda prize: everyone could see for themselves what barbarians they had to defend themselves against. The Russians had certainly massacred the local people, but when Goebbels sent a propaganda team to cover the atrocities, they also described other incidents that had nothing to do with Nemmersdorf.[10] The reports from Nemmersdorf should therefore be taken with a grain of salt. A large part of the 'facts' promulgated is information which fitted in with Goebbels' propaganda, but which is not entirely accurate.

The leadership in Berlin wanted to support army operations with a strong local defence based on the local people led by functionaries of the Nazi Party. The Gauleiters were to encourage a fight to the last man and Hitler named key cities, including Königsberg, as impregnable strongholds. Unfortunately for Goebbels, what happened was that the film campaign about the Soviet atrocities in Nemmersdorf instead encouraged the population to flee westward – as quickly as possible. What was worse was that, in several cases, it was the party officials who were the first to flee, with the Gauleiters and the mayors in the lead. This came as a considerable surprise to the leadership in Berlin, which had lost its grip on what was going on among the population.

---

10 Historians agree that a massacre took place in Nemmersdorf, but some of the atrocities described happened elsewhere. Twenty-three people were killed in Nemmersdorf and a further thirty-eight in the surrounding area. In addition, ten more deaths are mentioned without further information. There was probably only one person nailed up on a barn door and that was a man. It has thus been difficult to distinguish between facts and propaganda.

The situation at the end of 1944: the major war lines

Germans were now fighting on German soil. The Soviet forces had destroyed the original Army Group Centre, and the numbers of dead and wounded Germans continued to rise. The second half of 1944 had been a bloody period for the German forces. On the Eastern Front, they had lost 840,000 killed or missing, and in Western Europe the figure was 393,000. On the Eastern Front, the Luftwaffe was now only able to muster 1,900 aircraft, while its Soviet counterpart had 15,500 aircraft. The Soviet forces now had about 6.8 million men organised into fifty-five armies and six tank armies.

Italy had already left the war in 1943 and, in 1944, Finland, Romania and Bulgaria also left. Only Hungary could summon up any support. Germany's last major ally, Japan, was fighting desperately against US supremacy in the Pacific.

The pressure on the Eastern Front, and the Allied bombing of cities, oil installations, railways, bridges, shipping, ports and factories led to increasing problems in Germany on many levels, from war fatigue and scarcity of goods at one end of the scale, to lack of fuel for fighter planes, industrial supply problems, raw material shortages, lack of skilled labour, lack of suitable soldiers and a general lack of fuel (coal, oil and petrol) at the other end. Food shortages became increasingly noticeable. Civilian casualties from the bombing of the big cities were increasing. The railway system was under heavy strain, and maritime transport was hampered by the large number of mines.

Because of the large number of nightly over-flights, it was not possible to know whether new mines had been dropped into the waters concerned. Minesweeping therefore had to start all over again, and thus became an endless task. The increased risk of mines meant that Germany was using the Danish ports of Frederikshavn and Aarhus in Jutland for connections between Germany and Norway. This gave a reduced need for sailing, but it increased the pressure on the Jutland trunk lines. This meant that the SOE's need for railway sabotage and intelligence in Jutland increased.

On the Western Front, Hitler had staked much on the Ardennes Campaign, which took place at Christmas in 1944. It was based on bad weather, so the Western Allies could not use their air supremacy. As soon as flying weather returned for the Allied air forces, the German attack broke down. The situation was now getting more acute on both fronts.

During their advance in Eastern Europe, Soviet forces stumbled over the first death camps. In July 1944, the Red Army liberated the camp in Majdanek, and established that there had been extensive killing of prisoners, mainly Jews and Soviet prisoners of war.

When German forces had to gradually pull out of Estonia and Latvia, they maintained their hold on the ports longer than the other areas. The isolated forces in Courland were being supplied by sea up until the end of the war on 8 May 1945. In the beginning, this took place from Danzig, and from February 1945 from Stettin instead. When Soviet forces reached the Baltic coast near Memel in October 1944, the German forces continued to hold the city. The Russians deployed a number of motor torpedo boats and motor gunboats here – these had not sailed to the area but had been transported over land. Soviet air raids in mid-December sank or damaged at least twelve German transport ships.

The winter of 1944/45 was unusually severe, often with temperatures more than twenty degrees below zero, and it was clear that the situation was slowly becoming chaotic. German society, which in principle was well organised, gradually broke apart, despite the population being tremendously disciplined. There were too many authorities involved and they reacted too slowly because of maintaining the outward pretence that everything would come right when the wonder weapons that Hitler had up his sleeve were produced and used – everyone should just stay calm and do what they were told. In the last six months of the war, the Nazi Party, the SS, the German army, the Kriegsmarine, the Luftwaffe, industry and the civil authorities seemed like actors who were not working together on any overall common goal. The big shift in developments came in earnest when the city of Königsberg, the capital of East Prussia, came under threat from the middle of January 1945.

The Soviet Baltic Fleet forces its way out into the Baltic Sea once more

The sinking of *Nordstern* on 7 October 1944 gave Germany considerable evidence that Soviet submarines had slipped out and were now a threat to all shipping. On the night of 12/13 October 1944, the Danish freighter *Hilma Lau* from the Lauritzen shipping company was on its way from Danzig to Copenhagen with a cargo of coal. East of Bornholm, it was hit by two torpedoes from a Soviet submarine and sank in three minutes. Four Danish crew members perished. The submarine was the former Estonian submarine *Lembit*, now sailing under the Soviet flag. *Hilma Lau* had previously sailed with iron ore from Sweden to Germany.

On 21 November 1944, there was a German report about a Soviet submarine in Køge Bay, south of Copenhagen (although this does not mean that there actually was a Soviet submarine there). On 24 November, the Soviet submarine *L-21* sank the small passenger boat *Hansa*, which was en route from Nynäshamn in Sweden to Visby on Gotland. Eighty-four Swedish citizens lost their lives. The submarine commander thought he had sunk a large merchant ship on its way to Germany. On 12 December 1944, the Soviet submarine *Lembit* returned to Turku in Finland from a patrol. Because of bad weather, it was sailing at periscope depth when it collided with something; many years later this proved to have been the German submarine *U-479*, which had gone down with all hands.

Maritime operations in the central part of the Baltic Sea in the autumn of 1944

In October 1944, the head of the German naval staff, Admiral Wilhelm Meisel, wrote an instruction covering the Kriegsmarine's main task, which was to support army operations in the coastal areas and to protect supplies to army units on the Eastern Front. The Kriegsmarine notified the army, however, that it should not expect a level of ambition that corresponded to the Allied effort with its large artillery warships in Normandy. The Luftwaffe no longer had air supremacy in the areas where the Kriegsmarine was operating in the Baltic Sea, and there was no effective protection against the submarine threat, either. At the same time, there were problems with the training of crews for the big ships. The crews on the pocket battleship *Admiral Scheer* and the heavy cruiser *Admiral Hipper* had to practise providing artillery support for the army. The ships' ammunition was also running low and resupplies had to be fetched from the Kriegsmarine's depots in Norway.

Allied mines were now becoming a growing problem: British and US aircraft had begun to operate over East Prussia and Danzig Bay. The mines were mostly dropped in Danzig Bay, where submarine training and some of the submarine construction took place, as well as off ports and along the convoy routes. Soviet naval aircraft and submarines were also mining the German shipping routes. In January 1945, the Germans finally evacuated their bridgehead at Memel, and Soviet motor torpedo boats and motor gunboats were then based nearby, from where the first attack took place on 17 February 1945. At the beginning of 1945, the Seekriegsleitung calculated that there were constantly between three and six Soviet submarines on patrol. Admiral Kummetz therefore demanded the deployment of at least two anti-submarine flotillas. The only appropriate vessels were assigned to the commander of the submarine service. When the Seekriegsleitung refused to provide ships from here, because it would ruin the test programmes and exercises, no serious steps were taken to locate and destroy Soviet submarines in the Baltic Sea from the end of 1944 to the end of the war. On the other hand, the Soviet

The German light cruiser *Leipzig* was badly damaged in a collision north of Hela with the heavy cruiser *Prinz Eugen* in thick fog on 15 October 1944. *Leipzig* was almost cut in two when it was hit by *Prinz Eugen* making 20 knots; *Prinz Eugen* was repaired in less than a month, but *Leipzig* never regained operational status. (SMB arkiv)

Union protested to Britain over the RAF's minelaying in the central Baltic Sea. The British mines were hampering Soviet submarine operations and there was apparently no overall operational co-operation on naval warfare in the Baltic Sea in the last phase of the war. Britain wanted to halt the mobility of German submarines, while the Soviet Union wanted to paralyse German naval transports.

Sweden between 22 June 1944 and New Year 1945

Admiral Kummetz's problems with Sweden continued. In the beginning of July 1944, a German patrol boat observed a Swedish destroyer near the Baltic Coast – so instead of aircraft, Sweden was now sending a destroyer! During the next month, German vessels observed Swedish warships near the Irben Strait (the entrance to the Gulf of Riga) on three occasions. On one occasion, the Germans fired at a Swedish aircraft which was less than a mile from a German patrol boat, near Muhu Island. The Germans had not expected the Swedish plane to return fire, and Admiral Kummetz noted that it was the first time that Swedish forces had done so. Less than a week later, a German submarine exercise flotilla reported that there was a Swedish destroyer eighteen nautical miles north-northwest of Libau. This had Kummetz exclaiming, 'The Swedes are in the middle of our submarine exercise area.'

However, it should be made clear that Swedish reconnaissance operations served a defensive purpose, because there was a real threat of invasion by Germany. The Swedes received reports now and then of an imminent German invasion, and sometimes Swedish defence forces also had to back up government actions which were directed against German interests. It was thus possible that it would eventually cost something one way or another. The Swedish navy was primarily prepared for defensive operations, but on the Swedish east coast it also had to be able to act offensively. In addition to combating an invasion force, attacks could be required on German supply lines to the Åland Islands if they were occupied by Germany, as well as attacks on German supply lines in the Gulf of Bothnia, and on German bases on the coast between Tallinn and Libau. A major Swedish problem was that a German attack on Sweden could emanate from Germany, as well as from Norway, Denmark, Finland and the Baltic countries.

During the summer of 1944, it became clear to the Swedish government that Hitler could not win the war. It was therefore necessary for Sweden to rapidly distance itself from its past sins and its participation in the war on the German side. In August 1944, the Swedish government advised that Swedish ships could no longer be insured in German ports. This was a de facto rejection of aid being given to the German war economy by Swedish shipping, and a ban on participation in it.

Prompted by developments in Courland, the Swedish government reinforced the defence forces on Gotland in the beginning of September 1944. Hitler was of the opinion that as long as there were German troops in Courland, Sweden would have no desire to join the war on the Allied side.

Sweden had at this point in time been under much sustained diplomatic pressure from the Western Allies, who wanted to stop Swedish exports of ball bearings and iron ore to Germany (see page 187). Since the start of the war, between four and six ships daily had departed with Swedish iron ore for Germany, but it was now halted, and the last German transit through Swedish waters was conducted on 9 September 1944. On 27 September 1944, Sweden closed all its Baltic Sea ports to foreign shipping. Sweden finally ceased its exports of ball bearings to Germany on 12 October 1944. From 1941 to 1944, 40 per cent of iron ore exports to Germany had been transported by Swedish ships and 10 per cent by Finnish ships. Danish merchant ships had also participated in this traffic. Before supplies came to a halt in September, Germany had counted on importing 9 million tonnes of iron ore from Sweden in 1944. At this point in time, Germany was also having great difficulties in

256   THE NAVAL WAR IN THE BALTIC

procuring sea transport and fuel for its ships. From 29 September 1944, the Seekriegsleitung instructed all vessels under its command to avoid making border violations in Swedish territorial waters – purely to avoid sending Sweden over into the enemy camp as a belligerent party. Grossadmiral Dönitz was furious and said that 'these actions were an expression of the Swedes' fear of and dependence on Jewish capital'. The Kriegsmarine set out various aggressive plans, but Generalfeldmarschall Keitel cut things short on 15 October 1944 by declaring that it was in Germany's interest to avoid conflict with Sweden.

Sweden could also see that there were going to be major changes in the Baltic Sea. It began to get reports of Soviet submarines in the Baltic Sea from October. On 11 November 1944, the entire Baltic Sea was declared a war zone by Generaladmiral Kummetz[11] and the Seekriegsleitung stressed to German submarine commanders that they must not fire on a merchant ship until they were sure that it was not Swedish. The war zone made many things much easier, because if Sweden turned up with destroyers or aircraft, they could be fired on with a little more justification than earlier. He also pointed out that mines could disrupt links between Finland and Sweden, but Grossadmiral Dönitz's response to this was that the Kriegsmarine had no interest in this traffic. In late 1944, it was reported that the Swedish commander-in-chief of Defence, General Olof Thörnell 'was on the verge of tears about the German defeat'. His concerns probably included uncertainty about Soviet intentions.

The submarine net in the northern part of the Sound produced problems within the Swedish government. As the fortunes of war turned for the Germans, the Swedish government wanted to demonstrate that the net had been laid in violation of international law. The Swedish government was the sovereign authority on questions of passage in Swedish territorial waters, and this was how they wanted to present it to the Germans at this late stage of the war. There was one problem, though, namely that the Swedish people had absolutely no idea that a submarine net had been laid out, that it had been laid out by Germany, and that the Swedish government had collaborated with the Germans on the net throughout its extent between Denmark and Sweden. The government now took a stand and let the Swedish navy terminate the agreement around the net, but since the Swedish people had not been told that the net was there, it was left where it was. If official piloting and sailing directions were followed on the Swedish side, in the area of the net barrier, it would be possible to follow a mineswept route quite close to Viken, a small harbour between Helsingborg and Höganäs. This

---

11   Admiral Oskar Kummetz was promoted to Generaladmiral on 16 September 1944.

meant that shipping came very close to land – and around the submarine net – without otherwise becoming aware of the net's existence.[12] The outcome of the disagreement between Germany and Sweden was that on 21 October 1944, the Seekriegsleitung made demands about installing a further net barrier in the Sound. A German net barrier was thereby laid out between Drogden and Bredgrund in Danish territorial waters; it was completed on 21 November 1944.

The German trials with the V-1 and V-2 weapons at Peenemünde resulted in considerable British interest in having a presence and its own surveillance in the area. Intelligence personnel from the RAF managed to get permission from the Swedish authorities to set up a station in a summer cottage at Ottenby on the coast near the southern tip of Öland, from where they could follow the German trials. The condition was that a Swedish officer had to be present. The cover story was that 'the Swedish air force was holding trials here of a newly purchased British radar installation for future use in Sweden.' In reality, the British built their own radar station. This British operation on Swedish soil was a clear breach of neutrality. When a V-2 trial rocket fell in Bäckebo near Kalmar on 13 June 1944, Britain was sent the most important parts of the wreckage by courier plane after Sweden had first studied them. Since the German attack on the Soviet Union in 1941, Germany had flown regular courier flights over Swedish territory to northern Norway and Finland. They were civil Ju 52 aircraft, which have since proved to have been armed. The British used armed Mosquito aircraft, which were also flown by aircrew in civilian clothes. In principle, they were not military aircraft either, but it appears that all parties had their own interpretations of neutrality. Germany carried out 1,309 courier flights over Sweden in 1942 and they ended in May 1944. In 1944, Britain carried out 1,137 courier flights to Sweden. Together the Western Allies had a total of 3,333 courier flights, while the German total was 3,157. Allied aircraft could have been carrying diplomats, resistance fighters,[13] fleeing or interned flight

12 The chief editor of the Swedish local newspaper, the *Karlstadstidningen*, Manne Ståhl, got wind of the submarine net during the war and wanted to write about it, but the censors forbade him 'to write about defence installations. It could harm Swedish defences.' A year after the war and one year after Torgny Segerstedt's death, the *Göteborgs Handels-och Sjöfartstidning* (*Gothenburg Trade and Shipping Journal*) stated on 13 April 1946: 'It was near Viken, adjacent to the submarine net, that Sweden through its own Per Albin Hansson fell on its knees before Adolf Hitler for the first time … It was here that Hitler not only learned to correctly understand and appreciate our governing character and calibre, he also learned that he could go further. And he did too. Before long he came with his furlough trains.'

13 The Danish nuclear physicist Niels Bohr flew from Sweden to Britain in a Mosquito so he could travel on to the US to participate in the Manhattan Project, the production of the American atomic bomb.

crew, special steel and ball bearings. In 1944, a total of ten Germans, twenty Estonians and two Latvians took the opportunity to escape by aircraft from the Eastern Front to seek asylum in Sweden. They were placed in a special camp at Vägershult in southern Sweden.

The Swedish diplomat Sven Grafström, who was very critical of the Swedish government's conduct, wrote in his diary on 13 June 1944:

> We have today reached an agreement with Britain on the delivery of 50 radar systems for our aircraft. As compensation, we let 75 Allied pilots leave Sweden. To release the pilots in this way is obviously not in conformity with international law, but what does a poor girl do? Without these devices, we cannot protect ourselves from air attacks.[14]

A number of aircraft, belonging to both Germany and the Allies, were shot down by the Swedish air force. From 1943 until the end of the war, Sweden calculated that between 6,000 and 8,000 Allied aircraft violated Swedish airspace. These were mainly British aircraft operating at night. For example, about six hundred bombers flew over Swedish territory on the outward and return journeys in connection with the second major bombing raid on Königsberg on the night of 29/30 August 1944. They took the opportunity of avoiding the German air defences by deliberately flying over southern Sweden. In January 1945, it was said that the Swedish foreign minister, Günther 'was trivialising the Allied overflights and the protests in London were a mere formality.'

In the whole of 1944, 975 Britons and Americans and twenty Poles were released from internment and returned to Britain; 121 Russians were sent back to the Soviet Union. Germany got 328 Germans and twenty aircraft back.

In August 1944, a captain in the Swedish merchant fleet returned to a German port when he discovered two escaped British prisoners of war on board; the captain was blacklisted by the Allies. The case reached a British newspaper, which indicated that the captain had also been dismissed by the shipping company.

The threat of war against Sweden generally declined, according to Swedish understanding at the time, after the Normandy invasion and the Soviet advance in 1944, but Swedish intelligence services had to carefully watch the German retreat through the Baltic states in 1944 and 1945. These retreat operations could have led to acts of war directed against Gotland, Öland and the Swedish mainland. German fighters shot down three Swedish reconnaissance aircraft during this period.

---

14   Quoted from *Vårstormar – 1944 – Krigsslutet skönjes* (*Spring storms – 1944 – The end of the war discerned*), Bo Huldt and Klaus-Richard Böhme (Probus, 1995).

When Finland withdrew from the war, the Finnish President Mannerheim and the Swedish Prime Minister Per Albin Hansson came to an agreement that the Finnish radio detection service had to be evacuated to Sweden. It had achieved amazing results in locating and identifying Soviet units just by taking radio bearings and monitoring. Some of the messages could be deciphered, so it was possible to understand the content of the signals traffic. This was when Plan Stella Polaris was launched: in late summer 1944, three ships sailed cipher materials, radio equipment, two hundred filing cabinets and a large number of Finnish experts to Sweden, where they could continue their efforts aimed at their large neighbour in the east. Once there, they began to work for the FRA, which was later very grateful for this expertise during the Cold War.

The refugee situation in Sweden develops

In the autumn of 1944, the number of foreign refugees in Sweden increased dramatically: 30,000 from Norway, 15,000 from Denmark, 25,000 from the Baltic countries, 6,500 Estonian Swedes, 38,000 from Finland and 11,000 others. Among these unfortunate people, there were also spies, infiltrating agents, political defectors, fleeing war criminals, ordinary criminals and others who in one way or another could pose a threat to or a problem for Swedish society. Volunteers were recruited among the Danish and Norwegian refugees for military units which could be deployed in the events which were ending the war: officially, these were police forces.

Limited use of radio, radar and sonar in the war on the Eastern Front

The acts of war on the Eastern Front and in the Baltic Sea – in contrast to the air and maritime warfare in Western Europe – were not characterised by the latest technological advances. There was almost no use of radar and sonar on the Soviet side, but both warring parties took advantage of hydrophones for submarine hunting.

Many Soviet warships and aircraft had little or no radio communications, and this is one of the reasons why favourable tactical situations were not always exploited; another reason was the rigid command structure. The situation was similar in the Red Army units. Early Soviet radar was introduced, though, around September 1944 in some of the American-built Boston aircraft. They had Gneiss-2M radar, so they would be able to locate and attack ships at sea in all weathers. At the beginning of 1944, the Luftwaffe sent night-fighters and radar equipment to support the Finnish air defences.

The air war in the Baltic Sea

The operations of the Western Allies in the air war were in pursuit of a general collapse in Germany's industry, economy and infrastructure. In addition, they specifically aimed at stopping the production of advanced submarines, which they had no countermeasures against, and it can be said that these operations succeeded in the end. The Soviet contribution consisted primarily of the massive military pressure on the Eastern Front, where they tied down large forces and where they inflicted enormous losses on Germany – especially on its army – in the last year of the war.

In 1944, the RAF was ready for an increased effort in the Baltic Sea, partly with extensive minelaying operations and partly with air raids on coastal towns further east. Six to eight minelaying operations were carried out each month. In *British Maritime Doctrine*,[15] which is a kind of textbook on naval warfare, the RAF's minelaying in the Baltic Sea from 1943 to 1945 is described as an excellent example of the use of the principle of 'economy of forces'. For a relatively modest effort in terms of the loss of flight crews and aircraft and of the use of weapons, the air-dropped mines in the eastern part of the Baltic Sea had a very great effect. The RAF sacrificed a lot of resources to drop mines here, but this was due to the desire to cause difficulties for German submarine training, which was concentrated around 1. Abteilung der Ubootslehrdivision (1st Unit Submarine Training Division) in Memel and 2. Abteilung der Ubootslehrdivision in Gotenhafen on board the passenger ship *Wilhelm Gustloff*. The submarine training was hampered and delayed, and it was difficult for the new German submarines to be taken out on trial without hitting mines. In the last year of the war, it is estimated that the Kriegsmarine had allocated a total of 250,000 men to clearing mines. (The figure also includes German minesweeping and mine clearance outside the Baltic Sea.)

On the night of 29/30 August 1944, the RAF carried out a raid on two different targets in the Baltic Sea. The first was Stettin, the second Königsberg, which was at the maximum range of the British bombers. Königsberg had so far been spared major involvement in the war because of its remoteness. That night the city lost 40 per cent of its housing and 20 per cent of its industry, but the raid cost fifteen of the 189 attacking bombers. The local German

---

15 Naval Staff Directorate, *British Maritime Doctrine*, BR 1806, second edition (Stationery Office, London, 1999).

fighter defences had made themselves felt. The RAF had also tried to attack Königsberg three nights earlier, but most of the bombs had fallen in the eastern part of the city; that is, outside the industrial areas.

The changed situation in the air over northern Germany now led to frequent attacks on shipping in the Baltic region. The first attack took place on 1 October 1944 when Mustang P-51Ds and Mosquitoes attacked a submarine south of the Danish island of Als and the shipyard at Sønderborg in Denmark. This indicated a new era for German naval and commercial ships in Danish waters. From now on, it could only become increasingly difficult for Germany, and the threat of low-flying fighters, fighter bombers and bombers was part of everyday life. The USAAF carried out a number of daylight raids on German port cities. Conversely, this was not without its cost to the attackers. Submarines, other warships and merchant ships carried a lot of flak guns, and a lot of fighter aircraft, including night-fighters, were stationed at German air bases in Denmark. On the other hand, the Luftwaffe's fuel situation gradually deteriorated towards the end of the war.

On 18 December 1944, the RAF carried out a raid on the port of Gotenhafen where a number of warships and merchant ships were hit, among them *Schleswig-Holstein*, which was now a training vessel.

In 1944, the RAF withdrew two squadrons of radar-equipped Halifax bombers from minelaying operations. They were stationed in the Hebrides and were given new armaments, namely 0.75in/20mm guns and armour-piercing rockets, and with additional fuel tanks, they could cover the entire Skagerrak and Kattegat. They were now deployed against German shipping between Norway and Denmark.

Heading for the final collapse

In what follows, the progress of the war is depicted month by month. This is done in order to compare better the more or less simultaneous events on land and out on the Baltic Sea. In this way, the refugee situation will also be located in the actual time frame. Around the final collapse, land war, naval war and evacuation meld into one enormous chaos and mayhem.

9

New Year 1944/45 to the End of the War – Month by Month

An overview of the war

Around the turn of the year 1944/45, from the German point of view the military situation was deteriorating from going badly to being a disaster. The top political and military leadership was hoping that the so-called *Wunderwaffen* which were in production would have a decisive effect on the war. Conversely, the Western Allies were taking very strong action against those parts of the weapons' production that they could identify and attack from the air. Since the first bombing of Peenemünde, some of the production facilities had been moved to underground mines.

The Western Allies' invasion of Normandy had been successful, but the swift attack over the Rhine in September had stalled at Arnhem and this had led to another winter of war. Since May 1943, the German submarine threat had been reduced to something more amenable to the Western Allies, and a stream of supplies was therefore flowing from the US to Britain. France had been liberated. In Belgium, there had been some very heavy fighting when Hitler launched his Ardennes Campaign just before Christmas, a campaign which was intended to deprive the Western Allies of the possibility of getting supplies in through the Belgian ports. Moreover, the Germans had launched two campaigns with the new wonder weapons. On 13 June 1944, they had launched the V-1 campaign and, on 8 September 1944, the new ballistic missile V-2 had been taken into operation.

The Allies' air war was gaining momentum in the last year of the war. With the P-51D Mustang fighter aircraft – equipped with drop tanks – it became possible to provide fighter escort for daylight bombing raids on German cities. Fighter bombers were also gradually helping in destruction of the entire German infrastructure. In the last months of the war, Allied air forces attacked bridges, trains, railway hubs, fuel supplies, ships, ports, inland waterways, trucks and cars. The Western Allies had relatively high mobility, but it was logistics that were controlling activity. The crossing of the Rhine was given high priority.

In January 1945, the rapid Soviet advance provoked a stream of refugees across country from East Prussia's easternmost areas; people had to be evacuated from here by ship. The first major German cities did not fall until the end of March (Danzig) and the beginning of April (Königsberg).

German refugees from the East: Unternehmen Rettung (Operation Rescue) from 15 January to the end of May 1945

The refugee situation was to leave its mark on the remainder of the war in the Baltic Sea. In what follows, distances to reception ports, the threat from mines, submarines and aircraft, the ships available, the fuel situation, the winter, the administrative leadership, infectious diseases and much more, will be explained in detail. All of these factors cannot be considered individually, but have to be viewed in a larger context.

The background for the refugee situation was the Red Army's advance towards German territory. In several places, Soviet forces reached the coast, and German troops and civilians were thereby cut off from fleeing across country. Air transport was almost out of the question. There were no transport aircraft, aircraft fuel or fighter protection available on a large scale at this point in time. The Kriegsmarine now undertook the task of evacuating troops, as well as civilians, from the threatened areas in Courland, East Prussia and in the area around Danzig Bay.

In the last months of the war, the minesweept routes across the Baltic Sea came to the rescue of many German refugees from the Third Reich's most eastern areas, but the voyages demanded very considerable sacrifices. For most people, the sinking of the *Titanic* is regarded as the worst accident in maritime history, but during the winter and spring of 1945, the Baltic Sea was witness to at least four war events or accidents at sea which, when measured in loss of life, were much worse than the *Titanic* disaster. For various reasons, these events have not received nearly as much coverage. Three of the disasters included refugee ships bound for the west; ships which were sunk approximately sixty, eighty and a hundred nautical miles east of Bornholm. The last disaster involved thousands of concentration camp prisoners in two ships off Neustadt near Lübeck.

Developments on the Eastern Front were soon out of the German authorities' control. On the one hand, the 'system' (the Nazi Party) wanted to give the impression that everything was under control. As a result, it was considered far too early to initiate evacuations. On the other hand, people from the Eastern areas had prior knowledge of the Russian advance and what it meant.

The sea rescue operation is launched

Around 15 January 1945, without Hitler's full knowledge, the commander-in-chief for the Navy, Grossadmiral Dönitz, launched what was described as *Unternehmen Hannibal* or *Unternehemen Rettung* (Operation Rescue): the Kriegsmarine's evacuation of refugees and troops from the East. Dönitz had a highly skilled and competent naval officer on his staff as Seetra-Chef, that is, head of all naval transport. He reported directly to Dönitz and the two held regular meetings. His name was Kapitän zur See Konrad Engelhardt and he was promoted to Konteradmiral, 'so he would be in a better position to argue with the Field Marshals,' as Dönitz put it. His area of responsibility stretched from northern Norway to Courland in Latvia. Engelhardt's past as a captain in the merchant navy meant that he had many good connections there. In January 1945, it was clear to both Dönitz and Engelhardt that the navy had to become much more active in the Baltic Sea. In Berlin, there was no longer any sense of the realities of the situation and Hitler was not interested in the suffering of the people.

Dönitz was acutely aware that large groups of German people had to be rescued westward by sea. If this whole operation, along with the German retreat, took place in good order, he would have time to get his new weapons, the Type XXI and Type XXIII submarines, ready for action, which would be crucial for the outcome of the war. When the refugee problem began, it was really a land-based evacuation problem that the civil authorities should have taken care of. It could have been completed in plenty of time, but the authorities failed for political and ideological reasons.

The official part of the *Unternehmen Rettung* was the provision of supplies and troops to the army. The Kriegsmarine's ships also participated in air defence and bombardment in support of German army operations in coastal areas. Assistance was also to be offered with the retreat and evacuation of the wounded from the front. The less official part was to evacuate as many refugees westward as possible, and this could be done in connection with the evacuation of the large numbers of wounded. The evacuation operation should not detract from the Kriegsmarine's war-related operations, but it fitted in well with getting supplies in for the front, bombarding the advancing Red Army, and then returning with the wounded and refugees to a German port further west, where the ship could be refuelled and have its ammunition replenished. The operation was complicated by the rapidly changing situation and chaotic conditions in the evacuation ports.

It took a few days before the operation manifested itself in ship movements. It lasted until 10 May 1945, a total of 115 days. The operation is sometimes referred to as the largest rescue operation the world has ever seen. The naval staff had first to procure an overview of requirements and possibilities.

A plan had to be drawn up, suitable ships had to be acquired and, finally, facilities had to be arranged in the reception ports. Engelhardt was aware that he would have to use everything that could float for his task, but there was a catastrophic shortage of fuel. There were not enough resources or enough time to convert the available shipping capacity so that it could operate with large volumes of refugees and wounded. OKH had not prepared the commander of naval transport for the size of a task that demanded a great deal of preparatory work with respect to ships' interiors, stocks of freshwater, sanitation, food provision, fitting out berths, and in particular the provision of doctors and nurses. Added to this, there were problems with the lack of crews, weather conditions – particularly the ice situation – escort vessels, convoying, minesweeping, and threats from enemy mines, aircraft and submarines. Lifesaving equipment often had to be ignored.

Engelhardt wanted to use the large passenger ships for the evacuation: Germany's largest passenger ships had mostly been lying idle since the start of the war. Most of them had been converted into hospital ships and had hardly sailed at all. They had been built for the routes to North and South America and for Kraft durch Freude (Strength through Joy) – which was the Nazi party's holiday organisation for model workers – but the ships were now suffering from poor maintenance.

The first evacuations took place around 21 January 1945. On 24 January 1945, the situation came so much to a head that the Kriegsmarine was ordered immediately to initiate evacuations from Königsberg and Pillau. The passenger liners *Steuben*[1] and *Berlin* had to collect 10,000 wounded immediately and 20,000 wounded later. One of the first ships in the operation took about three thousand refugees on board and sailed west with them. The ship was still not fitted out for refugee transport and had only one toilet on board.

Pressure was soon put on Admiral Skagerrak, Hans-Heinrich Wurmbach, who had now been promoted to Admiral. Could he find room for refugees in Denmark? As the plenipotentiary in Denmark, SS-Obergruppenführer Dr Werner Best could not refuse to receive German refugees and shortly after there came a Führer directive about it. Dr Best reported to the German authorities that room could be created for 150,000 German refugees in Denmark, but by that time the evacuation was already in full swing. On

---

1 *Steuben* was originally built in 1922 at the Vulkan shipyard in Stettin for the Norddeutscher Lloyd shipping line and bore the name *München*. It sailed the North American routes and, after a fire in 1930, it changed its name to *General von Steuben*. It was named after a German general (1730–1794) who went to the United States in 1777 and helped George Washington to organise the US Army during the American War of Independence. When the German-American relationship was on the wane in Nazi Germany, the ship changed its name again in 1938 to *Steuben*.

4 February 1945, Adolf Hitler issued the following directive: 'In order to reduce the strain on the transport system in the Reich, I order that the groups coming from the Reich's eastern areas, in addition to being quartered in the Reich, can also be quartered in Denmark.'

In total, up until the end of the war, Denmark received about 250,000 German refugees, ie about 10 per cent of the total stream of refugees.

Distances between loading ports and reception ports
The main distances are reproduced below: 1 nautical mile = 1.15 miles = 1,852m.

Pillau–Hel:	38 nautical miles
Pillau–Danzig:	45 nautical miles
Danzig–Hel:	13 nautical miles
Pillau–Swinemünde:	210 nautical miles
Pillau–Copenhagen:	275 nautical miles
Pillau–Kiel:	320 nautical miles

The distances in themselves were not so important. When the route had been chosen, escort vessels had to be found and, before that, minesweeping had to be completed. Minesweeping, in particular, put restrictions on the transports. The convoys had a turnaround time between the collection areas and Swinemünde of seven days, while they had to count on ten days to Copenhagen.

The fuel situation and merchant ships available in the Baltic Sea
In 1944, according to Engelhardt's information, forty-four large vessels, totalling 101,000grt, from the German merchant fleet had been sunk in the Baltic Sea, and a similar number had had to be scrapped because of war damage and accidents. Among the non-operating passenger ships, Engelhardt could commandeer *Cap Arcona* (27,561 tonnes), the sister ships *Robert Ley* and *Wilhelm Gustloff* from the Kraft durch Freude organisation (each approximately 26,000 tonnes), *Hamburg* (22,117 tonnes), *Hansa* (21,131 tonnes) and *Deutschland* (21,046 tonnes). Ships between 10,000 and 20,000 tonnes included *Potsdam, Pretoria, Berlin, Steuben, Monte Rosa, Antonio Delfino* and *Winrich von Kniprode*.[2] In addition, there were approximately twenty-five freighters between 5,000 and 10,000 tonnes, and a host of smaller boats, barges and special ships.

The freighters had been through some tough years during the war, when they had been sailing a lot, and they had hardly been maintained. They were

2   *Winrich von Kniprode* was named after the Grand Master of the Teutonic Order of Knights, 1351–1382. This order was part of the ideological baggage of the SS.

The fast passenger liner *Antonio Delfino* was used for evacuation of troops, wounded soldiers and refugees. (Old Ship Picture Galleries)

rusty, ropes and cables were missing, the fuel was of poor quality, and the machinery in poor condition. They suddenly had to be made ready to sail and had to be provided with crews. From the end of 1944, most of the deck crews and some of the engine-room crews had been called up for the *Volkssturm* (the people's attack, in which Hitler called up all those between fifteen and sixty who were not already in a military unit into a kind of Home Guard for a final, last-ditch effort), so the ships were manned by Croats and sometimes by Ukrainians, often without proper training. The sailors who were still on the ships were not covered by the military war pension because they had not officially been in war service. They were hired as sailors in the merchant navy. As one of the sources puts it: 'For the sailors, there was no heroic death, only work accidents with fatal outcomes.'[3]

The evacuation of the German population groups up until the end of the war

Within the German cities which, one by one, were being surrounded and captured by the Russians was an administrative chaos which, in simple terms, generally boiled down to there being so many rival agencies involved and to their responsibilities not being clearly defined. Hitler and Goebbels demanded

---

3   See Jürg Meister, *Der Seekrieg in den osteuropäischen Gewässern 1939–1945* (J F Lehmanns Verlag, Munich, 1958).

that the people should 'Stand firm, fight and win or die.' This meant that the Nazi Party had the same attitude. The evacuations were therefore not started in time. The Gauleiters were under the command of Reichsleiter Martin Bormann. All mayors had to be party members and thus, in practice, worked for him and, generally speaking, the urban governments worked reasonably well right up until the end of the war, but the higher echelons of the Nazi Party were not as brave as their rhetoric would have them appear, so they usually took the opportunity to make themselves scarce before the general population realised what was happening, and they had their cars and petrol rations to ease the hardships of flight. The result was that the commanders of army and naval units frequently and suddenly found themselves with the responsibility for a huge mass of people who had to be evacuated far too late, after the means of transportation had already collapsed and the responsible leaders had disappeared. The most glaring examples were the Gauleiters in Königsberg and Breslau, but each in their own way. Gauleiter Erich Koch from Königsberg will be mentioned later. Gauleiter Karl Hanke[4] defended Breslau in a manner which attracted both Hitler's and Goebbels' attention. In the last days of the war, when Hitler discovered that Himmler had various peace overtures ongoing, he was stripped of all his posts and Karl Hanke was then appointed Reichsführer SS. When Breslau fell, Karl Hanke was not left lying on the battlefield. He flew out in a light Fieseler Storch aircraft which had been well hidden. The runway had been built by young people, especially from the Hitler Youth, many of whom died during the work.

Refugees from the eastern areas tried to get to the Baltic coast and from there further west, either by sea or across country, but the tactical situation could quickly change. Suddenly, a major German army in Courland was bypassed by Soviet forces, who reached the coast. By late January 1945, most of East Prussia had also been cut off and it was no longer possible to escape across country. The refugees therefore tried to get to the ports of Königsberg and Pillau for a passage by ship over Danzig Bay. From Gotenhafen-Oxhöft (now Oksywie in the Polish port of Gdynia) and from the two nearby ports of Gotenhafen-Neufahrwasser (now Gdańsk Nowy Port) and Zoppot (now Sopot), it was possible to get a passage to Kiel, Flensburg and Copenhagen. Gotenhafen-Oxhöft was a hub, and one of Germany's largest passenger ships, MV *Wilhelm Gustloff*, 26,000 tonnes, was berthed here as a training ship for the Kriegsmarine's 2. Abteilung der Ubootslehrdivision (2nd Unit Submarine Training Division). Crews for the new German Type XXI submarines were being trained here. Because of the submarine school's activities in Danzig

---

4   After the war, Karl Hanke was interned by the Allies while he was living under a false identity. He was shot while trying to escape and identified as a wanted war criminal afterwards.

Bay, the RAF regularly sent heavy bombers to mine the bay and the coastal routes along the German Baltic coast. American and British aircraft also bombed Danzig towards the end of the war.

German refugees in Denmark

The last months of the Second World War brought the war closer to Danish territory, and the German administration was now sending refugees in large numbers to Denmark. In recent years, there has been some focus on the previously taboo topic of the treatment of the refugees in Denmark and the suffering inflicted on them during the final months of the war, as well as their treatment until repatriation. In Denmark, the refugee problem has been a delicate subject. On the one hand, one could feel sorry for the large numbers of people who, under great human suffering, had been expelled from their homelands and now found themselves in a strange land, ravaged by hunger and disease. Innocent children died during the flight to Denmark and the subsequent stay in the country – some have since asked whether Denmark shares responsibility for their deaths.

On the other hand, the Danish population regarded the German refugees as accomplices in the war. The German population had itself chosen war and supported Hitler and, when the refugees came to Denmark in humiliating circumstances in the last months of the war, some of them behaved with a supremacist mentality, still convinced of the final victory and the righteousness of the German cause. Daily life in Denmark at the turn of 1944/45 was characterised by shortages and rationing, so it did not make the foreigners who were being forced on the country more welcome. The refugees consisted mainly of women, children and the elderly. Men between fifteen and sixty years of age had been conscripted into the armed forces or the Volkssturm. The refugees were often malnourished and their long journeys, where they were subjected to acts of war in up to twenty degrees of frost, had injured them in different ways. Infant mortality was high, due partly to measles and scarlet fever, but also to malnutrition, and the cold claimed victims among the smallest.

The massive Soviet offensive on the Eastern Front caused hundreds of thousands of German soldiers to be wounded. Many of the wounded came west in different ways with the refugee ships, but the possibilities of providing them with necessary care and treatment along the way were fading. In the last months of the war, there was a lack of surgical equipment and of the most basic analgesics, as well as anaesthetic and morphine preparations, dressings and much more.

The German authorities used Copenhagen as a destination for many of the refugee ships and many of the schools in Copenhagen were requisitioned as refugee centres, so the schools had to close to teaching. At negotiations with the

German authorities between 16 and 25 March 1945, the permanent secretaries' administration presented requests for improving conditions for Danish prisoners in German prisons and concentration camps. These were refused by the Germans. Dr Best stated that the prisoners were under German jurisdiction. The Danish Board of Health and the doctors' organisations took part in the meetings. That refusal formed the background for the German refugees in Denmark, in turn, not being admitted to Danish hospitals. There was a clear agreement that the German refugees in Denmark were a purely German affair. If the Germans had prioritised medicines, bandages and hospital berths, they could have managed the situation, but they were instead prioritising submarine production, V-weapons and much more. Germany had opted out of caring for its own people, but the issues surrounding ethics, responsibility and morality in Denmark in this situation were quite complicated. When the refugee stream began, there were quite a few German military doctors and nurses in Denmark to take care of the large numbers of wounded combatants, who were cared for at German military hospitals. They also took care of the large numbers of refugees and, in the beginning, it seemed to be going quite well, but in March and April, this system broke down because more refugees were arriving and supplies to hospitals were dwindling because of the widening German collapse. Danish doctors, nurses and midwives were urged not to provide help, except in life-threatening circumstances. Another exception was infectious diseases such as typhoid, paratyphoid, typhus and dysentery. The authorities had to prevent cases in the German camps or refugee centres spreading to the Danish population. Before the liberation of Denmark on 5 May 1945, 4,132 refugee children and 2,448 adult refugees died in Denmark. One of the arguments of the Danish Freedom Council was that Denmark should not do anything which, viewed in the big picture, helped to prolong the war.

Some of the criticism directed at the Danish position towards the German refugees refers to circumstances after liberation on 5 May 1945. The situation was now changed, but Danish resources were still limited and there was no popular support or sympathy for the refugees.

The Danish interior ministry's statutory notice from 1945,
issued 3 April 1945

Medical treatment of German Refugees. The question of hospitalisation of German refugees in Danish hospitals has been discussed by the National Board of Health and the doctors' organisations. On the basis of these negotiations, the Ministry of the Interior has issued the following statutory notice through the County Prefects to the Hospital Boards:

Any patients among the German refugees should be turned away from Danish hospitals, unless special circumstances, particularly the character of the illness, make it necessary that the person or persons in question be treated in a Danish hospital. The German authorities have declared that patients among the refugees will as an absolute general rule be referred for admission to the German field hospitals and thus it will only very exceptionally be a question of hospitalisation in a Danish hospital.

As guidance for the Hospital Boards with regard to in which cases it may be regarded as necessary to admit patients from among the refugees, it should be noted that patients suffering from typhoid, paratyphoid, dysentery and typhus should be received in hospitals to ensure the combatting of the disease or in any case to make it possible for the spread of the infection to be prevented. Patients suffering from diphtheria and scarlet fever should on the other hand only be admitted as an exception since the people concerned, who as a rule are not in danger of spreading an infection, will be isolated at their place of residence in agreement with the regulations of the Epidemic Act.

In cases where immediate medical attention is required to avert an imminent danger of death, the patient should at least be admitted for initial treatment.

The Ministry further declares that, if the referral is not made by a Danish doctor, it will consider it proper that, as a condition of hospitalisation, a written declaration be required from the referring German doctor about the type of illness in question (the diagnosis) and also, in cases where immediate medical attention is required, that both treatment of the patient on the spot and transportation to the nearest German field hospital will lead to imminent danger of death for the patient.

If such a declaration should prove to be materially incorrect in the opinion of the hospital doctor, a complaint to this effect should be forwarded as soon as possible to the German authorities, possibly through the National Board of Health or, as far as Jutland is concerned, through County Prefect Herschend's office in Silkeborg.*

---

*   Quoted from Søren Hansen, *Daily reports on events during the German occupation* (Bianco Luno, 1946).

Refugee problems in Schleswig-Holstein, northern Germany

In Schleswig-Holstein, a similar problem arose, in that the small local population in the spring of 1945 was supplemented by approximately 300,000 refugees, who were clearly regarded as a burden by the local people, and in that desperate situation of shortage, people did not wish to share food and shelter with what were perceived as totally alien population groups with infectious diseases. For the German nation, the ethnic cleansing which the final stages of the war led to has also been a very sensitive topic. Different German population groups were subjected to violent attacks, but because of extensive German war crimes in the occupied countries, there was little sympathy to be gained by mentioning it for many years after the war.[5]

Sweden between New Year 1944/45 and the end of the war

Three of the British boats in the Lysekil transports were again ready in September 1944, but now it was for Operation Moonshine, which was the supply of arms, ammunition and explosives to the Norwegian and Danish resistance movements. Because of equipment problems and bad weather, only a single successful trip was carried out, which took place on 13 January 1945 when the three boats delivered over 100 tonnes of weapons and ammunition to the Danish resistance movement in Sweden. At this stage of the war, the willingness of the Swedes to co-operate was somewhat more pronounced than previously. The weapons were partly sent via the Danish navy's transport organisation and the good ship *Glory* to Denmark.

At the beginning of 1945, the German military attaché in Stockholm proposed that V-1 and V-2 weapons could be directed at Stockholm, in order to rid the Swedes of any desire to participate in the war. Hitler rejected Swedish involvement in the war at that point in time, and this somewhat extreme proposal did not enjoy any further consideration in German planning.

In the last six months of the war, the USAAF was operating from bases in northern Sweden in a series of operations in support of the Norwegian resistance movement; 550 flights were made, which were led by the Norwegian-American Colonel Bernt Balchen.[6]

On 9 February 1945, Generaloberst Jodl wrote to the German forces: 'Sweden's entry into the war was unlikely and that Hitler would not be issuing special directives in this regard.'

---

5   In recent years, however, a wave of discussion has arisen, partly because of Günter Grass's novel *Crabwalk* about the sinking of the refugee ship *Wilhelm Gustloff*. It is a work of fiction based on real events. Grass himself came from Danzig.

6   William Colby, a major in the paratroopers who took part in operations in northern Norway, later became head of the CIA.

May 1945. Danish and British officers, along with a captured German officer, inspecting a German Marder one-man midget submarine at Lynæs Fortress, Denmark. RAF Halifax aircraft from the Hebrides attacked the German steamer *Feodosia* on 4 April 1945 in the Kattegat. The ship was hit by at least two 500lb/227kg bombs and exploded. It presumably went down with all hands – more than three hundred – and thirty Marder one-man midget submarines, which in total would have contained more than 8 tonnes of explosives.

In the last months of the war, the RAF set up a station in the attic of the British consulate in Malmö. From here, they could support bombing operations directed at northern Germany.

In the final days of the war, Count Folke Bernadotte made a great humanitarian effort. He negotiated with Himmler for the release of Nordic concentration camp prisoners, as a result of which large numbers of these escaped from Germany in April and May 1945 in the white buses which Folke Bernadotte had organised in co-operation with the Swedish authorities. Folke Bernadotte's daring operation in northern Germany undoubtedly saved the lives of many Danes and Norwegians.

The Royal Air Force takes out the big German warships

Near the end of the war, the RAF expanded its minelaying campaign and dropped a total of 3,000 mines along the German Baltic coast between January and March 1945.[7] The RAF also slowly stepped up its minelaying in Danish

---

7   A post-war analysis has provided some evidence that mines dropped by the RAF in the first three months of 1945 sank sixty-seven German ships.

waters. It is difficult to quantify the results of a mine war, partly because it is very difficult to calculate what the enemy's deployments would have been if the threat from the mines had not been present. In Danish waters alone, and in the adjacent areas of the Sound and the Kattegat over towards the Swedish coast, it is calculated that the RAF dropped 6,746 mines during the war. Almost 10 per cent of them probably damaged or sank a ship, while the Germans probably disarmed about 15–20 per cent of the mines by minesweeping.

In April, the Allied air effort over Danish waters was again intensified. On 4 April, some RAF Halifax aircraft from the Hebrides spotted a German convoy in the Kattegat between Læsø and Gothenburg. One of the ships, the steamship *Feodosia*, was hit by at least two 500lb/227kg bombs and exploded. The ship presumably went down with all hands – more than three hundred – and thirty Marder one-man midget submarines, which in total would have contained more than 8 tonnes of explosives. On 16 April 1945, the RAF raided Swinemünde, where the pocket battleship *Lützow* was subjected to attacks by fifteen Lancasters with Tallboy[8] bombs. One of the bombs landed very close to the ship and ripped the side open; *Lützow* sank in shallow water.

During the last week of the war, Allied aircraft were swarming over Danish waters. British aircraft had been ordered to sink all ships evacuating troops and equipment from Germany in order to sail to Norway and continue the fight from there. This meant that everything that sailed in Danish waters was under the threat of air attack. It affected thousands of concentration camp prisoners who were on ships in the Lübeck area, as well as vessels with refugees from eastern Germany. The Allied air forces probably had some knowledge of the concentration camp prisoners, but this did not reach the pilots in time. The situation regarding concentration camp prisoners and refugees will be clarified later. The East Asiatic Company, a Danish shipping company, had three vessels laid up in Nakskov Fjord in southern Denmark and they were subjected to a fierce air raid on 3 May 1945.

The bombings did not halt the submarine projects, but they delayed them, as both submarines and production facilities were hit. A growing problem for Germany, however, was the implications of this bombing and minelaying for the inland waterways which were used for transport, including the Kaiser Wilhelm Kanal (Kiel Canal), the Mittelland Kanal and the Dortmund–Ems Kanal. The submarine sections for Type XXI, which could no longer be transported by train, now came through the river systems and, in the spring of 1945, traffic on the rivers and canals ground to a halt. Dönitz pointed out to Hitler that if they could not secure the exit from the Baltic Sea, submarine

---

8   These were the so-called 'earthquake' bombs, which were fitted with a thick steel casing and an aerodynamic shape, so they achieved a high descent speed and great penetration. The warhead consisted of 5,200lb/2,358kg of explosives.

The pocket battleship *Admiral Scheer* photographed in Swinemünde port in February 1945. During the German army's retreats along the Baltic coast in 1944/45, the ship gave the army covering fire.

On 9 April 1945, during an RAF raid on Kiel, the pocket battleship *Admiral Scheer* was hit by five 12,000lb/5,443kg Tallboy bombs, after which it capsized and sank. In the same raid, the heavy cruiser *Admiral Hipper* and the light cruiser *Emden* were so badly damaged that they could not be used any more during the war. The picture shows the wreck of *Admiral Scheer* in Kiel harbour after the RAF attack on 9 April 1945. Unfinished bow sections for Type XXI submarines can be seen in the foreground. (SMB arkiv)

warfare would collapse. On several occasions, both shipping routes and submarine training areas in the Baltic Sea had to be closed because of the danger presented by mines.

Overview of mine warfare

The use of sea mines has many consequences. The immediately visible effects of mines are ships sinking. Crews and passengers are killed, and the cargo does not reach its destination. In the long run, a country's maritime trade can be restricted, or grind to a halt. Mines also work by influencing an enemy's available options and deployments. It may be necessary to redirect or suspend shipping. Mine warfare from 1939 to 1945 was a high-tech war which required input from scientists and industrial resources. The disarming of mines required the building of minesweepers with special equipment, demagnetising equipment, the building of 'barrier breakers' and a lot more that demanded people, money and other resources. In the last months of the war, mines contributed to the paralysation of Germany. As can be seen, it became difficult for Germany to establish mineswept routes during Operation Rescue. Troops and refugees would have been transported faster if there had been mineswept routes available, and several German submarines would have been able to reach Norway. The mines – Soviet as well as British – certainly shortened the war considerably but, on the other hand, they were a threat to sailors and fishermen long after the war.

The end of the war, month by month

The Baltic and East Prussia in January 1945: operations on land
It should be mentioned at the outset that the Red Army did not advance in straight lines. It often surrounded the German forces and then continued its advance. In some places it reached the coast, thereby cutting off the German retreat. In the case of Danzig, the Soviets advanced past the city and then attacked it from the west. Troop movements must therefore be understood with the help of the overview which a map can give.

From 25 January 1945, Army Group North's forces in Courland became known as Army Group Courland on Hitler's orders, while Army Group Centre was renamed Army Group North, and Army Group A became Army Group Centre.

On 17 January 1945, Warsaw fell to Soviet forces, which included Polish divisions of the Red Army. On 30 January 1945, the first Soviet units reached the River Oder, just north of Küstrin (now the Polish town of Kostrzyn). They crossed the river, formed small bridgeheads and examined the possibility of building bridges. The very rapid advance resulted in a need for improvisation by the tactical air forces, which established thirty-two new air bases and took over fifteen former German air bases in the space of twelve days during this advance. At some of the new bases, the runways simply consisted of a stretch of the German autobahn (motorway).

The 3rd Belarusian Front attacked north of the Masurian Lakes up towards the Baltic coast and, on 27 January 1945, Soviet forces captured Hitler's headquarters, Wolf's Lair, near Rastenburg (now Kętrzyn in northeast Poland). Hitler had spent about 850 days here between 1941 and 1944; that is, almost the entire war on the Eastern Front. The complex was started in the spring of 1940 and consisted of approximately eighty bunkers, which in themselves constituted a small town with its own power plant. The construction was launched under a cover story that a dangerous chemical factory, Chemische Werk Askania, was going to be built. Hitler stayed at this complex, where there were representatives from the German army, Kriegsmarine, Luftwaffe, SS, OKW and the foreign ministry, until December 1944. He then moved to the Führer-bunker in Berlin, while the OKW went to Berlin-Dahlem, the army to Zossen, the Kriegsmarine to Bernau[9] and the Luftwaffe to the Ministry of Aviation in Wilhelmstrasse. Wolf's Lair was blown up on Hitler's orders on the night of 24/25 January 1945. When the Russians overran the area two days later, they had no idea what they had captured.

On 21 January 1945, the Red Army captured Tilsit (now the Russian town of Sovetsk) and the following day, Soviet tanks stood between Insterburg (now the Russian town of Chernyakhovsk) and the Curonian Lagoon. The demolition of Memel was prepared. Further south, the Soviets were closing in on Allenstein and pushing on further towards Elbing. On 22 January 1945, the railway station in Marienburg (now the Polish town of Malbork) fell to the Red Army, but a naval regiment in the fifteenth-century castle

---

9   When Dönitz became commander-in-chief of the navy, the Kriegsmarine's headquarters were moved to Bernau, about 12 miles/20km north-north-east of the centre of Berlin: in a forest 1.2 miles/2km north of Bernau, there was a system of bunkers above and below ground. The Kriegsmarine set up its headquarters here in a communications bunker called Lager Koralle (the Coral Camp). The headquarters remained here until 19 April 1945, when it was moved to Objekt Forelle in Plön, Holstein, northwest Germany. On 27 April, it moved on to Flensburg-Mürwick, close to the German border with Denmark, where it remained until the war ended.

of Marienburg[10] held out until March. The Kriegsmarine's regiment was composed of elite submarine personnel, non-commissioned officers, training personnel and the crew of *Schleswig-Holstein*. On 23 January 1945, Soviet forces reached Elbing. East Prussia was hereby cut off – apart from the 43-mile/70km-long, narrow Vistula Spit, which is a row of dunes between the Baltic and the Vistula Lagoon that was slowly beginning to freeze. Numerous horses and carts and refugees on foot turned up here. Streams of refugees came from the areas north of Königsberg along the corresponding 98km-long Curonian Spit that lies west of the Curonian Lagoon. The refugees were fired upon by Soviet aircraft.

On 23 January 1945, Memel was under threat and could no longer be held. The next day, Hitler gave permission for the evacuation of the city, which was carried out at night between 27 and 28 January. The port areas were now being shelled by Soviet artillery, while ammunition and important spare parts were being loaded onto ships. At the same time, refugees were being taken on board. After this, the port was demolished, that is, the facilities were destroyed so the enemy would not be able to use the wharves, cranes, warehouses and so on. The transports to Courland had to be continued, however, while the Curonian Spit had to be held in German hands. The German forces in East Prussia now had the defence of Königsberg and Pillau as their main task. Hitler was hoping to secure Königsberg by recovering the entire peninsula of Samland northwest of the city, but his generals had other plans.

The garrison in Memel came under General Hans Reinhardt's command (commander-in-chief of Army Group North/Centre from August 1944 to January 1945). As mentioned earlier, Hitler had no intention of giving up the whole of East Prussia, but Reinhardt wanted to leave the whole of Samland, including the city of Königsberg, and break through to the west to join up with the German forces around Elbing. General Otto Heidkämper, who was Reinhardt's chief of staff, discussed the matter with General Walther Wenck, who at the time was head of operations at the OKH. The whole thing was complicated by the fact that, on 23 January 1945, the commander of the 4th Army, General der Infanterie Friedrich Hossbach, began an attack on his own initiative in order to break out. Marshal Rokossovsky threw Soviet reinforcements in and stopped the attack, whereupon Hitler fired Hossbach, Reinhardt and Heidkämper for having carried out this attack, despite the fact that the latter two had no knowledge that their subordinate commander had been planning it. After this, the situation around Königsberg and Pillau developed quite disastrously for Germany.

---

10 Marienburg Castle was the headquarters of the Teutonic Order of Knights in the fifteenth century.

At the end of January, Soviet forces were about 12 miles/20km from Königsberg and, on 28 January, they cut off the road between Königsberg and Cranz and thus the connection out to Pillau. When Königsberg was under threat, Erich Koch held a rousing speech on the radio. He was a Gauleiter and *Reichsverteidigungskommissar Ostpreussen* (the National Defence Commissioner of East Prussia). The city of Königsberg was the *Landeshauptstadt*, ie the East Prussian capital. In his speech, he assured the people that the situation had improved and that the German positions were being held against the Red Army at the Deime Line. The Deime is a river east of Königsberg, which runs northwards from Tapiau (now the Russian town of Gvardeysk) and out into the Curonian Lagoon. The theme of the speech was that 'everyone should dig their heels in, stand firm and contribute to the defence of the fatherland.' He himself fled the same day on an icebreaker along the sea canal from Königsberg out to Pillau. There were rumours that he had the party's coffers and his mistresses with him. The SS were keeping watch on a dozen fishing boats, which in an emergency could take him and his whole entourage safely across the sea to Hel. This was at the last moment, because on the morning of 29 January, Königsberg was surrounded by Soviet forces. The following day, the Panzergrenadier-Division Grossdeutschland managed to breach the encirclement, which allowed the city's civilian population to flee towards Pillau. In the last days of January, sixty-five ships managed to leave from Pillau and thirty-one ships from Königsberg. Pillau's population in 1944 was 5,000 people. On 25 January 1945, there were approximately forty thousand refugees on the quayside in Pillau and, on 30 January, Pillau announced that, in recent days, about three hundred thousand refugees had passed through the town. Now the whole population of East Prussia was on the move away from the advancing Russians.

On 29 January, it was clear that the Red Army had succeeded in splitting the German forces in East Prussia into four groups. The Russians now stood on the shore of the Curonian Lagoon both west and south of Königsberg. Generaloberst Rendulic was ordered to establish contact with the various groups and to hold Königsberg. He requested support from the Kriegsmarine. The German army initiated a counter-attack on 29 and 30 January, supported by a naval force consisting of the heavy cruiser *Prinz Eugen*, the destroyers *Z5 Paul Jacobi* and *Z25*, along with the torpedo boats *T23* and *T33*. Later, a German land attack was begun from the fishing village of Fischhausen (now the Russian village of Primorsk) where the pocket battleships *Lützow* and *Admiral Scheer* gave supporting fire. Smaller German warships gave artillery support from the sea canal connecting Königsberg and Pillau.

German refugees in Pillau embarking on *Sanga* (right) from the German Africa Line and the freighter *San Mateo*, still carrying the hull number *H-27* from Operation Seelöwe, the planned invasion of Great Britain in 1940. 'H' was used to designate the port of embarkation for this ship: Le Havre. (SMB arkiv)

The commander of the 4th Army, General der Infanterie Friederich Wilhelm Ludwig Hossbach tried to fight his way down to the south, to the mouth of the River Vistula, where he counted on establishing a new front and stabilising the situation along with the 2nd Army. Hossbach, as mentioned earlier, was suddenly sacked by Hitler on 30 January and replaced by General F W Müller. It took a while before it dawned on the people involved what had happened. The reason was that Gauleiter Erich Koch had sent a signal to Reichsleiter Martin Bormann, which read: 'The 4th Army is in cowardly flight and trying to break through to the homeland. I am struggling on with the Volkssturm in the defence of East Prussia.'

Koch[11] had no idea what was going on and, as also mentioned, he had himself retreated to safety. The 2nd and 4th armies had tried to stabilise the situation by moving down towards the other German units and establishing a new, common defence line at Elbing, but this was contrary to their instructions from Hitler. Much further south, about 28 miles/45km west of Krakow, the

---

11 On 23 April 1945, Erich Koch fled on the icebreaker *Ostpreussen* to Copenhagen and arranged his continued journey under false papers as 'Major Berger' to Flensburg. Two wagons with his acquired wealth had been sent westward. He was arrested by British authorities in 1949, extradited to Poland and here sentenced to death. The sentence was changed to life imprisonment. He died in prison in 1986.

Soviet forces reached the Polish town of Oświęcim on 27 January 1945.[12] Here they found the network of concentration camps known as Auschwitz-Birkenau, where the SS had initiated a systematic elimination of the regime's so-called 'enemies', mainly the Jews and the Roma.

Pomerania and West Prussia in January 1945
At the end of January 1945, Hitler established a new army group called Heeresgruppe Weichsel (Army Group Vistula). It was supposed to prevent the Red Army from isolating East Prussia with an advance on Danzig. Army Group Vistula included the long-suffering 9th Army and the equally long-suffering 2nd Army, which stood at the mouths of the rivers Nogat and Vistula. The newly established SS-Panzer-Armeeoberkommando 11 (11th SS Tank Army) was to fill the gap between the two. Moreover, the staff from the 3rd Panzer Army were to join up with Army Group Vistula, which was going to prepare an attack from Stargard to defeat the Russians on their way towards the River Oder and restore a secure route through to East Prussia.

The Soviet advance from the Vistula to the Oder had gone incredibly fast, and Hitler had felt that, at this particular moment, he had to put a staunch man on the case. Reichsführer-SS Heinrich Himmler was appointed as commander of the new Army Group Vistula and he turned out to be a disaster as a military commander.

Work in a high command in wartime requires a large amount of planning, often at night; it is hard work and the generals are in charge. If a new situation arises, one has to start completely from scratch to analyse and work out new, detailed plans. Himmler had no professional background for leading an army into war. He had an excellent organisational talent, but otherwise he achieved his 'results' first and foremost through intimidation. Himmler had his own personal train, Sonderzug Steiermark, moved forward to the town of Schneidemühl (now the Polish town of Piła). The train had only a single phone line and no other communications equipment was brought on board. Himmler announced unequivocally that he did not want to be woken up or disturbed in the morning before 1100, by which time he would have had his breakfast and had a massage from his personal masseur who had travelled with him. It is impossible to lead an army in this way when retreating from a tremendously superior force. Hitler was very concerned about the loss of Pomerania and, to Goebbels' great delight, he blamed Himmler for the disaster. Generaloberst Guderian pressed Hitler to abandon Himmler as an army commander and General Wenck took over instead, but he was injured in a traffic accident soon after.

---

12 Now 27 January is marked internationally as Auschwitz Day or Holocaust Day.

Naval operations in the Baltic Sea in January 1945

From 3 January 1945, the Kriegsmarine no longer held exercises because of fuel shortages, except for submarine training.

On 5 January 1945, the Germans observed a Soviet submarine off Brüster Ort (Cape Taran), northwest of Königsberg, but the Kriegsmarine now lacked accurate intelligence on the Soviet submarine threat. Shortly after, Soviet air attacks were directed against German shipping along the coast at Hel and Rixhöft, which showed that the Baltic Fleet air force was extending its former operational area.

At the beginning of January 1945, the Kriegsmarine ensured that the German forces in Memel received two months of supplies. The two remaining pocket battleships *Admiral Scheer* and *Lützow* and the heavy cruiser *Prinz Eugen* were ordered to be on three hours' notice.[13] The large vessels were also running short of fuel.

German hospital ships and hospital trains

In German, a distinction is made between hospital ships (*Lazarettschiffe*) and patient transport (*Verwundetentransporten*). The first type is protected by the Hague and Geneva conventions. These are ships which are clearly marked as Red Cross ships, the movements of which are published via the Red Cross monthly in advance between the warfaring nations. Only four weeks into the war, the Soviet government announced that they: 'would not take German hospitals, patient transports or hospital ships into consideration because of the German government's systematic and treacherous violations of international agreements and conventions.'

From the beginning of the war, most of the wounded from the Eastern Front were brought home by hospital train (*Lazarettzuge*). It was now only possible to evacuate the wounded from Courland by sea, and from East Prussia it soon became necessary to use ships, as the railway networks were overloaded, broken down or had been captured by the enemy. Germany initially only had eight small hospital ships at its disposal. In the final months of the war, approximately 600,000 wounded soldiers were sailed west.

---

13 Preparedness for leaving a port is often referred to as 'notice'. On an order for departure, the ship must be able to depart from the port/anchorage within the time that the notice specifies. Three hours' notice means that fuel consumption can be kept low, as boilers and engines do not need to be kept warm.

The Seekriegsleitung and the head of naval transport noted that, in January 1945, twice as many merchant ships had been lost as in December 1944.

The German submarine *U-679* (Type VIIC) was sunk on 9 January 1945 in the Gulf of Finland between Porkkala and Tallinn by depth charges from a small Soviet anti-submarine vessel, *MO-124* (MO for *Malyi Okhotnik*, which means 'little hunter').

On 15 January 1945, Soviet forces captured the large coal mining areas in Upper Silesia. After this, coal was distributed from Hamburg and Stettin. The seriousness of the situation could be read from Konteradmiral Engelhardt's decision to order anti-aircraft guns, a total of 250 machine guns, for river barges engaged in coal transportation on the rivers in northwest Germany.

On 18 January, Grossadmiral Dönitz transferred a regiment of 3,000 men from the Kriegsmarine to the German army. Two days later, after a meeting with Hitler, he offered the army an additional 20,000 men from the Kriegsmarine. On 22 January, he offered to send 1,500 men from the 2nd Unit of the Submarine Training Division in Gotenhafen to protect Danzig, but Hitler refused as these were irreplaceable specialists. Most of them probably went down with *Wilhelm Gustloff* a week later. On the same day, Dönitz issued a declaration that the submarine war should be continued and intensified. All the other forces in the navy were to help the army in every possible way. A few days later, he offered an additional 10,000 men to the army.

Between 19 and 22 January 1945, Dönitz had several meetings with Hitler about the loss of Danzig meaning an end to the submarine war. On 23 January, Hitler explained that the most important area was the Hungarian oil fields and the terrain east of Vienna. After these, he prioritised Danzig Bay and the industrial area of Upper Silesia. At the end of February, Dönitz was called in by Hitler to explain to him the importance of Stettin and Swinemünde for naval warfare. Dönitz declared that all troop transports and supplies emanated from here. There was now a very great mine threat in the shallow waters in the western Baltic Sea and the supply routes to Courland and East Prussia would be considerably longer with the loss of the other ports. If the Russians attacked with a powerful naval force consisting of cruisers and destroyers, a German counter-attack would have to be initiated from Swinemünde. If Germany was to lose these two ports, shipyard capacity would decrease significantly. If Germany also lost the exercise area east of Bornholm, only the shallow waters where it was difficult to carry out submarine training would remain. Hitler concurred and Dönitz then conferred with the chief of staff in the OKW, Generaloberst Alfred Jodl. On 23 January, Seekriegsleitung ordered a destroyer flotilla and a minesweeper flotilla to sail from Norway to the Baltic Sea. On 22 January, the army chief of staff, Generaloberst Guderian, tried to reinforce the Königsberg garrison with various units from the Volkssturm. The Seekriegsleitung emphasised the importance of holding on to Pillau, which was a prerequisite for holding Königsberg. Generaloberst Guderian, at the Kriegsmarine's behest, thereafter declared Pillau a 'stronghold'. Since orders had been given to evacuate Memel, the first priority of the German forces in East Prussia then became the defence of Königsberg and Pillau.

On 21 January 1945, Soviet forces captured the large Tannenberg memorial,[14] built to commemorate the German army's victory over two Russian armies in August 1914. The sarcophagi with President Hindenburg and his wife lay here. Before the Russians had arrived, the memorial had been demolished and the two sarcophagi transferred to Königsberg. They were taken on board the light cruiser *Emden*, which was in the harbour with engine trouble. Hitler had wanted the transport of the sarcophagi to take place with a certain pomp and ceremony. On the afternoon of 23 January, Hindenburg's son, Generalleutnant Oskar von Hindenburg[15] and his adjutant, Hauptmann Zöllenkopf, were expected, but they did not turn up until 2200. A guard of honour[16] had been lined up and floodlighting set up on the banners from the mausoleum in Tannenberg and on the sarcophagi. It was a very atmospheric event and the general did not leave the cruiser until three o'clock the next morning. *Emden* then departed from Königsberg, but the engine was not yet ready, so the cruiser was towed along the sea canal to Pillau, where the sarcophagi were transferred to the passenger ship *Pretoria*, which was being equipped as a hospital ship. *Emden* had her engine fixed so that the ship could leave Pillau on 1 February at 7 knots. *Pretoria* sailed west with refugees and wounded. The sarcophagi ended up in a salt mine in Marburg.[17]

On 28 January, the Kriegsmarine decided to vacate the submarine strongholds in Gotenhafen and Danzig. *Wilhelm Gustloff* was being used as an accommodation ship for the submarine training in Gotenhafen-Oxhöft. Dönitz was not very much in favour of giving up the ports in the eastern

---

14 The memorial had been built to commemorate the tenth anniversary of the victory in 1914. It was in the East Prussian city of Hohenstein, which today is called Olsztynek and is located in the northeastern part of Poland.

15 He had a peculiar career as he had been adjutant to his own father, the president. He probably had a significant influence on 30 January 1933 when the president finally gave in and allowed Hitler to be appointed Reichskanzler.

16 A guard of honour on board a ship is a relatively small contingent of soldiers or sailors parading on the quarterdeck. The historical background (approximately seventeenth century) is that the commanding officer often paid for the fine uniforms for the soldiers protecting him from the crew. When guests came on board, he would show them the fine soldiers/sailors to impress them.

17 They were found here by the Americans at the end of the war. The Americans buried the sarcophagi in the Protestant Elizabeth Church in Marburg an der Lahn at a ceremony in 1946. Hindenburg was a freeman of the city.

Gotenhafen-Oxhöft with *Wilhelm Gustloff* in the background (centre). The former liner was berthed here as a training ship for the Kriegsmarine's 2. Abteilung der Ubootslehrdivision (2nd Unit Submarine Training Division). It was evacuated on 30 January 1945, still with 918 future submarine crew members on board. In the background (right) is *Cap Arcona*. (SMB arkiv)

Seven unfinished Type XXI submarines damaged by RAF bombings of the building yard. (SMB arkiv)

Baltic. Danzig was one of the three ports where the new Type XXI submarines were being assembled and Gotenhafen was a base for submarines as well as surface ships. The evacuation was necessary to get the trained Type XXI crews to safety at Kiel.[18]

On 29 January 1945, the Kriegsmarine announced that every effort should be made to bring the refugees and the wounded home. The centre for this operation was Pillau and an evacuation route from Pillau to Gotenhafen was to be established. A few days earlier, on 26 January, Pillau had been hit by a huge explosion in one of the city's forts. Fort Stiehle, which was a torpedo factory with a workforce partly made up of slave labourers from Stalag 1A, was now being used as a mine depot, and one night the whole depot containing 2,000 sea mines and 1,500 depth charges blew up.[19] Everyone in the depot was killed and the explosion did extensive damage to the city. Pillau continued as an embarkation port for three months, and was the port from which most of the refugees were collected at the start of the evacuations. As far as possible, refugees were collected from Pillau and transported to Gotenhafen or Danzig, but it did not solve the refugee problems, because the rapidly developing situation meant that the people of these two cities would also need to be evacuated fairly soon – preferably by sea.

The naval transportation service brought the III SS Panzerkorps (3rd SS Tank Corps) from Libau to Stettin around the turn of January/February 1945; Hitler gave his assent, giving the Reich Commissioner for Naval Transport thirty ships at his disposal for a week to continue the evacuation of troops from Courland to Swinemünde and Stettin. In the receiving ports, however, the administration and reception system was falling apart because it was not possible to process the large numbers of people that were amassing. Train services from the western ports were about to collapse, and the large volume of refugees could not be moved onward. At the anchorage off Warnemünde, eight vessels lay at anchor with further refugees, and Gauleiter Hildebrandt did not want them in the harbour because rail transport was now exclusively reserved for troop transports.

The refugee ships in January 1945
In the middle of January 1945, there were forty-three ships at anchor off Swinemünde, but just two days later the number had increased to 101 ships.

---

18 Kiel suffered heavy Allied bombing and the production of Type XXI submarines therefore became difficult. There were many submarines which were almost finished, but only four were operational and only two of them succeeded in making it out to the North Atlantic before the end of the war.

19 The total amount of explosives in this accident must have been in the region of 1,000 tonnes of TNT.

All of them were waiting for minesweeping to be completed, so that they could continue on their way. On 23 January 1945, four ships had to be left in Sassnitz, six in Kolberg (now Polish Kołobrzeg) and fifteen in Pillau, because now there was also a lack of escort ships. An escort usually consisted of less impressive vessels – patrol boats, naval cutters and armed trawlers. On rare occasions, torpedo boats were included in the escort.

On 25 January 1945, 7,100 refugees were evacuated by ship from Pillau to the west. By three days later, 62,000 people had been evacuated. One of the first ships which docked at Pillau was *Gotenland* (5,266grt), from the Norddeutscher Lloyd shipping company. The ship had had makeshift repairs done after two hits by bombs, and it lacked both anchors and capstans. The captain took 3,500 women on board and brought them to Swinemünde. The smaller ships only took the refugees directly across the bay to either Hel or Gotenhafen, but the situation here was also worsening day by day. In the area between the two neighbouring cities of Danzig and Gotenhafen, 50,000 wounded soldiers had accumulated, and there were more arriving daily. The wounded needed special transport, nursing, medicine, bandages and much more, all of which there were less of as time went on. In the last days of January, refugee transports also started from Hel, and 850 people were evacuated from there. The former passenger liner *Potsdam* (17,528grt) from the East India route sailed in late January at high speed towards the Swedish coast and then on to Copenhagen. The ship was faster than both the enemy submarines and the escorts, and it arrived safe and sound with its cargo of 7,000 refugees.

In order to ensure that no men capable of fighting were travelling with the transports from the evacuation ports, the army sent patrols on board the departing ships. It was usually the Feltjägere (military police), who were known among the soldiers as *Kettenhunde* (chained dogs), due to the metal badge with the Feltjäger emblem which they carried on a chain around their necks. The patrols were looking for boys from fifteen to sixteen years and men up to sixty years of age who were trying to evade military service.

On 28 January 1945, the anchored steamer *Viborg* from the Danish Dannebrog shipping company was sunk, probably by a Soviet submarine torpedo off Rügenwalde (now Polish Darłowo). The ship was not part of the refugee transports, but was sailing a cargo to Denmark. The entire crew was rescued.

On 31 January 1945, the Soviet submarine commander, Commander Konovalov, from the guard submarine[20] *L-3*, tried twice to carry out an attack against the fully-laden passenger liner *Cap Arcona*, but neither of the attacks

---

20 Soviet units from the army and navy could be awarded the honorary title of 'guard unit' for exceptional war efforts.

The German passenger liner *Berlin* as a *Lazarettschiff* (hospital ship). The ship detonated two mines off Swinemünde on 1 February 1945. Before the tugboats could get to it, the ship was aground in 43ft/13m of water with some of the superstructure above the water. The ship was later salvaged and taken over by the USSR as *Admiral Nakhimov*. (SMB arkiv)

succeeded. On the same day, the passenger liner *Berlin* was at anchor near Swinemünde, waiting to join a convoy which was going to enter the port.

There was a lot of ice in the sea, and a mine suddenly detonated under the ship. It drifted and brought about the explosion of yet another mine. Before the tugboats could get to it, the ship was aground in 43ft/13m of water with some of the superstructure above the water, so that the rescue operation the next day was manageable. On the same day, the submarine depot ship *Memel* struck a mine close to the approach buoy off Swinemünde. It was the lead ship in a refugee convoy and 600 of the approximately 900 on board perished. On the previous day, 30 January 1945, the first major shipping disaster in connection with the evacuations had taken place.

Wilhelm Gustloff
1937–1945

The sinkings of *Wilhelm Gustloff*,
Steuben and *Goya*

Memel

Wilhelm Gustloff
30 January 1945.
Sunk by Soviet
submarine *S-13*

Goya 16 April 1945.
Sunk by Soviet
submarine *L-3*

Bornholm

Pillau

Königsberg

Steuben 10 February 1945.
Sunk by Soviet submarine *S-13*

Hela

Danzig

DANZIG

EAST
PRUSSIA

Oder

GERMANY

Wisła

POLAND

0   40   80 miles

1939 BORDERS

The world's greatest shipwreck: MV *Wilhelm Gustloff*[21]

The flagships of the Kraft durch Freude[22] were the sister merchant ships *Wilhelm Gustloff* and *Robert Ley*. In January 1945, *Robert Ley* had come safely westward from Pillau with 6,000 refugees on board. On 28 January, as the Soviet forces were approaching Gotenhafen, Grossadmiral Dönitz gave the order for *Wilhelm Gustloff* to deploy to Kiel. The ship was made ready to receive wounded, as well as refugees; the refugees were to be taken

---

21 The ship was named after a particularly insignificant German who had helped to organise the Nazi movement in Switzerland. He was murdered there by a German Jew on 4 February 1936 in revenge for the Nazis' persecution of the Jews and he was given a state funeral in Germany – and a large ship named after him.

22 Kraft durch Freude (Strength through Joy) was a Nazi organisation which provided holiday accommodation, trips and cruises for German model workers.

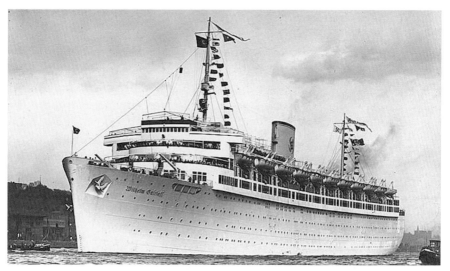

The Kraft durch Freude passenger liner *Wilhelm Gustloff* shown here before the war. (Old Ship Picture Galleries)

to Flensburg. On the first day, 6,000 refugees came on board, and initially there was tight control of the numbers. This control was maintained in the first few days via an efficient system involving handing out food coupons, but more people kept coming. There were far from enough lifejackets on board and ten of the ship's eighteen lifeboats had been requisitioned into service for laying smokescreens in the harbour during air raids. There were probably only four of the original lifeboats on board, plus a number of random lifeboats and life rafts.

The commander of the submarine training unit on board *Wilhelm Gustloff* was Korvettenkapitän Wilhelm Zahn, who had previously been commander of the submarines *U-56* and *U-69*. The master was 63-year-old Kapitän Friedrich Petersen. Zahn had not had any reports of enemy submarine activity and there were no orders for zigzagging (evasive manoeuvres to make submarine attacks difficult) for the convoy.

The Soviet submarine *S-13* had departed from Turku on 3 January 1945 towards the new Soviet base at Hanko. On 10 January, it left here with icebreaker assistance to go on patrol along the Baltic coast. The submarine commander was the half-Ukrainian, half-Romanian Lieutenant Aleksander Marinesco.[23] When the submarine commander was informed that the Red

---

23 Marinesco's foreign blood contributed to his being out of favour after the war: Stalin was sceptical about foreigners. Marinesco was not given recognition for his war efforts until 1963, when he was awarded the Gold Star and made a Hero of the Soviet Union, which was

Army had captured Memel, he redirected his submarine on the surface towards the lighthouse at Rixhöft on the north coast at the western end of the Hel Peninsula. He had noticed that the lighthouse had been turned on, which might be an indication that a convoy was on its way. Then he moved the submarine up towards the east side of Stolpe Bank (now Polish Słupsk Bank) between Danzig Bay and Bornholm, where the routes divided.

The passenger situation on board *Wilhelm Gustloff* got slowly out of hand in the following days. The departure was now scheduled for noon on 30 January 1945. It was so cold that the convoy was given icebreaker assistance on departure. On the way out of the harbour, *Wilhelm Gustloff* met the small freighter *Reval* with refugees from Pillau. There were so many people on board *Reval* that they stood shoulder to shoulder out on the deck, and many of those on the outside had frozen to death. Between 500 and 1,800 refugees from *Reval* were probably taken on board *Wilhelm Gustloff*.[24] The uncertainty about the number from *Reval* underlines the uncertainty about the total number of passengers on *Wilhelm Gustloff*. One of the problems for the navigators was whether they should choose the coastal route, which could be mined, or Zwangsweg 58, which was the minesweept mandatory route which the Kriegsmarine normally used. The convoy chose the latter route, which went north of Stolpe Bank and south of Dueodde on Bornholm. Stolpe Bank, with its shallow waters, is located off the Polish coast between Stolpmünde (now the Polish town of Ustka) and Rügenwalde. To avoid the danger of collision in the convoy, it was decided to use the side lanterns on *Wilhelm Gustloff*. The ship's main diesel engines had not been in use for years, and the hull had not been cleaned of fouling: the ship could therefore only travel at 12 knots, and not the original cruising speed of 16 knots. The convoy had a very inadequate escort; the smallest warships had to give up because of the weather, and the only escort unit remaining on departure was the torpedo boat *Löwe* (ex-Norwegian *Gyller*), 700 tonnes. *Löwe* was supposed to zigzag in front of the convoy, but because of the bad weather, she was having difficulty just keeping the ordered course and speed. *Löwe* had been equipped with radar, but on that evening, the radar was iced up and out

---

a very high distinction. His submarine was due to depart from Turku on 31 December 1944, but the commanding officer did not turn up (with the assistance of the military police) until 3 January 1945, after a rather intense shore leave marked by alcohol and women. The political officer wanted him punished, but the squadron commander wanted to avoid this: Marinesco was proficient and they had no other submarine commanders to put in his place.

24 Great uncertainty is associated with most declarations of the number of people on board. In the listed sources, there are sometimes wide variations. One of the survivors, Heinz Schön, has more or less dedicated his life to this experience. His calculation says that 9,343 people died in the sinking, but there are very great reservations surrounding this figure.

Admiral Scheer in Swinemünde, February 1945. At the top are the rangefinder and the artillery radar.

of operation. Not much importance had been assigned to the escort, as the convoy was later going to meet up with the heavy cruiser *Admiral Hipper* and the torpedo boat *T36*.

That evening, 30 January 1945, at 1910 German time, the lookout on submarine *S-13* saw a green lantern, the side lantern of *Wilhelm Gustloff*. Visibility at the time was three nautical miles when there were no snow showers. The wind was blowing from west-northwest at 12–14 knots, the air temperature was −18°C, and the water temperature +4°C. The submarine was on the surface and its commander decided to circumnavigate the relatively large target on the surface, taking two hours to go unobserved astern of the ship. Afterwards, the submarine was in a position to attack from landward – still on the surface, at a relatively low water depth of less than 98ft/30m. The submarine was now sailing awash.[25] The attack was carried out at a distance of around 2,000ft/600m. Three torpedoes were fired at 2108, and all three

25 'Awash' means that the submarine is trimmed to lie so deep that the whole hull is under water, and that only the conning tower is above water. It is dangerous, since the conning tower hatch is open so that the submarine commander and the lookout can get down into the boat again when it dives.

hit the target. A fourth torpedo started in the tube but got stuck. *Wilhelm Gustloff* sank slowly, setting her bow towards the bottom and disappearing from the surface in an hour and ten minutes.[26] The wreck lies at a depth of 157ft/48m at 55° 07′ N, 17° 42′ E, east of Stolpe Bank; the position is about 12 nautical miles/22km from the coast, just north of Łeba. The submarine's hydrophone operator reported all the sounds to his commander as the ship went down; the engine foundations broke free, the bulkheads collapsed, etc. The other ships in the convoy rescued 1,239 people alive, but of them only 904 survived the next twenty-four hours. The water temperature meant that it was only possible to stay in the water for a few minutes and there was not much rescue equipment to assist potential survivors.

How many people went down with the ship is pure guesswork – perhaps nine thousand people. She was originally built to sail with 1,463 passengers; there were 4,500 juveniles on board and less than a hundred of them escaped from the sinking alive. The lifejackets were trimmed incorrectly; if an adult lifejacket was used for a child, the child would tip round and go feet up. For most survivors, the sight of so many children's feet sticking up out of the icy water has been seared into their memories. The survivors were put off at Sassnitz, Kolberg, Swinemünde and Gotenhafen. Some survivors were thus brought back to the port they were so eager to leave, in the meantime having been exposed to unimaginable tragedy.

The cruiser *Admiral Hipper* reached the position within an hour, but its commanding officer did not want to tempt the Soviet submarine commander further. In addition to the cruiser's crew, there were 1,529 other people on board: 349 wounded soldiers, 152 shipyard workers, 968 women and sixty infants, and the cruiser disappeared westward to the astonishment of the survivors. Among the other ships in the convoy, *Oceana* reached Kiel and *Antonio Delfino*, Copenhagen.

On the same evening that *Wilhelm Gustloff* was sunk, Adolf Hitler spoke on the radio. It was 30 January, the twelfth anniversary of his seizure of power, and the main theme of the speech was that: 'the eastern regions of the Reich have surely suffered a cruel fate, but despite all these trials, the German people will succeed in holding the nation together and will come through the conflict victorious.'

It was also the same evening that the first Soviet patrols got a foothold on the west side of the River Oder. Hitler was informed the next afternoon about *Wilhelm Gustloff*, but it did not particularly interest him. Grossadmiral Dönitz explained that, after all, in the big picture the losses were limited.

---

26 In the 1950s, Soviet and Polish divers blasted their way into the wreckage to remove valuables and, among other things, to check if the famous amber panel (6 tonnes) from the Catherine Palace outside Leningrad happened to be here. It did not.

The sinking of *Wilhelm Gustloff* was kept secret from the German people. 'It could have destroyed the mood of endurance,' as the author Günter Grass put it later, but rumours spread.

East Prussia and the Baltic states in February 1945

The 4th Army was struggling to hold as much as possible of the area near the Vistula Lagoon. There were about a million refugees around Heiligenbeil (now the Russian town of Mamonovo) on 1 February 1945. The Kriegsmarine and the naval transportation service were still able to provide 2,000 tonnes of supplies daily to the forces, but the next problem was that, although there was certainly some transport capacity, the army was starting to lack necessary supplies. The naval transportation service arranged for flat-bottomed vessels from the Mediterranean, Denmark and Norway to be brought to the Vistula Lagoon, where they could bring people over to either Pillau or the Vistula Spit. From Heiligenbeil and Balga, some of the refugees moved onward to Pillau. Many tried using small boats to get from Pillau to Neutieff on the other side, so they could then come across country along the Vistula Spit, heading south towards Kahlberg (now the Polish town of Krynica Morska), and then on towards Danzig. An eyewitness has reported that on 1 February, Soviet artillery pounded the entire port area in Pillau, and Soviet planes dropped bombs into the large crowds gathered there.

General of the Army Ivan Danilovich Chernyakhovsky's 3rd Belarusian Front received orders on 9 February to complete the destruction of the German 4th Army by 25 February. Chernyakhovsky, at thirty-eight years of age, was the youngest general in the Red Army. Colonel-General Bagramyan's 1st Baltic Front was pulled out of Courland and ordered to storm Königsberg. Despite the impending storming of Berlin, where the Red Army would have to use great firepower, Colonel-General Bagramyan planned his attacks against Königsberg with 5,000 artillery pieces, 300 Katyusha rocket launchers, 538 tanks and self-propelled artillery pieces and 2,444 aircraft. In addition, two to three whole armies were deployed, plus parts of an additional two air armies and aircraft from the Baltic Fleet air force. Besides the front's normal engineer units, Bagramyan received an additional sixteen engineer brigades. Chernyakhovsky's front met fierce opposition when they attacked on 10 February, and on 18 February, the general was killed by a piece of shrapnel. Three days later, Marshal Aleksandr Mikhailovich Vasilevsky[27] was already in place in his new position as successor to the slain front commander. Bagramyan's forces were also stopped by strong German

---

27 Marshal Vasilevsky, together with Zhukov, had led the planning of the Soviet operations on the Eastern Front. When the Soviet Union entered the war against Japan in August 1945, Marshal Vasilevsky was made commander-in-chief of this force.

Soviet Petlyakov Pe-2 medium bombers, mainly used to support operations by the Red Army. (SMB arkiv)

resistance and the Soviet war leadership, the Stavka,[28] decided to join the two fronts together into the 3rd Belarusian Front, with Vasilevsky as commander-in-chief and Bagramyan as his chief of staff. The Russians now changed their plans. Instead of going after three targets simultaneously, they decided to first eliminate the German 4th Army, then clear Samland of German troops, and finally, to capture Königsberg. According to Stalin's next order, the German 4th Army was to be defeated by 22 March. It consisted of the remains of nineteen divisions and was holding an area of about 30 miles/50km of coastline with a depth of approximately 12 miles/20km around Heiligenbeil, known as *Heiligenbeiler Kessel* (the Heiligenbeil Cauldron). The attack on Königsberg was to be started in early April. The stubborn German resistance did not make it easy for the Russians, though, and Königsberg, in fact, fell before the rest of Samland had been captured.

On 19 February, German troops succeeded once more in fighting their way to the surrounded Königsberg. This was done in collaboration with the German forces inside the city, and with artillery support from the heavy warships; the counter-offensive took the Russians completely by surprise. The OKH now ordered that Königsberg, Gotenhafen and Danzig were to receive

---

28 The Supreme Soviet war council, with Stalin as chairman.

three months of supplies. The commander of naval transportation shook his head at this, because at that point in time there were not enough supplies for the battling armies in Courland, East Prussia and West Prussia, so there was absolutely no point in setting up large stores, and thus nothing more came of the matter. Up until the end of February, the German forces consolidated their positions, and they managed to keep the roads and railways between Königsberg and Pillau open for the extensive evacuation.

At the end of February 1945, approximately 560,000 men, about a quarter of the German forces on the Eastern Front, were isolated in Courland and East Prussia, and they were unable to participate in the defence of the rest of Germany. During February 1945, the Russians brought up some very heavy rail guns, which fired on Libau; they were converted 7in/180mm ships' guns which were manned by sailors from the Baltic Fleet.

Pomerania and West Prussia in February 1945
On 8 February 1945, the Stavka instructed Marshal Konstantin Konstant-inovich Rokossovsky of the 2nd Belarusian Front to defeat the German forces in Pomerania and to capture the ports of Danzig, Gotenhafen and Stettin, so that the coast as far as the estuary of the River Oder came into Soviet hands. On 10 February 1945, Rokossovsky attacked the German 2nd Army but, due to both bad weather and determined opposition, his exhausted divisions were not able to accomplish much and the attack was stopped on 19 February. Because of the previous fierce pace of the advance, the Red Army had run out of supplies and needed time to recuperate and replenish its units.

Generaloberst Guderian judged that, even though the Russians had made tremendous progress in recent weeks, the Soviet forces were overburdened. He proposed a pincer attack from Pomerania and Silesia to cut off the foremost Soviet forces and thereby reduce the threat to Berlin. Hitler decided that there should only be an attack from Pomerania and, after the failure of the Ardennes Offensive, he ordered the 6th Panzer Army directly to Hungary in order to protect the important oil fields there, instead of using the force in Pomerania.[29] The German forces in Pomerania attacked with more than twelve divisions from Stargard towards the south to free the area north of the River Warta (a tributary of the Oder) and retain Pomerania in German hands. The offensive began on 15 February, but petered out after three days. This gave Stalin a short break, but the attack was important in the sense that Stalin became anxious about the flanks. The attack on Berlin was now postponed for two months until the area had been made secure

---

29 The 6th Panzer Army was a regular army unit until 2 April 1945, after which it was transferred to the Waffen-SS. It had always had the legendary SS Oberstgruppenführer Josef 'Sepp' Dietrich as commander.

against further offensives. Stalin had been made aware that the Germans could still hit back.

Marshal Rokossovsky's 2nd Belarusian Front now attacked to the northwest, towards the Baltic coast of West Prussia. To the south was the 1st Belarusian Front, which now had Marshal Zhukov in charge. The advance from the Vistula to the Oder in January had gone unbelievably quickly and – like Rokossovsky – he needed both to consolidate his position and to rebuild logistics. It was quite a performance to advance about 375 miles/600km in just thirty days, in freezing weather in an area where there was virtually no infrastructure. Marshal Zhukov wanted to move on rapidly to Berlin, but Stalin hesitated, even though the attack on Berlin was important. South of Marshal Zhukov's front was Marshal Ivan Stepanovich Konev with the 1st Ukrainian Front. Altogether, the three fronts commanded by Rokossovsky, Zhukov and Konev had more than 190 divisions, 6,100 tanks and self-propelled artillery pieces, and 7,500 combat aircraft at their disposal. Zhukov alone had overall command of eight armies and two tank armies.

On 24 February 1945, Marshal Rokossovsky attacked Army Group Vistula at the line dividing the German 3rd Panzer Army and the 2nd Army. Even though the Germans were able to read from a captured Soviet map on 28 February that Rokossovsky wanted to fight his way out to the Baltic coast between the 3rd Panzer Army and the 2nd Army east of the city of Köslin (now Polish Koszalin, between Kolberg and Rügenwalde), these two German armies could not put up any defence and the following day, units from the Soviet 3rd Guard Tank Corps reached the coast. Rokossovsky's goal was to reach the coast at Köslin and then turn eastward to wipe out the 2nd Army in the area around Danzig and Gotenhafen.

Units from the Red Army were now approaching Peenemünde, where the missile tests had been terminated on 31 January 1945 and the German army's installations had been evacuated. The Luftwaffe's research centre still existed and, on 8 February 1945, a spectacular escape took place here. One of the concentration camp prisoners, Mikhail Petrovich Devyatayev, along with nine other prisoners, managed to capture a Heinkel He 111 aircraft during their lunch break, start it and fly behind the Eastern Front and land. None of the Germans knew that Devyatayev was a fighter pilot, and it was the airbase commander's personal aircraft they had 'borrowed'. Lieutenant Devyatayev was immediately imprisoned by the NKVD after landing behind Soviet lines. Their argument was that he had to be a spy, because they could not believe that anyone could steal a German aircraft without the active participation of the Germans. He remained in prison until November 1945 and was only vindicated in 1957 when he was awarded the Gold Star and made a Hero of the Soviet Union.

In the area east of Swinemünde, on the coast near Miedzyzdroje on the island of Wolin, the Russians found the research facilities for another retaliatory weapon, the V-3, known as the Hochdruckpumpe (high-pressure pump), which could fire shells a distance of approximately 100 miles/165km.

The Kriegsmarine in February 1945

In February 1945, the Seekriegsleitung urged the German army to hold on to the Narvik–Tromsø area in northern Norway, despite the advancing Soviet troops. This area was going to be an important base area for the new submarines. This probably explains why there were still around 380,000 German troops in Norway up until the end of the war.

In the same month, Dönitz announced that any naval officer, regardless of rank, who participated in the destruction of morale, would be made available to the army. He had no use for such officers.

From 28 January to 1 March, the ships in the 2. Kampfgruppe (2nd Battle Group) fired a total of 7,120 heavy shells (shells of between 6in/150mm and 11in/280mm) in support of army operations. They were using ammunition which could no longer be produced. Hitler's interest in this artillery support was clear in his meetings with Dönitz. Even though the 2. Kampfgruppe was particularly visible in the fighting – and the Soviet air force now had air supremacy – the Russians never made any organised air attacks on the force, which surprised the Germans.

On 11 February 1945, Dönitz had to come to the Führer headquarters to set out the Kriegsmarine's views, partly in connection with the evacuations from the east and the sinking of the two large refugee ships, *Wilhelm Gustloff* and *Steuben* (see the following sections on refugee ships). The naval commander-in-chief wanted to reduce the Soviet submarine threat with frequent aircraft patrols, which could attack the submarines on the surface and thereby 'put pressure on them'. The Luftwaffe's fuel situation no longer allowed for such flights, so the convoys were solely reliant on protection from the Kriegsmarine's escort ships. The possibilities of transport across country had dwindled away, and there was now only naval transport left. If the idea was to avoid transporting the wounded on large vessels, the monthly transportation capacity would fall from 57,000 men to 17,000 men, according to the naval commander. There was therefore nothing else to do, but to continue to use the big ships and accept the losses that this decision brought with it. Until Dönitz made this decision, the Kriegsmarine had successfully brought 76,000 wounded home by ship from Pillau and the losses had been relatively modest, considering the situation. Hitler concurred, but the topic did not interest him.

During one week in February 1945, the Russians sank two ships that were bringing replacement personnel to Courland. One of those, the transport ship *Göttingen*, had 1,500 soldiers on board, of whom 500 went down with the ship off Libau. The sailings with replacement personnel continued almost to the end of the war. Of the thirty-five German divisions in the Courland area, eight of them were successfully evacuated in January–February 1945, but with heavy losses during transportation.

The evacuations were centred on Gotenhafen, Danzig and Hel, and in order that embarkations could be carried out, an effective air defence system had to be established to keep the large numbers of Soviet aircraft at a distance. This became a task for the Kriegsmarine's flak guns. In the coastal areas, the Baltic Fleet's aircraft from the 9th Air Support Division under Lieutenant-Colonel[30] Slepenkov were on patrol, along with the 8th Minelaying and

---

30 The Soviet naval air force used the same rank designations as the Red Army.

Torpedo Aircraft Regiment under Colonel Kurochkin. Slepenkov later had a role in connection with the air raids on Bornholm.

The refugee ships in February 1945

By mid-February 1945, 228,455 civilian refugees, active soldiers and wounded soldiers were registered as having left Königsberg and Pillau by ship. From Danzig and Gotenhafen, the figure in the same period was 220,233 people. In total, that amounts to almost half a million people. The German retreats were intended to shield the coastal areas and slow down the Soviet capture of the embarkation ports. During the whole of February, the naval transport service sent a total of 250 ships westward: 147 ships from Königsberg and Pillau, and 103 ships from Danzig, Gotenhafen and Hel.

The sinking of the former Atlantic liner, ss *Steuben*

A former passenger ship from Norddeutscher Lloyd, *Steuben* departed Pillau on 9 February amid panicky scenes with about 2,500 wounded soldiers and 1,300 refugees and a crew of 450 men, including medical personnel. *Steuben* had been a hospital ship for the entire war and there was an experienced staff consisting of thirty doctors and 320 nurses on board. In case of panic breaking out among the wounded, the doctors and medical staff were armed with handguns, but this was normal procedure. On the evening of 9 February 1945, the

The passenger liner *München*, later *General von Steuben* and later again just *Steuben*, was used as a hospital ship, evacuating wounded soldiers from the east. Sunk by Soviet submarine *S-13* on 10 February 1945. (Old Ship Picture Galleries)

Soviet submarine *S-13* was again lying in wait for coastal traffic north of Stolpe Bank, and Lieutenant Marinesco spotted a big target which he wanted to attack. As he lay in position to attack, torpedo boat *T196* came straight towards the submarine and he was forced to dive. The target proved to be *Steuben*. Around midnight, the submarine was in position again, and it fired four torpedoes, two of which hit the target; the bow sank immediately and sat on the seabed. When the stern rose, the ship broke in half where the aft torpedo had struck, and both halves sank after thirty-three minutes. Only 659 of the probable 4,267 persons on board survived; they were rescued by *T196*, *TS1* and a German submarine. Almost none of the seriously wounded soldiers was able to get away from the ship and survive in the cold water. The news of the loss of *Steuben* and the large number of lives lost reached the Swedish newspapers during March.

East Prussia in March 1945
The 3rd Belarusian Front overcame the Heiligenbeil Cauldron during 13–29 March and the surviving German troops and refugees fled over the Vistula Lagoon, either northward to Pillau, in the hope of being shipped out, or southward along the Vistula Spit. The fighting in East Prussia has been described by a writer who later became world-famous.[31]

Pomerania and West Prussia in March 1945
The 2nd Belarusian Front reached the Baltic coast north of Köslin on 4 March, hereby isolating the German 2nd Army with about sixteen divisions in Pomerania and West Prussia. Köslin was captured, thus cutting off the last railway line to the west. Up until then, the Germans had still been able to send daily trains with refugees or wounded soldiers, but now there was only the sea route.

On 1 March, Marshal Zhukov attacked to the northwest, to the surprise of the German commanders, who had been expecting an attack directed at Berlin. Three days later, Zhukov's two tank armies fought their way through to the coast near Kolberg and reached the Oder on 5 March, close to Cammin (now the Polish town of Kamień Pomorski). The German 3rd Panzer Army was thus pushed back west of the Oder. This time the Soviet offensive went in accordance with the plan. The 1st Guard Tank Army went directly towards Kolberg, while the 2nd Guard Tank Army turned to the northwest towards the Oder estuary.

On 5 March, Marshal Zhukov released the 5th Tank Army to Marshal Rokossovsky, so it could be sent towards Danzig Bay. Two days later, the 2nd Belarusian Front attacked towards Danzig and Gotenhafen. The German 2nd

---

31 Artillery Officer Aleksandr Isayevich Solzhenitsyn wrote the extended poem Прусскйее ночи (*Prussian Night*s) about this period.

Army pulled back slowly along the coast near Rixhöft with artillery support from the heavy cruiser *Prinz Eugen* from 10 March. This won them time to evacuate more refugees. On 15 March, the fleet was increased by the armour-plated warship *Schlesien*, along with the gunboats *Soemba*, *Joost* and *Ostsee*, and the artillery training ship *Drache*.

On 22 March, Marshal Rokossovsky's forces were 12 miles/19km from Gotenhafen, which was being subjected to artillery and air attacks. The remnants of the German 2nd Army were fighting near Danzig and Gotenhafen. Around 6 miles/10km southwest of Danzig, the 4th Panzer Division was in a battle. The German forces were fighting with their backs to the port area, and their bridgehead was slowly shrinking. The Kriegsmarine's vessels were providing artillery support. On 25 March, the Russians had split the 2nd Army into three forces: one in Danzig, one in Gotenhafen and one in the base at Hel. Gotenhafen fell on 28 March, but the defenders hung on to a small bridgehead near the harbour in Gotenhafen-Oxhöft. The Soviet forces captured Danzig after a lot of hard fighting on 30 March 1945, and the German armies were pushed back to the Vistula estuary.

The Kriegsmarine's activities in March 1945

At the beginning of March, the refugee situation in Kolberg came to a head. They had previously received 250,000 refugees here from ships and sent them on by train, but the last eighty thousand or so had not yet left when the Soviet forces reached the suburbs of the city on 4 March. The Polish 3rd, 4th and 6th divisions were part of these Soviet forces, and the encirclement was completed on 7 March. On 9 March, according to the German authorities, there were still around forty thousand refugees remaining who had to be evacuated by sea. The defenders of Kolberg held the town for fourteen days, so that all the refugees, as well as the soldiers themselves, could be evacuated. This was only possible because of the heavy artillery cover provided by the destroyers. It was also their artillery cover which was a prerequisite for the completion of the evacuation of the last soldiers from the harbour and beach on the night of 18 March between 0200 and 0300. Overall, the Kriegsmarine calculated that they had rescued 70,915 people out of the burning town of Kolberg. Propaganda Minister Goebbels had shortly before had a colour film produced about the siege of Kolberg in 1807. It was intended to instil respect and create hope for the entire population of Germany. The film was based on a historical event where Major von Gneisenau (later Generalfeldmarschall) held out during Napoleon's siege, and where the fortunes of war turned at the very last moment.

On 6 March, off Sassnitz on the German island of Rügen, the hospital ship *Robert Möhring* was hit during an air raid by the RAF. The ship had

737 wounded and twenty refugees on board; it caught fire and 353 of the wounded died. On 9 March, the Seekriegsleitung determined that half of the Kriegsmarine's ships in the Baltic Sea were no longer operational, and that the only harbours that could be used by warships were those at Swinemünde and Kiel.

When the Russians advanced closer to Stettin and Swinemünde, the pocket battleship *Lützow*, the destroyer *Z34* and a number of smaller vessels pounded the advancing forces. On 12 March, *Z34* arrived at Swinemünde with refugees on board as an air-raid alarm sounded. It turned out to be a large-scale daylight raid by 700 American bombers. *Z34* increased speed, reached the public bathing area where the ship could turn, and then sailed out of the harbour. *Z34* made it out to sea with its refugees, but seven ships at the quayside with refugees on board suffered heavy losses. One of the ships, *Andros*, was in the process of disembarking people when she was hit by two bombs, and sank by the quay with 570 killed.

The Kriegsmarine now sent the big artillery vessels to defend Gotenhafen and Danzig. On 21 March, *Schlesien* had to be taken out of the fighting when the intensity of the firing made the rivets in the hull open up so that the ship sprang a leak, but from 23 March, *Lützow, Prinz Eugen, Leipzig, Z31* and *Z34* took part in shelling the advancing enemy. On 27 March, the hull of the battleship *Gneisenau* was sunk as a blockship in Gotenhafen harbour. In March 1945, German forces lost the industrial area of Upper Silesia to the Russians, and Churchill called upon Stalin to capture Danzig quickly, so that at least one of the three submarine production areas could be taken out of the reckoning. This happened on 30 March.

One of the Kriegsmarine's most important units was in Hel. This was the Ausbildungsgruppe für Front-U-Boote, which was responsible for the operational training of submarine crews before they were deployed in the battle for the North Atlantic. The group's submarines practised attacks on convoys and had up until then been able to use German shipping for target practice. On 23 March 1945, the organisation moved to Rønne on the island of Bornholm while torpedo firings were moved to Travemünde. The submarines were ordered partly to the waters around Bornholm and partly to Norwegian waters, while some of the staff were evacuated in three ships that put in at German Baltic ports further west. That same day, five new Type XXIII submarines sailed to Rønne. These were the *U-2334, U-2356, U-2357, U-2359* and *U-4701. U-2361* (Type XXIII) arrived later due to rudder problems. The submarines *U-2533, U-3522, U-3025* (Type XXI) and *U-1007* (Type VIIC) arrived at Rønne on 28 March with a total of 185 Hitler Youth members on board in addition to their own crews. One of the group's other submarines struck a mine on its way out and all the crew were lost. It turned out later that on board the submarine were the submarine commander's wife and several relatives of the other crew members. This was not normally permitted, but the situation could not be described as normal. Three Type XXI submarines, *U-3012*, *U-3013* and *U-3529*, brought fifty flak soldiers and an unknown number of refugees to Bornholm.

The Luftwaffe could still get hold of fuel for the Seenotflotille 81, the special rescue unit which was stationed on Rügen. It was a unit with seaplanes and rescue vessels which could recover downed flight crews and others in distress at sea. The seaplanes flew a number of flights to Pillau with morphine, bandages and other critical supply items, and took some of the severely wounded back with them. At the beginning of March, these aircraft had evacuated a camp containing children relocated from the big cities, on the German coast southeast of Bornholm. More than two thousand children and a few adults in the camp were airlifted out when Soviet tanks suddenly prevented the planned evacuation by bus. While the pilot of one of the planes was busy keeping an eye on the Soviet tanks, he handed over the boarding to the other crew members. The Dornier Do 24 aircraft[32] was designed to carry the crew plus fourteen passengers, but when the plane landed they counted, in addition to the crew, seventeen adults and ninety-nine children, which shocked the pilot. On 17 March, the seaplanes took part in the evacuation of Kolberg and flew a total of 2,356 people westward. During embarkation, they were covered by destroyers at the anchorage.

The refugee ships in March 1945
In March 1945, the head of naval transportation, Konteradmiral Engelhardt, drew up an overview. He had 470 ships available: 75 per cent of them were coal-fuelled, 7.5 per cent used heavy fuel oil, and the remaining 17.5 per cent were motor vessels which used diesel fuel. Coal deliveries would be the easiest way to improve the transport situation. There were only 80,000 tonnes of coal available and his ships used 8,000 tonnes per day. If the situation was to be improved, coal had to be brought from the mines to the quaysides. The German authorities managed to seize 2,000 tonnes of coal from Denmark and a similar amount from Norway – a total of half a day's consumption.

During the Soviet advance, the German administration slowly began to break down. Reports now began to come in to the naval transportation service that the Armaments Minister Albert Speer wanted to have 1,200 employees picked up from an aircraft factory in Stolp (now the Polish town of Słupsk). In addition, 1,600 *Luftwaffehelferinnen* (plotters from the German equivalent of the WRAF) had to be fetched from Danzig and 1,000 workers

---

32 The Dornier Do 24 was a three-engined seaplane.

from the Schichau shipyard in Elbing. The shipyard had been transferred to Gotenhafen and an additional 11,000 shipyard workers had to be picked up from here. The war was gradually approaching its end, but Engelhardt's task continued, and the desperation of the people of East and West Prussia and Pomerania was rising. At the beginning of March, Engelhardt directed fourteen ships to Stolpmünde from where they managed to evacuate 18,000 people.

In the last days of January, when Soviet forces reached the Oder, the Seetra staff themselves had to move westward and Engelhardt's staff got a new office in Hamburg. It was bombed while he was in East Friesland (near the German/Dutch border) to help the army with an important evacuation there. In Sønderborg in Denmark, he found the German freighter *Malaga*, which was not ready to sail because of engine failure. The ship had an excellent radio station, so it became his new headquarters. It was towed to Flensburg, where it was connected up to the telephone and telex network, so he could control his fleet of transport vessels between Norway and Courland from here. The collapse was now becoming almost total. If Engelhardt was to get round to where things were happening, his only means of transport now was a service car. Air transport was no longer an option. The railway system was about to collapse because of daily air raids and shortages of coal and rolling stock.

Off Sassnitz, an air raid came in daylight on 6 March; *Z28* was hit at the Sassnitz anchorage and the destroyer sank shortly before midnight. Eyewitnesses could see the RAF planes coming in and dropping mines by parachute. The entire armada of merchant ships at the Sassnitz anchorage was now in a minefield. When the passenger liner *Hamburg* (22,000 tonnes) tried to leave the area anyway, two mines exploded beneath the ship and she sank. Almost simultaneously, her sister ship *Hansa* struck a mine at Warnemünde and sank in 56ft/17m of water. During an RAF raid on Hamburg on 9 March 1945, the KdF ship *Robert Ley* (sister ship to *Wilhelm Gustloff*) was hit by bombs and set on fire.

On 12 March 1945, *Gerrit Fritzen* (1,761 tonnes), the minesweeper *M3137* and the submarine hunter *UJ303* were sunk by Soviet naval aircraft. On 14 March, the torpedo boat *T3* struck a mine off Hel and sank with three hundred crew members and refugees on board. On 23 March, the passenger liner *Deutschland* left Gotenhafen with 11,145 people, who were safely brought west. On 28 March, *Deutschland* made another trip and brought 11,295 people to safety. The passenger liner *Potsdam* followed with 9,000 refugees, but on the ship's next trip, new problems arose for the overloaded German administration. Someone had got the idea of sending the big ship *Potsdam* (17,528 tonnes) to Sassnitz with refugees. The ship was too large to get into the harbour and it had to spend ten days out at the anchorage sending the 7,500 refugees ashore with fishing boats, thereby consuming an extra 200 tonnes of fuel which could have been used in much better ways. The doctor on board had suspected that there were cases of both typhoid and typhus on board, which did not make it any easier, neither for the authorities on the ship nor for those ashore.

Between 10 March and 2 April 1945, the passenger liner *Cap Arcona* came to Copenhagen three times from the eastern areas, each time with eight to ten thousand refugees and wounded. It could take more than a week to find space on shore for so many refugees and it was very cramped onboard ship as the facilities were not designed for passenger transport on this scale.

Around 22 March, there were fourteen merchant ships at Swinemünde that could not help out in the evacuations because they did not have any coal. On 23 March, Engelhardt succeeded in getting the big whaling mother-ship *Walter Rau* to depart from Danzig with about six thousand refugees and after a few days, the ship reached Copenhagen.

The Danish Resistance

Even though the German armies were in retreat everywhere, circumstances in Denmark in early 1945 were characterised by stringent conditions. The German security police had obtained an overview of most of the Danish Resistance and were now in a position to unravel the whole organisation.

By agreement with the SOE, the Resistance had the job of handling the sabotage of Danish companies which were supplying weapons and equipment to the German armaments industry, including parts for the German V-1 and V-2 programmes. The agreement was intended to ensure minimal damage to the Danish population in relation to the massive bombings being carried out by the Western Allies' air forces. In addition, the Resistance was to sabotage the railway network in order to delay German military transports from Norway to the Eastern and Western Fronts. Troops were being sailed from Norway to either Frederikshavn or Aarhus in Jutland, and from there they were sent on by train. Although there were still a lot of German forces in Norway at the end of the war, they had been thinned out during the final years. The Danish Resistance was being equipped by the SOE with agents, weapons and explosives via nightly airdrops carried out by the RAF.

Other members of the Resistance were ordered to keep a low profile, but to report all German movements (army, navy and aircraft), so that the Western Allies knew what forces were in the area when the front reached Denmark. Afterwards, the Resistance groupings could support the advancing Allied troops. Due to lack of training, it was not possible to deploy them independently in direct fighting against a well-organised German military force.

Because of the threat of arrests and executions of the entire resistance movement, the SOE representative in Denmark, Major Ole Lippmann from the Royal East Kent Regiment (known as 'The Buffs') decided to ask the RAF to bomb Gestapo headquarters at the Shell House in Copenhagen. This was intended to serve two purposes: first, to kill as many Gestapo employees and henchmen as possible and, secondly, to destroy the Gestapo's archives of the Resistance which were stored on the first floor. However, there was a big problem. The Gestapo had installed a *Hausgefängnis* (house prison) in the attic, which was housing thirty-four hostages from the Resistance.

The operation was called Operation Carthage and was carried out on 21 March 1945. The task had been given to elite units of the RAF; eighteen Mosquito aircraft carried out the attack, covered by thirty-one Mustang P-51D fighters. Two more Mosquito aircraft were responsible for photo coverage of the attack. The time of the attack was set for 1115, at which point, because of the approaching lunch break, most of the Gestapo staff would be in the building and the archives would be open and in use. The attack was a military success: approximately a hundred Gestapo people were killed and the archives destroyed – the Gestapo was thus paralysed until the end of the war six weeks later. Eight of the thirty-four hostages in the attic were killed. The military success was marred, though, by a horrible accident. One of the low-flying Mosquito bombers hit a lamp post and crashed near a Catholic school, which was then bombed by some of the aircraft following; eighty-six children and eighteen adults were killed in this incident – most of the adult victims were nuns. Three more of the Mosquito aircraft and two Mustangs were shot down, partly by anti-aircraft fire from the light cruiser *Nürnberg* in Copenhagen harbour. Nine men from the RAF died and one was taken into captivity.

Langebro sabotaged

The reason for the bombing of Langebro, a bridge across Copenhagen harbour, was that sixteen of the forty-two largest Danish merchant ships moored in Copenhagen South Port had already been requisitioned by the Germans. The shipowners could expect the other ships to be requisitioned soon too. There were many motives for not allowing the ships to come into German service, not the least of which was concern for the crews. From a national point of view, the ships had to be ready when the war was over and goods would again have to be exported, imported and moved around the country. The shipowners also wanted to protect the value of their assets. The SOE and the Freedom Council did not want to support the German war machine or to prolong the war, and none of them wanted the Danish ships to be used as long as the mines in the surrounding waters had not been swept.

The Freedom Council had been concerned for some time about the German refugee transports, which required a lot of ships and many German ships had been sunk or damaged. Now there was a need for more ships. On 27 March 1945, the Danish resistance group BOPA therefore carried out sabotage against Langebro. A bomb was placed in a freight train that passed over Langebro. It was detonated as the train passed the bridge's machine house. After this, the bridge could not be opened for a few weeks and the sixteen ships were trapped in the harbour.

East Prussia and Courland in April 1945

A showdown was imminent between the massive Soviet army units backed by thousands of aircraft, and German Generalmajor Otto Lasch, who, with five worn-out divisions, some Volkssturm units and various other forces totalling 130,000 men, had the task of holding the Königsberg stronghold at any cost. Marshal Vasilevsky ordered a four-day artillery bombardment beginning on 2 April 1945 to soften up the German defences, which consisted of three concentric circles or defence rings placed around the city. On the fifth day, Vasilevsky sent 246 bombers in and, when they were finished, their raid was followed by 516 close air support fighters. The following day, 456 bombers escorted by 124 fighters were deployed west of the city where the German reserves were concentrated. At the same time, 108 fighters were sent to patrol over the city while the bombers were on the way in. Twenty minutes before the bombing raid, the Russians started a massive attack against the two largest Luftwaffe bases in the area to keep the German fighters away and, in this situation, there was nothing the Luftwaffe could do. A breakout attempt west of Königsberg was defeated from the air. On 10 April 1945, Königsberg fell to the Russians. Despite the late stage of the war, Königsberg was the first major German city to fall. (Danzig had fallen eleven days earlier, but it was not originally German.) After this, Marshal Vasilevsky continued towards the Samland Peninsula. The northern part was captured quickly on 13 April and, by 15 April, the Germans were only holding a small bridgehead around the harbour in Pillau. Fischhausen (Primorsk) was captured on 16 April and the Germans pulled back slowly southward along the Vistula Spit. They retreated calmly along this long, thin strip of land in the last days of the war. The Russian speed of advance in this area also decreased.

During the fighting in Samland, a Soviet force commander, who was himself Jewish, revealed that in January, SS units had driven a large group of Jewish prisoners on foot from an *Aussenlager* (branch camp) of Stutthof concentration camp, just east of Danzig, out towards Palmnicken (now Russian Yantarny) on the Samland peninsula. There were originally 7,000 prisoners, mostly women, but only about 3,000 survivors remained when they came out to the coast. These were murdered here by the SS, and only fifteen are thought to have survived the Palmnicken massacre. The bodies were found in April, when the Soviet commander forced the local people to bury the numerous victims.

At the end of April 1945, the OKW estimated that the German troops in Courland only had enough supplies for three weeks. Ships from the Kriegsmarine were still getting through, but to a very inadequate extent.

German suicide operations prepared

The German military situation was reflected in the decision to introduce suicide pilots. In April, the military leadership was so desperate that selected pilots of the Luftwaffe were encouraged into carrying out *Selbstopfer* (self-sacrifice) by crashing planes with bombs into the many bridges which the Russians had established over the Oder to build their beachhead before the final storming of Berlin. Between 17 and 20 April 1945, thirty-five pilots from the special *Selbstopfer* unit (the 5th Wing or Battle Group 200, also known as Leonidas) crashed their planes into the bridges over the Oder.[33] The word *Selbstopfer* did not have the correct ideological ring, so the euphemism *Total-Einsatz* (total effort) was used instead. The Luftwaffe's female personnel were invited to be loving and obliging towards these martyrs of the system. The *Selbstopfer* attacks stopped on 21 April when the Russians were approaching the air base at Jüterbog, south of Berlin, from where they took off.

Stalin's final intrigues: the road to Berlin

On 1 April 1945, Stalin informed General Eisenhower about his plans. Eisenhower had previously explained the Allies' views. The British had been left behind a bit here and the views put forward were mainly American. 'Berlin has lost its former strategic importance and only secondary forces will be sent in that direction,' advised Stalin – a declaration that has been called 'modern history's greatest April Fool' by a historian. Eisenhower was concerned about rumours and intelligence that the Germans would retreat to an Alpine stronghold and fight on from there. The Americans, therefore, concentrated large forces in southern Germany, and Stalin advised that he agreed and that his forces would do the same. In this way, Soviet and American forces would meet in southern Germany. Soviet forces would begin their advance towards southern Germany around the middle of May. Stalin added that he could not exclude that corrections might be made to the plans if circumstances changed.

---

33 According to the British military historian, Antony Beevor, the thirty-five aircraft only succeeded in temporarily interrupting the railway bridge at Küstrin. (Mentioned in the book *Berlin, The Downfall*).

On the same day that Eisenhower was being notified by Stalin, Marshals Konev and Zhukov both had a meeting with Stalin in Moscow. Zhukov was in the process of building a huge bridgehead at Küstrin, just east of Seelower Höhen. From here, Highway 1 went straight to Berlin. South of here were Marshal Konev's forces. Stalin first asked both of them: 'Who is going to take Berlin – us or our western allies?' Before Zhukov could answer, Konev had said it: 'We're going to.' That was what Stalin had expected. So he drew the line dividing the two fronts, the 1st Belarusian Front and the 1st Ukrainian Front. Stalin only drew the dividing line halfway towards Berlin. Both marshals immediately got Stalin's idea. Whoever came first would be the conqueror of Berlin, and thereby a kind of winner of the Second World War. If Konev arrived at the end point of the pencil line first, then he could just swing northwest and capture Berlin himself. It was Stalin's way of creating competition between his officers, and something that ultimately would cost the lives of many thousands of Soviet soldiers. Stalin's way of going about it increased the pace of the advance for the two fronts considerably. The marshals stayed in Moscow until 3 April, after which – in great haste and with only two minutes between them – they each took off in their plane towards the front.

On 16 April 1945, Marshal Zhukov completed his deployment and launched the final attack on Berlin. The overall bridgehead had by now been expanded to a width of 27 miles/43km in a north–south direction. It had taken a long time to build and secure the bridgehead, and to get all the heavy equipment across the River Oder. The Germans had concentrated their forces around Seelower Höhen, where Zhukov met fierce resistance. It was easier for Konev further south, and Stalin gave Konev permission to push on towards Berlin. Around 19/20 April, Marshal Zhukov's forces reached the Berlin suburbs. Neither of the two marshals took their own losses into consideration.[34] According to Stalin's orders, the conquest of Berlin should have taken place on 1 May, the most important day in the Communist calendar. The battles lasted until 2 May. After a little more than two weeks – and some of the bloodiest battles of the war – Zhukov had captured Berlin, and thereby the power centre of Nazi Germany. It was thus the Soviet Union which captured Berlin – and thereby accepted the heavy losses involved. In the Western Allies' areas, German soldiers had just surrendered in their hundreds of thousands. Still left were the German forces in the Netherlands, northwest Germany, Denmark and Norway.

---

34 The British military historian Christopher Nigel Donnelly from Sandhurst (the British Army's military academy) has estimated the Soviet military casualties from 16 April 1945 to the end of the war in Europe as greater than the total British casualties during the entire Second World War.

American troops were part of Field Marshal Montgomery's 21st Army Group. The Americans captured Schwerin, and British paratroopers from the 6th Airborne Division captured Wismar on 2 May. Wismar is located 31 miles/50km east of Lübeck, where the 'Iron Curtain' later went down. It was the most eastern point on the coast that the Western Allies reached, but they had cut off the Russians from further advancement, and the liberation of Denmark then became a matter for the 21st Army Group. The following day, they met the farthest advanced Soviet units in Wismar.[35]

The Kriegsmarine in April 1945

Soviet forces captured Gotenhafen on 28 March 1945, but from the very nearby quayside of Oxhöft, the Germans made a remarkable escape from a small beachhead on the night of 4/5 April 1945: 8,000 men from the 7th Panzer Corps, a fair amount of equipment and approximately thirty thousand refugees were picked up during Operation Walpurgisnacht, when the Kriegsmarine deployed twenty-five naval trawlers, twenty-seven ferry barges, five auxiliary gunboats and five other vessels. The meticulously planned operation was conducted in the five hours of darkness by the commander of the 9th See-Sicherungsdivision (naval security division), Fregattenkapitän Adalbert von Blanc. The pocket battleship *Lützow* and some destroyers and torpedo boats covered the vessels during the interim transportation to Hel. Three days later, *Lützow* and two destroyers had to leave the operation due to fuel shortages.

When the Russians moved westward towards the coast after capturing Königsberg, 70,000 German refugees were cut off. Some made it to safety by getting over to the Vistula Spit. Others tried to obtain a passage on a ship, but two of the large ships of over 5,000 tonnes which came to the rescue were sunk by Soviet aircraft. The air defence for the area consisted of five auxiliary gunboats and the artillery training ship *Drache*. *Drache* was sunk during a Soviet air raid on 18 April.

On 13 April 1945, Soviet motor torpedo boats were seen in Danzig Bay, but there were no longer any German warships which had enough fuel to fight them. There were still no Soviet destroyers deployed in the Baltic Sea, which amazed the German naval commanders. Generaladmiral Kummetz calculated that Stalin did not want to sacrifice the big ships in battle against the Germans, but wanted to retain them for a possible showdown later with the Western powers. The light cruiser *Leipzig* had been transferred to Aabenraa

---

35 It came to a shoot-out when the Soviet troops tried to force their way into a local hospital which had a large number of nurses, and where the British troops had already established themselves with copious amounts of alcohol and female company. Six slain Russians lay on the battleground afterwards.

in southeast Jutland, from where 100 men of the crew had been sent to the defence of Berlin. Admiral Hans-Heinrich Wurmbach, Kommandierender Admiral Skagerrak, paid the cruiser a visit and recommended that the ship took up the fight against the advancing British, but the ship had used up all its 6in/150mm ammunition at Gotenhafen in March. A truck was therefore sent to Hamburg for more ammunition, but it did not turn up before the end of the war.

In Rønne, four submarine crews were about to finish battle training. They were *U-2354*, *U-2365*, *U-4701* and *U-4707*, all Type XXIII. Because of fuel shortages, all training exercises were suspended from 20 April.

The refugee ships in April 1945

On 9 April, the steamer *Neuwerk* left Pillau with about 1,025 people on board. In the rush, the ship had not been notified of its *Erkennungssignal* (recognition signal).[36] The ship came a little adrift of its convoy, and when it was called up with a flash signal by the motor torpedo boat *S-708* and did not respond correctly, it was sunk. When the motor torpedo boat then approached the sinking ship, the misunderstanding was cleared up, but they only managed to save seventy-eight of those on board. The next day, the Russians bombed the freighter *Molktefels* in the anchorage off Hel. There were 4,000 refugees on board and after several hits the ship burned up totally, but 3,500 were saved from the burning ship. The hospital ship *Posen* was nearby; that was also hit and set on fire, killing approximately three hundred refugees and wounded. The following day, the small, overcrowded steamer *Karlsruhe* (898grt) was on its way from Pillau via Hel to Copenhagen with 1,083 people. It was sunk by a Soviet torpedo aircraft and 970 people went down with the ship. On 16 April, the transport ship *Cap Guir* (1,536grt) was subjected to an air attack off Libau in which 770 people died.

As the Kriegsmarine's vessels dropped out one by one – because of lack of fuel, mines or air attacks – the losses increased among refugee ships, especially because of air raids. Between 7 and 14 April 1945, Soviet aircraft also sank *Flensburg* (5,450 tonnes), the navy supply ship *Franken* (10,850 tonnes), the workshop ship *Hans Albrecht Wedel*, the submarine hunters *UJ301* and *UJ1102*, two minesweepers, and the merchant ships *Albert Jensen* and *Wiegand*. During air raids on 19 and 20 April, the freighter *Altengamme* (5,897 tonnes) and some smaller ships were sunk by Soviet aircraft. On 25 April, the merchant ship *Emily Sauber* (2,435 tonnes), was sunk by Soviet

---

36 An optical signal corresponding to the British system of 'Challenge and Reply': a call with an answer, both of which change periodically, which should ensure identification of friendly vessels.

The wreck of the Dutch ship *Wuri* was put across Copenhagen harbour and sunk by Knippelsbro on 20 April 1945 by the resistance movement (Langebro and Knippelsbro were the only two bridges across Copenhagen harbour, connecting two large areas of Copenhagen). The following day, the small Danish motor vessel *Japos* was sunk as an additional barrier. The remaining ships in the south harbour were now unable to get out, because all the tugboats were in Sweden. (Maritime Museum of Denmark, Elsinore)

The German freighter *Molktefels*, with 2,700 refugees, 1,000 wounded and 300 soldiers on board, was hit by bombs from Soviet aircraft and caught fire in the Hel roads on 10 April 1945. About five hundred were killed, but the German naval authorities managed to save 3,500. (SMB arkiv)

torpedo boats, which were now able to operate from the harbour area at Neufahrwasser in Danzig.

On 20 April, the liner *Eberhard Essberger* left Hel with 6,200 refugees and the following day, *Lappland* sailed with 7,700. On 28 April, seven merchant ships sailed with 24,000 evacuees and the total number of evacuees from Hel in April amounted to 387,000 people. On the night of 24/25 April 1945, the Kriegsmarine's barges brought a total of 19,200 people away from Pillau. It was a mixed group of both troops and civilians and that was the end of the evacuation from Pillau.

In a co-ordinated action, Danish tugboats are sent to Sweden
On the orders of the Freedom Council, the Danish resistance movement ensured that a total of one major freighter, *Røsnæs*, two salvage pontoons and sixteen tugs came to safety in Sweden through a carefully planned action which stretched from 7–9 April 1945. A grounding by *Røsnæs* was faked south of the island of Ven, after which tugs from A/S Svitzer and Forenede Bugserselskab (United Salvage Company) came to the rescue. This meant that these ships were also excluded from participation in the German Operation Rescue (*Unternehmen Rettung*).

The sinking of MV *Goya* on 16 April 1945
The port of Hel was one of the last collection points along the Polish Baltic coast. It is located at the tip of the Hel Peninsula, on the southern side. The peninsula is a 21-mile/33km-long spit which is less than a mile wide. In an atmosphere of rising desperation, the number of people on every single refugee ship also increased. The seized Norwegian MV *Goya* (5,230grt) departed from Hel with a convoy on 16 April 1945 as soon as night had fallen. The convoy, known as GO712, was on its way to Copenhagen and consisted of five merchant ships protected by two minesweepers; all of them were instructed to go north of Stolpe Bank. The convoy was carrying 21,000 soldiers and 14,000 refugees. The Soviet guard submarine *L-3* was on patrol not far from the positions where *Wilhelm Gustloff* and *Steuben* had previously been sunk. The submarine commander had captured German charts on board which showed Zwangsweg 58 (the mineswept compulsory route). The convoy had to reduce speed from 11 to 5 knots because of engine problems. At 2345, *L-3* fired a salvo of four torpedoes at *Goya*, of which two hit the target: *Goya* broke in two and sank in just seven minutes. Dönitz informed Hitler that probably up to seven thousand people had gone down with *Goya*. There are discrepancies in the estimates among the sources; after the war, the number rescued was calculated at 165 people, while 6,220 people are estimated to have gone down with *Goya*. One of the other ships in the

The Norwegian freighter *Goya* from the shipping company J Ludwig Mowinkel A/S in Bergen, sailing in home waters. *Goya* was seized and requisitioned for German refugee transports. On 16 April 1945, she was sunk east of Bornholm by the Soviet submarine *L-3*. About 6,220 people went down with the ship. (Maritime Museum of Denmark, Elsinore)

convoy, *Mercator*, reached Copenhagen with 5,500 refugees. The same day, the rescue ship *Boelcke* was sunk by Soviet IL-2 aircraft: she was in a convoy from Pillau and twenty men were killed.

BOPA's two sabotage actions against the cruiser *Nürnberg* in Copenhagen Freeport

The Danish resistance movement was anxious to immobilise the German light cruiser *Nürnberg*, but it was well guarded in Copenhagen Freeport. In February 1945, BOPA had placed a bomb in a nearby sewer, but it caused only minor damage to the cruiser when some cranes fell on her, so a renewed action was required. BOPA decided that a diver might provide the solution and they made contact with an able seaman from the Danish navy diving school on 24 April 1945, the same day as he completed his qualification as a heavy diver. This was the 26-year-old Henry Chirholm, who had previously been involved in illegal work. Chirholm succeeded in placing a bomb of 220lb/100kg under the bottom of the cruiser, but the trip along the bottom of the harbour had been very difficult. Chirholm had been forced to drag the bomb about 1,000ft/300m across the harbour bottom and under the cruiser's ammunition magazine. For some mysterious reason, the bomb did not explode and a new attempt was planned, but liberation put an end to

The passenger liner *Cap Arcona* before the war. Thousands of concentration camp prisoners were embarked on this ship by the SS in May 1945 for unknown reasons. The RAF mistakenly attacked her as a troop transport ship heading for Norway. (Old Ship Picture Galleries)

that.[37] From 23 April, it was reported that the Germans were preparing the demolition of the outer harbour, but activity was halted on 1 May.

The tragedy of the concentration camp prisoners in Neustadt Bay: the story of *Cap Arcona*

The last of the great tragedies at sea took place in Neustadt Bay, north of Lübeck. Through negotiations with Himmler, Count Folke Bernadotte had been trying to have Scandinavian concentration camp prisoners transported to Sweden. As head of the SS, Himmler was responsible for all concentration camps and negotiations took place regularly in February and March 1945. Himmler had apparently begun double-dealing on a grand scale. On the one hand, he wanted to be seen in a good light in the future, so he tried to contribute to some Jews being allowed to travel to neutral countries like Switzerland and Sweden, and on the other hand, he had issued an order to the SS that no concentration camp prisoners were to fall into the hands of

---

37 On 16 May 1945, Chirholm dived down once more to locate and dismantle the bomb, which was still under *Nürnberg*.

the Allies alive, and that all traces of the concentration camps should be removed. As British forces approached Hamburg in late April, Count Folke Bernadotte was given the opportunity to arrange transportation to Sweden for the Scandinavian prisoners in Neuengamme camp, which was located near Hamburg. The remaining approximately eighteen thousand prisoners were driven on foot in the direction of Lübeck and Neustadt. In Lübeck harbour, there were an additional four barges, which had been towed from the Stutthof camp near Danzig,[38] full of concentration camp prisoners.

At the end of April 1945, Konteradmiral Engelhardt had assembled some large ships in Neustadt Bay, north of Lübeck. These included liners previously used on the routes to the Americas which used large amounts of fuel, something Engelhardt's organisation had found very difficult to obtain throughout 1945. It was therefore predominantly smaller freighters that were being used for refugee traffic, but one of the great liners had just been brought into use. This was the Hamburg South America Line's flagship, *Cap Arcona*, built in 1927, which had just been to Copenhagen with 8,000 refugees and now lay at anchor off Neustadt. Engelhardt got a telephone call from the SS that *Cap Arcona* had been requisitioned as a floating concentration camp. He became angry and said that the ship had been allocated to the Kriegsmarine's transport organisation, which was under his command. As far as he was concerned, he only took orders from Grossadmiral Dönitz. It is supposed, but it is not known for certain, that Dönitz had in some way sanctioned the decision, or not tried to resist it. Engelhardt had to make this and other ships nearby available to the SS. It is also supposed that the SS wanted to sink the ships with all the prisoners on board, but this has never been determined. The first 2,000 prisoners were taken on board on 26 April and, by 29 April, the ship's command estimated that there were 7,500 prisoners on board *Cap Arcona*. New prisoners were still being brought on board, and on 3 May, the freighter *Thielbek* was nearby, loaded with further prisoners. The liner *Deutschland* also lay at anchor in the area, but without prisoners.

During the British advance towards Schleswig-Holstein, it was feared that the remaining German armies would retreat in order to continue the fight in the north. There was particular unease about the concentration of ships and the RAF were given the priority of ensuring that no ship transports departed towards Norway with troops who could continue the fight from there. The British armies received heavy air support, mainly from Hawker Typhoons from the RAF's 2nd Tactical Air Force.

---

38 It was in this camp, southeast of Danzig, that Danish Communists were interned. Some of them were sent westward on the 'death march' without food, while others were transported westward in barges – also without any food. This has been described by the Danish Communist Martin Nielsen in three books published between 1947 and 1949.

On 3 May, four squadrons from 123 Wing carried out several attacks on German shipping in the Lübeck area. These were Hawker Typhoon fighter bombers from 184, 263 and 198 squadrons, which were equipped with machine guns and rockets, while 197 Squadron was armed with machine guns and bombs. The second attack of the day was led by Group Captain Johnny Baldwin RAF, commander of 123 Wing; they targeted ships in Neustadt Bay. The first three squadrons were carrying some new rockets whose effectiveness against shipping targets was very much in doubt, and this needed to be tested. The large numbers of aircraft first attacked the liner *Deutschland*, which only had a crew of eighty men and a hospital staff of twenty-six; there was a Red Cross sign painted on one side of one funnel. The next attack was launched against a liner with three funnels, and a small freighter at anchor nearby. Both ships were hit by forty and thirty rockets respectively. In the space of a few minutes, *Deutschland*, *Cap Arcona* and *Thielbek* had been hit by rockets, bombs and fire from machine guns from many aircraft. The rockets caused extensive fires. The two big ships were totally destroyed by fire and lay on their sides in the low water, with one side of the ship out of the water. *Thielbek* sank and only about fifty of the more than 2,750 prisoners survived. On *Cap Arcona*, it is surmised that somewhere between 4,150 and 5,400 additional prisoners were killed, but a few thousand of the prisoners miraculously escaped out of the wreck and got to land. The big barges with prisoners from the Stutthof camp were in Lübeck harbour, as well as the 1,936-tonne large steamer *Athen* with 2,300 prisoners on board, which was not hit. The pilots did not know what they had been attacking. A few hours later, Lübeck was captured by British forces. Up until then, the SS men had killed those prisoners they could manage to get hold of in Lübeck itself and on the beaches between Lübeck and Neustadt.[39] Some of the locals in Lübeck had tried to draw the attention of the British forces to the ships and their cargoes, but the information did not get through to the RAF squadrons in time. Presumably there existed a message of one kind or another which did not reach all the way down the command chain to the pilots. Some of the British records on this tragic episode remain classified until 2045, presumably to protect the names of the RAF people involved.

On 3 May 1945, Generalfeldmarschall Erhard Milch of the Luftwaffe met the British Brigadier Derek Mills-Roberts, commanding officer of No. 1 Commando Brigade, Royal Marines, to surrender. Mills-Roberts had just come back to Lübeck after inspecting the widespread killings on the coast at Neustadt. When Milch saluted with a '*Heil Hitler*' and handed his marshal's baton to the brigadier, the latter took the baton and broke it over Milch's head.

---

39 Local people were reported as having assisted the SS in apprehending escaped concentration camp prisoners.

The Kriegsmarine's operations in May 1945 and the end of the refugee transports

Between 1 and 8 May, barges and small vessels from the 13th Landing Flotilla ferried a total of 150,000 refugees and troops to Hel from Schiewenhorst (now Polish Świbno) at the mouth of the Vistula, just east of Danzig. From here, the transport ships *Sachsenwald* and *Weserstrom* and the torpedo boats *T36* and *T108* carried a total of 8,850 people to the West on 3 May. The remnants of the 2nd Army held the Vistula estuary and the peninsula of Hel until Germany surrendered on 8 May.

Schlesien went towards Greifswalder Bodden (the bay south of Rügen) to cover the bridge at Wolgast, where the refugees were streaming across the River Peene. The ship hit a British mine on 3 May 1945 off Zinnowitz near Swinemünde. The next day, it was hit by a large number of bombs dropped by Soviet naval aircraft, put aground and then blown up.

As late as 3 May 1945, Seekriegsleitung sent a signal to the submarine commanders that the submarine war was to continue from Norway, if northern Germany fell to the Allies. At that point in time, sixteen Type XXI submarines had been delivered: ten of them were in Norway, three in Denmark and three in North German ports. Twenty of the small Type XXIII submarines had been delivered and seventeen of them were now in Norway. It is mainly due to the RAF and USAAF bombing of Kiel and Bremen that the number of operational submarines did not match the production figures. Dönitz had plans ready for an attack against the invading forces near the end of the war. If the Allies came to the Dutch coast, the big ships would not have been deployed, but if, on the other hand, an invasion of Denmark and southern Norway was threatened, then they would have been. This plan was approved by Hitler before his death and it was linked to the deployment of the new submarines. The submarines did not come to play the decisive role that had been intended, but they could have done if they had been deployed earlier and in large numbers, according to a later US study. Overall, submarine production took 80 per cent of total electricity production near the end of the war. Huge quantities of steel were used, which could instead have been used to produce 5,100 tanks; 40,000 men worked solely on the production of Type XXI submarines. A number of the submarines which in the final climactic days were transferred from Germany to Norway were sunk, or the crews, on hearing of the surrender, chose to scuttle them. Two submarines made it all the way to Argentina without surrendering.

On 4 May 1945 at six in the morning, a German convoy from Frederikshavn in north Jutland arrived in Copenhagen. It was escorted by the destroyers *Z6 Theodor Riedel*, *Z10 Hans Lody* and *Z14 Friedrich Ihn*, the torpedo boats *T7* and *T17*, and a naval ferry barge equipped with artillery.

The closer to the end of the war, the more desperate were the means of transport. German soldiers were evacuated on merchant ships, warships, river barges, and floating docks. Here soldiers are evacuated by a *Marinefährprahm* (naval ferry barge), *F879*. (SMB arkiv)

German Dornier Do 24 from Seenotflotille 81 in Guldborgsund, Denmark in May 1945. (Aage Boding)

On 4 May, Seenotflotille 81 from the Luftwaffe's sea-rescue service made ready to transfer from Rügen to Denmark. The next morning, fifteen Do 24 seaplanes and a single Arado 196 seaplane flew to Guldborgsund (the sound between the southeastern Danish islands of Falster and Lolland), where they remained for a month. At the same time, ten of the unit's rescue vessels arrived. The planes and boats were carrying mechanics, secretaries, spouses and girlfriends. Moreover, there were ample supplies in both the ships and the aircraft. They had also brought a number of live pigs,[40] so the personnel could be fed for some time.

On 5 May 1945, a floating dock ran aground on the southern tip of the island of Langeland in the Great Belt. The tugboats had cast off during transportation – probably while being attacked from the air. On board were 1,500 concentration camp prisoners.[41] They were Russians and French, whom the local people on Langeland had to take care of in the midst of the general confusion surrounding liberation.[42]

Around the time of Denmark's liberation on 5 May 1945, German naval headquarters wanted to ensure that German warships and other vessels in German and Danish waters which were still sailing quickly put their refugees ashore and conducted a further trip to Hel. The order came in a signal at 2107 on 5 May and it was added at the end that Field Marshal Montgomery had given his oral approval. The freighters *Linz*, *Ceuta*, *Nautik*, *Pompeii*, *Sachsenwald* and the auxiliary cruiser *Hansa* came from Copenhagen to Hel on 6 May with the destroyers *Z6 Theodor Riedel*, *Z10 Hans Lody*, *Z14 Friedrich Ihn*, *Z25* and *Z34*, and the torpedo boats *T17*, *T19*, *T23*, *T28* and *T35*. Along with a number of minesweepers, training ships, *Sperrbrecher 11* and *Sperrbrecher 17*, they brought a total of 43,000 refugees to Copenhagen. On the way out, they met the destroyers *Z38* and *Z39* and the torpedo boat *T33*, which were coming from Swinemünde. In transit, the naval force fought off an attack from Soviet torpedo boats now operating from Kolberg. A Soviet motor torpedo boat was sunk and its crew were put ashore in Copenhagen by the Germans. British aircraft flew over the German convoy, but did nothing else than signal with flashlight to the ships on their way eastward. On the way back with many people on board, the convoy was subjected to Soviet air attacks. The wounded were allowed to remain on board after arriving in Copenhagen, and all the ships with the wounded were later assembled

---

40 A very zealous Danish resistance fighter felt that the German pigs should not have been transferred to Danish pigsties. He felt that it would not be good for Danish pigs to be associating with those 'Nazi pigs', so they were moved.

41 The French were accommodated at Skovsgård manor house. The Russians were split up and later they were all sent back to the Soviet Union.

42 The floating dock was later towed to Copenhagen and used by the Royal Danish Navy.

in a new convoy by agreement with the British. It sailed north of Zealand and through the Great Belt to Kiel. All the able-bodied German troops in Denmark had to walk home to Germany.

From the 'Nanny' anchorage south of Drogden, German ships were able to sail over to Hel to pick up refugees and military personnel until 8 May at 2359 (Moscow time). Seekriegsleitung sent out the following signal 7 May 1945:

An alle in der Ostsee befindlichen Schiffe: Infolge Kapitulation müssen sämtliche See- und Sicherungsstreitkräfte sowie Handelsschiffe die Häfen in Kurland und Hela bis 9. Mai null Uhr verlassen haben. Transport deutscher Menschen aus dem Osten daher mit höchter Beschleunigung durchführen. Seekriegsleitung.

To all ships in the Baltic Sea: As a result of the surrender, all naval and security vessels as well as merchant ships which are in the harbours in Courland and Hel must have left by no later than 9 May, 0000. Transportation of German people from the eastern areas must therefore be stepped up immediately. Naval operations staff.

In the final days of the war, it was important for Germany to keep the ports open as long as possible for the sake of the ongoing evacuations from the various 'pockets'. Generaladmiral Hans-Georg von Friedeburg, Dönitz's successor as commander-in-chief of the Kriegsmarine, in accordance with the conditions of the surrender to the Allies, had agreed that no German ship might leave north German or Danish ports, but that ships at anchor

The German destroyer *Z-39* with a double 6in/150mm turret. The heavy armament made these ships unstable. The trainable antenna on top of the bridge is a 20ft antenna for the FuMO 24/25 radar working at 368 MHz. (SMB arkiv)

The passenger ship *Ubena* in Copehagen roads brought over three thousand soldiers ashore from destroyers and torpedo boats before their final rescue trip to Hel. (Old Ship Picture Galleries)

or at sea were not covered. On the other hand, each ship had very limited stocks of fuel available, whether coal or oil, because the German fuel supply system had totally collapsed. After the next peace treaty in Reims on 7 May, the British and the Germans tried to bend the rules. The British admiral in Denmark, Vice-Admiral R Vesey Holt RN allowed the Germans to continue the evacuation operation, as long as it did not include ships that departed from Danish ports or territorial waters. The deadline expired at midnight on 8 May, Moscow time, ie on 8 May at 2000 GMT. It would be too difficult for the merchant ships to make another trip before the deadline, so only the fast warships were sent off.

The participants in the last trip were therefore five warships anchored south of Drogden. The passenger ship *Ubena* was sent from Copenhagen harbour to pick up the more than three thousand soldiers who were still on board the destroyers and torpedo boats from the trip they had just completed. They had to be disembarked before the ships departed. At the same time, the ships concerned took the remaining fuel from the other ships at the anchorage. The two freighters *Weserberg* and *Paloma* and the little steamer *Rugard* were in Hel. They escaped an attack from three Soviet torpedo boats on 8 May and reached the west with a total of 7,230 soldiers and refugees.

The destroyers *Z14 Friedrich Ihn*, *Z20 Karl Galster* and *Z25*, and the torpedo boats *T23* and *T28* took part in the last trip. They departed from the Drogden area on the morning of 8 May and reached Hel at 1900. They departed for Kiel before 2100 with refugees on board, arriving the next day. Now the war was over. The refugees caused chaos in the days after liberation in Denmark. At the anchorage in Sønderborg in south Jutland alone, there were ships with ten to fifteen thousand refugees and 1,500 wounded soldiers on board. There were fifty ships at Korsør in west Zealand. Copenhagen was a distribution centre for refugees. There were refugee ships in Copenhagen harbour and out in the anchorage, as well as all the way down at Drogden, southeast of Copenhagen airport. There was a lively traffic of small boats taking the refugees ashore from the anchorage. Some of the large numbers of sick and wounded refugees had died during the transport from Germany. The bodies were piled up in warehouses in Copenhagen. German troops organised transport from here, often with horse-drawn carriages, out to the West Cemetery, where there is still a section for German victims of the war.[43]

The war also ended in Courland on 8 May, where all ships had to have left the ports before midnight Moscow time. The German army decided to evacuate all the sick and wounded soldiers; they had only the slightest chances of survival in Soviet captivity. One officer and 125 men from each division, preferably soldiers with children in Germany, were also selected to be taken to the West. Four convoys left Libau with about 14,400 men and an unknown number of refugees, distributed in sixty-five ships. The convoy consisted of everything that could sail and float in the area. Similarly, two convoys left Ventspils with 11,300 men in sixty-one ships. When the last convoys left Libau, the advancing Soviet forces fired on the ships and captured two tugboats with three hundred soldiers on board.

There were almost sixty thousand men left in Hel, and a pocket on the estuary of the Vistula consisting of some forty thousand men. More than two hundred thousand men[44] from the 16th and 18th armies, part of Army Group Courland, were left behind. All of these troops fell into Soviet captivity, which many of them did not survive. The last survivors came home in 1955.

On 9 May, a lot of ships sailed close to Christiansø, an island off the east coast of Bornholm. Many of them came from Libau and Ventspils, but there were also some from the pockets at Hel and on the estuary of the Vistula. When passing Christiansø, they were subjected to an air raid – after the end of the war – by a large number of Soviet aircraft. The fighting could be followed from Christiansø and Bornholm. The tanker *Liselotte Friederich* and the artillery ferry barge *F517* were sunk off Christiansø with the loss of

---

43 In Denmark, there are a total of approximately ten thousand graves of German soldiers and fifteen thousand graves of German refugees from the war.

44 The Soviet figures say 189,112 men, including forty-two generals, plus about fourteen thousand Latvian soldiers.

ten and five men respectively. Throughout the following summer, countless bodies drifted up onto the shores of Bornholm from all the ships sunk during the previous months.

Only three of the Kriegsmarine's large vessels escaped destruction during the war and they were all in a Danish port when the war ended. At the surrender, the heavy cruiser *Prinz Eugen* had a crew of approximately 1,500 men. The light cruiser *Nürnberg* had 870 men on board. They were both in Copenhagen, while *Leipzig*, as mentioned earlier, was in Aabenraa. The ships had been prepared for blasting/sinking. The Germans would have liked to have had permission from the British to sail another trip to Hel with *Prinz Eugen* and *Nürnberg* to fetch a shipload of refugees and German troops, combat-ready troops as well as wounded, but the British did not allow the big ships out of harbour. The German crews had also received orders not to surrender to the resistance movement, who were regarded as a street mob, or lawless partisans. They were only allowed to surrender to British forces.

Unternehmen Rettung: the rescue operation in numbers

On 22 March 1945, the local naval headquarters in Danzig drew up a status report. Up until then, 1,108,191 people had been rescued and taken to the West. The official explanation was that the people of the eastern areas had to be evacuated from the war zones of the Eastern Front, but the real purpose was to transfer as many of the German people as possible to areas that would be captured by the Western powers and not by the Russians. The German leadership did not know where the boundary between the Allies was going to go.

Between 21 March and 10 April, 157,270 German wounded (exclusively military personnel) were evacuated via Hel. On 21 April 1945, the largest number of people in a single day was evacuated: 38,000 people were brought westward from Hel. In the month of April, 264,887 people were evacuated from the ports in Danzig Bay: Pillau, Kahlberg, Schiewenhorst and Oxhöft. Since 21 January, almost half a million people had been evacuated from Pillau.

Between 25 January and 8 May 1945, 1,420,000 civilian refugees were evacuated from the area around Danzig Bay and from the Pomeranian coast. A further approximately six hundred thousand had been taken westward by ship over shorter distances. This amounts to the world's largest ever rescue operation by sea, in which more than two million people were picked out of the 'pockets' and brought westward; 500,000–600,000 wounded soldiers were also evacuated.

A German assessment mentions that 495,810 people were evacuated to the West from Hel alone in the last four months of the war. On 8 May, there were about eighty thousand soldiers, refugees and wounded in Hel. The last

Two of the worst tragedies experienced at sea: *Wilhelm Gustloff* (left) and *Cap Arcona*, here shown in a peaceful moment before the war. *Gustloff* is regarded as the largest loss at sea ever, sunk by the Soviet submarine *S-13*. *Cap Arcona* was mistakenly attacked by the RAF while thousands of concentration camp prisoners were on board. (Old Ship Picture Galleries)

'turnaround' of ships from Copenhagen and Glücksburg probably saved about twenty-two thousand of them.

According to Grossadmiral Dönitz's own account, in the period from 23 January to 8 May 1945, 2,022,602 persons were sailed to safety westward. Approximately thirty-three thousand people died in connection with the transport ships, which were subjected to acts of war or accidents. This figure does not include the concentration camp prisoners who were killed on the ships in Neustadt Bay. It gives a loss ratio of 1.63 per cent. If the transports had been organised across country under war conditions and winter weather, the losses would probably have been significantly higher.

The Kriegsmarine saved large numbers of people from being left behind the front line of the advancing Soviet forces. It used more than eight hundred ships, of which about 160 large ships were sunk by the Russians or by the Western Allies' aircraft and mines. During the operation, a total of 245 ships – large and small – were lost. It is thought-provoking that about half of the 33,000 who died just happened to find themselves on three ships, *Wilhelm Gustloff*, *Steuben* and *Goya*.

Sweden's involvement in the liberation of Denmark and Norway

The defence staff in Stockholm had been busy with plans since December 1943 to intervene in Norway and Denmark when the war ended. The plans were included in two main sets of plans referred to as RN and RD, which stood for *Rädda Norge* (Save Norway) and *Rädda Danmark* (Save Denmark) respectively. Under RD, there were two sub-plans RDS and RDB, which stood for invasions of Sjælland (Zealand) and Bornholm, respectively. The precondition was that Germany's war potential hardly existed any more. One of the main problems for the planners was whether the two operations could be conducted in parallel. If there was strong resistance on Zealand, the action on Bornholm would be postponed.

Plan RD was ready in draft by 10 April 1945. Preparations were complete by 27 April and, on the same day, Swedish photo reconnaissance flights were begun over Bornholm. RDS was to be led by the commander of the 3rd Army Corps, while RDB was to be led by the head of the south coast naval district. The overall plan included virtually the whole of the Swedish navy, 300 combat aircraft and large army forces. About two regiments were to be deployed on Bornholm: the operation against Bornholm was relatively detailed, but there were large uncertainties attached relating to German air forces and German naval vessels, especially submarines and mines. Resistance from German army forces on the island was not discussed in detail. (It is an interesting thought experiment to imagine RDB being implemented right under the nose of the planned Soviet invasion of Bornholm – or even implemented on the same day!)

The liberation of Bornholm

The liberation of Bornholm proceeded quite differently from the rest of Denmark. Prior to the liberation, no specific agreements on Bornholm had been made among the Allies, but since the summer of 1944, the Soviet foreign ministry had been toying with the idea of a Soviet liberation of the island, whereby it could come under Soviet influence. Tactical developments in the final days of the war took place quickly, and neither General Eisenhower nor Field Marshal Montgomery had probably given the island much thought, but the Russians had. In relation to the German surrender on 4 May 1945 on Lüneburg Heath south of Hamburg, Bornholm belonged to the rest of Denmark. On the other hand, Montgomery came with only 6,000 British soldiers during the liberation days, and there were still some 250,000 well-armed German troops in Denmark. Major-General Richard Henry Dewing accepted the German surrender in Denmark on Montgomery's behalf. On 7 May, General Eisenhower made it clear to the British that Bornholm had the same status as the rest of the country. If the Danish government had demands about British troops on the island, it could just make them. This request never came, although Dewing had some troops ready to be sent to Bornholm. There were thirty-four Sterling bombers from the RAF in Copenhagen airport, and there were units from the airborne forces present in Copenhagen. On 8 May, Eisenhower took the liberty of asking the Russians whether it was contrary to their plans if a British delegation was sent to the island. The British Foreign Office was informed about developments and disagreed with Eisenhower's approach. There was an important difference here in the perception of the two Western Allies. The Americans, including the new president, Harry S Truman,[45] reckoned that Stalin could be trusted; the British had seen the writing on the wall. In this case, the Russians just sat back and waited without answering. Meanwhile, preparations were being made for the capture of the island.

The Russians had been following developments, but they were already set to go on 7 May. A little before noon, Soviet naval aircraft from the 51st Mine and Torpedo Air Regiment bombed Rønne and Nexø. From a Soviet point of view, it was a natural thing to do, because before a major attack 'the main objectives had to be softened up', either by artillery bombardment or bombs. In the evening, the Russians dropped more bombs on the towns, as well as leaflets with Russian text. They contained a call for the island's German commander to surrender to the Russians the next morning. To that end, he had to come to Kolberg before ten o'clock. The sea journey would be made safe, it said. The flyer was signed by 'Lieutenant-Colonel Slepenkov, Commander of the air units'.[46]

The flyers were simply stencilled sheets of paper. When the surrender had not taken place, a renewed bombardment of Rønne and Nexø came on 8 May, but by now the towns had been evacuated. Ten civilian Bornholmers died. The bombing raid came around nine o'clock, since the Russians were not aware of the time difference, and that their ultimatum had not yet expired. The bombardment of Rønne and Nexø, and the subsequent Soviet capture of the island was an opportunity the Russians just suddenly grabbed. A strong indication of the improvisation involved was the self-same flyers. Usually, Soviet army units had excellent opportunities for printing newspapers and distributing propaganda material to the troops. It was part of the whole Soviet agitprop (agitation and propaganda) system, which also included the political organisation of the armed forces. If there was a situation where a Soviet division wanted to accept a surrender from the Island Commander of Bornholm, they could just have printed something more elegant, flawless and bombastic than this flyer. The signature should at least have been from a

---

45 President Franklin D Roosevelt had died on 12 April 1945 and was succeeded by the vice-president.
46 Lieutenant-Colonel Slepenkov was commander of the 9th Air Support Division of the Baltic Fleet air force.

major-general and not a lieutenant-colonel. In this case, the local commander of a unit belonging to the Baltic Fleet air force had written a message, had it stencilled and immediately had it dropped on the island without otherwise clarifying what time zone the Germans on Bornholm were in.

In the general confusion during the liberation days, many Danes thought that the German commander on the island had to be mad when he would not surrender. The war was clearly lost and thereby over. The situation was more complicated than that, however, and there were many decision-makers involved. The 42-year-old Kapitän zur See Gerhard von Kamptz, Island Commander of Bornholm, was a naval officer and reported to Kommandierende Admiral Westliche Ostsee (Admiral of the West Baltic), who had his headquarters in Naval Command East in Kiel, which in turn reported to the Kriegsmarine headquarters in Flensburg-Mürwick. He had only been on the island since 5 March 1945 and, according to his instructions, he could only surrender to the British. Neither the naval headquarters, the German army headquarters in Silkeborg in central Jutland, nor the German plenipotentiary in Denmark, Dr Werner Best, could get a clear message from the British about what their intentions were with Bornholm. So the instruction to von Kamptz was that he should defend himself in the case of a Soviet attack. He was in the process of carrying out *Unternehmen Rettung*, which was an operation that continued until the official end of the war on 8 May at 2100. In fact, this operation continued until the end of May, when the Kriegsmarine eventually discontinued the round trips to the many surviving pockets of refugees and soldiers.

On 6 May, General der Artillerie Rolf Wuthmann arrived on Bornholm with the remainder of a grenadier regiment of about eight hundred men. He had been given the task of defending the island so that, among others, the 2nd Panzer Army could be evacuated safely to the west. A tacit agreement was concluded between Wuthmann and von Kamptz, under which von Kamptz remained the island's commander, but Wuthmann would take care of any fighting on land.

The Russian landing took place after the war had ended. It was on the afternoon of 9 May, when five Soviet motor torpedo boats with about a hundred marines on board took Rønne harbour without a fight. The German forces did not put up any resistance. Among the German officers on the quay was Wuthmann's chief of staff. The war had ended the previous evening at 2100 on 8 May.

On the evening of 9 May, Kapitän zur See von Kamptz was transported to the Baltic Fleet staff in Kolberg by Soviet motor torpedo boat. The Russians wanted to fly him to Tallinn and make him the commander of the German mine-clearing force that would clear the Finnish and German mine barriers in the Gulf of Finland, but von Kamptz did not want to work for the Russians and refused.[47]

The case of the liberation of Bornholm came up in the British House of Commons in late May 1945 when the Foreign Minister Anthony Eden was asked about progress by the Honourable Member for Wallsend, Miss Irene Ward. Eden was evasive and instead stated that it was simply the military situation that decided who came first. He did not mention that the British could easily have flown to Bornholm and received the German surrender. The British had felt obliged to ask the commander-in-chief, who was American. Eisenhower had, out of courtesy, asked the Russians, who had not responded to the inquiry.

It was thus pure chance that decided the fate of Bornholm. The German collapse had left its mark on the island's garrison, but the island was also affected by *Unternehmen Rettung*. A ship with troops and refugees, about six hundred in all, had arrived at Nexø just as the first Soviet air raid took place and it was hit. There were a total of approximately sixteen thousand troops on the island – among others, forces from the Waffen-SS. A portion of the latter were volunteers from the Baltic countries, and some of the SS men were immediately executed by the Russians; the other Germans were transported to Kolberg as prisoners of war. The Gestapo had apparently taken the opportunity to disappear from the island without trace, between the transmission of the message of liberation and the arrival of the Soviet forces.

Kapitän zur See von Kamptz has left a strange legacy. Dönitz had given him the task of making sure that as many soldiers and refugees as possible came west and he was probably stubborn, tough and uncompromising – as well as being a staunch Nazi. The Russians respected him and he was not convicted of anything after the war. He would have liked the island to be handed over to the British, but since that could not happen, he delayed the arrival of the Russians so much that thousands of German refugees and soldiers reached safety in the West and the people of Bornholm paid the price. Seen from the German side, many people were saved by his intransigence. The liberation of Bornholm should thus be seen in conjunction with a number of other major events of the war which were far outside the influence of the local people.

The final air and naval warfare in the Danish straits

In the last month of the war, the fighting came very close to Danish waters, where Allied air forces were operating in the air with both fighter bombers and large four-engined aircraft fitted out for anti-submarine and anti-surface operations. No warships from the Western Allies entered Danish waters

---

47 Gerhard von Kamptz was a Soviet prisoner of war from 9 May 1945 to 1 January 1954. He died in 1998.

before the end of the war. The air attacks during the last month of the war give an indication of the intensity of the fighting in Danish waters at the time – as can be seen below, the last days were very eventful.

Examples of the fighting in April and May 1945

4 April   The freighter *Feodosia* explodes in the northern Kattegat; approximately three hundred killed. The ship was carrying thirty Marder one-man midget submarines from Aarhus to Oslo.

9 April   Three submarines sunk in the northern Kattegat: *U-804* and *U-843* (both Type IXC) and *U-1065* (Type VIIC). Twelve men were rescued from *U-843*. The other 144 crew members perished. One of the attacking Mosquito aircraft was shot down.

19 April   The submarine *U-251* (Type VIIC) sunk southeast of the island of Anholt in the Kattegat; thirty-nine killed. The minesweeper *M403* sunk close to the same position by twenty two Mosquito IV escorted by twelve Mustang P-51Ds from the RAF and RNoAF. The entire minesweeper crew of sixty-eight perished.

21 April   The minelayer *Ostmark* sunk south of Anholt; 109 killed.

2 May   The submarine *U-2359* (Type XXIII) sunk northeast of the island of Læsø; twelve killed.

3 May   The minesweeper/patrol boat *Vs 524* sunk in the Langeland Belt (southern part of the Great Belt).
The German freighter *Diana* sunk in the Langeland Belt; twenty killed.
The tanker *Taifun* sunk in the Langeland Belt; twenty-seven killed.
The East Asia Company's *Java*, *Jutlandia* and *Falstria* damaged in Nakskov Fjord (Lolland).

4 May   The submarine *U-2338* (Type XXIII) sunk in the Little Belt; twelve killed.
The motor torpedo boat *S-103* sunk off Mommark in the Little Belt; twenty killed.
The freighter *Wolfgang L M Russ* sunk off Helgenæs (east of Aarhus); twenty-five killed.
The minesweeper *M301* sunk off Helgenæs; twenty-one killed.
The German gunboat *K1* (ex-Dutch) sunk off Helgenæs; 114 killed.
Additional vessels damaged at the Battle of Helgenæs: the Chilean freighter *Angamos*,[48] the gunboat *K3* and the minesweeper *Stettin*; unknown number of deaths.
The minesweeper *M36* sunk in the Langeland Belt; twenty killed.

------

48 Seized by the Germans at Aalborg shipyard.

The salvage ships *Ernst Hugo Stinnes* and *Else Hugo Stinnes* sunk off Marstal; forty killed.

5 May   The submarine *U-534* (Type IXC) sunk off Anholt; three killed.

An attacking Liberator aircraft from the *RAF* was shot down; ten killed.

The submarine *U-2521* (Type XXI) sunk at Anholt, forty-three killed.

The submarine *U-579* (Type VIIC) sunk east of Aarhus; twenty-four killed.

6 May   The submarine *U-3523* (Type XXI) sunk north of the Scaw; fifty-eight killed.

9 May   The tanker *Liselotte Friederich* sunk off Christiansø; ten killed.

The artillery ferry barge *F517* sunk off Christiansø; five killed.

The end of the war – and the new submarines heading for Norway

The advance towards Denmark developed into an improvised race. Field Marshal Montgomery received his secret national instructions from Churchill around 18 April 1945.[49] He was to move in the direction of Lübeck to cut off the Soviet advance along the coast. Eisenhower and Montgomery were not in agreement about the situation. The Allies each had priorities of their own, with the Russians having set their sights on Fehmarn and possibly the Danish straits, but it was not to be. Montgomery and the British government were aware that if the Red Army was involved in the liberation of Denmark, the straits into the Baltic Sea could become Soviet territory, or at least a high-priority Soviet sphere of interest. This was in clear violation of British foreign policy.

During the spring of 1945, the Western Allies feared that, in the moment of defeat, the German forces were planning to retreat to the Alps and fight a last battle there. When it came down to it, this fear proved to be unfounded. Eisenhower had diverted large US forces to southern Germany and the retreating German forces from the Eastern Front surrendered here in large numbers in April and May 1945. A lesser known, but in turn more well-founded fear, was the Germans' plans to fight a last battle for '*Führer und Vaterland*' (Leader and Fatherland) in Norway, even though Germany itself had fallen to Soviet, American and British forces. Hitler and Dönitz had been planning since 1943 for the new submarines to force Britain out of the war. The construction of the submarines and the training of the crews

---

49 See Antony Beevor, *The Second World War*, p746.

were progressively delayed, but the original plan had not been completely unrealistic. It could have given the Western Allies major problems if the RAF had not raised the priority of its operations against this submarine production. In 1944 and especially in 1945, the basis for the new German submarine operations was slowly but surely eroded, because of the RAF's efforts with mines and bombs, as well as the widespread collapse caused by refugee flows, the Russian advance, and much more. However, Hitler's suicide did not change Dönitz's plans. On 30 April 1945, he was appointed Hitler's successor and he continued to equip German submarines for the battle of the Atlantic. The submarines were sent north towards Trondheim and Narvik in Norway and this continued until around 5 May 1945. From the turbulent days between Hitler's death to the final German surrender, a wide range of strange and somewhat contradictory decisions were made.

The explanation seems to be that Dönitz held a meeting on 3 May with the participation, among others, of the Nazi leadership from Norway and Denmark. From Norway came Reichskommissar Josef Terboven, and the commander-in-chief of the German military forces there, General der Gebirgstruppe Franz Böhme, and from Denmark came Dr Werner Best from

The German submarine base at Trondheim. One of the main reasons for the occupation of Norway was access for German submarines to the North Atlantic. (SMB arkiv)

The German submarine Type XXI submarine, *U-2518*. Although Hitler was dead and Berlin had fallen, German submarines were sent towards bases in Norway on 3 May 1945 to continue the fight in the Atlantic. (Old Ship Picture Galleries)

Copenhagen, and Generaloberst Georg Lindemann from army headquarters in Silkeborg. Both generals offered to fight on. Lindemann had previously been accused by Hitler of laxity and relieved of the command of Army Group North on the Eastern Front, and he is quoted as having said at the meeting, 'that in Denmark we could fight one last decent battle – and fight to the last bullet'. It was decided to continue the submarine war, despite the loss of Germany itself. What the real purpose of continuing the submarine offensive was supposed to be is still uncertain – it would probably have meant an extension of a few months. At that point in time, there were still around 380,000 German troops in Norway, some of whom belonged to the SS. The morale of the troops was higher than one would immediately have expected – the Swedes had gathered that information by systematically reading the German soldiers' letters which were transported through Sweden. A conquest of Norway – from the north by Soviet units and from the south by British and American units – would have been an expensive and meaningless affair for all parties in terms of both lives and money.

Dr Best argued at the meeting that the large numbers of German refugees in Denmark could be exposed to attacks if there was an insurrection or outright battles on Danish territory. In this way, the German refugees in Denmark perhaps became the decisive argument for giving up on continuing to fight in the country. Dönitz had that morning put out the first overture – an officer delegation – to Montgomery. It was to inquire whether the three German armies on the Eastern Front could surrender to the British, and large numbers of civilians from Mecklenburg could be saved into the British troops' area. Montgomery's response was that the refugees could not be taken care of, and the units on the Eastern Front could surrender to the Red Army. Individual people could surrender to the British. This led, in turn, to the sending of a renewed delegation to Montgomery the following day, which resulted in the unconditional surrender of all German forces in the Netherlands, northwest Germany and Denmark. Remaining were the German forces in Norway, which did not surrender until 7 May. The British could not accept more refugees unless the submarine war and operations in Norway ceased – there should be an unconditional surrender. This would explain the conflicting decisions of the German authorities. The German forces in Norway thus surrendered on 7 May, including the submarine force, and then the refugees could again stream into the new American and British occupation zones in Germany.

The German military commanders continued to be in doubt about what was really going on. Some of the German generals continued to believe for four or five days after the war finally ended that their forces would now be made available for the final battle against the Russians – in co-operation with American and British forces. In any event, there is no clear picture of a logical sequence of events in the new German leadership from 30 April until the final peace settlement. An order that the crews should sink their own submarines was apparently released around 4 May, and withdrawn again around 5 May.

One of the war's many paradoxes is the number of German submarines. The Kriegsmarine built a total of approximately 1,170 submarines. Hitler had fifty-seven operational submarines when the war started on 1 September 1939 and fifty-three submarines when it ended in May 1945. In the meantime, about thirty thousand men had died in German submarines.

10

The End of the War

Aftermath and Retrospect

The days following liberation in Denmark

On 4 May 1945, a British naval force on its way to Murmansk received orders to go back to its base at Scapa Flow in the Orkney Islands and take large amounts of food on board; the crews were told that they were going to liberate an occupied country. On 6 May, the light cruisers *Birmingham* and *Dido*, and the destroyers *Zealous*, *Zephyr*, *Zest* and *Zodiac* departed from the islands once more. The naval force had been ordered to Copenhagen, where it arrived on the morning of 9 May after having sailed down the coast of Sweden in Swedish territorial waters, where there was the least danger from mines. They were accompanied by the Swedish warships *Karlskrona*, *Klas Horn*, *Ehrensköld* and *Nordenskjöld*. The crews did not, in fact, need all the food they had brought with them for the people of the city, but in return, the crews were lavishly entertained by the Copenhageners, and the sailors from the Royal Navy tasted food and drink that they had not been able to get in their home country for the last six years. Meat, butter, whipped cream, beer, etc, were enjoyed in large quantities.[1]

Vice-Admiral Reginald Vesey Holt RN was appointed Flag Officer Denmark. The takeover/surrender operation was carried out by another naval force under Vice-Admiral Rhoderick Robert McGrigor RN. It came to Copenhagen a few days later and consisted of two escort carriers (very small aircraft carriers), *Searcher* and *Trumpeter*, the heavy cruiser *Norfolk*, and the destroyers *Carysfort*, *Zambesi*, *Obedient*, *Opportune* and *Orwell*. The two German cruisers moored in Copenhagen Freeport were handed over by Vizeadmiral Wilhelm Meendsen-Bohlken. The British made the German sailors take the cruisers' ammunition ashore under heavy guard on 20 May. In Copenhagen, the Germans left the following ships to be transferred to the British: the two cruisers *Prinz Eugen* and *Nürnberg*, three destroyers, ten torpedo boats, thirteen flak ships, two armed merchant ships and nineteen patrol boats. The German cruisers were escorted to Wilhelmshaven by British destroyers later in May.

---

1 Around the fiftieth anniversary of the liberation, the author met representatives from the destroyer crews in London.

Bornholm after the end of the war

Bornholmers regarded the Russian occupation with some trepidation: they did not know what it would mean and whether it would be permanent. The Russians remained on the island until 5 April 1946. Shortly before, Denmark had indicated that it was now able to take care of the island itself, and the need for Soviet troops had thereby ceased. After the war ended, there was a maximum of 7,700[2] Russians on the island, and they stayed mainly in their barracks area. In general, there were not the problems that might have been expected. There were individual incidents, but they were probably no worse than if the Americans or the British had provided the liberation/occupation troops. It is reported that one of the Soviet soldiers was executed at the former German barracks at Galløkken just south of Rønne after a rape, and that another was executed after a theft committed earlier in Germany. On 1 June 1945, one of the ships that shuttled back and forth between Rønne and Kolberg was sunk. This was the rescue ship *Vesterhavet*, which struck a mine just outside Kolberg harbour. Only eight of the 225 Soviet soldiers on board, and only one of the Danish crew of twelve, were rescued. The ships being used sailed German POWs away from Rønne and brought Soviet troops in the opposite direction.

The bombings on 7 and 8 May 1945 had caused extensive damage to buildings in Rønne and Nexø. The Swedish government donated 300 wooden houses for the reconstruction of the towns.

When the Russians left Bornholm, Denmark could take over the German barracks and other installations free of charge, as long as Denmark did not in turn make financial claims on the Russians for damage, deforestation, and so on. However, the Soviet Union wanted 500,000 Danish kroner for the new buildings which they had built themselves. A Danish commission estimated that they were worth a maximum of 200,000 kroner. Only a few hours before departure, the Soviet commanding general said he was prepared to accept 300,000 kroner in cash. The Danish county prefect managed to raise this amount from the local banks.

Exercise Post Mortem

On 25 June 1945, a strange and unusual exercise called Exercise Post Mortem began at Fliegerhorst Grove (later Karup airbase). Here, the RAF had taken over an entire sector of the German air-warning system, which was intact

---

2   One source stated that, around the end of the war, there were 9,900 Soviet soldiers on the island, but this figure was quickly brought down to 7,700.

and undamaged, and the personnel still present. Led by Generalmajor Boner of the Luftwaffe, most of the air-warning system was activated with ten large radar stations covering a total of forty radar installations. The RAF provided personnel who looked over the shoulder of each German staff member, while a large force of British bombers conducted simulated attacks where electronic countermeasures ('jamming') were used. The exercise lasted for more than a week. Although the RAF was not popular with the Luftwaffe staff, there was a certain understanding of the situation, because Generalmajor Boner, like many other German generals, expected that it would only be a matter of a few months before the Western Allies were at war with the Soviet Union.

Danish navy operations between 29 August 1943 and 5 May 1945

Under the leadership of Kommandørkaptajn K Lundsteen, and with Vice-admiral A H Vedel's tacit approval, Danish naval personnel slid smoothly into a mutually beneficial co-operation with the Freedom Council and the rest of the Resistance, and did not experience the antagonism that the Danish army was subjected to. In September 1944, the Western Allies (SHAEF) had wanted Viceadmiral A H Vedel as the designated commander of the underground army in Denmark if it should come to the Western Allies having to conquer the country. Vedel politely declined, partly because it would probably be more of an army operation, and he suggested that the commander-in-chief of the army, Generalløjtnant E Gørtz, was appointed instead, which he was.

During the occupation, the Danish naval personnel consisted of about 160 permanent officers and 850 regular recruits. In addition, there were reserve personnel, conscripts and a number of civilian employees, to which group numerous employees at the naval dockyard also belonged. Between 29 August 1943 and 5 May 1945, the Danish navy suffered a total of forty-five fatalities. More than fifty men were in concentration camps in Germany and another fifty were in German prisons in Denmark at the liberation in May 1945. Two men had been sentenced to death on 2 May 1945, but the sentences were not carried out before time ran out. Eight of the Danish naval officers had been sent by aircraft from Stockholm to Britain so that they could be part of the Royal Navy and the RAF. Seven of the Danish naval pilots flew for the Allies and two were shot down and killed over the Netherlands and Belgium, respectively. The navy's personnel had managed to rectify the awkward impression that Viceadmiral Rechnitzer's inaction on 9 April 1940 had caused.

One of the Danish navy's most important tasks was to set up an effective intelligence service that could forward news of Kriegsmarine and German ship movements to London. This was done in close co-operation with all areas of domestic shipping. Using information supplied by pilots, harbourmasters, fishermen, ships' captains, mates and other crew members, it had been possible to describe very thoroughly what was happening in Danish waters. During Field Marshal Montgomery's visit to Copenhagen in May 1945, he uttered the famous words 'Second to none'. This was not about the Danish resistance movement, but about the intelligence efforts of the Danish army and navy.

Ammunition accidents, destruction of captured equipment and dumping of munitions

The end of the occupation gave rise to a series of disposals, not all of which will be looked on very kindly by posterity. However, some of the events must be seen in the light of the extensive nature of the task and the very limited resources at the time. Munitions were thrown into the sea, and not always at practical locations. All processing of ammunition was dangerous: the munitions were manufactured under war conditions, often by slave labour; they could be chemically unstable or bear manufacturing defects, since their production had had to be as cheap as possible. There had been some very large explosive accidents not caused by acts of war: Aarhus harbour on 4 July 1944; Bergen harbour on 20 April 1945; the mine depot at Pillau on 26 January 1945, and others. There was a further accident in Flensburg near the German-Danish border on 14 June 1945, when eighty-eight people are believed to have died. In the summer of 1945, large quantities of German ammunition were dumped at the seaward approach to Kalø Vig, an inlet north of Aarhus. About twenty-five years later, when a power plant was going to be constructed nearby, the waters had to be cleared of explosives so that there would be no risk to the large ships that would be delivering the fuel.

The British destroyed vast quantities of German military equipment on Danish soil, in particular, large numbers of aircraft at the German airbases, especially Grove (Karup). The British formally owned all German materials left in Denmark. This was part of the agreement between the Allies.

The war seen as a pollution disaster

While the war in the Baltic Sea was in progress, there were not many who were concerned about its pollution aspects. This applied, incidentally, to the war in other seas too. Since that time, especially in the Baltic Sea, quite a lot has been done to determine what was actually sunk, where it was sunk, and the consequences it may have on the environment for posterity. We are talking here about shipwrecks, mines, torpedoes, depth charges, and the dumping of conventional munitions and large quantities of chemical weapons. The shipwrecks may contain large amounts of fuel and unspecified cargoes.

In 1939, Germany sank about ten Polish warships. In 1940, there were only a few sinkings in the straits caused by mines. In 1941, there was an estimated total of 145 ships lost in the Baltic Sea. These were mainly in the Gulf of Finland and include about eighty Soviet ships and sixty-five German and Finnish ships. In 1942/43, about two hundred ships were sunk in the Baltic Sea. In 1944, the war at sea intensified and an estimated 639 vessels were registered as sunk and, from New Year 1945 to the end of the war, the estimate is 381 ships, mostly German. This gives a total of approximately 1,375 ships. It is a very rough statistic and the numbers should be accepted with some caution. The calculation covers both large and small vessels.[3]

Those ships which were sunk by large explosive charges, for example, by a mine or a torpedo, have probably also lost most of their fuel stocks in connection with the sinking, as their bottom tanks must have been split open. The other wrecks may contain larger amounts of fuel which is slowly being released to the surrounding environment. In the final months of the war, however, German ships were sailing round with only minimal fuel stocks. A large number of the merchant ships were coal-fired, and coal does not pollute the sea.

Germany had produced large quantities of chemical weapons but had not used them, because it was feared that using them would probably bring about retaliation with similar weapons by the Allies. Some of the discovered German chemical weapons were dumped in the Skagerrak after the war in very deep water (about 2,300–3,000ft/700–900m). Chemical munitions were dumped in multiple locations in the Baltic Sea. The two biggest dumps were carried out in areas to the east of Bornholm and the east of Gotland.

Bornholm fishermen, however, have often come in with chemical munitions in their nets, even though they have been fishing far outside the dumping zones. Immediately after the war ended, the Soviet navy sailed out with chemical munitions from Swinemünde to the area east of Bornholm. There were Soviet crews aboard the ships concerned, but the hard work of taking the munitions on board and then later throwing them overboard was handled by German prisoners of war. In interviews with former prisoners of war many years later, it has been revealed that the jettisoning of the

---

3   The information comes from Professor Antoni Komorowski's report in August 2000, 'Prolonged Consequences of the Second World War for the Environment of the Baltic Sea', which also quotes from E Kosiarz, *Druga wojna światowa na Bałtyku* (*The Second World War in the Baltic Sea*), 1988.

munitions started immediately after leaving port, so the dangerous chemical munitions were spread over large areas where fishing trawls have later moved it around. This explains why chemical munitions are being found far outside the established dumping zones.

The mine war in the Baltic Sea

The number of mines in the Baltic Sea was massive. In 1946, an international minesweeping commission estimated that between 1939 and 1945, in the Gulf of Finland alone, 68,080 sea mines and explosive minesweeping obstacles had been laid. More than two hundred ships took an active part in the Finnish part of the post-war minesweeping, which lasted a few years into the 1950s; twenty-eight men from the Finnish navy were killed in this connection and approximately ten thousand mines and minesweeping obstacles were rendered harmless or blown up.

In Danish waters alone, it is estimated that approximately 4,700 people died during the war, of whom about 90 per cent were German; 600 ships were wrecked or were severely damaged, and 312 Danish sailors and fishermen were killed. Since the war and well into the 1950s, a further approximately 120 sailors and fishermen have lost their lives because of mines in Danish waters; forty-eight people were killed when a mine blew up DFDS's passenger ship *København* on 11 June 1948. The number of mines in Danish waters has been estimated by one source as 23,640. The RAF and the Baltic Fleet air force laid a large number of mines in the Baltic Sea in 1945. After the war, it was estimated that seventy German ships were sunk by these mines during that year.

Immediately after liberation, it was clear that the minesweeping in Danish waters would have to be very extensive, and that the Danish navy lacked both the appropriate equipment and manpower. Initially, British minesweepers came with Danish crews to take care of the task. The first task was to open the sea routes between the country's regions, but the actual minesweeping lasted for more than twenty-five years.

The large numbers of wrecks from the war

During the next several years, the Baltic region was scarred by the large numbers of shipwrecks. There were many wrecks sticking out of the water, especially along the German Baltic coast and in the German ports. Some were cut up on the spot, others towed closer to land and broken up; a few of the ships could be raised and reconditioned. This was because the ships of the time, unlike today, did not include extensive electrical and electronic components, so a lot of the material could stand up to salt water for long periods, and engines could sometimes be renovated. Sunken ships were salvaged if it was cost effective to raise and recondition them; if they were getting in the way of navigation, they were raised and towed away or blown apart on the spot. The cargo or fuel supply could be removed beforehand if it posed a threat. Over the years, there have been reports of great treasures in some of the sunken vessels. The German submarine *U-534*, which was recovered near Anholt in 1993, did not include the treasure that the investors had hoped for. In the early 1950s, Soviet and Polish divers were down in the wreck of *Wilhelm Gustloff* to search for valuables, but the result is not known.

In 1957, West Germans raised the sunken Type XXI submarine *U-2540* and reconditioned it. The Bundesmarine began using it in 1960 as a test submarine under the name of *Wilhelm Bauer*, a role it played until 1982. It had been on a training voyage to Bornholm in April 1945 and had been scuttled by its crew near Flensburg light vessel on 4 May 1945.

The international legal aspects of the refugee transports

There have subsequently been discussions or rationalisations about the international legal aspects of the entire evacuation operation, but during the actual process there were not many who emphasised the importance of that aspect of the matter, let alone made any statements about it. None of the German ships named earlier were protected by the Red Cross while carrying out those tasks and they were not bearing any Red Cross markings.[4] They were combatants who were sailing under a naval flag and were carrying anti-aircraft artillery, battle-ready soldiers, military equipment and so on. On departure from Gotenhafen in 1945, *Wilhelm Gustloff*, for example, had been painted grey like a warship, equipped with anti-aircraft guns and was under the command of the Kriegsmarine. The ship was carrying 918 submarine crew members who were ready to be deployed in the war in the North Atlantic. Moreover, there were 373 uniformed Marinehelferinnen (equivalent to British WRNS) on board, as well as 162 seriously wounded soldiers and many others with minor injuries. The ship was thus a legitimate target.[5]

---

4   As mentioned earlier, during the RAF attack on 3 May 1945, the liner *Deutschland* had a Red Cross marking on one side of one of its funnels, but it was not on a Red Cross mission.
5   Günter Grass said in an interview in connection with the launch of his novel *Crabwalk*: '*Es war eine Katastrophe, aber kein Verbrechen.*' (It was a disaster, but not a crime.)

In Germany, there has also been a debate about guilt. In this it has been mentioned that, by mixing military personnel and civilians, Grossadmiral Dönitz had made everyone a legitimate target. It is largely a question of whether the Soviet response would have been different if there had been a clearer separation between civilian and military targets. The war on the Eastern Front was, to a great extent, 'a total war', which was not fought according to existing conventions. The Kriegsmarine took an independent initiative where no one else was doing anything. The motive was to help as many as possible to be brought into areas that would be occupied by the Western Allies, but it was never expressed in that way.

Mutinies, murders and executions on the German side after liberation

The Germans maintained their discipline to the last. This also applied to the German forces on Bornholm under Kapitän zur See von Kamptz. The German Oberstleutnant Henschel had been evacuated from the 18th Army in Courland and admitted to the German field hospital. Here he made some statements which could have affected the morale of the troops, not least because they had come from a senior officer, and he was executed at Galløkken outside Rønne on 6 May 1945 for defeatism.

Executions were carried out on the quarterdeck of the former Bornholm ferry *Hammershus*,[6] which had been renamed *Buea* by the German occupation forces and served as a depot ship for a flotilla of motor torpedo boats.

A mutiny on the minesweeper *M612*, on its way out of Fredericia harbour on the morning of 5 May, went awry. The officers had been locked up, but before the ship arrived at Sønderborg, the crew's strange behaviour – without officers on the bridge – had been reported by the officers on a couple of motor torpedo boats which had passed it in the Little Belt. Upon arrival, the ship was prevented from leaving the port again and the mutineers were overpowered. This resulted in eleven death sentences, which were carried out on the aft deck of the minesweeper while it was anchored in Sønderborg Bay.

Similar executions – in total probably about twenty-eight – took place in Flensburg for crew members who refused to participate in the continuing evacuation operations from the eastern Baltic Sea. Despite the end of the war, the Kriegsmarine had continued with the evacuation of the various armed pockets along the Baltic coast and, according to the Kriegsmarine, this required the continued maintenance of discipline. The executions continued

---

6   In 1968, *Hammershus* was taken over by the Danish navy and the ship became part of the Submarine Squadron as a depot ship under the name *Henrik Gerner*.

until the end of May 1945, when the evacuations were discontinued. The sailings emanated mostly from Flensburg and were by motor torpedo boats and minesweepers. The British did not intervene in what they regarded as internal matters[7] in the German barracks and they did not have many troops to put into Schleswig-Holstein. The number of German executions after the end of the war has, later on, probably surprised the British too. Many years later, it emerged that Germans in the prison camps in the following years also made sure that they took the lives of fellow prisoners who had not complied with the German disciplinary or moral code. There are reports that as late as the home transports to Germany in 1955 from Soviet prison camps, there were prisoners who were killed during the rail journey because of their collaboration with the Soviet authorities.

---

7 The matter first became widely known in 1967 through the publication of an article in an East German magazine solely to discredit West Germany. The West German government was reluctant to take any action against those responsible, who now all sat in relatively high positions in West German society. The argument was partly that the commanding officers responsible had no knowledge of the conditions of surrender, and partly that there had still been a requirement for maintaining discipline in connection with the Kriegsmarine's continuing evacuations from eastern areas. The cases against many in the West German judiciary lasted until about 1979. They had all been military prosecutors and sentenced soldiers to death after the war ended – using Nazi law as a basis.

11

Postscript

Germany

Hitler as naval commander-in-chief and the Kriegsmarine's options
Generally, it can be said about Hitler as a naval commander that – like Napoleon – he knew nothing about naval warfare and had no prerequisites to be able to deploy naval vessels. General der Infanterie Günther von Blumentritt put it a different way to the British historian B H Liddell Hart after the war: 'It was only the admirals who had a happy time during the war. Hitler knew nothing about naval warfare, whereas he thought he knew everything about waging war on land.'

In addition, he probably suffered from seasickness and did not want to take any part in voyages at sea, as this might cause him to reveal signs of weakness. His instructions in relation to the operations of the major warships were basically the reason for their lack of success. Grossadmiral Raeder resigned as a result of his vehement discussions with Hitler. Despite intense quarrels with '*der Führer*', the new naval commander-in-chief, Grossadmiral Dönitz, was soon sticking firmly to Raeder's positions and it took Hitler more than fourteen days to 'cool down', and accept that the big ships should not be scrapped. Most naval operations with battleships, cruisers and destroyers contain moments of offensive action, and a naval force commander generally expects that his commanding officers in the offensive units 'act with the necessary boldness'.[1] The Kriegsmarine could have got much more out of the fighting potential of their surface warships if the commanding officers had just been given offensive powers.

Assessment of the German war effort
Overall, one of Hitler's biggest mistakes was that he did not observe the first of the *Ten Principles of Warfare*: 'Selection and Maintenance of the Aim'.[2]

---

1 At the Royal Danish Naval College at Holmen, the midshipmen can be inspired on the main staircase by Niels Iuel's motto in Latin: '*Nec temere nec timide*' (Neither reckless nor timid).
2 A continuation of Carl von Clausewitz's theories, which in their present form date from the British review of the Second World War in 1947.

During the war, he was constantly changing his objectives; for example, in the attempted conquests of Stalingrad, Leningrad, Moscow and the oil fields of the Caucasus.

The Kriegsmarine initially put a lot of effort into keeping the British out of the Baltic Sea, and this effort turned out to be a good investment. After the neutralisation of the Soviet Baltic Fleet, the Baltic Sea could be used as a transport route and a training area. The overall intention from 1941 thereby succeeded. On the other hand, the Baltic Fleet had not been put definitively out of action, and the Kriegsmarine had quickly had to grasp the fact that much more effort had to be made than planned to keep the Soviet submarines locked in. In this context, it was clearly a mistake from the German side not to have captured Leningrad in 1941 when they had had the opportunity to do so.

The 2nd Battle Group's extensive artillery support in the coastal areas led to the Soviet advance being delayed and the evacuations of German army personnel and refugees therefore being continued. The Soviet submarines, torpedo boats or naval aircraft did nothing to prevent the activities of the big German warships.

The Kriegsmarine's officers and crew were well trained and highly professional. From a technological point of view, the ships were probably the best in the world, but Germany had only been a significant naval power for about fifty years, whereas its main naval opponent had more than three hundred years' experience of using naval power. It was a strong performance by Germany to produce as many submarines, and implement the effective training of as many crews, as they actually did during the war. The war came earlier than planned for the Kriegsmarine and, when it became a fact, the Luftwaffe was unable to prevent Allied aircraft flying over Germany. That Hitler's ideological successor was to come from the Kriegsmarine was probably a surprise to most people.

The Soviet Union

Stalin as naval commander-in-chief – and the immediate future of the Baltic Fleet

In the 1930s, Stalin wanted a major ocean-going navy, but when the war came suddenly in 1941, the Soviet navy had not been developed and there was no sign of any professionalism. When viewed from the very large perspective of the war, the Soviet naval efforts were only marginal.

The Soviet Baltic Fleet's efforts in retrospect

In 1941, the Baltic Fleet had little influence on the war in the Baltic Sea. The efforts of the Soviet submarines in 1942 gave the Germans a fright, which led to the blockading of the Gulf of Finland the following spring. After the breakout from Leningrad, Soviet naval warfare in the Baltic Sea was characterised by smaller vessels, such as submarines, motor torpedo boats and motor gunboats, and by naval aircraft; the large vessels did not come out. The threat to German warships and merchant vessels came primarily from Soviet submarines, mines and naval air forces. Soviet motor torpedo boats and motor gunboats also took part in large numbers but, on the other hand, they did not achieve any operational results of importance. The submarines only fired 152 torpedoes from 1 January 1945 until the end of the war. Motor torpedo boats fired fifty-five torpedoes from February 1945 until the end of the war. None of the larger German warships was sunk by Soviet surface units in the war's final phase. On the other hand, the Baltic Fleet air force had been particularly active from around October 1943, and throughout the advance westward in 1944 and 1945. The naval aircraft, however, had suffered huge losses, and among torpedo planes alone, the Baltic Fleet air force lost 101 Douglas A-20G Boston aircraft in 1945.

In the final stages of the war in the Baltic Sea, the Soviet Union showed an amazing lack of flexibility and tactical initiative. Operations were controlled very centrally, without the possibility of deviation if a favourable opportunity should emerge. On the other hand, the officers and men generally delivered a heroic effort, even though personnel losses were unnecessarily large. The major Soviet artillery vessels, the battleships, cruisers and destroyers, did not come out of the Gulf of Finland in 1944 and 1945, when mineswept routes were opened. The Soviet leaders were not sure whether the recently concluded war against Germany would develop into a continuation against the US and Britain. For the same reason, the German Nashorn barrier across the Gulf of Finland was not removed until 1947.

When the Allies were preparing the occupation zones in Germany in 1944, the island of Fehmarn was included in Soviet demands. As the war was drawing to a close, a race developed between the forces of Field Marshal Montgomery, who was coming from Hamburg, and those of Marshal Rokossovsky, which were following the Baltic coast westward. The British forces reached the Baltic coast at Lübeck and Wismar. The race between Montgomery and Rokossovsky was a result of how the situation developed and not detailed military planning, but both sides were aware of the importance of the Danish straits.

The final settlement of the war took place on land, but the Baltic Fleet contributed to the victory

The final settlement of the war took place on land, where huge Soviet army and air forces destroyed the German forces. The war in the Baltic Sea did not give rise to any major battles. The individual events of the war at sea were not in themselves battle-decisive, but the Soviet Baltic Fleet made a considerable contribution to the wearing down of Germany. The warfare was characterised by sea mines in very large numbers, combined with submarine operations and the efforts of naval air forces. The Russians have traditionally been good at mine warfare and, after a not very impressive start against Finland, the Soviet mines and mining operations later in the war gave both Germany and Finland big problems. The Soviet Union showed great ingenuity around the construction and laying of sea mines. To be fair, the same also applied to both Finland and Germany.

The Soviet Union's naval spoils of war

At a conference in Berlin after the war, the USSR was allocated the following ships:

- the aircraft carrier *Graf Zeppelin* (badly damaged and incomplete);
- the light cruiser *Nürnberg*;
- ten German destroyers;
- the armour-plated warship *Schleswig-Holstein*;
- the Italian battleship *Giulio Cesare*;
- the Italian light cruiser *Filiberto Duca d'Aosta*;
- four Italian destroyers;
- fourteen Italian torpedo boats;
- two submarines;
- six Japanese destroyers;* and
- a number of smaller Italian and Japanese* vessels.

(*decided at a subsequent meeting).

When the war ended, the victors became the beneficiaries of German technology. The United States, Britain and the Soviet Union each had their own national programme, which was aimed at acquiring as much German know-how, technology, and as many German scientists as possible, not least the nuclear physicists. In the maritime area, the new German submarines and their means of propulsion were particularly on the wish list. Along the Baltic coast, the Soviet Union found unfinished ships, shipyards and factories, as well as technical and scientific data. Anything that could be dismantled, was dismantled and sent east.

The heavy cruiser *Prinz Eugen* in Copenhagen at the liberation in May 1945. The man in the centre is a resistance fighter with armband. The two others are German crew members from the cruiser. (Old Ship Picture Galleries)

The Soviet Union secured Germany's only aircraft carrier, *Graf Zeppelin*. She was sunk after a number of attempts in which the ship served as an aircraft carrier target for the Soviet navy's various offensive weapons. There were probably several reasons for this. The aircraft carrier was far from being finished, and there would be big problems keeping her in operation, but by sinking her, they could get this set off against the allocations of the total spoils among the victors. She was sunk north of Łeba on the current Polish coast on 16 August 1947, and was rediscovered here in 2006 in connection with examination of the seabed before laying a gas pipeline from Russia to Germany. When Denmark was liberated, the cruiser *Nürnberg* was in Copenhagen Freeport. She became part of the Soviet Baltic Fleet under the name *Admiral Makarov*[3] until 1959. The Russians had a lot of problems operating the engines in the technically advanced and complicated German vessels. For this reason, a number of boilers were burned out on board

3   Named after Admiral Stepan Osipovich Makarov, who was a multi-genius in the tsarist fleet (a skilled torpedo-boat commander, a polar explorer, a naval architect and a force commander). When the Russo-Japanese War began in 1904, Admiral Makarov was called in to sort out the slack leadership and he succeeded. He was killed by a Japanese mine which exploded under the ammunition magazine in the flagship, the battleship *Petropavlovs*k, on 13 April 1904, just six weeks into the war.

Admiral Makarov. Some of the German submarines which they had managed to have completed were wrecked during their sea trials.

The devastation of war and Soviet casualties
When the war ended, the western part of the Soviet Union lay in ruins. The Soviet Union's total loss of life during the war was set very low in 1945, and the numbers have grown steadily ever since. There are now reckoned to be over 27 million dead, of whom 11 million fell in the armed forces and 16 million were civilian victims. Because of Stalin's atrocities in the 1930s, the starting figures could have been tampered with. The casualty figures could therefore be adjusted upwards in the future, for there are, even today, many uncertainties: Russian historians are still trying to clarify them. For some of the dead Soviet citizens, it is relevant to ask whether it was actually Hitler or Stalin who was responsible for their deaths.

The outcome of the war in the Baltic Sea, seen through Soviet eyes
When the war ended, Stalin had neutralised Finland and occupied the three Baltic countries. Finland had to cede the Pechenga (formerly Petsamo) nickel deposits in the north and Karelia, as well as lease out the Porkkala Peninsula southwest of Helsinki as a Soviet base. Poland ended up in effect as an occupied country after the Soviet liberation, and Poland's borders were moved far to the west. Eastern Poland was annexed into Belarus and the Ukraine. Most of the Germans in the new Polish territories were expelled. East Prussia was annexed into the Soviet Union as Kaliningradskaja Oblast (the Kaliningrad exclave), and the German population here was also hounded out. The Soviet occupation zone in Germany developed into an independent nation, East Germany (DDR), completely controlled, however, by the German Communist Party faithful, and supported by the Soviet armed forces and the secret police. One of the results of the war was that, from 1939 to 1945, the Soviet Union had expanded its access to the Baltic Sea coast, and its sphere of influence, from a confined area at the eastern end of the Gulf of Finland from Sestroretsk to Narva, to going instead from Vyborg all the way round to the Bay of Lübeck. Soviet troops left Bornholm in April 1946. A number of the Baltic Fleet's new bases, including Kaliningrad (formerly Königsberg) and Baltiysk (formerly Pillau), were noted for normally being ice-free in winter.

Partisan movements and agents behind the Iron Curtain
The relationship between the former allies quickly cooled, because of Stalin's ambitions for the introduction of the 'people's democracies'[4] in the new buffer

---

4   As the word 'democracy' in Greek means government by the people, the appellation 'people's democracy' was linguistically not particularly well chosen by the Communist

zone which he had established between the Soviet Union and Western Europe. It was in fact a Soviet occupation of Central and Eastern Europe. Western intelligence sought to follow developments within the Soviet Union, and give partial support to the large number of resistance groups which continued to exist in the Ukraine and the Baltic states, among other places. Some of the former local Waffen-SS volunteers and other opponents in the Baltic states had gone underground and participated in partisan activities directed against the Communist regime. There were plenty of weapons in circulation, and the men could live in the woods and get a certain amount of support from the local population, but that ended with the forced collectivisation of Baltic agriculture. When small, deserted farms and smallholdings were closed down, the NKVD had better control of the situation.

Between 1948 and 1955, the British conducted Operation Jungle, where they tried to smuggle agents in and out of the Baltic states and Poland. The British intelligence organisation MI6, in co operation with the CIA, was responsible for the operation. Transport took place via the British Baltic Fishery Protection Service (BBFPS), which was a front organisation created for the purpose. The BBFPS was officially supposed to be protecting West German fishermen from harassment by the Soviet Union. It made use of one of the Royal Navy's German S-boats[5] and former personnel from the Kriegsmarine. The skipper was a former motor torpedo-boat commander in the Kriegsmarine, Kapitänleutnant Hans-Helmut Klose.[6]

The agents were put ashore near Palanga in Lithuania, Užava and Ventspils in Latvia and on the island of Saaremaa in Estonia – and also at Ustka (formerly Stolpmünde) in Poland. The exchange of agents often happened several miles from land, under poor visibility and darkness. The sailings emanated from Bornholm, where the S-boat would wait for the final 'go' signal from London. The agents and the operation were compromised by British double agents,[7] above all by Kim Philby. The NKVD/KGB's countermeasures were called Operation Lürssen-S after the manufacturer of the E-boats and S-boats.[8] Almost all of the forty-two agents landed were picked up by the

---

leaders – and under no circumstances was there any democracy involved.

5 The Royal Navy had had two S-boats since 1945, one of which was reconditioned and given increased speed and tank capacity.

6 Later Vizeadmiral and commander-in-chief of the Bundesmarine (the Federal German Navy). When the author was a Danish torpedo-boat commander, Hans-Helmut Klose was Kapitän zur See and flotilla commander for the German motor torpedo boats. Klose was a very professional, respected and charismatic commander.

7 Known as the Philby, Burgess and Maclean affair – all three were educated at Cambridge University in the 1930s.

8 The Kriegsmarine's S-boats were built according to a design from the Lürssen shipyard in Bremen.

Soviet authorities and most of the agents were turned and obliged to co-operate with their captors.

From 1952, the second British S-boat also took part in the operations. Its commander was Klose's former deputy commander, Oberleutnant zur See E G Müller. Later on, the organisation continued to conduct radio reconnaissance from boats directed against the Soviet forces in the coastal areas. It took place in collaboration with Organisation Gehlen, Generalmajor Reinhard Gehlen's intelligence organisation, which immediately after the war took advantage of German specialists and the former German network of agents in the Soviet Union and Eastern Europe in co-operation with the Americans. When West Germany joined NATO, Klose and his boats and crews went over to the Bundesmarine, and his radio reconnaissance people were transferred to the Bundesmarine's special unit for radio reconnaissance. Gehlen's organisation evolved into the Bundesnachrichtendienst (BND), the Federal German Republic's intelligence service in Pullach near Munich.

A summary and evaluation of Sweden's war operations

It is widely believed that Sweden was neutral during the Second World War, but this perception is flawed and incorrect. As mentioned earlier, Sweden was poorly prepared for the war before it broke out. When it happened, the most influential circles in the country were characterised by a centuries-old grudge against Russia, as well as a certain admiration for strong German leadership. At the beginning of the war, when Germany looked like winning, there was no hesitation in complying with German political pressure, which was mainly put on Sweden after 9 April 1940, when Germany invaded Denmark and Norway, and critical opposition was subjected to censorship – not even Charlie Chaplin's film *The Great Dictator*[9] was allowed to be shown in Swedish cinemas. Sweden delivered raw materials, mainly iron ore but also industrial products, and Germany accounted by and large for the entire Swedish export market, whereby the import of strategic goods could also be accomplished. When the Soviet Union was attacked, Sweden supported German military operations by providing rail transport, convoy protection, workshops, depots, warehouses, and much more. Seen with Soviet eyes, most of the bullets that claimed Soviet victims during the war were, partly or wholly, 'made in Sweden'. To what extent Sweden's contribution prolonged the war is difficult to define exactly. A number of factors put a strain on Swedish-Soviet relations in the post-war period: the Wallenberg case; the

---

9   Charlie Chaplin's 1940 film, a parody of Hitler's behaviour, was banned in Sweden until the end of the war.

sinking of *Bengt Sture*; the shooting-down of two Swedish aircraft in 1952; Baltic refugees, and other factors.

Sweden's foreign policy situation throughout the war was quite difficult. In the late 1930s, it became clear to the Swedish government and the Swedish military leadership that not only the Soviet Union but also Germany could pose a future military threat, for which Sweden was not adequately prepared. The start of the war in September 1939 resulted in complicated trade relations across the oceans, which were also theatres of war. Sweden was trying to avoid a repeat of the bad experience from the First World War: the Wallenberg brothers tried to take care of this. When Denmark and Norway were occupied, the military threat increased, and Sweden headed down the slippery slope which the concessions to Germany amounted to from a security point of view. Sweden actively supported German war operations against the Allies, and pretended that it was neutral. In many of the occupied countries, the large industrial groups and dynasties were looking to hedge their bets by having good relations with both sides, and this also came to apply to Sweden.

It is a moot point what Sweden should have done differently. In Britain, there was a certain understanding of Sweden's difficult situation, but as time went by, there was little respect left for the country's actions. The Swedish government, however, carried out some very capable and persistent work on circumventing the concept of neutrality in ingenious ways, by which the Western Allies, especially the British, also got some concessions, which opened up some opportunities for co-operation. Maintaining neutrality had its price for the Swedish navy. In total, 163 men from the navy lost their lives during the war.

In 1942, there were those in Germany who wanted to disclose detailed information about the extermination of the Jews. Bishop Otto Dibelius[10] had become aware of '*Die Endlösung der jüdischen Frage*' ('the final solution to the Jewish question') – now known as the extermination of the Jews, or the Holocaust, via a German who is believed to have gone into the SS solely to reveal its activities. The SS officer in question, Kurt Gerstein,[11] had also tried to pass on his knowledge to Göran von Otter, the Swedish embassy adviser at the Berlin embassy. The German bishop passed on his information to the Swedish archbishop, Erling Eidem, but Archbishop Eidem remained silent in Sweden about his knowledge of the Holocaust until his death in 1972. The

---

10 Otto Dibelius was the German Evangelical Church's Bishop of Berlin.
11 Kurt Gerstein committed suicide on 25 July 1945 while he was imprisoned in Paris. However, there are a number of uncertainties about his motives for applying for entry into the SS, but it is beyond doubt that, from 1942, he tried to make Bishop Dibelius aware of the German pogrom against the Jews, and that Dibelius tried to pass on his knowledge.

Swedish foreign ministry tried to hush up von Otter's account. When the case against Adolf Eichmann began in Israel in 1961, the Israeli prosecutor wanted answers to the question of what the Swedish foreign ministry had actually done in connection with the information about the extermination programme. The answer from Sweden was that Władysław Sikorski, the Polish president in exile, had already spoken about it in a speech on the BBC and that, in the general turmoil of war, some people had just regarded it as scaremongering propaganda. 'As it was already known about, nothing was done about it,' said the Swedish foreign ministry in a rather unconvincing explanation. The ministry responded in this case, as in so many others related to Sweden's relationships during the war, by saying as little as possible, as late as possible. Stockholm was well aware of what was going on in Germany in the last three years of the war.[12]

Many Swedish individuals and organisations made a commendable effort: Sweden took care of Danish Jews from 1943. So-called police forces were given training so that they could be deployed in Denmark (the Danish Brigade) and Norway at the end of the war. Many refugees were accepted into the country, and downed Allied airmen and Polish submariners were sent to Britain. Ball bearings were exported to Britain, and the Danish resistance movement received British weapons the other way: 3,000 Husqvarna submachine guns were manufactured in Sweden for the Danish resistance movement and were paid for by A P Møller (the founder of the Maersk Company). The Norwegian resistance movement received support via northern Sweden, and the Danish resistance movement's presence in Sweden was tolerated. In the last months of the war, Count Folke Bernadotte made a particularly big effort in Germany, especially for Danish and Norwegian concentration camp prisoners; his work was supported by the entire Swedish diplomatic corps. The effort was commendable and saved many human lives. Seen with the Swedish government's eyes, it was probably a welcome opportunity to disguise its very pro-German position at the start of the war. From a cynical historical perspective, the official Swedish support for Bernadotte's activities was probably a last-minute attempt to cast a mere ounce of decency and humanity over Swedish policy from 1939 to 1945. About fifteen thousand Scandinavian concentration camp prisoners were brought home in the final days of the war. From 27 June to 26 July 1945, the Swedish government and the Swedish Red Cross, in co-operation with British forces in Germany, organised further transport and hospital care for 9,273 concentration camp prisoners from a pick-up

---

12 The account of Gerstein, von Otter, Dibelius and Eidem can be read in the book *My Dear Reich Chancellor* by Staffan Thorsell (Borgen, 2007).

point in Bergen-Belsen. On thirty-six trips they were brought from Lübeck to Sweden on five Swedish white-painted ships with Red Cross markings.

For good reasons, there was no judicial settlement in Sweden after the war, in which unfortunate and unpatriotic conduct could have been addressed, as all of the political and economic actions were sanctioned by the legally elected government of unity, but the Nuremberg trials had offshoots in Sweden. One of the Wallenberg brothers, Jacob Wallenberg, was thought by the Americans in 1946 to have been a front for Hitler's economic policy with regard to the exposure of the so-called Bosch affair. He was banned from travelling to the United States and the family bank, Stockholms Enskilda Bank (SEB), was blacklisted until 1947. Only a few individuals had dared to persevere with ethical arguments and moral attitudes in opposition to Nazism. The best known was Torgny Segerstedt from *Göteborgs Handels-och Sjöfartstidning*, who was originally a theologian and historian of religion, and not a journalist. He spoke with the voice of conscience, which incidentally made Hitler, Goebbels and Göring absolutely furious.

The Swedes had not laid their cards on the table during the war, but then there were not many others who did. On the other hand, one could also say that Sweden bet on all the horses, and that duplicity was successful. The nation came through the Second World War without being directly involved, and the Swedish welfare state and Swedish jobs had been preserved. Swedish industry had not been troubled by the war and stood ready to participate in the reconstruction of Europe. On the other hand, Sweden's reputation got some serious scratches on the paintwork, which could have made it difficult – and still makes it difficult – to take Swedish politicians seriously. When Swedes consider themselves to be a better and more peaceful people than others, they base it solely on the illusion and hypocrisy which have been the two cornerstones of Swedish foreign policy since 1939. In the post-war period, Sweden asserted its 'non-alignment in peacetime and neutrality in wartime.' Once again, the Swedes were neither neutral nor non-aligned while they were exporting weapons to questionable regimes. Arms exports have been crucial for Sweden's economy all the way back to around 1560. Swedish security policy experience from the period 1939–1945 was that it had, in reality, gone well.

The level of Swedish support for Germany was surprisingly large. As mentioned earlier, Goebbels' enthusiasm was so great that he noted it in his diary. Sweden was, indeed, hard-pressed in some of the tenser situations, but at no time did Sweden stand up and be counted, nor was it considered that there was any public call for an adjustment to the pro-German line taken. With the return of the Baltic refugees to the Soviet Union after the war, Swedish indulgence of totalitarian regimes continued at great human cost.

The Baltic states and the Baltic refugees

The situation regarding the Baltic states is rather complicated to explain in a few words. The Baltic peoples were sandwiched between two great powers – Germany and the Soviet Union. The Soviet annexation of the three Baltic countries led to the deportation of elements whose influence constituted or could pose a threat to the Communist regime. For some, the German attack on the Soviet Union in 1941 represented liberation. For the Jewish population, it meant extermination.

Shortly after Operation Barbarossa in 1941, young men in the Baltic states were threatened with the choice of either entering the Arbeitsdienst (labour service) in Germany, or joining the armed forces, which, however, were not part of the Wehrmacht, but only the Waffen-SS. When local historians from the Baltic states attempt to describe the situation, it will often be given a rosy glow of 'defence of the homeland', 'the Home Guard', 'freedom fighters', and so on. However, that is only a small fragment of the story. The Baltic people knew what the Red Army and NKVD could get up to if they came back, and therefore there was a certain empathy with Germany's 'anti-Bolshevik' policy. The other part of the story is that many of the Baltic peoples carried out war crimes for the Germans, and some of the local people took part in the hunting down and killing of the Jewish population during the German advance in the summer of 1941. Many of the Baltic 'volunteers' took part as guards around the Jewish ghettos which were established and even later as guards at concentration camps.

When the Soviet Union returned in 1944, the regime had become even more heavy-handed. Many among the Baltic population were ready to bear arms against the advancing Russians, and there was a partisan movement which had been living in the forests for years and continued attacking Soviet security forces[13] for many more years after the war. For the Baltic states – as for the Finns – it was the Soviet Union, not Germany, who constituted the real enemy.

When the war ended, the Soviet Union wanted its Baltic refugees sent back from Sweden to the three Baltic Soviet republics – the refugees in question were aware of the consequences. Sweden gave in to political pressure and handed them over. Many of them attempted suicide or inflicted injuries on themselves to avoid extradition. The refugee ships from Sweden were received by the NKVD, which screened out refugees with a Waffen-SS background: there are examples of rank and file veterans being sent to Siberia for fifteen years, while officers and petty officers were executed on the quayside.

---

13 The Soviet security forces and border troops belonged to the NKVD and later (from 1946) to the KGB.

Finland

Finland had only become involved in the war because of Stalin's need to secure the Soviet Union's borders. Despite a proficient military intervention in both the Winter War and the Continuation War, Finland ended on the losers' side – without having supported Hitler's Germany ideologically in any way.

Finnish naval warfare during the war itself was successful, but it was, of course, carried out in close collaboration with German forces. Finland's sea lines of communication to other countries, mainly to Sweden, had always been open during the war, but that in itself was not enough to turn the tide. Finland contributed to the blockading of the huge Soviet Baltic Fleet right up to 1944.

The Peace Treaty of Paris in 1947 established the following restrictions on the Finnish forces: the strength of the army must not exceed 34,400 men; the strength of the navy must not exceed 4,500 men, and a total displacement of 10,000 tonnes; and the air force must not exceed 3,000 men and sixty combat aircraft.

Finland was not permitted to acquire offensive weapons systems such as bombers, submarines and missiles. The arrangement was eased in 1963 when air defence missiles were allowed, and Soviet air defence missiles purchased.

In 1948, a mutual co-operation and assistance treaty with the Soviet Union was forced upon Finland, which among other things said that 'if Finland – or the Soviet Union through Finland – is subjected to an armed attack from Germany or any state allied with Germany, Finland should defend itself if necessary in co-operation with the Soviet Union.' The treaty was renewed in 1955, 1970 and again in 1983. It was in force until the collapse of the Soviet Union in 1991, and when West Germany became a member of NATO in 1955, it meant that the treaty included an attack from NATO.

The territorial relinquishments meant that the population in Karelia and on the Porkkala Peninsula had to be moved. One might wonder why the Baltic states were occupied by Soviet troops in 1945 – but not Finland. After all, in Stalin's eyes, Finland was old Russian territory.[14]

Soviet losses in Leningrad

One of the war's greatest human disasters was the German siege of Leningrad. Immediately after the war, the Soviet authorities made it known that the

---

14 The author asked an officer from the Finnish border troops the question in the 1970s. He thought for a moment and replied: 'Stalin knew that we would fight.'

city's civilian casualties from hunger and disease during the siege had been 632,253 dead. Added to this, 16,747 had been killed by bombs and shells. The numbers had been set very low for several reasons. Stalin was jealous and, in his opinion, the people of Leningrad should not feel that it had been worse for them than it had been for the people of Moscow. He was also jealous of Party Secretary Zhdanov, who had emerged stronger from the siege, both as a leader figure and as a competitor. All in all, Stalin was not fond of competitors. At the Nuremberg trials in 1946, the Soviet authorities set the number of dead civilians in the city at 671,635, but researchers have now calculated that about 750,000 civilians perished during the blockade. If the military casualties in the area are included, the blockade of Leningrad cost the lives of between 1.6 million and 2.0 million Soviet citizens. This was for a city whose population was significantly below the total population of Denmark (under 4 million) during the war. Overall, Leningrad is the city which suffered the greatest human losses in the world during the Second World War.[15]

The Baltic Fleet's material losses during the war

The Soviet Baltic Fleet lost fifteen destroyers, four large torpedo boats, one gunboat, approximately sixty motor torpedo boats, forty-six submarines and hundreds of naval aircraft during the war. Many of the Baltic Fleet crews had to fight on land from 1941, and many thousands of these sailors died in the defence of Leningrad. A total of 137 men from the Baltic Fleet were honoured with the title of 'Hero of the Soviet Union'.

German war experience included in the reconstruction of the Soviet navy

The Kriegsmarine's two Grossadmirals, Raeder and Dönitz, each published their memoirs after the war, and they were read with great interest and attention to detail by admirals in the Soviet navy, especially by the renowned head of the Soviet navy from 1956 to 1985, Sergey Georgiyevich Gorshkov,

---

15 In order to put Leningrad's human losses in perspective, they can be compared with Denmark's losses during the war: Leningrad was, as mentioned, a city with fewer inhabitants than the whole of Denmark at that time. In the worst periods, more than eight thousand people a day were dying, ie more than the total number of Danes killed during the whole war, taking into account members of the Danish Resistance, civilian victims, sailors, fishermen, Eastern Front volunteers and people in Allied service. Leningrad's total losses were also greater than the combined military and civilian casualties of France, Britain and the United States.

Admiral of the Fleet of the Soviet Union, who rebuilt the Soviet navy to superpower status. It emerged from the German memoirs that at least 250 submarines were required to cut off supplies across the Atlantic, and that a navy had to have its own naval air force, and its own radio and radar intercept service. Admiral Gorshkov's own war experiences showed him that a navy had to be able to provide fire support from its own vessels during a landing operation. These thoughts helped shape the reconstruction of the Soviet Baltic Fleet after the war and, because at the same time the whole of Soviet society was undergoing reconstruction after the ravages of war, it took a long time.

The battle of the two major ideologies

The Great Patriotic War was not a war between evil and good. On the Eastern Front, two malevolent ideologies were at war with each other. The one ideology was no more sympathetic than the other, and the war was waged with incredible cruelty by both parties. It was a case of a 'total war', which laid waste to villages, towns, cities, industries and agriculture, and where a whole society's infrastructure was destroyed and civilian livelihoods removed. The terror that the two ideologies perpetrated was directed as much against their own people as it was against the people in the many countries affected by the conflict.

The occupation of Denmark – and the fate of Bornholm

Denmark experienced a German occupation in its mildest form, as Germany prioritised collaboration and a high yield from Danish industry and agriculture. The number of direct military operations, such as Allied bombing raids, was extremely limited. The Soviet liberation of Bornholm led to bombing raids on Rønne and Nexø. Further suffering for the Danish population was very limited in relation to the rest of Europe. On the other hand, the populations of Bornholm and Christiansø were witnesses to extensive war activity, with thousands of deaths in the surrounding waters. When the celebration of the fiftieth anniversary of the liberation was being planned in 1995, Ole Lippmann[16] was asked how it should be marked. He was a very modest man and said, 'Ring the church bells and thank God that it went as it did.' It was only chance and small differentials which meant that Denmark did not become a war zone around the end of the war and that Soviet forces did not battle their way through Denmark during a German withdrawal towards Norway.

---

16 The SOE's representative in Denmark; a member of the Freedom Council and, at the liberation of Denmark, the de facto leader of the Danish resistance movement.

The Baltic Sea since 1945: the Cold War develops

After the war, the Baltic Sea region became very tense. The Soviet Union remained a closed society that guarded its borders on land, at sea and by air with powerful armed forces, including the NKVD/KGB border troops. A US reconnaissance aircraft was shot down over international waters in the Baltic Sea in April 1950.[17] In June 1952, Soviet MiG fighters shot down two Swedish aircraft. The first was a reconnaissance aircraft[18] over international waters and three days later, a sea rescue aircraft – a Catalina – was shot down during the search for the first aircraft. In the latter case, the entire flight crew was rescued by a passing West German ship.

Summary and conclusion: the results of the war in the Baltic region

Britain and France had gone to war because of Germany's aggression against Poland in 1939. After the war, Churchill could not persuade Stalin that Poland should be restored to its former borders in 1939. Poland had lost large tracts of its original territory and about six million of its twenty-seven million inhabitants. The Baltic states had been occupied and incorporated into the Soviet Union as Soviet republics. Finland was impoverished and reduced in size after five years of war. The immediate victor in the Baltic region was Stalin, but apart from its huge armies, the Soviet Union was a much weakened and impoverished country after the ravages of war.

Sweden, on the other hand, was a kind of winner – largely untouched by the devastation. Banks, industries, including the arms industry, shipping and other businesses in Sweden were ready to take part in Europe's reconstruction. But Sweden was also ready with a raised finger towards what they considered morally offensive foreign policy, while the country's foreign ministry and the leaders of banking and industry blurred the traces of their own enterprising business initiatives and questionable actions during the war.

Throughout the long course of the war, the Baltic Sea played a very important role in the whole economy of the Third Reich. In addition to iron ore supplies, the Baltic Sea was also the supply route for the entire northern part of the Eastern Front. The Baltic Sea was an exercise area for the German submarine force which was under construction for operations in the North

---

17 One of the crew members possibly survived but, if so, he disappeared afterwards into the Soviet camp system.

18 A converted DC-3 aircraft designed to intercept Soviet radio and radar signals. All eight occupants, three flight crew members, and five radio and radar intercept operators from the FRA were presumed killed. The wreckage of the aircraft was salvaged in 2004.

Atlantic. The Baltic coast also constituted an experimental firing range for Germany's two most advanced weapons, the V-1 and V-2 missiles. Freedom of navigation in the Baltic Sea formed the basis of the entire German war industry from 1939 to 1944, and when Soviet submarines and naval aircraft put a stop to it, it became a contributing cause of the German collapse. The breakdowns of the Kriegsmarine, the German merchant fleet, the river traffic and the German railways all happened around April 1945.

Some observers might argue that the Western Allies did not participate very actively in the war in the Baltic Sea, but that is not so. British air operations were critical to the war in the area. The British had been able to establish a solid overview of the military situation, in which all available intelligence sources were taken into account. The deciphering of signals at Bletchley Park played a very crucial role in this. Based on the intelligence picture, the requirement for the bombing of key industries was drawn up, including docks, fuel supplies, training units and minelaying by aircraft, all in relation to how many bombing raids they were able to implement, because the British were operating with very limited resources. All the bombing raids, except in the very last days of the war, were carried out at night and may therefore have lacked visibility.

The military significance of the Germans' operations in *Unternehmen Rettung* (Operation Rescue – also known as Operation Hannibal) was relatively limited. Most of the two million people who were brought to the West were civilian refugees, and the military forces that were moved did not, for the most part, manage to be redeployed in new war operations; the collapse occurred before then. In the years after the war, some observers have wondered about Soviet aircraft continuing attacks against German ships on their way west after the actual cessation of hostilities. From the Soviet point of view, the ships were also transporting battle-ready troops and war equipment. The Soviet forces were trying to bring the fighting to an end and, in their eyes, that should be done by 'stopping where you were when the war ended'. Most German soldiers and refugees saw it another way. They did not want to fall into Soviet captivity, and they therefore sailed with everything that could float from East to West – and defended themselves along the way.

The people along the Baltic Sea experienced large movements of people. Today we would call it ethnic cleansing. Germans were driven out of the eastern areas; Finns had to leave the lost territories; and the Poles had to move to a completely new Poland further west. East Germans, Poles and Balts came to experience the Soviet advance as an occupation that lasted until 1989 and 1991, respectively. At the end of the war, Stalin had acquired a buffer zone in case of a new war, and Soviet propaganda now called the Baltic Sea 'the Sea of Peace', which should be understood as peace on Soviet terms.

At the start of the war, Denmark was in an area where the interests of the great powers – Britain, Germany and the Soviet Union – met. Denmark had escaped relatively cheaply through the turmoil of war, with few deaths and limited damage to the country's infrastructure and business. The war had come quite close to Denmark, but – apart from Bornholm – it ended just before it reached that far and there was no one in Denmark who had had very much influence on it. Denmark's reputation had only just been saved by the operations of the resistance movement to the benefit of the Allies, and the Russians left Bornholm again in 1946 without any problems. On the other hand, the waters around Denmark were infested with a lot of mines and wrecks for years afterwards.

Heads of state and naval commanders

Neither Germany nor the Soviet Union, who were both continental land powers, had been able to train competent, enterprising and independent naval officers. It is the ability that the British call 'the Nelson touch' which is so important for the professional exercise of naval craftsmanship. That was an ability the Soviet navy could have used during the Great Patriotic War in the big showdown in and around the Baltic Sea. It was probably the explanation for the failure of the Kriegsmarine too. The Russian and the German admirals were competent enough, but their heads of state or dictators were not.

Conclusion

The end of the war came about in a way that no one could have foreseen. There have been many different views about when it was obvious that Germany had been defeated militarily. The German military leadership ought to have given up when it was clear that the Normandy invasion had succeeded, at the same time as the Red Army was wiping out Army Group Centre. Hitler's special style of leadership prevented this, however, and he preferred everyone 'to be dragged down into an Armageddon now that Germany could not win'. The failure of the German military leadership to do more to stop the war – because of misguided loyalty and the oath of allegiance they had taken – continues to astonish both historians and military professionals. The attempted assassination of Hitler on 20 July 1944 never managed to get broad popular support before the uprising was stifled, but if the war had been ended in the summer of 1944, many lives on both sides would have been spared. The war was thus – quite unnecessarily – extended for nearly a year and thereby claimed millions of additional victims. During this final year, Grossadmiral Dönitz was trying to finish building the submarine fleet which was supposed to force Britain out of the war. In order to accomplish this, he required the industrial and shipyard capacity in northern Germany and an exercise area in the Baltic Sea. While his project was continuously being delayed, the Kriegsmarine managed to evacuate over two million people from eastern areas. Germany was now effectively defeated militarily on the ground, primarily by the Red Army. The German cities had been bombed to smithereens by British and American air power. Almost all the ships belonging to the Kriegsmarine and the German merchant fleet lay on the bottom of the Baltic Sea. The Luftwaffe was paralysed. Continued submarine warfare would not have made sense: the German collapse was total.

Appendix 1

Chronology of Key Events up to the Outbreak of War

1933

30 January	Hitler appointed German chancellor.
19 October	Germany withdraws from the League of Nations and breaks off negotiations with the major powers on German rearmament.

1934

26 January	Poland and Germany sign a non-aggression pact with a validity period of ten years.
2 August	President Hindenburg dies. Hitler takes over as Führer and Reich Chancellor. The German state and the German Nazi Party hereby melt into one. The armed forces' pledge of allegiance shall hereafter not be given to the constitution, but to Hitler personally.

1935

26 February	In direct violation of the Versailles Treaty, Germany declares that it now has an air force called the Luftwaffe. The building of the new force is to be led by Hermann Göring.
16 March	Germany introduces conscription and builds an army of 600,000 men, which is also a violation of the Versailles Treaty. The armed forces are given the name Wehrmacht, comprising Heer, Kriegsmarine and Luftwaffe (army, navy and air force).
18 June	Britain and Germany enter into a bilateral naval agreement laying down the relative strength of the two countries to 100:35 in British favour. A German navy of this size is a violation of the Versailles Treaty, but Britain is hoping to gain control of German rearmament by the agreement. Britain does not consult any other European powers in this regard.
3 October	Italy invades Ethiopia/the Abyssinian Empire, despite French and British protests.

1936

7 March	The Wehrmacht reoccupies the Rhineland which, according to agreements, should remain a demilitarised zone. France considers making a military response, but because of an unstable domestic political situation and British pressure, the plans are not implemented.

17 July	The Spanish Civil War breaks out. Germany supports General Franco with the army and air forces of the Condor Legion.
1 August	In a secret directive, Hitler gives the Wehrmacht and German industry orders to be ready for war in four years. There is a sharp increase in production of war equipment.
25 October	After a visit to Germany by the Italian foreign minister, Count Ciano, the two countries begin a close collaboration.
1 November	As a result of the meeting with Count Ciano the previous week, the Berlin–Rome axis (Axis powers) is established.
7 November	Germany and Japan conclude the Anti-Comintern Pact directed against the Soviet-backed international Communist parties. They undertake to exchange information on the matter. Later this month, Italy joins the pact.
28 December	Italy sends fighter aircraft to Spain to support Franco.

1937

26 April	The Luftwaffe and Italian aircraft bomb the Basque town of Guernica, where 1,600 people are killed. This was the Luftwaffe's first act of war.

1938

12 February	Hitler demands that Chancellor Schussnigg in Austria include Nazis in his government. Schussnigg appeals in vain to Britain and France, which refuse to give assistance.
16 February	The Nazi Arthur Seyss-Inquart is admitted to the Austrian government.
11 March	Chancellor Schussnigg is forced from power and Seyss-Inquart takes over as head of government.
12 March	German troops enter Austria, which hereby implements the Anschluss (connection) without resistance.
12 September	Hitler demands autonomy for the Germans in the Sudetenland in the western part of Czechoslovakia. This means that the area is to be incorporated into Germany.
28 September	*Fall Grün* (Operation Green – the conquest of Czechoslovakia) was scheduled to launch on this day, but because of the meeting the following day the operation was cancelled.
29 September	Meeting in Munich on Sudetenland between Hitler, Daladier (French prime minister) and Chamberlain (British prime minister). Czechoslovakia is not invited. Prime Minister Chamberlain returns to Britain and announces that there will remain 'peace in our time'.[1]

---

1   In the ensuing debate in the House of Commons, Winston Churchill told Prime Minister Neville Chamberlain: 'You were given the choice between war and dishonour. You chose dishonour – and you will have war.'

1 October	German troops march into the Sudetenland. This means that Czechoslovakia can no longer be defended, since the country's defence lines and fortifications lay in the border area in the Sudetenland.
2 October	Polish troops march into the border town of Těšín (Cieszyn) in Czechoslovakia, which must relinquish the town.
24 October	The German foreign minister, von Ribbentrop, offers Poland a renewal of the non-aggression pact on the condition that Germany can incorporate Danzig into the German Reich. Germany also wants to build railway lines and roads through the Polish Corridor to East Prussia. Poland refuses and the tension between the two countries increases.
29 October	Hitler orders German forces to prepare for military action to capture Danzig.
9 November	Kristallnacht in Germany where Jewish homes, businesses and synagogues are set on fire and Jews are murdered. The name Kristallnacht comes from the large number of windows broken during the action.

1939

14 March	Czechoslovakia is dissolved. Slovakia and Ruthenia declare their independence. Ruthenia is then annexed by Hungary. Bohemia and Moravia become German protectorates.
21 March	Germany takes over the administration of the city of Memel (Klaipėda) from Lithuania in a bloodless coup. This is Hitler's last bloodless annexation. Hitler demands of Poland that the free city of Danzig should come under German control and that there should be a corridor from Germany to the city. This demand should be seen in the light of the events in Memel the same day.
26 March	The German-Polish negotiations stall. Poland will not give in to German demands.
28 March	Madrid falls. Even though the fighting continues in Barcelona for a short while yet, it marks the de facto end of the Spanish Civil War with the victory of Franco and his Nationalists/Fascists.
31 March	France and Britain declare that they will guarantee the independence of Poland. The declaration contains a commitment to support Poland if the country is attacked by Germany.
3 April	Hitler instructs the OKW to prepare plans for an attack on the whole of Poland. The plan is drawn up by the army general staff.

7 April	Italy invades Albania, which is incorporated into Italy.
28 April	Hitler revokes the non-aggression pact of 1934 with Poland. Hitler also revokes the bilateral naval treaty with Britain from 18 June 1935.
20 August	General Zhukov's Red Army 1st Front takes up the fight against the Japanese Kwantung Army after many Japanese border violations along the border river Kalkhin Gol between Manchuria and Mongolia.
23 August	The Molotov–Ribbentrop Pact is signed in Moscow. It contains a secret additional protocol in which Hitler and Stalin outline their areas of interest. Poland is divided along the rivers Narew, Vistula and San. Stalin claims interests in Finland, Estonia and Latvia and the Romanian province of Bessarabia. Under the agreement, the Soviet Union will not intervene if Germany attacks Poland.
25 August	In London, the British government concludes a mutual assistance pact with the Polish government in which Britain undertakes to come to Poland's aid in the event of a German attack. German merchant ships receive radio instructions to head for German, Italian, Spanish or Japanese ports and to avoid international shipping lanes.
30 August	General Zhukov's forces of the Red Army inflict a decisive defeat on the Japanese Kwantung Army at Kalkhin Gol. The Japanese 6th Army is wiped out.
31 August	A fake Polish attack – actually by the Sicherheitsdienst (the Nazi intelligence agency) – is carried out against the German radio station in Gleiwitz (now the Polish town of Gliwice). Murdered concentration camp prisoners dressed in Polish uniforms were used to justify the German attack on Poland.
1 September	0447: the old pre-dreadnought battleship *Schleswig-Holstein* fires the first shots of the war at the fort at Westerplatte in Danzig (Gdańsk). The German attack on Poland consists of 1,500,000 men. Italy declares itself as non-belligerent.
15 September	Ceasefire between Japan and the Soviet Union. The Soviet Union could then transfer troops to its western borders.
17 September	The Red Army moves into eastern Poland.

Appendix 2

Glossary, Abbreviations, Ranks, Terminology and Explanations

Please note that titles and ranks in different services and nations are only approximately comparable. There are great variations in command relations, training, competence, authority, remuneration and prestige. Furthermore, many of the military units may vary considerably in size. Some of the organisations mentioned below underwent changes during the war. The following text is therefore merely for guidance.

General information

Asdic: Anti-Submarine Detection Investigation Committee; underwater detection system for submarines using active sound transmissions. Now called sonar (SOund Navigation And Ranging).

Displacement: The size of a warship is normally stated in tonnes, ie the weight of water it displaces (which is also the weight of the ship).

Division (army): In Germany, an army division from 1939 until 1942 comprised 17,734 men, then it was reduced to approximately 12,500. A Soviet division in 1941 was typically 14,500 men; the following year it was 11,000 men; at the end of the war, it was around 8,000 men.

FRA: Försvarets Radioanstalt. The Swedish radio signals interception service which tapped cable communications through Sweden and intercepted radio traffic. Enciphered messages were – if possible – deciphered and used for political, economic and military purposes.

HMS: His Majesty's Ship/His Majesty's Submarine.

KdF: Kraft durch Freude (Strength through Joy) was a German state-operated leisure organisation from 1933 with its own hotels and passenger liners. The organisation collapsed at the outbreak of war. The passenger liners *Wilhelm Gustloff* and *Robert Ley* belonged to KdF.

KGB: Комитет Государственной Безопасности (Komitet Gosudarstvennoi Bezopasnosti, or, State Committee for Security). Successor to the NKVD, the secret police in the USSR during the war. Established in 1946; from 1995 replaced by FSB.

Knots: Nautical miles/hour. 1 knot = 1 nautical mile/hour = 1.15 miles/1.852 km/hr.

LUT: Lage Unabhangige Torpedo. A German torpedo type that takes up a search pattern after a direct hit should have taken place.

Nautical mile: 1 nautical mile = 1.15 miles/1,852m.

NKVD: *Народный Коммиссариат Внутренних Дел* (Narodnyy Kommissariat Bnytrennikh Del, or, People's Commissariat for Internal Affairs). From 1934 to 1946, the designation for the Soviet secret police. The organisation comprised the ordinary police force, border troops, the secret police and the administration of the gulag camps. During the war, NKVD troops created stop lines for deserters behind the front. In 1946, the organisation was replaced by the KGB and the MVD.

OKH: Oberkommando des Heeres, the Supreme High Command of the German army. On the Eastern Front, the OKH co-ordinated the German war effort. From December 1941, it was under the personal leadership of Adolf Hitler. Located next to the OKW in Zossen.[1]

OKW: Oberkommando der Wehrmacht, Supreme Command of the German armed forces with responsibility for the war in the West (see also OKH).

ORP: Okret Rzeczyospolitej Polskiej, or, Ship of the Polish Republic.

RAF: Royal Air Force.

RN: Royal Navy.

RNoAF: Royal Norwegian Air Force (under the Norwegian government in exile in London).

SKL: Seekriegsleitung, the German naval staff.

SKF: Svenska Kullager Fabrikken (Swedish ball bearing factory).

SMS: Seiner Majestät Schiff (His Imperial Majesty's Ship – German naval ships until 1918).

SOE: Special Operations Executive, a secret British organisation which, in the words of Winston Churchill, should set Europe ablaze, through the co-ordination and collection of intelligence and giving support to all sorts of resistance groups in the German occupied territories.

SÄPO: Säkerhetspolisen, the Swedish security service/security police.

TNT: Trinitrotoluene. Common type of explosive for mines, torpedoes, shells, etc.

USAAF: United States Army Air Force.

---

1   The OKW and the OKH were both located in Zossen, respectively in the bunker complexes Maybach 2 and Maybach 1, but it was said that mentally they were thousands of miles apart.

Germany

The Nazi leadership

Adolf Hitler was chairman of the Nazi Party and Herman Göring was his deputy; third in rank was Rudolf Hess, also entitled deputy Führer. The party chancellery was run by Martin Bormann, who also acted as Hitler's private secretary. In these functions, he could effectively control access to Hitler from party members and others. Just below the chairman and his deputy there were eighteen Reichsleiters, who each controlled important sectors of society on behalf of the party. Heinrich Himmler was one of the Reichsleiters. The (approximately) forty-three Gauleiters worked under Bormann. A Gauleiter was in charge of the party structure in a large area of Germany and in a few of the 'new' territories. All Burgermeisters (mayors) had to be party-members, so in that way the Gauleiters controlled large parts of the German local administration. From December 1943, some officers worked under the direction of Martin Bormann on boosting the morale in the German armed forces via Nazi party propaganda, but those officers had no influence on combat operations.

The security system

Heinrich Himmler had gathered a number of organisations under his command. He was one of the Reichsleiters and in charge of the SS, in which he had the rank of Reichsführer-SS. Under him were the Waffen-SS, the Sicherheitsdienst (SD), the Gestapo and other police authorities. Part of the police force was organised into fighting units that took part in combat as well as war crimes. The guarding and daily running of the concentration camps also came under the SS remit. One of Himmler's ideas was that the SS should constitute the German elite. Some VIPs therefore received honorary ranks in the SS – parallel with their other ranks and titles.

The armed forces

As head of state, Hitler was commander-in-chief of the armed forces and, in that respect, the OKW and the OKH were under his command. From December 1941, he took over direct leadership on the Eastern Front from the OKH.

Officers' ranks in Waffen-SS and equivalent ranks in the German army

Note that the title Reichsführer-SS (Heinrich Himmler) is not related to Waffen-SS but the entire SS.

The various international reference lists vary at least one rank up or down on the list.

Waffen-SS	German army	British Army
SS-Oberst-Gruppenführer und Generaloberst der Waffen-SS	Generaloberst	No equivalent
SS-Obergruppenführer und General der Waffen-SS	General	General
SS-Gruppenführer und Generalleutnant der Waffen-SS	Generalleutnant	Lieutenant-General
SS-Brigadeführer und Generalmajor der Waffen-SS	Generalmajor	Major-General
SS-Oberführer und Oberst der Waffen-SS	No equivalent	Brigadier
SS-Standartenführer	Oberst	Colonel
SS-Obersturmbannführer	Oberstleutnant	Lieutenant-Colonel
SS-Sturmbannführer	Major	Major
SS-Hauptsturmführer	Hauptmann/Rittmeister	Captain
SS-Obersturmführer	Oberleutnant	Lieutenant
SS-Untersturmführer	Leutnant	Second Lieutenant

Naval ranks in the Kriegsmarine and their equivalents in the Royal Navy

The various international reference lists vary at least one rank up or down on the comparative list.

Kriegsmarine	Royal Navy
Grossadmiral	Admiral of the Fleet
Generaladmiral	No equivalent
Admiral	Admiral
Vizeadmiral	Vice-Admiral
Konteradmiral	Rear-Admiral
Kommodore*	Commodore
Kapitän zur See	Captain
Fregattenkapitän	Commander (senior grade)
Korvettenkapitän	Commander
Kapitänleutnant	Lieutenant-Commander
Oberleutnant zur See	Lieutenant
Leutnant zur See	Sub-Lieutenant

* This rank was introduced shortly before the war on 13 March 1939.

German ship designations:
FLAK-Schiff : AAA-ship (Anti-Aircraft Artillery-ship) with a large number of anti-aircraft guns to take part in local air defence.
Kreuzer: Cruiser. Normally divided into light cruisers with (approximately) 6in/150mm guns and heavy cruisers with (approximately) 8in/203mm guns.
Panzerkreuzer: The designation for the three pocket battleships with 11in/280mm guns.
Räumboote: Minesweepers which also could be used as minelayers and patrol vessels. Designated with an 'R'.
Schnellboot: Motor torpedo boat of about 110 tonnes. Designated with an 'S'.
Sperrbrecher: Means 'barrier breaker'. A large ship from the merchant navy with cables around the hull producing a heavy magnetic influence in front of the ship, bringing enemy magnetic mines to detonate far ahead at a safe distance.
Torpedoboot: A German designation for a small corvette or frigate of about 600–900 tonnes. From 1941, a new type of 1,754 tonnes was introduced. Both types had a minelaying capability. Designated with a 'T'. Not to be mistaken for Schnellboot.
U-boot: Submarine. Designated with a 'U'.
Zerstörer: Destroyer. Designated with a 'Z'. Z1 to Z22 also carried ship names, but from Z23 there was only the 'Z'-number. They carried heavy artillery (5in/127mm or 6in/150mm guns) and had a large minelaying capability.
Vorpostenboot: Patrol vessel or patrol cutters (small). Designated with a 'V'.

The Soviet Union

Guard units: An honorary designation won in battle. Used by all services: Guard Division, Guard Submarine, Guard Air Army, etc.
Front: A Soviet designation for a military unit comprising at least two armies. It can include naval and air units. At the end of the war the Soviet forces facing Germany were organised in ten fronts. A Soviet front was often compared to a US/UK army group.
Stavka: In the Russian imperial era, it was the war council. It was reintroduced in the USSR on 23 June 1941, the second day of the war, as the supreme headquarters of the Soviet armed forces. Stalin was chairman of the Stavka. In that capacity, he was generalissimo/generalissimus.

Soviet officers' ranks
The list below gives an idea of the ranks around 1945. Not all ranks have an unambiguous British or American equivalent at the time. The Soviet system

of ranks and rank badges changed during the war. Please note that officers in the naval air force and the naval infantry used army titles such as colonel and general. Translation of the Russian word for the military rank is in parenthesis.

Soviet army	Soviet navy	British equivalent
Marshal of the USSR	Admiral of the Fleet of USSR	Field Marshal/Admiral of the Fleet/Marshal of the RAF
Marshal	Admiral of the Fleet/Admiral	As above
General of the Army	Admiral of the Fleet/Admiral	General/Admiral/Air Chief Marshal
Colonel-General	Admiral	As above
Lieutenant-General	Vice Admiral	Lieutenant-General/Vice-Admiral/Air Marshal
Major-General	Rear Admiral	Major-General, Rear-Admiral/Air Vice Marshal
Colonel*	Captain (Captain 1st Rank)	Colonel, Captain/Group Captain
Lieutenant-Colonel**	Commander senior grade (Captain 2nd Rank)	Lieutenant-Colonel/Commander/Wing Commander
Major	Commander (Captain 3rd Rank)	Captain/ Lieutenant-Commander/Squadron Leader
Captain	Lieutenant-Commander	Lieutenant/Sub-Lieutenant/Flying Officer
Senior Lieutenant	Senior Lieutenant	Second Lieutenant/Midshipman/Pilot Officer
Lieutenant	Lieutenant	As above
Junior Lieutenant	Junior Lieutenant	As above

* The Russian word for a regiment is *polk* and a colonel is *polkovnik*, meaning regimental commander.

** Similarly a lieutenant-colonel is called *podpolkovnik*, thus meaning sub-regimental commander.

Appendix 3

Cross-reference List of Place Names in Various Languages

Below is a list of place names with more than one designation in two or more languages. A few of them have not been mentioned in this book, but the list can be useful for readers of Second World War literature and users of older maps. All the names are listed alphabetically in the left column. The right column indicates other versions of the same place and in what language. Such a list can be neither absolutely complete nor correct as some of the names are in dialects and in some languages a foreign word is used for the place name.

In Finnish, the suffix *-joki* means 'river' and the suffix *-saari* means 'island'. *Rajajoki* means 'border river'.

Languages	*(abbreviated)*
Czech	CZ
Danish	DA
English	EN
Estonian	ES
Finnish	FI
German	GE
Latin	LT
Latvian	LA
Lithuanian	LI
Polish	PL
Prussian	PR (Local dialect)
Russian	RU
Swedish:	SW

Alphabetical	Other languages	
Aabenraa	Apenrade	GE
Åbo	Turku	FI
Aistmarės	Vistula Lagoon, Zalew Wiślany,	EN, PL,
	Kaliningradskii Zaliv, Frisches Haff	RU, GE
Apenrade	Aabenraa	DA
Arensburg	Kuressaare (on Saaremaa)	ES
Aspö	Haapasaari	FI
Auschwitz	Oświęcim	PL
Baltiysk	Pillau, Piława	GE, PL
Baltiyskaya Kosa	Vistula Spit, Frische Nehrung,	EN, GE,
	Mierzeja Wiślana	PL
Björkö	Koivisto, Beryozovye Ostrova	FI, RU
Bolshoy Tyuters	(Great) Tutters, Tyterskär, Tytärsaari	EN, SW, FI
Breslau	Wrocław	PL
Bromberg	Bydgoszcz	PL
Brüster Ort	Cape Taran, Mys Taran	EN, RU
Bydgoszcz	Bromberg	GE
Cammin	Kamień Pomorski	PL
Cape Taran	Brüster Ort, Mys Taran	GE, RU
Chernyakhovsk*	Insterburg	GE
Chudskoye Ozero	Peipussee, Peipsi Järv	GE, ES
Cieszyn	Teschen, Těšín	GE, CZ
Copenhagen	København	DA
Cranz	Zelenogradsk	RU
Curonian Lagoon	Kurshskii Zaliv, Zalew Kuroński,	RU, PL,
	Kurishes Haff, Kuršių marios	GE, LI
Curonian Spit	Kuršių nerija, Kurshkaya Kosa,	LI, RU,
	Kurisches Nehrung, Kuršu kāpas	GE, LA
Dagö/Dagø	Hiiumaa	ES
Darłowo	Rügenwalde	GE
Danzig	Gdańsk	PL
Deima	Deime, Deimena, Deyma	GE, LI, EN

*   Named after General of the Army Ivan Danilovich Chernyakhovsky who was killed at the
     front in East Prussia on 18 February 1945.

Alphabetical	Other languages	
Deime	Deima, Deimena, Deyma	RU, LI, EN
Deimena	Deima, Deime, Deyma	RU, GE, EN
Deyma	Deima, Deime, Deimena	RU, GE, LI
Dirschau	Tczew	PL
Dorpat	Tartu	ES
Elbing	Elbląg, Truso, Ilfing	PL, PR, DA
Elbląg	Elbing, Truso, Ilfing	GE, PR, DA
Elsinore	Helsingør	DA
Fischhausen	Primorsk, Rybaki	RU, PL
Frisches Haff	Zalew Wiślany, Vistula Lagoon,	PL, EN,
	Kaliningradskii Zaliv, Aistmarės	RU, LI
Frische Nehrung	Mierzeja Wiślana, Vistula Spit,	PL, EN,
	Baltiyskaya Kosa	RU
Gangut	Hanko, Hangö/Hankø	FI, SW/DA
Gatchina	Kranogvardeisk	RU
Gdańsk	Danzig	GE
Gdingen	Gdynia, Gotenhafen	PL, GE
Gdynia	Gdingen, Gotenhafen (1939–1945)	GE, GE
Gleiwitz	Gliwice	PL
Gliwice	Gleiwitz	GE
Glogau	Głogów	PL
Głogów	Glogau	GE
Gogland	Hogland, Suursaari	SW, FI
Gothenburg	Göteborg	SW
Gotenhafen (1939–1945)	Gdynia, Gdingen	PL, GE
Great Tutters	Tyterskär, Tutters	SW, EN
	Tytärsaari, Bolshoy Tyuters	FI, RU
Grossendorf	Władysławowo	PL
Gumbinnen	Gussew	RU
Gussew	Gumbinnen	GE
Gvardeysk	Tapiau	PR
Göteborg	Gothenburg	EN
Haapasaari	Aspö	SW

Alphabetical	Other languages	
Hadersleben	Haderslev	DA
Haderslev	Hadersleben	GE
Hangö/Hankø	Gangut, Hanko	RU, FI
Hanko	Hangö, Gangut	SW, RU
Heiligenbeil	Mamonovo	RU
Hel	Hela	GE
Hela	Hel	PL
Helsingfors	Helsinki	FI
Helsingør	Elsinore	EN
Helsinki	Helsingfors	SW
Hiiumaa	Dagö/Dagø	SW/DA
Hogland	Gogland, Suursaari	RU, FI
Hohenstein	Olsztynek	PL
Hungerburg	Narva-Jõesuu	ES
Ilfing	Elbląg, Elbing, Truso	PL, GE, PR
Insterburg	Chernyakhovsk	RU
Kahlberg	Krynica Morska	PL
Kaliningrad	Königsberg, Królewiec	GE, PL
Kaliningradskii Zaliv	Vistula Lagoon, Zalew Wiślany,	EN, PL,
	Frisches Haff, Aistmarės	GE, LI
Kamien Pomorski	Cammin	GE
Kętrzyn	Rastenburg	GE
Klaipėda	Memel	GE
Koivisto	Björkö, Beryozovye Ostrova	SW, RU
Kolberg	Kołobrzeg	PL
Kołobrzeg	Kolberg	GE
Koszalin	Köslin	GE
Kotlin	Retusaari	FI
Kranogvardeisk	Gatjina	RU
Krasnoje Selo	'The beautiful/red village'	RU
Królewiec	Königsberg, Kaliningrad	GE, RU
Krynica Morska	Kahlberg	GE
Kuressaare	Arensburg (on Saaremaa)	GE
Kurisches Haff	Kurshkii Zaliv, Kuršių marios,	RU, LI,
	Zalew Kuroński, Curonian Lagoon	PL, EN

Alphabetical	Other languages	
Kurische Nehrung	Curonian Spit, Kuršių nerija,	EN, LI,
	Kurshkaya Kosa, Kuršu kāpas	RU, LA
Kurshkaya Kosa	Kurische Nehrung, Kuršu kāpas,	GE, LA,
	Curonian Spit, Kuršių nerija	EN, LI
Kurshkii Zaliv	Kurisches Haff, Curonian Lagoon,	GE, EN,
	Zalew Kuroński, Kuršių marios	PL, LI
Kuršių marios	Kurisches Haff, Curonian Lagoon,	GE, EN,
	Zalew Kuroński, Kurshkii Zaliv	PL, RU
Kuršių nerija	Curonian Spit, Kurshkaya Kosa,	EN, RU,
	Kurische Nehrung, Kuršu kāpas	GE, LA
Kuršu kāpas	Curonian Spit, Kuršių nerija,	EN, LI,
	Kurshkaya Kosa, Kurisches Nehrung	RU, GE
Köningsberg	Kaliningrad, Królewiec	RU, PL
København	Copenhagen	EN
Köslin	Koszalin	PL
Lauenburg	Lębork	PL
Lavansaari	Lövskär, Moshchny Ostrov	SW, RU
Lębork	Lauenburg	GE
Leningrad	Petrograd, Saint Petersburg,	RU, EN,
	Sankt Peterburg	RU
Libau	Liepāja	LA
Liepāja	Libau	GE
Lomonosov	Oranienbaum	GE
Lövskar	Lavansaari, Moshchny Ostrov	FI, RU
Mamonovo	Heiligenbeil	GE
Mayakovskoye	Nemmersdorf	GE
Memel	Klaipėda	LI
Międzyzdroje	Misdroy	GE
Mierzeja Wiślana	Frische Nehrung, Baltiyskaya Kosa,	GE, RU,
	Vistula Spit	EN
Misdroy	Międzyzdroje	PL
Moon	Muhu	ES
Moshchny Ostrov	Lavansaari, Lövskär	FI, SW
Muhu	Moon	GE
Möwenschanze	Nabrzeże Mew	PL

Alphabetical	Other languages	
Mys Taran	Brüster Ort, Cape Taran	GE, EN
Nabrzeże Mew	Möwenschanze	GE
Naissaari	Nargön, Naissar	SW, ES
Nargön	Naissaari, Naissar	FI, ES
Narva-Jõesuu	Hungerburg	GE
Nemmersdorf	Mayakovskoye	RU
Neufahrwasser	Nowy Port	PL
Neustadt	Wejherowo	PL
Nowy Port	Neufahrwasser	GE
Nöteborg	Schlüsselburg, Petrokrepost,	GE, RU,
	Schlisselburg, Pähkinälinna	RU, FI
Odensholm	Osmussar	ES
Oksywie	Oxhöft (part of Gotenhafen)	GE
Olsztynek	Hohenstein	GE
Oranienbaum	Lomonosov	RU
Öresund/Øresund	The Sound	EN
Ormsö	Worms, Vormsi	GE, ES
Ösel/Øsel	Saaremaa	ES
Osmussar	Odensholm	SW
Oświęcim	Auschwitz	GE
Oxhöft	Oksywie (part of Gdynia)	PL
Palmnicken	Yantarny	RU
Pähkinälinna	Schlüsselburg, Schlisselburg,	GE, RU,
	Nöteborg, Petrokrepost	SW, RU
Pechenga	Petsamo	FI
Peipsi Järv	Peipussee, Chudskoye Ozero	GE, RU
	Lake Peipus	EN
Peipussee	Peipsis Järv, Chudskoye Ozero	ES, RU
	Lake Peipus	EN
Penisaari	Malyi	RU
Peterhof	Petrodvorets	RU
Petrodvorets	Peterhof	GE
Petrograd	Leningrad, Saint Petersburg,	RU, EN,
	Sankt Peterburg	RU

Alphabetical	Other languages	
Petrokrepost	Schlüsselburg, Nöteborg,	GE, SW,
	Schlisselburg, Pähkinälinna	RU, FI
Petsamo	Pechenga	RU
Piła	Schneidemühl	GE
Piława	Pillau, Baltiysk	GE/PR, RU
Pillau	Baltiysk, Piława	RU, PL
Pleskau	Pskov	RU
Pomerania	Pomorze ('By the Sea'), Pommern	PL, GE
Pommern	Pomorze, Pomerania	PL, EN
Pomorze	Pommern, Pomerania	GE, EN
Posen	Poznań	PL
Poznań	Posen	GE
Primorsk	Fischhausen, Rybaki	GE, PL
Pskov	Pleskau	GE
Puck	Putzig	GE
Putzig	Puck	PL
Rajajoki	Sistroetsk, Siestarjoki, Systerbäck	RU, FI, SW
Rastenburg	Kętrzyn	PL
Retusaari	Kotlin	RU
Reval	Tallinn, Tallinna	ES, FI
Rixhöft	Rozewie	PL
Rozewie	Rixhöft	GE
Rügenwalde	Darłowo	PL
Rybaki	Fischhausen, Primorsk	GE, RU
Saaremaa	Ösel/Øsel	SW/DA
Saiskaari	Seitskär	SW
Sambiya	Samland, Semba	SW, LI
Samland	Sambiya, Semba	PL/LT, LI
Saint Petersburg	Leningrad, Petrograd, Sankt Peterburg	RU, RU, RU
Sankt Peterburg	Leningrad, Petrograd, Saint Petersburg	RU, RU, EN
Schiewenhorst	Świbno	PL
Schlisselburg	Schlüsselburg, Nöteborg,	GE, SW,
	Petrokrepost, Pähkinälinna	RU, FI
Schlüsselburg	Nöteborg, Petrokrepost,	SW, RU,
	Schlisselburg, Pähkinälinna	RU, FI

Alphabetical	Other languages	
Schneidemühl	Piła	PL
Seitskär	Saiskaari, Seskar	FI, RU
Semba	Samland, Sambiya	SW, PL/LT
Seskar	Seitskär, Saiskaari	SW, FI
Sestroretsk	Rajajoki, Siestarjoki, Systerbäck	FI, FI, SW
Siestarjoki	Rajajoki, Sestroretsk, Systerbäck	FI, RU, SW
Skagen	The Scaw	EN
(The) Scaw	Skagen	DA
Słupsk	Stolp	GE
Sonderburg	Sønderborg	DA
Sopot	Zoppot	GE
Sõrve	Sworbe	GE
(The) Sound	Öresund/Øresund	SW/DA
Sovetsk	Tilsit	GE
Stettin	Szczecin	PL
Stolp	Słupsk	PL
Stolpmünde	Ustka	PL
Sukhodolskoye Ozero	Suvanto	FI
Suomenlinna	Sveaborg	SW
Suursaari	Gogland, Hogland	RU, SW
Suvanto (lake)	Sukhodolskoye Ozero	RU
Sveaborg	Suomenlinna	FI
Świbno	Schiewenhorst	GE
Swinemünde	Świnoujście	PL
Świnoujście	Swinemünde	GE
Sworbe	Sõrve	ES
Systerbäck	Rajajoki, Sestroretsk, Siestarjoki	FI, RU, FI
Szczecin	Stettin	GE
Sønderborg	Sonderburg	GE
Tallinn	Reval, Tallinna	GE, FI
Tallinna	Reval, Tallinn	GE, ES
Tapiau	Gvardeysk	RU
Tartu	Dorpat	GE
Tczew	Dirschau	GE

Alphabetical	*Other languages*	
Terezín	Theresienstadt	GE
Teschen	Cieszyn, Těšín	PL, CZ
Těšín	Cieszyn, Teschen	PL, GE
Theresienstadt	Terezín	CZ
Thorn	Toruń	PL
Tichwin	Tikhvin	RU
Tikhvin	Tichwin	GE
Tilsit	Sovetsk	RU
Toruń	Thorn	GE
Truso	Elbląg, Elbing, Ilfing	PL, GE, DA
Tsarskoye Selo	Pushkin	RU
Turku	Åbo	SW
Tutters	Tytarsaari, Tyterskär, Great Tutters, Bolshoy Tyuters	FI, SW, EN, RU
Tytarsaari	Great Tutters, Tyterskär, Tutters, Bolshoy Tyuters	EN, SW, EN, RU
Tyterskär	Great Tutters, Tytarsaari, Tutters, Bolshoy Tyuters	EN, FI, EN, RU
Ustka	Stolpmünde	GE
Vaindlo	Stenskär	SW
Ventspils	Windau	GE
Viborg	Viipuri, Vyborg	FI, RU
Viipuri	Viborg, Vyborg	SW, RU
Vistula	Weichsel, Wisła	GE, PL
Vistula Lagoon	Zalew Wiślany, Kalingradskii Zaliv, Frisches Haff, Aistmarės	PL, RU, GE, LI
Vistula Spit	Baltiyskaya Kosa, Frische Nehrung, Mierzeja Wiślana	RU, GE, PL
Vormsi	Worms, Ormsö	GE, SW
Vuoksa	Vuoksi, Vuoksen	FI, SW
Vuoksen	Vuoksi, Vuoksa	FI, RU
Vuoksi	Vuoksen, Vuoksa	SW, RU
Vyborg	Viborg, Viipuri	SW, FI
Weichsel	Wisła ,Vistula	PL, EN

Alphabetical	Other languages	
Weichselmünde	Wisłoujście	PL
Wejherowo	Neustadt	GE
Windau	Ventspils	LA
Wisła	Weichsel, Vistula	GE, EN
Wisłoujście	Weichselmünde	GE
Władysławowo	Grossendorf	GE
Wolin	Wollin	GE
Wollin	Wolin	PL
Worms	Vormsi, Ormsö	ES, SW
Wrocław	Breslau	GE
Yantarny	Palmnicken	GE
Zalew Kuroński	Curonian Lagoon, Kurshskii Zaliv, Kurisches Haff, Kuršių marios	EN, RU, GE, LI
Zalew Wiślany	Vistula Lagoon, Kalingradskii Zaliv, Frisches Haff, Aistmarės	EN, RU, GE, LI
Zoppot	Sopot	PL

Sources and Bibliography

A large number of books have been published about the Second World War in recent years. Danish historians have described the German occupation of Denmark, while Swedish historians wrote about circumstances in Sweden during the war. Much of this knowledge is based on new research, but some of the topics are still very hard to get access to because some archives are still closed. Shortly after the fall of the Soviet Union, some Russian archives were made accessible, but they were closed again after a while. The archives belonging to the Swedish Wallenberg family are still closed to researchers looking for insight into industrial co-operation with Hitler's Germany.

The German naval archives

A large part of the knowledge of German naval activities during the war, especially for the last months, stems from studies by historians of the Tambach archives. The records contain the German naval archives from mid-eighteenth century to 1945. They were brought to light by personnel from the US Navy and the Royal Marines in April 1945 at Tambach Castle near Coburg.

Sources and bibliography

The following list of books and reports have been used as sources and are recommended for further reading.

Books

Achkasov, V I, *Krasnoznamehennyi Baltiskii Flot v Bitve za Leningrad 1941–1944 gg* (*The Baltic Red Banner Fleet in the Battle for Leningrad, 1941–1944*) (Nauka, Moscow, 1973)

Åhlund, Bertil, *Svensk marin säkerhetspolitik 1939–1945* (*Swedish Naval Security Policy 1939–1945*) (Kungliga Orlogsmannasälskapet, Marinlitteraturforeningen No. 78, 1994)

Amirkhanov, L I, *Morskie pushki na zheleznoi doroge* (*Naval Railway Guns*) (Ivanov and Leshchinskij, Saint Petersburg, 1994)

Andree, Johan, *Kanonerna på Djuramåsa – Öresunds lås under femtio år* (*The Guns at Djuramåsa – the lock on the Sound for fifty years*) (Svensk Militärhistoriskt Bibliotek, 2007)

Åselius, Gunnar, *The Rise and Fall of the Soviet Navy in the Baltic, 1921–1941* (Frank Cass, London and New York, 2005)

Bahm, Karl, *Berlin 1945 – Die letzte Schlacht des Dritten Reichs* (*Berlin 1945 – The Last Battle of the Third Reich*) (Kaiser, 2004)

Bech, Poul, *Søkrig i danske farvande* (*Naval Warfare in Danish Waters*), 2 vols (Schønberg, 2008/2009)

Beevor, Antony, *The Second World War* (Weidenfeld & Nicholson, London, 2012)

Bekker, Cajus, *Das grosse Bildbuch der Deutschen Kriegsmarine 1939–1945* (*The Big Picture Book of the German Navy 1939–1945*) (Gerhard Stalling AG, Oldenburg, 1973)

——, *Hitler's Naval War* (Doubleday & Company, New York, 1974)

Bidlack, Richard, and Nikita Lomagin, *The Leningrad Blockade 1941–1944 – A New Documentary History from the Soviet Archives* (Yale University Press, 2002)

Bjerg, Hans Christian, *Ligaen – Den danske militære efterretningstjeneste 1940–1945* (*The League – The Danish Military Intelligence Service 1940–1945*), 2 vols (Gyldendal, 1985)

Bredt, Alexander, *Weyers Taschenbuch der Kriegsflotten, Jahrgang 1939, 1940 und 1941* (*Weyer's Pocket Book for the Navies, vols 1939, 1940 and 1941*) (J F Lehmanns Verlag, Munich/Berlin, 1939, 1940 and 1941)

Breyer, Siegfried, *Die deutsche Kriegsmarine 1935–1945* (*The German Navy 1935–1945*) (Podzun-Pallas Verlag, Friedberg/H, 1986)

Christiansen, Jens Erik, *I nabovenligt samarbejde* (*In Friendly Co-operation among Neighbours*) (Maritim Kontakt, 2010)

Christiansen, Lisbet, and Jesper S Thomsen, *Danmark i Østersøregionen* (*Denmark in the Baltic Region*) (report from the DUPI conference, 27–28 November 1997)

Clemmesen, Michael H, and Marcus S Faulkner, *Northern European Overture to War, 1939–1941: From Memel to Barbarossa* (Brill, Leiden and Boston, 2013)

Dahl, Hans Fredrik, Hans Kirchhoff, Joachim Lund, and Lars-Erik Vaale, *Danske tilstande – norske tilstande* (*Danish Conditions – Norwegian Conditions*) (Gyldendal, 2010)

Dobson, Christopher, John Miller, and Ronald Payne, *The Cruellest Night* (Little Brown & Company, 1980)

Dornberger, Walter, *V-2* (Viking, London, 1954)

Ekman, Per-Olof, *Havsvargar: Ubåtar och ubåtskrig i Östersjön* (*Sea Wolves: Submarines and Submarine Warfare in the Baltic*) (Schildts, 1983)

Erickson, John & Ljubica, *Østfronten i billeder 1941–1945 – Den største konflikt i Anden Verdenskrig* (*The Eastern Front in Pictures 1941–1945 – The Greatest Conflict in the Second World War*) (Nyt Nordisk Forlag Arnold Busck, 2005)

Frick, Lennart W, and Lars Rosander, *Bakom hemligstampeln: Hemlig verksamhet i Sverige i vår tid* (*Behind the Secret Stamp: Secret Activity in Sweden in our Time*) (Historiska Media, Lund, 2004)

Grass, Günter, *I krebsegang* (*Crabwalk*) (Mariner Books, 2002)

Grier, Howard D, *Hitler, Dönitz and the Baltic Sea. The Third Reich's last hope, 1944–1945* (Naval Institute Press, 2013)

Gröner, Erich, *Die deutschen Kriegsschiffe 1815–1945* (*German Warships 1815–1945*), vol 2 (J F Lehmanns Verlag, Munich, 1968)

Hansen, Jørn, *Svitzer-aktionen i 1945* (*The Svitzer Action in 1945*) (2000)

Hansen, Ole Steen, with Anette Betke, *1945 – Kampen for Europas og Danmarks befrielse* (*1945 – The Battle for the Liberation of Europe and Denmark*) (Borgens Forlag, 2005)

Hansen, Søren, *Daglige Beretninger om Begivenheder under den tyske Besættelse* (*Daily Reports about Events during the German Occupation*) (Bianco Luno, 1946)

Hastings, Max, *All Hell Let Loose: The World at War 1939–1945* (Harper Press, 2012)

Haws & Hurst, *The Maritime History of the World*, vol II (Teredo Books)

Heinamies, Vilho, *Sju minuter på havet – pansarbåten Ilmarinens undergang* (*Seven Minutes at Sea – the Loss of the Monitor Ilmarinen*) (Svenska Militärhistoriskt Bibliotek, 1946/2005)

Herzog, Bodo, *Die deutschen Uboote 1906 bis 1945* (*German Submarines 1906 to 1945*) (J F Lehmanns Verlag, Munich, 1959)

Hildebrand, Hans H, Albert Rohr, and Hans-Otto Steinmetz, *Die Deutschen Kriegsschiffe* (*German Warships*), vol I (Koehlers Verlagsgesellschaft MBH, Herford 1979)

Huldt, Bo, and Klaus-Richard Böhme, *Vårstormar – 1944 – krigsslutet skönjes* (*Spring Storms 1944 – the end of the war can be sensed*) (Forlaget Probus, 1995)

Irving, David, T*he Mare's Nest* (William Kimber, 1964)

Jackson, Robert, *Battle of the Baltic: The Wars 1918–1945* (Pen & Sword Maritime, 2007)

Jones, Michael, *Leningrad – september 1941 til januar 1944* (*Leningrad – September 1941 to January 1944*) (Borgen, 2008)

Jones, Reginald Victor, *Most Secret War. British Secret Intelligence 1939–1945* (Hamish Hamilton, London 1978)

Keskinen, Kalevi, and Jorma Mantykoski, *Suomen Laivasto sodassa 1939–1945* (*The Finnish Navy at War 1939–1945*) (Tietoteos, Espoo, 1991)

Kieler, Svend, *Skandinavien i maritim strategisk belysning i det 20. århundrede* (*Scandinavia seen in the maritime strategic light of the 20th century*) (Tidsskrift for Søvæsen, December 1972)

Kijanen, Kalervo, *Finlands ubåtar i fred och krig* (*Finnish Submarines in Peace and War*) (Marinlitteraturforeningen No. 70, Karlskrona, 1986)

Koburger, Jr, C W, Captain US Coastguard, *Naval Warfare in the Baltic, 1939–1945: War in a Narrow Sea* (Praeger, Greenwood Press, 1994)

Kosiarz, E, *Druga Wojna Swiatowa na Baltyku* (*The Second World War in the Baltic*) (Gdansk, 1988)

Kotelnikov, Vladimir, *Bostony v Sovjetskom Soyze* (*Boston Aircraft in the Soviet Union*) (Airmuseums, Edition No. 1, 2010)

Krasnopyorov, Pavel Yevdokimovich, *Slava Baltijskaya* (*Glory to the Baltic Fleet*) (Eesti Paamat, Tallinn, 1971)

Krivosheev, Grigoriy Fedorovich (ed), *Rossiya i SSSR v voinakh XX veka* (*Russia and the USSR at War in the 20th Century*) (Olma-Press, Moskva, 2001)

Lenton, H T, *German Surface Warships*, vols 1 and 2 (Macdonald, London, 1966)

Leverkuehn, Paul, *German Military Intelligence* (Weidenfeld and Nicholson, London, 1954)

Levine, Joshua, *Operation Fortitude: The Greatest Hoax of the Second World War* (Collins, 2011)

Linder, Jan, and Lennart Lundberg, *Ofredens hav, Östersjön 1939–1992* (*The Sea of Trouble: The Baltic 1939–1992*) (Infomanager Förlag Jan Linder, 2002)

Lund, Mogens, *Tilintetgørelseskrig – Krigen på Østfronten 1941–45* (*War of Annihilation: The War on the Eastern Front 1941–45*) (Ellekær, 2013)

Lusar, Rudolf, *Die deutschen Waffen und Geheimwaffen des 2. Weltkrieges und ihreWeiterentwicklung* (*German Weapons and Secret Weapons from the Second World War and their future development*) (N Spearman, 1960)

Martelli, George, *Manden der reddede London* (*The Man Who Saved London*) (Hasselbalch, 1960)

Meister, Jurg, *Der Seekrieg in den osteuropäischen Gewässern 1939–1945* (*The Naval War in East European Waters 1939–1945*) (J F Lehmanns Verlag, Munich, 1958)

——, *The Soviet Navy*, vols 1 and 2 (Macdonald, London, 1972)

Mitchell, Donald B, *A History of Russian and Soviet Sea Power* (Andre Deutsch, 1974)

Naval Staff Directorate, *British Maritime Doctrine BR 1806*, second edn (London: The Stationery Office, 1999)

Nielsen, Kay Søren, *Soldaterne den 9. april 1940* (*The Soldiers on 9 April 1940*) (Cultours, 2010)

Nørby, Søren, *Flådens sænkning – 29. august 1943* (*The Navy Scuttled – 29 August 1943*) (Region, 2003)

O'Hara, Vincent P, *The German Fleet at War, 1939–1945* (Naval Institute Press, 2004)

Orlenko, I F, *My – 'Tallinskie'* (*We – the Guys from Tallinn*), booklet about 51. Mine- and Torpedoregiment from the Baltic Fleet, liberating Tallinn and later bombing Bornholm (Eesti Paamat, 1982)

Outze, Børge, *Danmark under Anden Verdenskrig* (*Denmark during the Second World War*) (Steen Hasselbalchs Forlag, Copenhagen, 1962)

Pleysier, Albet, and Alexey Vinogradov, *The Blockade and the Battle for Leningrad* (Publishing House LEMA, Saint Petersburg, 2010)

Pope, Dudley, *73 North: The Battle of the Barents Sea* (McBooks Press, 1958)

Poulsen, Niels Bo, *Den Store fædrelandskrig – statsmagt og mennesker i Sovjetunionen 1939–1955* (*The Great Patriotic War: The Power of the State and the People in the USSR 1939–1955*) (Høst & Søn, 2007)

Price, Alfred, *Instruments of Darkness: The History of Electronic Warfare* (Macdonald & Jane's, London, 1977)

Raeder, Erich, *Grand Admiral* (Da Capo Press, 2001)

Reid, Anna, *Leningrad: Tragedy of a City Under Siege, 1941–44* (Bloomsbury, 2011)

Ruge, Friederich, *The Soviets as Naval Opponents 1941–1945* (Naval Institute Press, 1979)

Rystad, Göran, Klaus-R Böhme, and Wilhelm M Carlgren, *In Quest of Trade and Security: The Baltic in Power Politics, 1500–1990* (Chartwell-Bratt, 1996)

Salewski, Michael, *Die deutsche Seekriegsleitung 1935–1945* (*The German Naval Staff 1939–1945*) (Bernard & Graefe, Verlag für Wehrwesen, Munich, 1975)

Salisbury, Harrison E, *Rusland i krig 1941–1945* (*Russia at War 1941–1945*) (Politikens Forlag, 1980)

Sellwood, A V, *The Damned Don't Drown* (Bluejacket Books, Naval Institute Press, 1973/1996)

Showell, Jak P Mallmann (ed), *Führer Conferences on Naval Affairs 1939–1945* (Chatham Publishing, London, 2005)

Sikkerhedspolitisk Studiegruppe and Det Udenrigspolitiske Selskab, *Østersøen (The Baltic): Geography, History, Economics, the Law of the Sea, Defence and Security* (Schultz Forlag, 1979)

Sørensen, Egon, Ole Andersen, and Niels Christian Pihl, *Tyske og russiske aktiviteter på Bornholm under 2. Verdenskrig (German and Soviet activities on Bornholm during the Second World War)* (Bornholms Tidendes Forlag, 2004)

Søværnet, *For Flaget og Flåden – om marinens personel og dets virke 1943–45 (In Honour of the Flag and the Navy – about the naval personnel and their activities 1943–45)* (Søværnet (Royal Danish Navy), 1995)

Stjernfelt, Bertil, and Klaus-Richard Böhme, *Hitler anfaller Polen – Westerplatte 1. september 1939 (Hitler attacks Poland – Westerplatte 1 September 1939)* (Svenska Militärhistoriskt Bibliotek, 2007)

——, *Vägen til Westerplatte (The Road to Westerplatte)* (Militärhistoriska Studier No. 2, Marinlitteraturforeningen No. 65 1978)

Stoker, Donald, 'The Naval War in the Baltic, September – November 1939', *Baltic Security and Defence Review* (2009:2)

Tamelander, Michael, and Niklas Zetterling, *Den nionde april – Nazitysklands invasion av Norge 1940 (9 April 1940 – the German Invasion of Norway)* (Historiska Media, 2004)

Thomer, Egbert, *Torpedoboote und Zerstörer – eine Bildchronik aus zwei Weltkriegen (Torpedo Boats and Destroyers – Pictures from Two World Wars)* (Gerhard Stalling Verlag, Oldenburg and Hamburg, 1964)

Thoren, Ragnar, *Ryska ubåtskriget i Östersjön 1941–1945 (Soviet Submarine Warfare 1941–1945)* (Militärhögskolan No. 6, 1992)

Thorsell, Staffan, *Min käre Rigskansler. Sveriges kontakter til Hitlers Rigskancelli (My Dear Reich Chancellor. Swedish contacts with Hitler's Reich chancellery)* (Borgen, 2007)

Tortzen, Christian, *Kampen på havet – Danske søfolk under Anden Verdenskrig (The War at Sea – Danish Sailors during the Second World War)* (Informations Forlag, 2011)

Trotter, William R, *Den finske Vinterkrig 1939–1940 (The Finnish Winter War 1939–1940)* (Borgens Forlag, 2004)

Ulfving, Lars, *Rysk krigskonst (Soviet Art of War)* (Försvarshögskolan, 2005)

——, *Överraskning och vilseledning – sovjetiska och ryska vilseledningsprincipper i krig och fred (Surprise and Deception – Soviet and Russian Principles for Deception in War and Peace)* (Svenska Militärhistoriskt Bibliotek, Hallstavik, 2006)

Wechsberg, Joseph, *Leningrad* (Det Schønbergske Forlag, 1978)

Wendt, Herbert, *Der Kampf um die Ostsee (The Fight for the Baltic)* (Vier Tannen Verlag, Berlin, 1943)

Werner, Christopher, *Den blå boken, marina stridskrafter ur ett militärteoretiskt perspektiv (The Blue Book: Naval forces in a theoretical military perspective)* (Försvarshögskolan, 2002)

Wetterholm, Claes-Goran, *Dödens hav, Östersjön 1945* (*The Sea of Death: The Baltic 1945*) (Prisma Bokförlag, 2002)

Whitley, M J, *Destroyers of World War Two* (Naval Institute Press, 1988)

Zetterling, Niklas, *Hitler mod Stalin. Kampen pa Östfronten 1941–1945* (*Hitler against Stalin: The Battle on the Eastern Front 1941–1945*) (Informations Forlag, 2010)

Other articles and reports

'Bizarre Schrottwüste' ('Bizarre heap of scrap metal'), *Der Spiegel* 3/1994, p51

Komorowski, Antoni, 'Prolonged Consequences of the Second World War for the Environment of the Baltic Sea' (2000)

Lauring, Kåre, '*Wilhelm Gustloff*s forlis – krigsforbrydelse eller katastrofe?' ('The Sinking of *Wilhelm Gusloff* – War Crime or Disaster?'), *Berlingske Tidende*, 27 December 2002

Index of Ship Names

If the name is not known the hull number is used as name

Index of People